SCENIC
WONDERS
OF CANADA

Published by The Reader's Digest Association (Canada) Ltd.,
in conjunction with the Canadian Automobile Association

Reader's Digest

SCENIC WONDERS

OF CANADA

An Illustrated Guide to Our Natural Splendors

Acknowledgments The publisher acknowledges with thanks the major contributions of the writers of the Scenic Wonders articles: P. D. Baird, Harry Bruce, Fred Bruemmer, Neil G. Carey, Robert Choquette, Robert Collins, Paul Grescoe, Stan Handman, Ernest Hillen, Jack Hobbs, Harold Horwood, Ron Kerr, Bruce Litteljohn, David McFadden, Charles Magill, Fred McGuinness, Sid Marty, Lois Neely, Anker Odum, Sheila Thomson, Ian Walker, Alex Whitecross; the writers of the Closeup features: Wayne Clark, Eileen McKee, Joan Voukides; and Dr. John Elson, geological consultant for the entire book.

Thanks is expressed also to the Department of Energy, Mines and Resources (particularly the Canadian Permanent Committee on Geographical Names and the Geological Survey of Canada), Environment Canada (particularly the Canadian Wildlife Service and the Glaciology Division), the Department of Indian and Northern Affairs (particularly Parks Canada and the staffs of the national parks), Information Canada and Statistics Canada;

To the provincial departments of parks, natural resources and tourism; to provincial and regional tourist associations and tourist bureaus, museums, zoological societies and conservation authorities;

To the staffs of the natural history departments of Brock University, Carleton University, Lakehead University, Macdonald College, McGill University and the universities of Alberta, Calgary, Ottawa, Toronto and Waterloo, and to the following individuals, organizations and associations:

Arctic Institute
  of North America
Dr. Francis R. Cook
Selwyn Dewdney
Dr. Mike Dickman
Dr. Gordon Edmond
R. C. Elliott
Mrs. Hope Johnson
Val Macins
L. David Mech

National Museum
  of Natural Sciences
Dr. Gerry Osborn
Dr. Douglas H. Pimlott
Dr. Keith Ronald
Royal Ontario Museum
Dr. Dale Russell
Dr. Jack Souther
Dr. John Theberge
Westmount Library

EDITOR: Paul Minvielle
ART DIRECTOR AND DESIGNER: Lucie Martineau
ASSISTANT EDITOR: Don McNaughton
DESIGN ASSISTANTS: Jacques Lavigne, Michel Rousseau
EDITORIAL RESEARCHERS: Eileen McKee (chief), Keith Bellows, Susan Copeland, Horst D. Dornbusch, Pablo Fenjves, Janet Holmes, Eva Jacek, Lynda Leonard
PHOTO RESEARCHERS: Penelope Cowie (chief), Michèle B. Fitzgerald, Peter Hedrich, Lyne Young
COPY PREPARATION: Lynne Abell, Gilles Humbert, Margot Weinreich
CLOSEUP ILLUSTRATORS: Anker Odum (plants and animals) and George Buctel (geology and landforms), except: Paul Gerahty (pages 181, 197, 251, 303), Barry McKay (23, 59), George V. Kelvin (189), James B. Loates (45)
CARTOGRAPHY: Topographics Limited (physical relief map models), Cartex Inc. and Cartographie Québec (waterways scribing), Peter Brandt Studios Ltd. (map photography), Brian E. Priest (map design)
INDEXER: Carolyn McConnell
PRODUCTION: Mark Recher (manager), Holger Lorenzen

Book Department
DIRECTOR: Louis Hamel
MANAGING EDITOR: George Ronald
MANAGING ART DIRECTOR: James Hayes
COORDINATOR: Denise Hyde-Clarke

More Canadians than ever before are traveling across this great country and enjoying its scenic beauties. At the same time more of us are becoming aware of the vulnerability of our natural resources and of the need to protect them. We are coming to realize that the environment is affected by human attitudes and behavior. This book shows us what superb scenic wonders we have in Canada—and how much we stand to lose.

Many of Canada's best known scenic wonders are seen by millions every year. Other natural beauty is more remote. But all these wonders are a little more accessible—and perhaps a little more threatened—each year.

It is important that Canadians come to know and appreciate these treasures. Our wilderness is shrinking and if Canada is to preserve any of it we must have some knowledge of what is worth preserving.

In many cases governments are leading the way with new parks and wilderness preserves. Many areas described in this volume contain wilderness preserved and protected within such National Parks as Terra Nova, Kejimkujik, La Mauricie, Pukaskwa, Pacific Rim and Kluane. They range from our oldest National Park, Banff, to one of our newest, Auyuittuq.

Some 50,000 square miles of the Canadian landscape is preserved in 28 National Parks. But if we are to have a complete representation of all the types of landscapes that exist in this country, then we must create new National Parks.

I can tell that the stories and pictures in *Scenic Wonders of Canada* have been created with deep affection. We travel from Atlantic Canada up the St. Lawrence Valley to the Great Lakes and on to the Prairies. We roam the mountains of the west, then explore the Pacific coast. We stand amazed by the beauty of the vast Shield country in the north. We visit no fewer than 42 of the great scenic wonders—from the fjords of Gros Morne National Park to the Cypress Hills and the Nahanni—and we make shorter stops at hundreds of other attractions.

Scenic Wonders of Canada is a visual record of our incredibly beautiful and diverse natural heritage. Through its pages Canadians can revisit favorite places and discover others they might never have heard of before. But in this book we can see not only the beauty of the land but also how the variety of landscapes were formed, how they determine what plants and animals can exist and how everything fits in the natural scheme of things.

I hope that, with a deeper understanding of our unique natural legacy, Canadians not only will acquire a greater appreciation of our land but also will be much better equipped to resist the pressures to despoil it.

I would like to congratulate the Reader's Digest and the Canadian Automobile Association for publishing this fine book, which I am sure will do much to make Canadians more appreciative of our great natural heritage.

Foreword

Judd Buchanan
Minister of Indian Affairs
and Northern Development
Ottawa, January 1976

Contents

10-11 Finding the Wonders

ATLANTIC CANADA

12-15 Introduction

16 Terra Nova National Park
Map 21 Other Attractions 21-22 Closeup 23

24 Gros Morne National Park
Map 29 Other Attractions 29-30 Closeup 31

32 The Magdalens
Map 36 Closeup 37

38 Cape Breton Highlands
Map 43 Other Attractions 43-44 Closeup 45

46 North-Shore P.E.I.
Map 50 Other Attractions 50 Closeup 51

52 Kejimkujik National Park
Map 57 Other Attractions 57-58 Closeup 59

60 The Saint John
Map 65 Other Attractions 65-66 Closeup 67

FORILLON TO GATINEAU

68-71 Introduction

72 Forillon National Park
Map 77 Other Attractions 77-78 Closeup 79

80 The Saguenay
Map 85 Other Attractions 85-86 Closeup 87

88 La Mauricie National Park
Map 93 Other Attractions 93-94 Closeup 95

96 Mont-Tremblant Provincial Park
Map 101 Other Attractions 101-102 Closeup 103

104 Gatineau Park
Map 109 Other Attractions 109-110 Closeup 111

112 Thousand Islands
Map 117 Other Attractions 117-118 Closeup 119

THE GREAT LAKES

120-123 Introduction

124 Algonquin Provincial Park
Map 129 Other Attractions 129-130 Closeup 131

132 Niagara Falls
Map 137 Other Attractions 137-138 Closeup 139

140 Point Pelee National Park
Map 145 Other Attractions 145-146 Closeup 147

148 Bruce Peninsula
Map 153 Other Attractions 153-154 Closeup 155

156 Pukaskwa National Park
Map 161 Other Attractions 161-162 Closeup 163

THE SHIELD

164-167 Introduction

168 Quetico Provincial Park
Map 172 Other Attractions 172 Closeup 173

174 Lake of the Woods
Map 179 Other Attractions 179-180 Closeup 181

182　The Upper Churchill
　　　Map 187　Other Attractions 187-188　Closeup 189

190　Peace-Athabasca Delta
　　　Map 195　Other Attractions 195-196　Closeup 197

THE PRAIRIES

198-201　Introduction

202　Riding Mountain National Park
　　　Map 207　Other Attractions 207-208　Closeup 209

210　The Qu'Appelle Valley
　　　Map 214　Other Attractions 214　Closeup 215

216　The Big Muddy
　　　Map 221　Other Attractions 221-222　Closeup 223

224　Cypress Hills
　　　Map 229　Other Attractions 229-230　Closeup 231

232　Red Deer Badlands
　　　Map 238　Other Attractions 238　Closeup 239

THE WESTERN MOUNTAINS

240-243　Introduction

244　Waterton Lakes National Park
　　　Map 249　Other Attractions 249-250　Closeup 251

252　Creston Valley
　　　Map 257　Other Attractions 257-258　Closeup 259

260　Banff National Park
　　　Map 266　Other Attractions 266-268　Closeup 269

270　Jasper National Park
　　　Map 275　Other Attractions 275-276　Closeup 277

278　Mount Edziza Provincial Park
　　　Map 283　Other Attractions 283-284　Closeup 285

286　Tweedsmuir Provincial Park
　　　Map 291　Other Attractions 291-292　Closeup 293

294　The Fraser Canyon
　　　Map 300　Other Attractions 300-302　Closeup 303

THE PACIFIC COAST

304-307　Introduction

308　Pacific Rim National Park
　　　Map 314　Other Attractions 314-316　Closeup 317

318　The Inside Passage
　　　Map 322　Other Attractions 322　Closeup 323

324　The Queen Charlottes
　　　Map 330　Closeup 331

THE NORTH

332-335　Introduction

336　Kluane National Park
　　　Map 341　Other Attractions 341-342　Closeup 343

344　Nahanni National Park
　　　Map 350　Other Attractions 350　Closeup 351

352　The Mackenzie
　　　Map 357　Other Attractions 357-358　Closeup 359

360　The Barren Grounds
　　　Map 365　Other Attractions 365-366　Closeup 367

368　Auyuittuq National Park
　　　Map 373　Other Attractions 373-374　Closeup 375

376　Index

384　Picture Credits

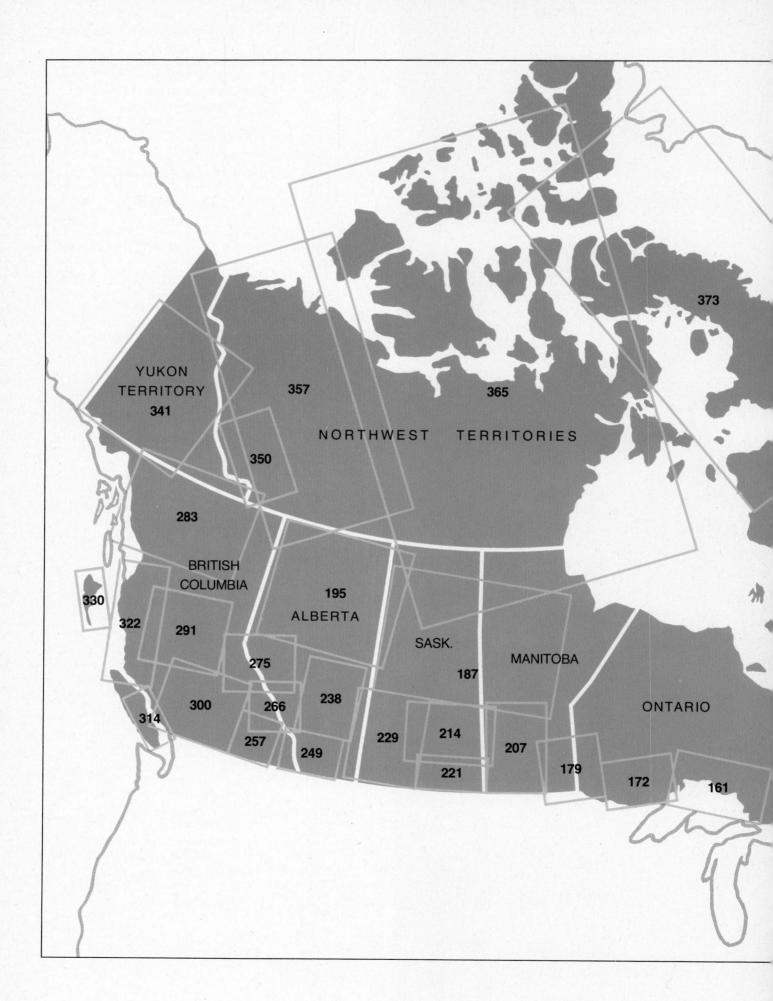

Finding the Wonders

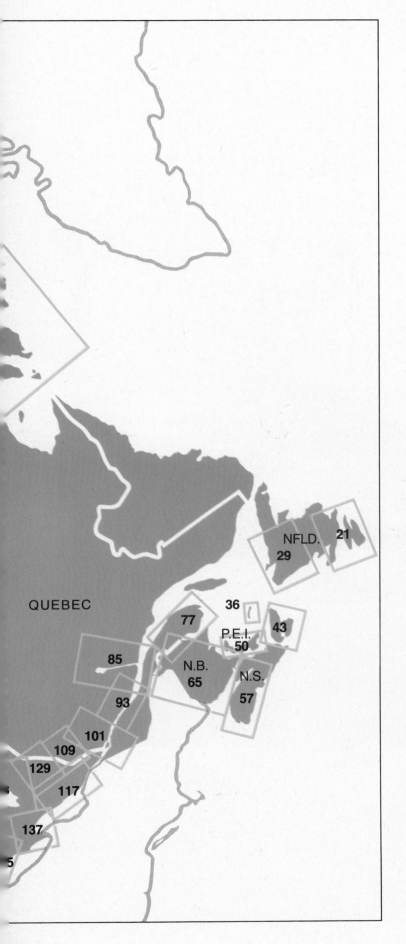

Forty-two of Canada's greatest Scenic Wonders are presented in this book by region, beginning with Atlantic Canada and ending with The North. A two-page picture, followed by a one-page picture and a page of text, introduces each region.

Within each regional section are stories and pictures that describe and show the individual Scenic Wonders. Following each story is a map locating the Wonder and showing the location of Other Attractions in that area. Accompanying the map is text describing the Other Attractions in alphabetical order; some are shown in photos. After each set of Other Attractions is a Closeup feature. With photos, text, diagrams and illustrations, the Closeup goes into detail about some intriguing special feature of the Scenic Wonder in question. Closeups are on beige-tinted pages.

On the maps:

▣ The main Scenic Wonder is outlined in yellow. The yellow border follows the boundaries of large Wonder areas. If a Wonder area is small, the border encloses more than the actual area.

△ Other Attractions are marked with yellow triangles and the names of the attractions. The accompanying text describes the Other Attractions in alphabetical order.

🏛 This symbol indicates a museum or exhibit that can contribute to better understanding and enjoyment of the scenery and wildlife of an area.

✈ Airports are shown where air travel is a comfortable alternative to land travel, or where air travel is the only way to visit a Scenic Wonder without great hardship.

⛴ This symbol shows ferry service. A ferry route is indicated by a dotted black line. Many ferry routes pass through great scenic areas.

▬ An exceptionally scenic road is represented by a solid red line and the route is described with the Other Attractions. Other roads are solid black.

▬▬ Hiking and nature trails and canoe routes are represented by broken red lines.

▬▬ This represents a railway line. Scenic railway routes are shown in red.

The incidence map at the left shows the areas covered by the maps in *Scenic Wonders of Canada*. The number inside a small map area represents the page on which the larger map of that area appears.

ATLANTIC CANADA

Wilderness, History and Always the Sea

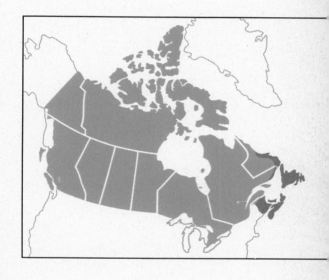

Atlantic Canada is the thunder of breakers against an ancient headland, the sigh of a spent wave on a lonely beach. It is the reedy cry of a wheeling gull, the raucous urgency of a colony of seabirds. It is the smell of the sea, of fish and weed and salt air, a tang that wafts inland to mingle with the heady scent of wild flowers. Atlantic Canada is four provinces and part of a fifth but less than one-twentieth of the total land mass of Canada. Yet in this 220,000 square miles are the Vinland of the Vikings, the Acadia of the French, a New Scotland and the Newfownd Lande of the Bristol fishermen who came to reap the bounty of the Grand Banks. This part of Canada seems synonymous with the sea, yet it contains vast inland areas that, like its seascapes, are among the most scenic in the nation. Atlantic Canada has unclimbed mountains and high tableland where caribou graze. There are huge wilderness areas so rugged and remote that the only reasonable way to penetrate their loneliness is by aircraft. There are dense forests that have never felt the bite of a logger's ax. There are rivers great and small, serene and turbulent, tamed and wild. Atlantic Canada is Gros Morne and Terra Nova and the broad beaches of Prince Edward Island. It is the Magdalens, the highlands of Cape Breton, Kejimkujik canoe country, the historic Saint John. And always the sea.

Opposite: *The Magdalen Islands.*
Preceding pages: *Ageless, changeless, relentless: the Atlantic.*

A Splendid Fjord and Pounding Sea Where Ice Parades Until Midsummer

A loon's eerie call shatters the silence of the pre-dawn twilight. The wild laughter skims across tidal flats and through mists that seep from bogs and meadows into the dark aisles of the forest. Then the bird comes planing through the valley of Big Brook, sending up plumes of spray as he touches down on the tidal pool at the river's mouth. Morning has come to Terra Nova National Park, on Newfoundland's east coast, 160 miles northwest of St. John's.

As echoes of the loon's mad notes fade into the hills, the ritual hunt for food begins again and hundreds of creatures stir 153-square-mile Terra Nova into wakefulness. Canada geese wing in from the outer reaches of Bonavista Bay, scouting the flats. Maintaining V formation, the flight lands near the center of the valley, then starts to search for a living meal in the shallow water.

Ragged lines of gulls settle a respectful distance from the geese. A fox at the edge of the forest sniffs the air cautiously, trots onto the flats. He sits, nose quivering. Two more foxes appear as from nowhere, so stealthy is their approach. Now all three industriously forage in the sand for worms and shellfish. Geese and gulls keep a wary eye on the foxes and the three occasionally lift their snouts and savor the heady scent of the birds—but no fox stalks prey it cannot catch.

Daybreak on Newman Sound.

As the day brightens, a reconnoitering flock of dowitchers circles three times. Then the long-billed birds alight on the flats and begin feeding on marine worms.

Beyond Newman Sound, where the sun now gilds the ridges, an angler climbs to his campsite beyond the valley. He too has found his breakfast—a string of fat sea trout from Big Brook. An otter slips noiselessly into the water to hunt fish the man missed.

In an upriver pool a mink, also a fish eater, leaves the den he has excavated from the soft bank. Farther upstream, beavers patiently repair dams and store birch and alder saplings underwater near their lodges.

Just south of Dunphy's Pond is a peat bog covering several square miles, its beautiful plant complex based on acid soil and sphagnum moss. The pitcher plant (Newfoundland's provincial flower and the largest carnivorous plant in Canada) is one of the most conspicuous in the bog. It traps insects in its jug-shaped leaves, then drowns and digests them in fluid near its base. More delicate are the bog orchids—dragon's tongue, broad-lipped twayblade, spotted coralroot—rare flowers but easy to find at Terra Nova in July and August. Hooded ladies' tresses—orchids called "scent bottles" because of their powerful perfume—are common too. Also plentiful here are pyrola, bog mirtle and twinflower. Bogland ponds and lakes have patches of white water lilies. In early summer clusters of marsh blue violets spread across adjacent wet meadows.

Flowering shrubs—northern fly honeysuckle, rhododendron, lamb kill, Labrador tea—fill the areas between the park boglands and surrounding forest.

Terra Nova is one of Newfoundland's best places for seeing wild animals close up. Moose saunter through campgrounds. Bears are sometimes live-trapped and removed to keep them from becoming a nuisance to campers. Even the shy Canada lynx is occasionally seen at dusk and dawn. It resembles a handsome overgrown cat but is suspicious and unfriendly.

Terra Nova National Park presents a rich contrast in colors, from the glittering gold bathing Newman Sound at evening to the brilliant scarlet tips of the red jacket (also called British Soldier), one of countless lichens found on rocks, trees and fallen logs.

Although the Trans-Canada Highway runs through the park, a few visitors arrive by sea. Docks and a launching ramp are provided for yachts and small boats. The landlocked waterways are open only to canoes and small boats and are safe in all weather. This is true of Broad Cove and the Southwest Arm of Alexander Bay at the north end of the park.

One canoe route takes in many of the park's best features. It starts at Sandy Pond, then goes into Dunphy's Pond, the park's biggest lake. The rest of the

route is recommended for experienced canoeists only. It involves portaging from Dunphy's Pond to Pitts Pond, outside the park. Then it's down the Terra Nova River into the Middle Arm of Alexander Bay and back into the park via the Southwest Arm of the bay into Southwest Brook. This two-day trip is through some of the loveliest wilderness in eastern Canada, including a splendid fjord with perpendicular headlands.

One of the finest views of the Atlantic shore anywhere is from the Blue Hills lookout tower—a pano-rama of forest, lakes, seashore, islands and mountains, with the distant lands of Bonavista Bay falling away in diminishing shades of blue and green, like hills in a Chinese landscape painting.

The real glory of Terra Nova is the sea and the towering headlands. Surf from the open Atlantic pounds against black rocks, shooting white curtains of spray high into the air. Sheltered sounds are lined with low shores of shingle and beach rock. Clode Sound, Newman Sound, Swale Tickle, Lions Den and Chandler Reach all open past groups of islands, many with seabird colonies, toward Cape Bonavista and the ocean.

Deep-sea fishing is a specialty of this part of Newfoundland. Bluefin tuna taken here are usually between 400 and 700 pounds. Less ambitious anglers fish for mackerel or flounder or jig for cod.

Bay seals are seen occasionally, harp seals between December and May, dolphins and small whales in summer. With a light boat you can drift into a "pod" of pilot whales and stay as long as you wish. If you do not frighten these gentle, two-ton beasts they will rise and sink beside the boat, breathing in puffs and snorts through their blowholes, standing upright in the water.

Pods of black and white killer whales are sometimes found here, feeding on schools of cod or even chasing

The dark green of Terra Nova's seemingly endless forested hills is interrupted occasionally by the lighter greens of low-lying meadows and bogs. Between the bogs and forests are flowering shrubs.

tuna. A great many specimens of giant squid have been found along this coast between Cape Norman at the north end of Newfoundland and St. John's. These rarely seen marine animals seldom surface. Most giant squid are 20 to 50 feet long, including tentacles, but monsters of more than 100 feet are thought to exist.

Another marine attraction at Terra Nova (although outside the park) is the parade of icebergs drifting south with the Labrador Current until midsummer. A few are mile-long islands of ice but the best are smaller— about the size of a cathedral or a castle and shaped somewhat the same, with soaring towers, turrets, buttresses and battlements. These bergs' fairy-tale quality is heightened by the shimmering gemlike colors of the ice—from deep blue to pale green. The highlight of a Terra Nova visit is often the sight of one of these crystalline giants, menacing as it looms from fog, enchanting as it sparkles in dazzling bright sunshine.

OTHER ATTRACTIONS

Fossils 500 Million Years Old and Islands Teeming With Birds

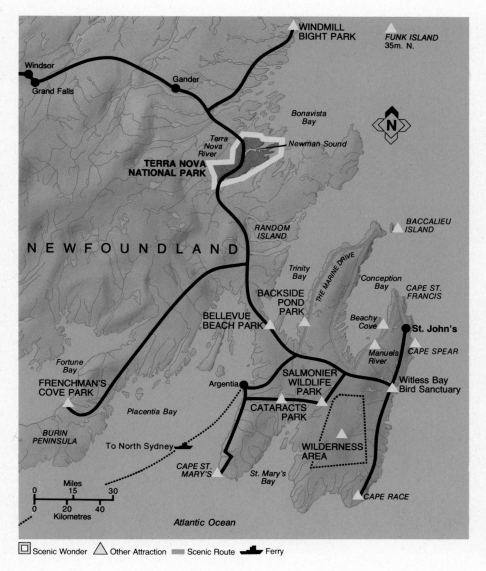

Scenic Wonder △ Other Attraction ▮ Scenic Route ⛴ Ferry

Cape Spear *Fingers of rock near Cape Spear, North America's most easterly point, reach toward Europe. About 250 million years ago this part of Newfoundland was attached to southwestern Europe.*

Baccalieu Island Although not a formal sanctuary, the island is a nesting ground for puffins, storm petrels, gannets, gulls, black guillemots, kittiwakes, murres and razorbills at various times from late April to October.

Backside Pond Provincial Park A freshwater pond and a seashore beach are connected by a footpath through the dense evergreen forest of this 1,390-acre park.

Beachy Cove A tiny, rocky inlet with a picturesque waterfall, a beach set between cliffs, and a rock formation called the Lion's Head.

Bellevue Beach Provincial Park Mussels can be picked in the saltwater pond here, protected from pounding waves by a barachois, a natural sand and gravel breakwater.

Cape Race Picture next page.

Cape St. Mary's Bird Rock, a 500-foot-high sea stack, is the home of one of North America's largest gannet colonies. Clouds of the streamlined, snow-white birds soar on wings that span six feet or more. When a gannet sights a fish, it dives from as high as 100 feet, plunging into the sea with a spectacular splash.

Cape Spear Picture this page.

Cataracts Provincial Park A 32-acre picnic site that boasts a 100-foot-high waterfall. Walkways make the falls accessible and easy to photograph. In winter, the cataract freezes, forming tall, shimmering icicles like giant candles.

Frenchman's Cove Provincial Park A natural pebble beach, a calm and protected barachois pond, a marsh and a stream: 125 acres of varied wildlife habitat.

Funk Island The flightless great auk once nested here in great numbers. But hunters who collected eggs and killed adult birds for their flesh and downy

21

breast feathers virtually wiped out the penguin-like bird. (The last great auks recorded were two captured off the coast of Iceland in 1844.) The rocky, 66-acre island is now a refuge for murres (probably a million), puffins, gannets, razorbills and kittiwakes.

Manuels River The fossil remains of uncounted prehistoric marine creatures called trilobites are buried in soft rock at the river's mouth. They can be dug by hand but a trowel or pick makes the job easier.

Salmonier Provincial Wildlife Park A one-and-a-half-mile nature trail winds through 200 acres of this 2,900-acre park. Animals typical of Newfoundland and Labrador are seen in areas fenced to protect their natural habitat.

The Marine Drive Built to follow the Atlantic coast north of St. John's, this highway runs to Cape St. Francis, connects with other shore roads, and at Topsail joins what Newfoundlanders call the Road Around the Bay (Conception Bay). At Old Perlican the 280-mile Marine Drive turns south along the shore of Trinity Bay and intersects the Trans-Canada Highway at Whitbourne Crossing.

Wilderness Area A caribou herd roams this 335-square-mile wilderness in the Avalon Peninsula. The region is sparsely forested with spruce and balsam fir.

Windmill Bight Provincial Park A freshwater pond and a mile-long sand beach that faces the cold North Atlantic surf. Icebergs are frequently seen during the summer about a mile off the 182-acre park.

Witless Bay Bird Sanctuary Parts of Gull Island are honeycombed with the burrows of an estimated 1,250,000 Leach's storm-petrels, but the entrances are concealed by vegetation and the birds do not stir when incubating. Anyone could be in the middle of a colony without knowing it. When not on their nests the swallow-like petrels range far out to sea and return only after dark to relieve their incubating mates. For a time there is great activity but at daylight the colony again appears deserted. Other birds on Gull Island include kittiwakes, herring gulls and some 200,000 puffins. Green Island has gulls, black guillemots, kittiwakes and 100,000 murres. Puffins and storm petrels are found on Great Island.

Cape Race *An arm of the ocean cuts between ancient cliffs near Cape Race. The world's richest find of Precambrian fossils—nature's record of animals that flourished some 500 million years ago—was made at nearby Mistaken Point in 1968. Among the fossils still imprinted in a sloping rock face is one of a three-foot-long creature thought to be 600 million years old.*

A Place on the Cliff

A cliffside gives sea birds ready access to fish and protection from predatory animals. Just as each species has evolved wings, feet and a beak suited to its way of life, so each has chosen its own kind of nesting site at a certain level on the cliff. Competition for space is eliminated and the birds can concentrate on breeding and raising their young. Black guillemots lay eggs among rocks at the foot of the cliff. At the next few levels black-legged kittiwakes fashion nests on narrow ledges. Higher still are murres that lay pear-shaped eggs on bare rock shelves, and razorbills that prefer the meager protection of a crevice or hole for their eggs. Where the cliff slopes, common puffins excavate breeding chambers. Great black-backed gulls and Leach's storm-petrels live on the cliff tops.

Gannets share ledges with murres and kittiwakes or gather in dense colonies on the flat tops of islands or seastacks.

Leach's storm-petrel

Great black-backed gull

Common puffin

Razorbill

Common murre

Thick-billed murre

Black-legged kittiwake

Black guillemot

Although they share a common larder—the sea—marine birds have developed beaks which vary greatly in appearance and purpose.

Leach's storm-petrel. The nasal tube atop this black, hooked bill is an adaptation to sea living. It enables the bird to blow out fluid containing excess salt.

Great black-backed gull. Young birds, as soon as they are hatched, have an urge to peck at the red spot near the tip of this heavy, yellow bill. This stimulates the parent to regurgitate food.

Common puffin. At breeding time this bill takes on exotic coloring and grows in size, allowing the bird to carry more of the slender fish it feeds its young.

Common murre. A baby murre eats just one fish at each meal—but it can be longer than the chick! The fish is carried with its head inside the parent's throat and its tail protruding past the tip of its slender black beak so that the tougher part of the fish is predigested.

Thick-billed murre. This bill is distinguished from that of the common murre by being shorter and thicker and, in the breeding season, having a thin whitish line along the upper cutting edge.

Razorbill. This bird's membership in the auk family is indicated by its short, deep, grooved bill, which has a vertical white line. The razorbill closely resembles the extinct great auk.

Black-legged kittiwake. Although this bird prefers fish, its plain all-purpose beak allows it to eat a wide variety of food. Its durable nest is a neat cup of seaweed, grass and moss, cemented with mud.

Black guillemot. The long, slender bill of the black guillemot is in keeping with the rest of its streamlined diver's body. These birds, anxious to protect their eggs, sometimes lay them in crevices too deep to allow incubation.

23

Storm clouds over Bonne Bay.

GROS MORNE NATIONAL PARK

Brooding, Flat-Topped Mountains Behind a Coast of Endless Variety

High above the dark waters of Bonne Bay broods the ancient bulk of Gros Morne, a giant's quilt of green and black—sparse alpine vegetation alternating with stark rock faces. The 2,644-foot mountain and other peaks that punctuate the 750 square miles of Gros Morne National Park are the most spectacular of the Long Range Mountains along the west coast of Newfoundland.

Only 75 miles northeast of Corner Brook, the park is a blend of deep lakes flanked by near-vertical cliffs . . . waterfalls so powerful and so high (some more than 300 feet) that water turns to dense mist before it can reach the land below . . . a desolate boulder-strewn tableland . . . highland tundra . . . salmon rivers cascading through rocky gorges . . .

But the flat-topped mountains dominate the landscape. On a map the Long Range appears to be an extension of the Appalachian Mountains, which run up the New England coast, northeast through New Brunswick and the Gaspé and, apparently, into Newfoundland. In fact, the Long Range is far older than the 600-million-year-old Appalachians. The base rocks, more than 1,500 million years old, were part of the leading edge of the North American continent when Newfoundland's eastern rocks were attached to southwestern Europe. The shifting and folding of the earth's crust millions of years later created Newfoundland and the mixture of rocks in Gros Morne National Park. Lava was forced up through cracks in the earth's crust to form new mountains—such as Gros Morne Mountain and other nearby peaks on top of the Long Range.

This massive movement of the land, with erosion by water and ice—and some volcanic eruption—created an intriguing variety of terrain and some of the most dramatic scenery in eastern Canada. Much can be seen from a car but the park's most awesome sights are reserved for those who boat on the fjord-like lakes or roam the highlands around the Western Brook gorge or hike to the peak of Gros Morne (which Newfoundlanders pronounce Gross Morn).

Marks of the Ice Age are everywhere in the park: glacial valleys, moraines of sand and gravel and boulders, bedrock furrowed by stones embedded in ice, and fjord-like lakes—ancient river valleys that were widened and deepened by mile-thick ice and then flooded. Although fjords were created the same way, these glacial trough lakes, as geologists call them, do not extend to the sea, as do fjords. The Western Brook gorge is one of these. In it is Western Brook Pond, 544 feet deep.

About 13,000 years ago, when the ice melted away

from this part of Newfoundland, the land began to rebound. At many places along the shore are high terraces that once were sea-level beaches. Just below the surface of these terraces are still found shells and skeletons of marine animals.

Treeless barrens atop the Long Range Mountains are pasture for the Newfoundland caribou. This handsome animal, the most plentiful of North American woodland caribou, has an extraordinary rack of antlers. The herd size is difficult to determine because the animals are never all together (as are the smaller Barren Grounds caribou) but they number about 17,000 in Newfoundland, between 75 and 100 in the park.

The mountains are home to such birds as the bald eagle and osprey. Eagles are seen in cliff faces and mountains, ospreys in river estuaries. Majestic gyrfalcons are sometimes sighted.

Arctic hares—white in winter, pale gray in summer, with black-tipped ears year round—are found here singly and in pairs and, infrequently, in threes and fours. These 10-to-12-pound animals often bound on hind feet only, like kangaroos. To see hares in summer you must visit the barren uplands. In winter they move down to the tree line to feed on low shrubs and on branch tips broken down to snow level by moose.

Near the coast the mountains give way to foothills. They end in a 2,000-foot escarpment of highly folded sedimentary rock, a ragged ridge pointing seaward.

The poorly drained coastal plain is crisscrossed by small rivers. Covered with bogs and prairielike grassland, this plain is broken by higher, well-drained ridges. In summer many of the ridges blaze with arctic rhododendron. Massed beds of blue flag, a wild iris, fill the wet meadows, and in the intervening bogs are

A jumble of ocher-brown volcanic rock high above Bonne Bay is one of Canada's weirdest landscapes. The main highway into Gros Morne National Park skirts this six-by-nine-mile wasteland, where toxic chemicals in the rock restrict plants to a few hardy species. Also in the park, near Green Point, are gray rocks smoothed by centuries of wave action.

showy lady's-slipper, pitcher plants and delicate orchids. The woodland glades glow with yellow lady's-slipper and light-purple moccasin flower. Many fields are blanketed with silver-white or orange-bronze cotton grass.

A Krummholz forest of stunted spruce and fir, known as tuckamoor or tuck, covers some of the more exposed ridges of the coastal plain, as well as some mountain

27

slopes that face the sea. Wind and snow have pruned and woven these trees into a shrubby carpet two to six feet thick, extending up to 100 feet inland.

The park is fringed by 45 miles of seacoast in endless variety. Cliffs fall sheer into deep water. Great sea stacks just offshore are the remnants of headlands reduced to rubble by pounding waves. Mud flats shelter clams, food for huge flocks of migrating shorebirds and such nesting species as the spotted sandpiper, the semipalmated plover and the greater yellowlegs.

Whimbrels (Hudsonian curlews), unlike most other shorebirds, feed inland on berries, often in large flocks, and sometimes with black-bellied plovers.

The flat-topped mountains of Gros Morne are prime grazing land for the handsome Newfoundland caribou.

Along the Gros Morne coastline are countless tidal pools with sea urchins, starfish, sponges and sea anemones. Beds of red, green and brown seaweed slope into the deeps. Moon jellies and other jellyfish are common along the shore. At night some phosphorescent jellyfish and other organisms make the water glitter with tiny explosions of yellowish-white light.

Beyond the shoreline gulls wheel and keen, sometimes mewing like cats, the twin arcs of their wings mastering the wind. Cormorants skim the sparkling waves as they cruise the offshore islands. When storm clouds gather, the Gulf unleashes its fearsome power on the land. And over all, ever present, are the dark mountains of Gros Morne National Park, with their air of mystery and eternity.

OTHER ATTRACTIONS

A Bay of Islands, and Rocks Like a Ship's Topsails

Barachois Pond Provincial Park A two-mile nature trail climbs through a forest of birch, spruce and fir to the barren summit of Erin Mountain. The 1,000-foot peak provides a panoramic view of the surrounding area.

Bay of Islands Picture next page.

Blow Me Down Provincial Park A two-mile hiking trail leads to a lookout with a splendid view over Bay of Islands. The densely-forested, 550-acre park is reputed to have buried treasure.

Blue Ponds Provincial Park Limestone on the bottoms of the park's two lakes accounts for their turquoise color. Both are drained by underground sinkholes.

Cape St. George Picture this page.

Crabbes River Provincial Park Spawning salmon fight upstream in June and early July.

Grand Lake There is magnificent scenery along the 90-mile waterway formed by Grand Lake, Sandy Lake and Birchy Lake. A short portage extends the waterway into Sheffield Lake, set amid heavy forest below Mount Sykes and Mount Seemore.

Humber Valley Some of Newfoundland's finest scenery is in the lush valley of the Humber River, in the shadow of the Blomidon and Long Range mountains. Towering cliffs rise sharply out of the water on both sides of Humber Arm. Some of the best salmon fishing in the world is in the headwaters of the Upper Humber.

Cape St. George *Bitter winter wind and waves batter this westernmost point of the Port au Port Peninsula.*

John T. Cheeseman Provincial Park The park is in a valley surrounded by the barren terrain of Cape Ray. At one end is a saltwater barachois, or inlet, cut off from the sea and the chilly Labrador current by a bar of sand and gravel called a barachois.

Mummichog Provincial Park This park on the Little Codroy River is named for a fish found in a dank lagoon — and in few other places in Newfoundland. The mummichog, usually three or four inches long, can survive with little oxygen in stagnant water. This 204-acre park has hiking and nature trails. The lagoon is a mixture of fresh and salt water; as the tide comes in, it mixes with the fresh water of the Little Codroy River. Bacteria colors the lagoon shore purple.

Bay of Islands *Guernsey, Tweed and Pearl islands are strung across the horizon at the outer reaches of Bay of Islands, 20 miles northwest of Corner Brook.*

Otter Bay Provincial Park A forest of shrubs two feet high covers most of this barrenland park's 400 acres. Parts of the terrain are rocky and covered by a variety of bright green, yellow, orange and black lichens.

Piccadilly Head Provincial Park A number of small marine creatures lie exposed on sand flats at low tide. A walking trail leaves the beach and penetrates the forest of balsam fir. The 100-acre park also has limestone cliffs—some drop more than 40 feet to the sea—from where migrating waterfowl may be seen in the fall.

Port au Port Evidence of forces that shaped this region some 500 million years ago is seen in layered, folded and faulted rock along the Gulf of St. Lawrence shore. Mostly dolomite and limestone, the formations contain fossils of marine animals.

Red Rocks Hurricane-force winds funnel out of the Long Range Mountains and through a dry gulch to the sea here. Gusts sometimes exceed 100 miles an hour; they have frequently derailed railway cars.

Sandbanks Provincial Park The park is accessible only by boat or on foot. A path follows the sandbanks along nearly three miles of beach.

Scenic Route The 28-mile highway from Channel-Port aux Basques to Rose Blanche passes through treeless, rocky barrens with gushing streams, tumbling waterfalls and wild seascapes.

Sir Richard Squires Memorial Park Salmon are seen bypassing 30-foot-high Big Falls by means of a fish ladder on the Humber River. The river flows through a gorge which cuts through the 3,890-acre park.

Sop's Arm River Provincial Park The horseshoe-shaped park rises about 70 feet above the Main River, providing a view of the islands in Sop's Arm. A mile north of the park is a canyon with walls of greenish soapstone.

The Topsails Some of the high rock outcroppings that rise from flat barrens in this area are named for the topsails of a square-rigged ship: Gaff Topsail, Main Topsail and Mizzen Topsail. They tower 300 to 500 feet above the surrounding barrens. Mostly granite, they have resisted erosion. Freight trains cross the barrens but carry no passengers. The only way into the area for tourists is by aircraft or by hiking 15 miles from Sheffield Lake.

Wilderness Area Few roads penetrate this 2,500-square-mile wilderness in south-central Newfoundland. Covered partly by thick forests, partly by barrens, the territory is a labyrinth of lakes, rivers and streams, and should be visited only with a guide.

The Awesome Mark of a Glacier

The rugged beauty of the Western Brook gorge in Gros Morne National Park is a testament to the awesome power of glacial erosion. The gorge is more than 2,500 feet deep: cliffs tower some 2,000 feet above the surface of fjord-like Western Brook Pond—and the pond is 544 feet deep. The gorge was gouged from the rock during the Ice Age, when most of Newfoundland was covered much of the time by a massive ice cap.

The weight at the center of the cap spawned glaciers—great rivers of ice flowing toward the sea. One glacier dug ever deeper into the valley of the river now called Western Brook. Even when the ice cap ebbed (it shrank and expanded at least three times during the Ice Age), glaciers persisted in the valleys.

When finally the ice retreated, the once shallow Western Brook valley had been transformed into a deep U-shaped gorge, its western end blocked by glacial debris. Because the glacier that cut the gorge never reached the sea, the Western Brook gorge did not become a true fjord. (Parsons Pond, Portland Creek Pond, St. Pauls Inlet, Bonne Bay, Hawkes Bay and Bay of Islands, all on Newfoundland's west coast, are true fjords.)

During the Ice Age, the sheer weight of the ice pressed the land down. With the ice gone the land began to "float" upward. That process continues even today as the land returns to its pre-Ice Age level. Western Brook, which runs through the glacial debris to the sea, cuts ever deeper as the land continues to rise. In time the stream could become a series of waterfalls. Its source would then be a high-altitude lake now called Western Brook Pond.

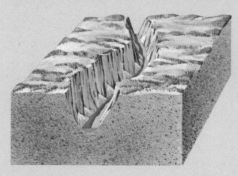

Two million years ago: Western Brook flows down a valley that cuts through the Long Range Mountains, which form a high plateau.

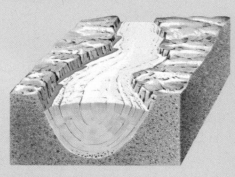

12,000 years ago: At times the entire landscape has been covered by an ice sheet as much as a mile thick. But now the ice has temporarily receded, exposing the highlands on both sides. The glacier lingers stubbornly in the deepened valley of Western Brook, now a gorge.

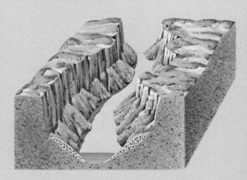

Today: Some 10,000 years have passed since the ice released its grip on the land. The Western Brook gorge is steep-sided, U-shaped and about half a mile deep. One end is partly blocked by glacial debris. Western Brook Pond fills the bottom to a depth of 544 feet.

31

Remote, Enchanting, a Tiny Archipelago of Superb Beaches

The Magdalens—remote, strange, sometimes eerie—are among the most beautiful of all Canada's scenic wonders. Yet few Canadians know even where the islands are. Not many have taken the ferry from Souris, P.E.I., or flown from Charlottetown or Gaspé to discover the haunting charm of this eternally windswept ocean outpost of French Canada.

Physically, the 60-mile-long archipelago in the Gulf of St. Lawrence is a string of rocky outcrops, once part of a broad expanse of land but isolated during the past 10,000 to 12,000 years as the sea level rose. Administratively, the islands are a part of Quebec. Historically, they are a promised land for the threatened.

Although some 800 of the 13,500 Madelinots speak English—their ancestors were Cape Breton Scots or the survivors of shipwrecks—almost all others descend from Acadian French who fled British rule in Nova Scotia after 1755. Most modern Madelinots trace their families back to political and religious refugees who chose the islands as a place of freedom.

The dozen major Iles de la Madeleine lie roughly 70 miles off the northeast tip of Prince Edward Island. They are 100 miles from Newfoundland, 60 miles from the Cape Breton Highlands and 160 miles from Gaspé.

Their geological core, 270 to 350 million years old, is partly sedimentary, partly volcanic. It breaks out

Headland on Ile du Havre aux Maisons.

33

along miles of shoreline in glowering cliffs of greenish-gray sandstone, in blazes of white gypsum, in intricately sea-sculptured bluffs, arches, tunnels and caves of red sandstone so soft that it leaves a rusty smear on clothes.

This seascape defines the outer limits of three collections of stubby hills—on which most of the people live. One is Ile du Havre Aubert (Amherst Island) and nearby Ile d'Entrée (Entry Island). Another includes Ile du Cap aux Meules (Grindstone Island) and Ile du Havre aux Maisons (Alright Island). The third has Grosse Ile, Ile de l'Est and Ile de la Grande Entrée (Coffin Island). French names are official, but many a boat bears the English name of its port.

As once they were a political and religious refuge, the Magdalens—and particularly the beaches—are a supreme escape from the outside world. The road that links the islands wanders along two parallel beaches. The Atlantic rolls in through the Cabot Strait and onto the eastern shores. A few feet away, dune grass whispers at the edge of a huge, shimmering lagoon. Across the lagoon is another skinny strip of sand snaking into a misty distance, and beyond is the sea again, the blue Gulf. At any moment, you imagine, the ocean may shrug and inundate everything in sight.

The utter loneliness of some beaches, the mysterious shifting of dunes, the rustling grass, the sea's clatter and growl, the way the wind wails in the cliffside caves . . . these are why the Magdalens abound in stories of hideous apparitions, fiends that walk by night, dwarfs, sirens, hermits, buried treasure and the frightful cries of tormented souls. Yet in the fragrant heat of a sunny midsummer afternoon these deserted beaches—with the beauty of their grassy dunes, their sumptuous width, the powdery fineness of their pink, gold and white sands—are among the most seductive in the world, a beach connoisseur's dream of heaven.

The main island group has at least 75 miles of flawless ocean beach. That does not include the saltwater frontage along the lagoons that split the Magdalens throughout most of their length. Behind some beaches are hard, sand flatlands hundreds of yards wide. You can leave the ferry at Cap-aux-Meules, drive for miles along these flats, then pitch a tent beside the surf, exploit the infinity of driftwood for your bonfire, and forget whatever it is you go to beaches to forget. Chances are there will be no other camper in sight— but perhaps a rusty wreck: more than 180 ships have gone down on and around the Magdalens. As a "graveyard of the Atlantic," they rival Sable Island.

Generations ago, islanders cut most of the larger trees. Now the hills are bare of all but grass, clumps of scrubby spruce and wild flowers that seafarers swear

This rock arch, formed by pounding seas, will eventually collapse, leaving a tiny island off the Magdalens coast. In time even the island will crumble. A late sun filtering through a slight haze turns the beach along Dune de l'Ouest into a study of light and shadow.

they sniff from miles offshore. Houses on these hills wear the bright colors of rural Quebec. They are built to face the view each family likes best, even in the little conglomerations that pass for towns, and tumble toward the sea like blocks a child has spilled.

Madelinots are not farmers, although some try to scratch a bit of food from the sandy soil. Island men have always preferred to harvest the ocean. Each year this skinny little archipelago lands more than one quarter of the tonnage of all fish caught in Quebec.

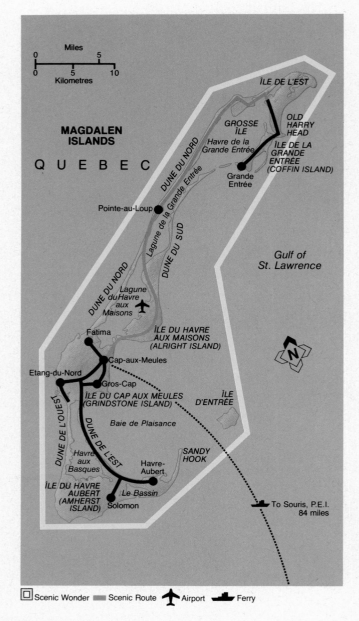

MAGDALEN ISLANDS

QUEBEC

Miles
0 · · · 5
0 · · · 5 · · · 10
Kilometres

ÎLE DE L'EST

GROSSE ÎLE

OLD HARRY HEAD

DUNE DU NORD

Havre de la Grande Entrée

ÎLE DE LA GRANDE ENTRÉE (COFFIN ISLAND)

Lagune de la Grande Entrée

Grande Entrée

Pointe-au-Loup

DUNE DU SUD

Gulf of St. Lawrence

DUNE DU NORD

Lagune du Havre aux Maisons

Fatima

ÎLE DU HAVRE AUX MAISONS (ALRIGHT ISLAND)

Cap-aux-Meules

Etang-du-Nord

Gros-Cap

ÎLE DU CAP AUX MEULES (GRINDSTONE ISLAND)

ÎLE D'ENTRÉE

DUNE DE L'OUEST

DUNE DE L'EST

Baie de Plaisance

Havre aux Basques

Havre-Aubert

SANDY HOOK

ÎLE DU HAVRE AUBERT (AMHERST ISLAND)

Le Bassin

Solomon

To Souris, P.E.I. 84 miles

□ Scenic Wonder ▬ Scenic Route ✈ Airport ⛴ Ferry

The islands are dense with evidence of the people's dependence on the sea: smelly, ancient shacks for smoking herring, little canneries, refrigeration plants, rusty anchors among the wild flowers, and quaint harbors with as many bobbing boats as wheeling gulls. Even inland (never more than a couple of miles from shore) you see boats abandoned in the fields, a dory full of flowers, boys selling clams at the roadside, old fishing nets rigged as softball backstops or soccer and lacrosse goals. And everywhere there are lobster traps.

The isolation of the Madelinots has always fascinated outsiders. As recently as the late 1940s the then infrequent tourists marveled at not only the contentment and good health of the islanders (a result, supposedly, of their distance from mainlanders' germs) but also their never having seen trains, street lights, skyscrapers or beauty parlors.

Air travel, electric power, television and the spread of government services have since destroyed the islands' air of cultural isolation. But it is doubtful that anything will ever change their geographical isolation, their mid-ocean aura of being both a deadly trap and a safe haven for ships, their place as a remote and favorite haunt for a dazzling variety of birds, their dependence on sea and wind for their very shape.

The birds are a wonder in their own right. The islands have been their refuge for thousands of springs and autumns, since before any man knew the archipelago existed. Ile aux Goélands (Gull Island), close by the village of Etang-du-Nord, swarms with herring gulls and great black-backed gulls. On Ile aux Loups Marins (Seal Island) are great blue herons and double-crested cormorants. Ile Brion, to the north of the main island group, harbors great black-backed and herring gulls, great cormorants, eiders and guillemots.

Even on the major islands birds noisily assert their right to be there. Migrating pintail and black ducks, blue-winged and green-winged teal, Canada geese and shorebirds gather by the thousands beyond the sedges, dune grass, cattails and bulrushes of the tidal lagoons and off Ile du Havre Aubert in Baie de Plaisance.

Like many of the birds, some people of the Magdalens move on and off the islands in seasons. Months before Christmas, they book all the late December flights to Montreal to visit friends and relatives who live in the city; all summer the little airport at Havre-aux-Maisons seethes with activity as those who've settled elsewhere come home for a while. "The Maggies," even for a onetime visitor, are memorable; for a Madelinot born and bred they are unforgettable.

On Rochers aux Oiseaux (Bird Rocks), some 20 miles northeast of Ile de l'Est, are huge colonies of jabbering, squawking razorbills, puffins, kittiwakes, murres and gannets, the latter with six-foot wingspreads.

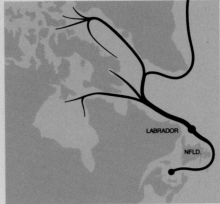

For most of the year harp seals range the North Atlantic as far as the Arctic Circle. But in March some 1,250,000 gather on the ice in the Gulf of St. Lawrence and off southern Labrador and northern Newfoundland where northwest Atlantic harp seals mate, and where their young are born.

Harp Seals Range the Seas, Rendezvous in the Gulf

Within a month of giving birth on the ice, a female harp seal mates again. A two-month delay in development of the embryo ensures that the new birth will coincide with the return to the ice the following March, when food will be plentiful. The annual visit lasts six to eight weeks.

A newborn seal (right, top) is about 2½ feet long and weighs some 20 pounds. Because of its mother's rich milk, it can gain up to five pounds a day (right, bottom) during its first two weeks. When weaned it weighs nearly 100 pounds. By the fourth week the pup has lost the thick coat sought by sealers and is covered with gray and black hair. The marking on its back for which the species is named—it resembles a harp or saddle—does not appear until the seal's seventh year.

The harp seal is so streamlined that even its earflaps have disappeared. The internal ear openings and nostrils are closed under water. Even out of the water, the seal's nostrils are kept closed (for as long as 10 minutes at a time), opening only when the animal takes a breath. A thick layer of blubber serves as insulation against the cold and as a reserve store of food. To minimize the loss of body heat, the entrances to blood vessels in the skin can be constricted, allowing through only enough blood to keep the skin from freezing. The flippers are important in regulating body heat. In cold conditions they are kept colder than the rest of the body. Arteries and veins are arranged so that blood that surges into a flipper releases heat to blood flowing back into the body.

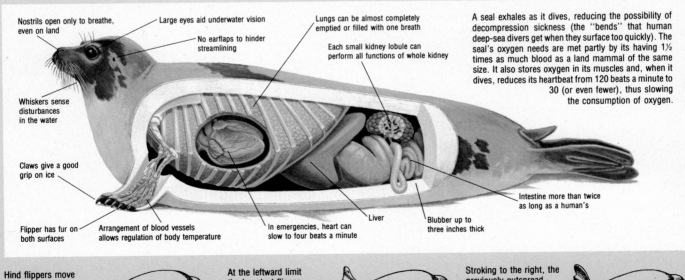

Nostrils open only to breathe, even on land

Large eyes aid underwater vision

No earflaps to hinder streamlining

Whiskers sense disturbances in the water

Claws give a good grip on ice

Flipper has fur on both surfaces

Arrangement of blood vessels allows regulation of body temperature

In emergencies, heart can slow to four beats a minute

Liver

Lungs can be almost completely emptied or filled with one breath

Each small kidney lobule can perform all functions of whole kidney

Intestine more than twice as long as a human's

Blubber up to three inches thick

A seal exhales as it dives, reducing the possibility of decompression sickness (the "bends" that human deep-sea divers get when they surface too quickly). The seal's oxygen needs are met partly by its having 1½ times as much blood as a land mammal of the same size. It also stores oxygen in its muscles and, when it dives, reduces its heartbeat from 120 beats a minute to 30 (or even fewer), thus slowing the consumption of oxygen.

Hind flippers move together from side to side, one bunched, the other outspread.

At the leftward limit the bunched flipper opens, the other closes, ready to swing right.

Stroking to the right, the previously outspread flipper now is bunched and leading.

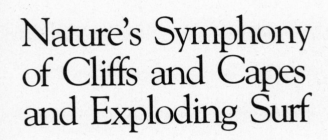

Nature's Symphony of Cliffs and Capes and Exploding Surf

Forever windblown, forever beautiful, the great Cape Breton Highlands wage endless war with the sea. Bare rocks expose the awesome record of the age-old conflict, and the infinite sounds of sea on stone give up-to-the-second news of the ocean's latest offensive.

Thick forests of hardwood and evergreen, like some bright new dress, drape the round shoulders of the ancient inland hills. As little rivers tumble their lacy way through these hills, sometimes in gorges a thousand feet deep, the ocean continues its ceaseless sculpturing of the shore. These moving waters not only shape the rock now but also reveal what it was before mankind was even a gleam in evolution's eye.

The national park near the northern tip of Cape Breton Island stretches from the Gulf of St. Lawrence on the west to the open Atlantic on the east. It is part of an upland that was beneath the sea 200 million years ago and at sea level 100 million years ago. Parts now are 1,700 feet above the ocean.

The 367-square-mile park is 75 miles north of Sydney. Its two entrances (near Chéticamp on the Gulf and at Ingonish Beach on the Atlantic) lie on the roughly circular 184-mile highway known as the Cabot Trail, one of the most beautiful drives in North America.

Near Chéticamp, N.S., along the Cabot Trail.

39

The shores along the trail are a symphony concert for the eye. The themes are these: cliffs that slope gently to seaward, then abruptly plunge 1,000 feet to the exploding surf; massive headlands and echoing coves; desolate capes and dazzling white bluffs of gypsum; beaches of gleaming sand; and slender barachois—nature's breakwaters of rocks and sand. Shorefuls of round stones make a deep and unforgettable sound as waves roll and rattle them in an eternal process that is slowly turning them to sand.

The rocky understructure of Cape Breton Highlands National Park was formed more than 800 million years ago. The earliest rocks were both sedimentary—solidified from sand, lime, mud, gravel and shells on the floor of an ancient sea—and volcanic. Some of the oldest rocks in the park—black, dark green, gray, silvery—are exposed by roadcuts in several places.

They are most remarkable on the western shore and along the steepest parts of the Cabot Trail just east of Pleasant Bay in the valley of the Grande Anse River.

Heat and immense pressures folded and broke the rock and bands of minerals were transformed into new kinds of rock. To this mix was added molten rock that forced up through cracks in the earlier composition. Spectacular pink and gray granites in cliffs and roadcuts on the east side of the park—notably along the tidemark between Black Brook Cove and Green Point— are a dramatic inheritance from this period.

For hundreds of millions of years, erosion cut deep into the rocky framework, exposing masses of what had been subterranean rock. About 330 million years ago, new sediment collected in shallow waters and river deltas; patches of this sedimentary rock now lie atop more ancient rock at Chéticamp, Pleasant Bay and Ingonish.

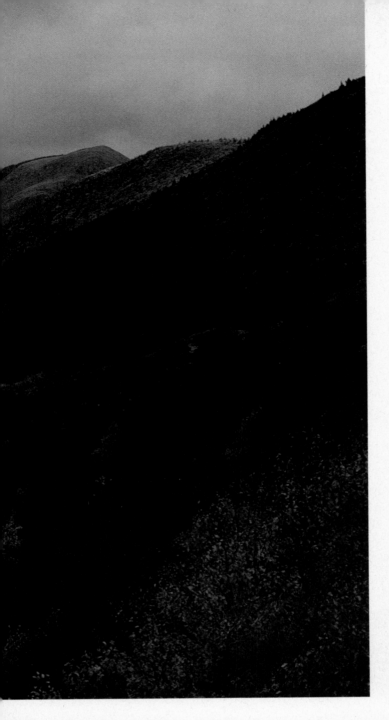

Twenty million years later, amid a breaking and splitting of the earth's crust, river erosion had transformed the fractured land into a plain. Then, as a block of ice floats higher in water as it melts, the land "floated" higher as erosion lightened its upper surfaces. This tableland is now 1,200 to 1,500 feet above sea level; rising above it are rounded summits of more than 200 feet. The Cabot Trail crosses the tableland between Pleasant Bay and Jumping Brook and between the North Aspy River and Grande Anse River valleys.

After 300 million years, by which time rivers had cut gorges and the sea had undermined cliffs, an ice cap covered Cape Breton Island. It gouged and scraped and polished and when the ice melted away, a mere 12,000 years ago, it left a blanket of debris 10 to 20 feet thick.

Glacial rubbish lies in layers atop freshly exposed bedrock in rock-cuts throughout the highlands. Some massive boulders are stranded on hilltops; others, at the shore, endure the ocean's never-ending battering. Little ponds and bogs in the park's remote interior are also partly an Ice Age hangover.

And now? Again a period of erosion. Waves and rivers continue to eat away at the land and to reshape it.

The Cape Breton glens, with their tumbling streams, and the seascapes, often half obscured by fleecy mists, are like those of the Scottish Highlands and the Isles, and Scots who settled Cape Breton Island felt at home here. The first European visitors to the island may have been Norse and Icelanders about A.D. 1000. English fishermen probably knew the coast in the late 15th cen-

Cape Bretoners, who proudly regard their whole island as a natural wonder, say their scenic crown jewels are the mountain-hugging sections of the Cabot Trail that loop and hairpin their dizzying way along the park's two coastlines. Villages such as Friars Head add charm to the trail.

tury. Italian-born John Cabot sailed from Bristol in 1497 and, on June 24, after some five weeks, claimed for England what almost certainly was Cape Breton Island. Near Cape North, just off the Cabot Trail, a small cairn marks Cabot's probable landfall.

For more than a century—until the 1740s—Cape Breton Island was French; in 1763 it was proclaimed a part of Nova Scotia. Scottish immigrants began to arrive in Nova Scotia in 1773 and by 1835 about 25,000 Gaelic-speaking highlanders had made their homes in Cape Breton. Gaelic is still spoken in some parts of the island. So is French, among the people of the western shore. Many are descendants of 14 Acadian families settled at Chéticamp in 1785-86.

In any coastal settlement in northern Cape Breton Island—whether Acadians or Scots are claimed as ancestors—odds are that for generations men have taken fish from the sea. The fishing villages are the man-made scenic wonder of the highlands.

The national park has a magnificently varied forest. On the hills are hemlock, white and jack pine, white and black spruce, white and yellow birch, red, striped and sugar maple, elm, beech, ash, trembling and largetooth aspen, balsam poplar and balsam fir. High in the central plateau is an eerie country of muskeg,

Sunset on a highland pond turns lily pads into an intricate brocade.

ponds, heath barrens and subarctic-like growth. The environment there and along the battered coastal headlands twists and stunts the few spruce into bizarre runts. Atop the salt-sprayed headlands are creeping and ground juniper, black crowberry and Scotch lovage.

The park's animal life includes lynx, snowshoe hare, black bear, red fox, short-tailed weasel, chipmunk, white-tailed deer, muskrat, flying squirrel, otter, mink, pine marten, Keen's bat, beaver and moose.

Bird watchers have recorded more than 185 species. Along the coast in summer can be seen gannets, terns, cormorants, ducks, geese, gulls and shorebirds. Grouse, hawks, barred owls and bald eagles are common. For serious bird watchers the Cape Breton Highlands' greatest attraction is perhaps the extraordinary variety of warblers, thrushes, finches and woodpeckers.

A drive through the park is a lyrical experience for anyone who keeps his brakes and gears in good shape, who does not suffer seriously from fear of heights and who loves magical seascapes. But the Cabot Trail touches only the edges of the highlands.

The best way to get *into* the park is to walk. Nature trails range from those no tougher than a stroll through a city garden to those that require modest hill-climbing ability. Together, these footpaths reveal all the diverse natural and geological marvels of a land where, for millions of years, mountains have met the sea.

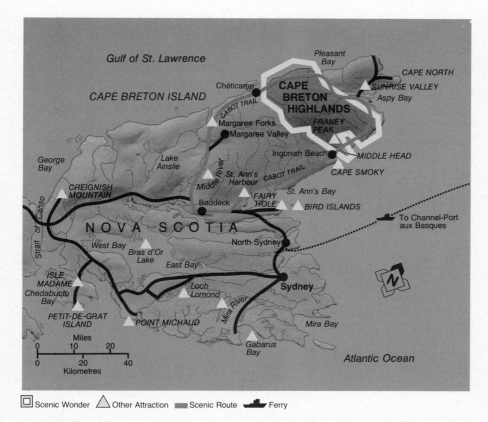

Scenic Wonder △ Other Attraction ■ Scenic Route ⛴ Ferry

OTHER ATTRACTIONS
The Cabot Trail and Bras d'Or

Bird Islands Picture this page.

Bras d'Or Lake This sparkling, 400-square-mile inland sea almost splits Cape Breton Island. Encircled by superb highland scenery, the virtually tideless lake resembles a Scottish loch, with scores of fine beaches and pine-clad islands. Two of Cape Breton's Micmac Indian reserves border Bras d'Or and one occupies Chapel Island in the lake. At Eskasoni, on East Bay, the Micmacs use an ingenious method of oyster farming based on Japanese practice.

Cabot Trail A modern two-lane highway, the 184-mile route is seldom far from the sea; many side roads lead to picturesque coastal communities, rocky inlets and magnificent headlands pounded by surf. Open all year, the trail is at its breathtaking best in September and October when the highlands are bright with autumn color. Seventy miles of the route pass through Cape Breton Highlands National Park. The trail is named for John Cabot, who is said to have landed at the island's northern tip in 1497. From Cabot's Landing, near Cape North, a hiking trail leads to the summit of 1,350-foot Sugar Loaf, which may have been the explorer's landfall.

Cape Smoky This 1,200-foot headland, often shrouded in mist, is best seen from across South Bay Ingonish at Middle Head, a two-mile-long peninsula that is a part of Cape Breton Highlands National Park.

Creignish Mountain Looming 850 feet above George Bay and the Strait of Canso, the mountain affords a spectacular view of the strait, the bay and mainland Nova Scotia.

Fairy Hole This limestone cavern of stalactites and stalagmites has a 50-foot-wide mouth but narrows abruptly to a mere crawl space.

Franey Peak A two-and-a-half-mile hiking and nature trail from Ingonish Centre leads up to the summit of 1,405-foot Franey Peak and a majestic

Bird Islands *Great cormorants stand guard over Ciboux and Hertford islands, where thousands of puffins, guillemots and razorbills nest. A two-and-half-hour boat tour from Great Bras d'Or circles the uninhabited islands.*

43

view of the Atlantic. Included in the panorama are Cape Smoky, Ingonish Island with its tall lighthouse, Middle Head and the hills of the national park.

Gabarus Bay Several lush patches of evergreen forest hug this low, irregular coastline almost to the water's edge. In open areas, the shore is carpeted with green and yellow marsh grasses.

Isle Madame Largest of the Chedabucto Bay islands, it is linked to Cape Breton by a bridge across Lennox Passage.

Loch Lomond Nestled between the East Bay Hills and Mira Hills, Loch Lomond is the largest lake in a chain that includes Lake Uist and Enon Lake.

Middle River *A lovely section of the Middle River near Cape Breton's Margaree Valley.*

Margaree Forks An aquarium here has specimens of salmon and trout. Nearby are some of Canada's best salmon fishing grounds at the Forks, Thornbush, Hut and Long pools.

Middle River Picture this page.

Mira River Broad and serene, the island-laced river is more like a lake. Forests reach to the water's edge. In places beaches line the twisting shore.

Petit-de-Grat Island This small, rocky island with its charming villages and jagged coastline is a favorite of artists.

Point Michaud Two miles of white sand make the crescent beach here one of Nova Scotia's most beautiful. Gray seals are found on and around the Basque Islands in the bay.

St. Ann's Harbour A scenic drive—part of the Cabot Trail—circles the harbor and runs to the end of a spit of land that separates the harbor from St. Ann's Bay. At its southern end the route passes sheer cliffs of gypsum; at the north it offers a clear view of the Bird Islands (and often of bald eagles soaring overhead); at most places in between it looks down from rugged bluffs to rolling breakers. The spit, which resembles an artificial breakwater, ends 300 yards short of Englishtown on the southern shore. A motorist blows his car horn to summon the ferry.

Sunrise Valley From surrounding hills, the view of valley and sea is spectacular. Fertile farmlands, stands of elm and brightly colored houses are scattered along the banks of the North Aspy River.

A ruffed grouse can nip off the tender buds of saplings without damaging the fragile twigs.

Porcupines strip large pieces of bark from trees, particularly pines, leaving tooth marks.

A conical stump that appears to have been felled with a chisel is the handiwork of a beaver.

Deer, elk and moose strip bark from trees, leaving patches. In spring these browsers leave broken twigs.

Bears use claws and teeth to make the long, vertical slashes that mark their territory.

In scraping the velvet from their antlers, moose, elk and deer leave sections of bark hanging in shreds.

Signs in the Forest and the Story They Tell

Cape Breton Highlands forests are typical of the Acadian Forest Region (which includes most forests in the Maritime provinces). Climax species—those which predominate when the forest is stable, mature and undisturbed—are sugar maple on good soil, hemlock on poor soil. Other trees include white pine, balsam fir, white and black spruce, red maple, birch, elm, beech, ash and aspen. But only climax species survive in areas which remain undisturbed for about 500 years. Jack pine is common in areas destroyed by fire within the last 50 years. On higher ground, the Cape Breton forests resemble the boreal evergreen forests farther north, with balsam fir the predominant species. The forest also tells the close observer much about wildlife, prevailing winds, past weather conditions, which way is north, and, it is said, whether it will rain soon. With practice, anyone can learn to "read" a forest.

In coastal areas, trees are often stunted and bent by salt spray blown onshore by prevailing winds.

Folklore has it that when fallen pine cones are tightly closed, it will rain. When they are open, fine weather is in the offing.

This cutaway view of a tree stump shows how a tree increases its girth and height each growing season. It is widely believed that the counting of these annual growth rings in a tree stump or at the end of a log reveals the tree's age at the time it was cut. This is only partly true. The "ring" of growth is actually a cone-shaped addition to the tree's bulk, and the added wood at the top of the tree creates the first ring at that level. The diagram shows fewer growth rings in the top cross-section than in the section lower down. The closer to ground level a tree is cut, the more accurate the computing of its age by ring counting. In years of heavy rainfall, the ring is thicker than those formed in years of drought. In a very dry year, it is possible that no growth will be formed at a tree's lower level, further complicating the dating of the tree.

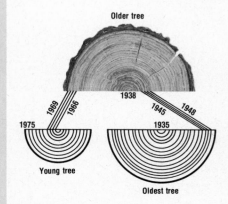

Older tree

1969 1966 1938 1945 1948

1975 1935

Young tree

Oldest tree

By matching especially large or small rings, known to have been formed in a particular year, from one tree sample to another, scientists have been able to establish a calendar dating as far back as 1,000 years. Buildings centuries old can be precisely dated by this method.

The outermost growth ring of a young tree represents the year it was cut down. With this year established, the young tree's growth rings can all be dated, and then compared and matched to the appropriate growth rings of an older tree. Once the dates of the older tree's growth rings are established, the age of any tree that was growing in the same area and sometime during the lifespan of the older tree, can be determined.

Rolling Dunes, a Tireless Wind, the Loving Grass

Y ou expect a kind of flowery prettiness in Prince Edward Island, but not the grandeur of the great dune lands of the north shore. They are like a strip cut from the mighty Sahara and set down between a storybook sea and a neat country garden.

The shaping of this coast—the shifting dunes, the beaches, the cliffs, the symmetrical sandspits—is the work of a conspiracy that began before even dinosaurs trod the earth, a marvelously intricate conspiracy of winds, tides, ice, ocean and river currents, tough grass and shrubs. The red sandstone of the cliffs is 250 million years old but the arrangement of the beaches and dunes is always newer than the newest sunrise.

The best place to experience both the naturalist's awe at the creation of the dunes and the sunny comfort of some of the finest beaches in North America is in Prince Edward Island National Park. This 25-mile stretch of sand, bluffs, salt marshes and freshwater ponds is at the heart of the north shore—at Cavendish, Rustico Island, Brackley, Stanhope and Dalvay.

A half-dozen roads fan north from Charlottetown, the provincial capital, to various corners of the national park; no drive takes more than 30 minutes. The eight-square-mile park—it is one and a half miles at its widest—is one of the smallest of the national parks. Yet it is among the most popular. Each year more than

Ocean currents shape the Blooming Point sandspit.

47

a million persons travel millions of miles to get there, some from as far as Australia, some from just down the road at Oyster Bed Bridge, Ebenezer and Pleasant Grove. Hundreds of thousands make the pilgrimage to Green Gables, the house that helped inspire Lucy Maud Montgomery's classic *Anne of Green Gables.*

Other hundreds of thousands find a deeper meaning in the park: a sense of the incredible complexity in the natural forces that—each millennium, each season, each second—make the dune country what it is. Prince Edward Island National Park could be a model for ecological studies—its lessons are inspirational.

Take, for example, the crucial importance of the humble marram grass. Its botanical name, *Ammophila arenaria,* means "sand loving." On north-shore Prince Edward Island the sand desperately needs loving, just to stay put. Marram grass obliges.

It is the first growth in nature's system for turning sand into something that can support life. Sand at the high-water line is dried by the sun, then freed by the wind from the wet hem of the sea—first to be caught on pebbles, seashell fragments and driftwood, then to rise in tiny mounds where the grass has sunk its roots. From these little sand hills grow great dunes.

The marram roots reach as much as 10 feet down in search of water, then spread into a deep, stringy network that helps hold the dune together. The grass survives because it can grow quickly to the surface after being blanketed with sand and because it is impervious to salt spray. But it is not hardy enough to withstand heavy human traffic. At Cavendish and Brackley, the park's most used beaches, there's been some deterioration of the dunes. Once the grass has gone, the wind often carves small depressions into giant holes called "blow-outs." Too many blowouts turn stable dunes into constantly shifting hills unable to support vegetation.

The pristine magnificence of the dunes can still be seen at the most inaccessible part of this highly accessible park. To get there, you walk west along the superb spit on Tracadie Bay to Blooming Point. The excursion is one of the finest hikes in Canada.

Marram grass is essential to the mutual support system that sustains the entire seascape. By settling the sand, the grass gives northern bayberry a chance. Sea rocket and seabeach sandwort fringe the beaches. Then crowberry, bearberry, ground juniper and wild roses fill the sheltered hollows of the dunes. In some places, a few feet farther inland, white spruce fight to grip the sand. Winds prune them, salt spray stunts them. Strange, twisted, older than they look (some trees 75 years old are only two or three feet high), they are the tough handiwork of the violent elements.

Yet only a few hundred feet away, where the high dunes offer shelter from winds and salt spray, the white spruce grow straight and tall, heralding the start of the coastal forest. Here also are red spruce, white and wire birch, red maple, balsam fir, trembling aspen and speckled alder. Rich, emerald-green ferns and mosses carpet the forest floor. And though it can't be seen from here, the faint sound of surf echoes in the trees.

In some spruce trees in the park, particularly on Rustico Island, are the huge nests of the great blue herons. A single tree may support up to four nests, some of them 40 feet above ground. There are more than 100 nests on Rustico Island, home to hundreds of the dignified gray-blue birds with their tapering bills, snakelike necks and six-foot wingspreads. Some are four feet tall and can be seen spearing fish in the marshes and ponds.

The great blue heron is but one of more than 210 species of land and water birds in the park. From May until early autumn migratory birds keep the wetlands

The rippling effect of wind on sand is seen in this grass-fringed dune at Brackley Beach. Marram grass surfaces quickly even after being covered by sand and its intricate root system works ceaselessly to turn shifting dunes into something permanent. Striking features of beaches such as Cavendish Beach (right) are headlands of reddish sandstone.

gently seething with activity. Blue- and green-winged teal, ring-necked and black ducks nest by the ponds. Great flocks of Canada geese feed on the Brackley marshlands each fall; and curlews, plovers, phalaropes, sandpipers, yellowlegs, godwits and dozens of other shorebirds visit the park throughout the summer.

The marsh hawk cruises effortlessly above the sand hills. The Savannah sparrow and the horned lark flit over the dune lands. The wave-chasing sanderling runs out behind the retreating surf, pecking at tiny crustaceans—then, at the exact moment the surf turns, the sanderling turns too, neatly avoiding the incoming wave. In the woodlands are chipping, song and white-throated sparrows, the slate-colored junco, red-eyed vireo, Swainson's thrush, flicker and many warblers.

The park is rich in animals that survive on terrain that sea and wind never stop remaking. The red fox has yellow eyes, a white-tipped tail and fur that ripples in the breeze like shot silk. He hunts field mice in the dense thickets and grass where dunes and forest meet.

The fox is king of the dunes but when in pursuit of the grass-eating snowshoe hare he roams inland. The elusive short-tailed weasel also hunts mice and hares, but mostly in fields and bush country farther inland. Skunks prefer the spruce woodlands. Raccoons feed at the edges of Long Pond and Lake of Shining Waters. Mink and muskrat live in park waterways and in the ponds are muskrat houses—mounds of mud and plants.

Sunset stills the park. But along its seaward edge the eternal conspirators build busily through the night. Great waves roll relentlessly to the land. White breakers curl, collapse, and foam up on the beaches, each in turn tracing a delicate new line of sand at high water. The wind—never still—teases and sweeps and scours the dunes and the spits, digging some depressions deeper, filling in others, tirelessly reshaping the sandy shore. And marram grass, the great lover, loves on.

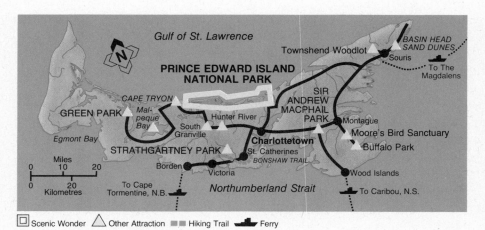

Scenic Wonder △ Other Attraction ▨ Hiking Trail ⛴ Ferry

OTHER ATTRACTIONS

Hiking Trails and Oyster Beds

Basin Head Sand Dunes Beachgrass, lichens and other vegetation fight for life along one and one-half miles of coast. Cranberries grow in sheltered spots. Foxes roam the dunes hunting meadow voles, shrews and woodland jumping-mice. Herring gulls, great black-backed gulls and crows are seen on the barren open center part of the dune system. Seven miles southeast is Souris, noted for beaches and deep-sea fishing and linked by ferry with Cap-aux-Meules in the Magdalen Islands.

Bonshaw Hills Trail This well-marked, 20-mile trail between St. Catherines and Victoria goes through woodlots and cool, dark hemlock forests, past placid ponds and babbling brooks and along a seaside beach.

Buffalo Park A herd of 20 buffalo in a 100-acre enclosure.

Cape Tryon Picture this page.

Green Park About 200 acres of fields and forest, the park is bordered by the Trout River, Campbell Creek, the Bideford River and Malpeque Bay.

Hunter River Fields and pastures are adazzle with daisies in early July.

Malpeque Bay Oysters are raised on underwater "clotheslines" (wires strung underwater between stakes) until large enough to survive in tidal rivers.

Moore's Bird Sanctuary Migrating Canada geese and a variety of ducks stop over on these islands.

Sir Andrew Macphail Provincial Park A small museum commemorates author-physician Sir Andrew Macphail. There is a trout pond and a nature trail.

South Granville A one-mile hiking trail follows the Old Princetown Road (once a wagon road) through gently undulating countryside and mature hardwood forests. Maples and white and yellow birch are abundant along the trail. It goes from Devil's Punch Bowl Provincial Park to South Granville.

Strathgartney Provincial Park A high grassy hill in this scenic 40-acre park provides a panoramic view of Northumberland Strait.

Townshend Woodlot Some 250 acres of mature maple and beech, typical of forest that was characteristic of Prince Edward Island 200 to 400 years ago.

Cape Tryon Sea stacks off shore near Cape Tryon were once headlands. Wave action isolated and will ultimately destroy them.

Nature's patterns in the sand are endlessly fascinating. The tiny granules—particles of disintegrated rock—are constantly being rearranged by wind, wave and tide. Each new creation is destroyed by the very forces that made it, then reshaped, destroyed again, reshaped anew. Water currents pick up sand from the ocean bottom, only to deposit it where some obstruction—a rock perhaps—creates turbulence. On land the wind pushes the tiny grains, nudges them, rolls them, carries them, now a few inches, now a few yards. Sand patterns give some clues to the nature of the creative forces.

Evidence of the awesome power of the elements, sand is also the canvas on which the wanderings of men and animals are recorded, then erased. A long, thin groove through wet sand may be the signature of a snail. A crab's pointed claws leave distinctive holes. Bird tracks can be identified—the triangular imprints of a gull's webbed feet, the three-pronged toemarks of small shorebirds, the scuffs the starling makes, dragging its rear toes when it walks . . .

Nature's Artistry in Sand

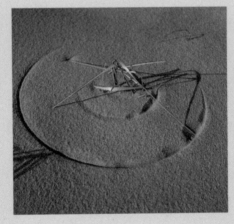

Capricious winds tease bent stalks of marram grass and their tips describe arcs and circles in the sand. Below: a sea worm burrowing in wet sand leaves a seemingly aimless but still elegant trail, an abstract that will be washed away by the next high tide.

Diagonal ripples (above) were caused by a current that covered this part of the beach at high tide. At the outgoing tide, vertical lines were formed by two obstructing stones. Pebbles on a beach created complex ripples (left). Below: when a single strong current is at work, unhindered by other currents or obstacles, parallel ripples are created.

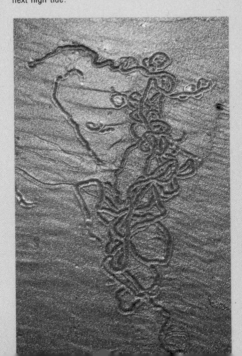

A Classic Wilderness: Calm Canoe Routes and Deep Solitude

Kejimkujik National Park is a lush jungle of shadowy trees and darkly strange rivers and lakes— a classic wilderness of mystery, calm and beauty. Roughly halfway between Annapolis Royal on the Bay of Fundy and Liverpool on the Atlantic Ocean, it is a remote land, a thick forest filigreed with waterways where engines rarely throb and loons still call.

It was to Kejimkujik (usually pronounced Kedge-uh-muh-KOO-jik) that the Micmacs came each year, leaving summer fishing grounds on the coasts, stroking their canoes to winter here under the great hemlocks in the country of the caribou. The canoe is still the best means of plunging into the forested depths of the 145-square-mile park. There are only about seven miles of paved road in the most crowded corner and campers' vehicles can go no farther. Outboard motors are allowed only on Kejimkujik Lake.

Ice molded the face of Kejimkujik thousands of years ago. Great sheets scoured the ancient rocks, gouged shallow lakes and shaped the soil into long, streamlined hills called eskers. As the ice relaxed its grip, plants moved in. Hardwood and coniferous forests mingled and grew up together. Despite heavy logging and burning, the mixed character of the woods is intact. Wire birch and balsam fir grow where men once farmed or

Deep in the Kejimkujik forest.

53

logged. Red oak, sugar maple, beech and white birch embellish the hills. Barely escaping the grasp of the bogs are larch and black and red spruce.

In the spring, swollen by runoff and rich with nutrients from the thick marsh grasses, the waterways rise to the trunks of red maples. White pine, some more than a hundred feet, grow everywhere. Some hemlocks are centuries old and so big that two men embracing a trunk from opposite sides cannot join hands.

Kejimkujik is an oasis where greenbrier and witch hazel thrive. Botanists speculate that these plants (not normally found as far north as Nova Scotia) entered over a coastal plain when the sea level was lower. As glacial ice melted, the rising sea flooded the plain, but the plants had established themselves in Kejimkujik.

In the spring, before the hardwoods have spread their canopy over the cool forest floor, the ground sparkles with mayflowers, starflowers, painted trilliums, lady's slippers, spotted coralroot, orchid bunchberries and wild iris. Crowning the bogs around the many waterways are hardier shrubs—rhodora, leatherleaf, Labrador tea and sheep laurel.

Most animals found in other eastern forests are common in Kejimkujik. White-tailed deer are often seen and red squirrels chatter in the hardwood forests. Porcupines roam the forest and grassy slopes, and black bears treat themselves in the berry patches. Muskrat and otter patrol the waterways, and at night bobcats, raccoons and northern flying squirrels are astir.

Along the grassy edges of lakes and rivers are the nesting grounds of great black-backed gulls and black ducks. Nearby tall trees support osprey nests. The songs of jays, robins, veeries, dark-eyed juncos, countless warblers and pileated woodpeckers enliven the woods. The cry of the loon breaks the abrupt hush of twilight.

Nature has been generous with Kejimkujik. Naturalists have discovered only in recent years that the scarlet tanager, great crested flycatcher and wood thrush make their home in the park. All were supposedly more southerly birds.

Kejimkujik has longer, hotter summers than most other areas of the province. Several of the park's reptiles and other creatures are normally found farther south: they may be descendants of life in a warmer climate some 4,000 to 7,000 years ago. Five species of salamanders, eight kinds of frogs and toads, five snake species and three varieties of turtles live here, surviving winter by hibernating in mud. The ribbon snake and Blanding's turtle are found nowhere else in the Atlantic provinces. Nor is the southern flying squirrel. In

The coloring of this young ruffed grouse makes it difficult to spot in the dense underbrush of Kejimkujik National Park.

54

Kejimkujik Lake (at 15 square miles the park's largest) and in many smaller lakes are eastern brook trout, European brown trout and white perch. There are whitefish in some lakes. Like several of the park's reptiles, they are something of a mystery; whitefish usually are found much farther west in North America. Although the inner geological structure of the park is ancient, most visible evidence of nature's sculpturing is only a few thousand years old. In the eastern half, the lowest rock structure is quartzite, believed at least 500 million years old. Almost as old and found above the quartzite is slate; it often appears as the crest of huge folds. The foundation of the higher northwestern parts of the park is mostly typical central Nova Scotian granite, 350 to 450 million years old.

Kejimkujik has been a national park only since 1969 but men have lived here for more centuries than anyone can say with certainty. Here and there on the

The dark color of the Mersey River and of most lakes in Kejimkujik National Park is caused by plant pigments that feeder rivers pick up in bogs and swamps. Many lakes are shallow and lined with dark rocks and shoals. Canoeists call one particularly hazardous area of Kejimkujik Lake the granite barrens.

shores of Kejimkujik Lake is fascinating evidence of early human existence. The slate is so soft that, with a harder rock, a knife or piece of bone, men could carve pictures and symbols on it. Some of these petroglyphs may predate the arrival of the Europeans. There are pictures of animals, of men fishing and hunting, ancient Micmac symbols, and a four-legged bird surrounded by stars—thought to be a Micmac deity. Later drawings show European traces in Micmac dress and one figure resembles a French cavalier. Some petroglyphs portray sailing ships with flawless rigging.

But perhaps Kejimkujik's greatest appeal lies in its solitude. Canoeists go from lake to lake through narrow channels whose openings are often hidden by overhanging trees. Parts of the seven canoe routes are as ancient as the Micmacs themselves. There are more than 40 miles of hiking trails, and an interpretative program includes guided walks, canoe outings, nature films and lectures. For snowshoers and cross-country skiers the Kejimkujik wilderness is quieter than ever.

Kejimkujik National Park. Its lakes and forest resemble areas of almost every other province, but a wondrous blend of glacial artistry, deep tranquillity and unique animals and plants makes it special indeed.

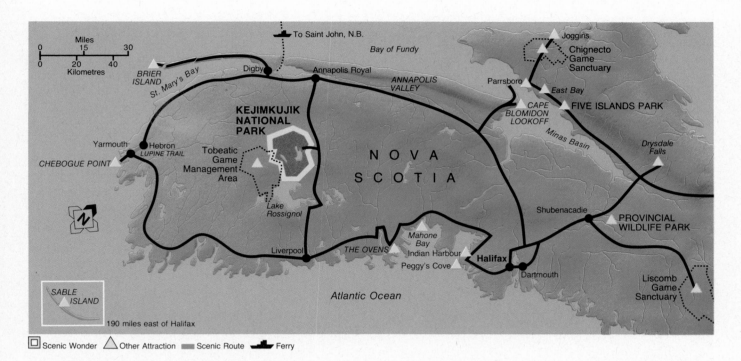

Miles
0   15   30
0   20   40
Kilometres

BRIER ISLAND
St. Mary's Bay
Digby
To Saint John, N.B.
Bay of Fundy
Annapolis Royal
ANNAPOLIS VALLEY
Joggins
Chignecto Game Sanctuary
Parrsboro
East Bay
FIVE ISLANDS PARK
CAPE BLOMIDON LOOKOFF
Minas Basin
Drysdale Falls
KEJIMKUJIK NATIONAL PARK
Yarmouth   Hebron   LUPINE TRAIL
Tobeatic Game Management Area
N O V A   S C O T I A
CHEBOGUE POINT
Lake Rossignol
Shubenacadie
PROVINCIAL WILDLIFE PARK
Liverpool
THE OVENS
Mahone Bay
Indian Harbour
Peggy's Cove
Halifax
Dartmouth
Liscomb Game Sanctuary
SABLE ISLAND
190 miles east of Halifax
Atlantic Ocean

☐ Scenic Wonder △ Other Attraction ▬ Scenic Route ⛴ Ferry

OTHER ATTRACTIONS

Apple Valley, 50-Foot Tides, a Shipwreck Island

Annapolis Valley This is one of the most famous apple-growing areas in Canada. In late May and early June, the 100-mile-long valley is filled with the fragrance of blossoming trees.

Brier Island Picture next page.

Cape Blomidon Lookoff This 760-foot cape (one end of a 120-mile ridge called North Mountain) is mostly red sandstone. From its top the view encompasses Minas Basin and many valleys.

Chebogue Point During June and July, masses of blue-violet and pink lupines cover the hills in this area. There is a fine view of the sea.

Chignecto Game Sanctuary A secondary highway crosses this 85-square-mile reserve, where extensive forestry experiments are conducted.

The Ovens *Three caves in a headland off Lunenburg Harbour can be seen from a concrete platform extending out over the water. One is this great "blowhole" where the sea rushes in, trapping and compressing the air at the back of the cave. At a critical point this mass of compressed air acts like a giant piston, shooting sea water out with an explosive roar.*

Drysdale Falls A ledge in a cliff enables visitors to walk behind this 120-foot-high falls near Balmoral Mills.

East Bay Footprints of a small dinosaur and prehistoric lizards are preserved in rock here. There are fossils of leaves, fish, lizards and amphibians.

Five Islands Provincial Park Picture next page.

Indian Harbour Although not as well known as Peggy's Cove, Indian Harbour is a similar settlement where weather-beaten fishing shacks perch on a barren shoreline.

Joggins Embedded in 100-foot cliffs along the shore of Chignecto Bay are sandstone casts of trees, and fossils of reeds, ferns, insects and marine animals that lived 300 million years ago. Frost and 35-to-40-foot tides crack and erode the cliffs, revealing more fossils.

Liscomb Game Sanctuary This game refuge has abundant wildlife, good trout fishing, a fine example of Nova Scotia virgin forest, and several lakes. A road

Brier Island *Dazzling white yarrow, yellow Scotch lovage, delicate bluebells and streaks of green lichens enliven the gray rock of a sheer cliff that juts from the sea.*

through the 175-square-mile sanctuary connects Sheet Harbour with Pictou County centers.

Lupine Trail Blue-violet and pink lupines are common throughout Yarmouth County. The road between Yarmouth and Hebron is called the Lupine Trail.

Mahone Bay Some 350 islands and coves make Mahone Bay fascinating to explore. One of the best views of the bay is from Chester.

Parrsboro Scenery along the Bay of Fundy shoreline, with the Cobequid Mountains in the background, includes rocky inlets and island-dotted bays along the rugged coast, and low-tide mudflats as much as one mile wide. Amethysts, agates and other semiprecious stones are found in several areas. Many of the stones are displayed at the Parrsboro Museum.

Peggy's Cove Great granite boulders are strewn about and piled one upon another around a quaint, rustic cove. Fishing boats rest peacefully in the calm natural harbor. The barren lighthouse point provides a sweeping view of the ocean.

Five Islands Provincial Park *Tides at this park in Minas Basin sometimes rise more than 50 feet and are among the world's highest. At low water miles of red sand are laid bare.*

Provincial Wildlife Park Dozens of kinds of animals can be seen in this 1,600-acre forested park near Shubenacadie. Moose and caribou roam woods and meadows in enclosures as large as 10 acres. Six dozen species of ducks and geese live here and migrating waterfowl feed in the park's ponds.

Sable Island Short, stocky horses roam this shifting crescent of sand. Harbor and gray seals bask along the shore and hundreds of species of migrant and stray birds find refuge here. The island is the only known breeding ground of the Ipswich sparrow; this breeding range is the smallest of any bird in Canada. Only hardy marram grass and a few shrubs prevent wind and waves from destroying the island. Even so, the western end is being steadily eroded. More than 200 ships have been wrecked here.

The Ovens Picture preceding page.

Tobeatic Game Management Area All mammals and most birds of Nova Scotia are found in this 190-square-mile area.

Amphibians and reptiles are often thought of as members of the same family. But they are distinct classes, each cold-blooded, each with land- and water-dwelling species, each having some members able to grow a substitute for a lost limb or tail. How can they be told apart? Amphibians (frogs, toads and salamanders) are wet-skinned. Because they absorb oxygen through the skin, it must be kept moist, like a lung. Most reptiles (snakes, turtles and lizards) have dry, scaly skin and breathe only through lungs.

From the Same Family? Not If One's Wet and One's Dry

AMPHIBIANS

The jelly-like substance encasing each egg is not complete protection against destruction by drying out. So amphibians lay eggs in water or a damp place. Most young go through a stage called metamorphosis, living in water and breathing through gills, like fish. Salamander larvae are recognizable as salamanders but frog and toad tadpoles look quite unlike their parents. During the last part of metamorphosis, tadpoles do not eat, getting nourishment by gradually absorbing their tails.

REPTILES

Because their eggs have leathery or calcified shells, reptiles need neither wet birth sites nor metamorphosis. Some snakes do not even lay eggs; the young are born as tiny reproductions of the adults. The northern ringneck snake appears to be somewhere in between. The egg has a very short incubation period and the young are unusually well developed when hatched. Like most shelled reptiles, the Blanding's turtle uses her hind legs to dig a nest in sandy soil in which to lay her clutch of dull white eggs.

LEOPARD FROG | FOUR-TOED SALAMANDER | NORTHERN RINGNECK SNAKE | BLANDING'S TURTLE

A gelatinous mass laid in shallow water may contain 5,000 eggs.

These salamander eggs are laid on sphagnum moss hanging over water.

These elongated eggs continue to grow after being laid, assuming irregular shapes.

The female fashions a nest in sandy soil in 45 minutes. It holds 6 to 11 eggs.

External gills disappear about a week after the tadpole is hatched.

Newly-hatched larvae leave the nest and wriggle down into the water.

Darker than its parents, the snakelet exhibits the golden gorget of its species.

Although they will live partly on land, baby turtles instinctively head for nearest water.

Front limbs grow inside, breaking through after hind legs are developed.

All four legs grown, larvae retain gills and tail fins until ready for adult life.

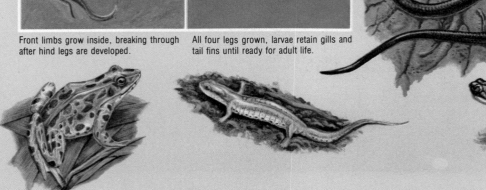

Long Reach, on the Saint John near Oak Point, N.B.

THE SAINT JOHN

A Great River, an Historic Valley and Serene, Persistent Beauty

Now wild, now pastoral, coursing through forest and farmland and primeval gorge, the Saint John River traverses New Brunswick from its remote northwest border with Maine to tidewater on the Bay of Fundy. It flows through some of the most varied countryside in the Maritimes. Ever more picturesque as it approaches the sea, it finally surges over a chute that twice a day turns into a rapids flowing *upstream*. But the greatness of this river lies in a persistent beauty that reaches almost the point of surfeit.

The Saint John follows a weirdly erratic course. It flows northeast out of Maine to Edmundston, turns southeastward to Grand Falls, then south to Meductic. After that it winds southeast, then northeast, before turning eastward to Fredericton. From there it twists and turns south to the Bay of Fundy.

In the dim geologic past the valley of the Saint John lay beneath a warm and shallow prehistoric sea, where coral grew. During the Ice Age, ice sheets widened and deepened parts of the valley. The weight of the ice depressed the earth's crust and, when the ice melted, the sea filled the valley as far upriver as where Fredericton was later built. The land rose, causing the sea to withdraw slowly, and glacial silt formed a delta that extends down the valley past Grand Lake. At one time the river had four outlets to the sea but, as the land continued to rise, three were abandoned and the present course was established.

Human history on the Saint John goes back at least 3,000 years, probably 10,000. Bones covered with red ocher—the mark of the Red Paint Culture—have been found in riverbank graves and dated to 1800 B.C. Farther north in Canada other graves of the same Maritime Archaic people (as they are now called) go back almost 5,000 years. There is reason to believe that the Saint John Valley has been inhabited intermittently almost from the end of the Ice Age some 10,000 years ago.

The Malecite Indians were the predominant tribe here when de Monts and Champlain named the river on the feast day of St. John, June 24, 1604. The Malecites still live here, along with descendants of French, English, Scottish and Dutch settlers. There were only a few hamlets until 30,000 political refugees, fleeing from their neighbors' wrath at the end of the American War of Independence, descended on the Maritimes, most of them in 1783. About 14,000 of these United Empire Loyalists, most from New York and New Jersey, settled in what now is New Brunswick. Their property had been confiscated, but they brought the education, skills and experience of lawyers, doctors, carpenters, shipwrights, blacksmiths, soldiers.

Until the 1940s the river was New Brunswick's principal transport route. Now the Trans-Canada Highway skirts the Saint John for most of its length in New Brunswick. In fact, paved highways follow its banks the 272 miles from Connors, N.B., to the sea. Except for farmers' boats and scows, and some ferries, the river carries little but pleasure craft.

Traveling upriver from Saint John past the gorge and Grand Bay, you come to Long Reach (the French

The "persistent beauty" of the Saint John: islands by moonlight near Jemseg and a placid bend at Kingston Creek. Islands in the great river are used for pasture and hay but seldom for homesteads. Most are swept by floodwater, ice and driftwood in the annual breakup—but the millions of tons of silt dumped by the river every spring make the lower parts of the valley among the most fertile farmlands in Canada.

called it *Longue Vue*). This lovely lake, flanked by impressive hills covered in hardwood and laced with trout streams, is a 20-mile stretch of the river. At the end of Long Reach is Belleisle Bay, one of the most beautiful of the Saint John's offshoots.

The river is quiet here, so filled with long, low islands that it is often impossible to distinguish the main channel. It is pastoral country, with deer, muskrat and almost every species of duck and wading bird native to eastern Canada. Lovely creeks, locally called bogans, tumble to the river from the surrounding hills.

The "capital" of this intervale region is charming little Gagetown, elm-shaded, typical of the Maritimes backcountry. It is surrounded by woodlands of white cedar, pine, maple, spruce, poplar, and great oaks that sprouted before the first Loyalist landed. Lilies of the valley and orchids grow in the damp woods, but the most abundant flower is the blue flag, a wild iris.

The short stretch of the Saint John from Fredericton upstream to the Keswick River is one of the most picturesque. The current flows swiftly between countless islands, giving the downstream canoeist a free and sometimes exciting ride. It is a run for experienced canoeists only.

Fifteen miles upstream from Fredericton is Mactaquac

At Grand Falls the Saint John plunges over its only escarpment, dropping 80 feet. It is still an impressive cataract although much of its water has been diverted into a power station.

Provincial Park. Not far away is Kings Landing, a representation of a mid-19th-century village. In it are farm buildings and homesteads that were moved when part of the shoreline was flooded after the Mactaquac Dam was built. Near the head of Mactaquac Lake is Meductic, where the folds of the hills enclosing the river create one of the most beautiful views in the Maritimes. Next is Woodstock, then Hartland and the world's longest covered bridge (1,282 feet).

Above Grand Falls the river flows through hill country 500 feet above sea level. The river forms the Canadian-American boundary for about 70 miles, with a road skirting each bank and little in sight but woodlot and farmland. Only once is its sleepy progress seriously interrupted—at booming Edmundston, the industrial capital of northwest New Brunswick. But the river is mostly narrow and placid and pleasure boats land on both sides. Nowhere else, perhaps, is an international border so accessible. Here the Saint John is simply a lovely stream winding through the foothills of a mountain chain, speaking peace to both its banks.

Above Edmundston is the true quiet of the north woods where a typical sound is the evening song of the hermit thrush. This is the land that Acadian pioneers saw in the mid-18th century, like "the forest primeval" of Longfellow's *Evangeline*. It is here that the Saint John most deserves to be called the loveliest of all of Canada's eastern rivers.

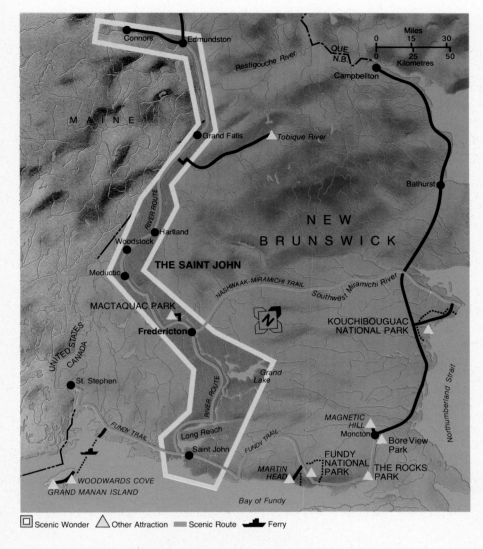

Scenic Wonder △ Other Attraction ▬ Scenic Route ⚓ Ferry

Bore View Park From this 15-acre park in Moncton is seen the tidal bore, a wave that surges up the Petitcodiac River twice a day. It ranges from a few inches to two feet high, reaching its greatest height in spring and fall. The wave is caused by the incoming tides from the Bay of Fundy. The phenomenon can be seen at night under floodlights focused on the river.

Fundy National Park Coves and inlets indent steep sandstone cliffs along the eight-mile Bay of Fundy shoreline of the park. Behind the coast the 80-square-mile park is an undulating plateau of forested hills, tumbling brooks and rivers, placid lakes and flower-filled meadows. In the dense forests moose, white-tailed deer, bear, bobcat and smaller creatures find shelter.

Fundy Trail This 156-mile route winds along the Bay of Fundy coast from St. Stephen, N.B., to Fundy National Park, and then along Chignecto and Shepody bays to Moncton. There are good lookoffs for watching the Fundy tides. Side trips include ferry rides to Deer, Campobello and Grand Manan islands off shore.

Grand Manan Island This island at the mouth of the Bay of Fundy is noted for towering cliffs, picturesque harbors and rolling landscapes. At Red Point, the

OTHER ATTRACTIONS

Grand Manan and the Miramichi

Woodwards Cove Gulls flock to a freshwater pond near Woodwards Cove on Grand Manan Island when their usual rock perches in the Bay of Fundy are submerged at high tide.

gray volcanic rock of the western half of the island overlaps the far older red sedimentary rock of the eastern half. A line can be seen where the two rock formations joined millions of years ago. Dulse, an edible seaweed rich in iodine, iron and minerals, is harvested and processed in great quantities by the Grand Mananers. The Grand Manan Museum at Grand Harbour contains the Allan Moses bird collection, in which are some 230 mounted specimens of sea and land birds taken on the island.

Kouchibouguac National Park A 15½-mile sweep of offshore barrier sandbars is a highlight of this 93-square-mile park on Northumberland Strait. Quiet tide-water lagoons offer fine swimming. The park has extensive peat bogs an estimated 10,000 years old, and salt marshes and dunes.

Mactaquac Provincial Park New Brunswick's 1,400-acre "Super Park" has

Martin Head *Ten miles west of Fundy National Park the Quiddy River snakes into the sea and, with the tides of the Bay of Fundy, shapes a green-tipped spit called Martin Head.*

golf, marinas, beaches, nature and hiking trails, playgrounds, an outdoor amphitheater, a rainy-day recreation center, and tent and trailer sites. The park is on the shore of the head pond formed when 133-foot-high Mactaquac Dam was built on the Saint John River.

Magnetic Hill Motorists seem to coast uphill on a gravel road here. The illusion is so powerful that it is difficult not to believe that cars are being pulled by a strong magnetic force.

Martin Head Picture this page.

Nashwaak-Miramichi Trail It generally follows the Nashwaak River north from Fredericton, then northeast along the Miramichi River to the sea. Along the way are spectacular scenery and the peace of central New Brunswick. At Boiestown, the geographical center of the province, northbound travelers get their first glimpse of the Miramichi, world famous for its salmon.

River Route A 250-mile drive through the Saint John Valley. From Edmundston, the route takes the traveler down

to Fredericton, New Brunswick's capital, and then to the seaport of Saint John. Most of the route follows the Saint John River. Travelers can cross the river at many places, over modern bridges, the world's longest covered bridge at Hartland, or via the free ferries that still operate.

The Rocks Provincial Park Top-heavy formations of soft rock resembling overgrown flowerpots stand near the mouth of the Petitcodiac River at Hopewell Cape. The reddish formations capped by balsam fir and dwarf black spruce were shaped by frost, wind and the tides that surge up the Bay of Fundy. At high tide the "flowerpots" become small islands.

Tobique River The restless Tobique flows past Mount Carleton, New Brunswick's highest peak, and provides some of the province's finest wilderness canoeing. The 85-mile route includes fast water, rapids, tight turns and the calm waters of the Tobique Reservoir.

Woodwards Cove Picture preceding page.

As the Moon Turns, Earth Bulges, Tides Run

Tides, the twice-daily rising and falling of the ocean, are caused by the gravitational attraction of the sun and moon. The range between high and low tide is inches in some parts of the world, but more than 50 feet in the Bay of Fundy between Nova Scotia and New Brunswick.

Since the 17th century, scientists have known that all objects exert an attractive force (gravity) upon one another. The more massive the objects, and the closer they are, the greater the gravitational "pull." All matter on earth responds to the gravitational forces of the sun and the moon. Since the

earth, sun and moon are constantly changing position, the effects of these forces at any particular moment are greater in some parts of the world than in others.

The moon, because it is much closer to earth than any other heavenly body, has the greatest effect on tides. As the moon revolves around the earth, it causes it to bulge at the points nearest to and farthest from the moon. Even the land rises and falls.

Because tides follow the moon's daily cycle of 24 hours and 50 minutes (rather than the sun's 24-hour schedule) high tide is always 50 minutes later than it was the day before.

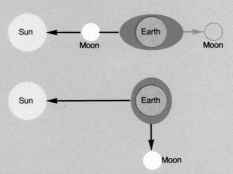

When the sun, earth and moon are aligned (top), the gravitational pulls of the sun and moon work together, creating the highest tides. But when the sun and moon are at right angles in relation to the earth (bottom), their pulls counteract each other, resulting in lower high tides.

Fishing boats at Alma, N.B., are stranded when the tide sweeps out of the Bay of Fundy. Incoming tides create waves (tidal bores) that rush up rivers emptying into the bay. The bore on the Saint John River creates a spectacular phenomenon: the Reversing Falls Rapids at Saint John (above, right). At low water there the river drops 14 feet over a ledge. The waterfall disappears under 28-foot tides that create rapids flowing upstream. The bore on the Petitcodiac River (below) can be two feet high.

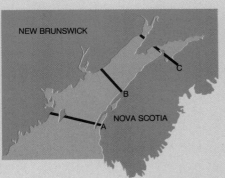

NEW BRUNSWICK

NOVA SCOTIA

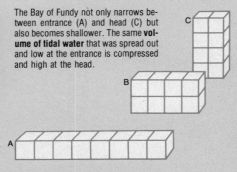

The Bay of Fundy not only narrows between entrance (A) and head (C) but also becomes shallower. The same **volume of tidal water** that was spread out and low at the entrance is compressed and high at the head.

Some of the highest tides in the world are in the Bay of Fundy, where the difference between low and high water is as much as 54 feet. They carry about 100 billion tons of water in and out of the bay twice a day and their great height is caused by the bay's funnel shape: wide and deep at the entrance, narrow and shallow at the head. The mouth of Fundy is about 50 miles wide and the tidal range about 13 feet. Some 120 miles to the northeast the bay is only 20 miles wide and the tidal range is more than 50 feet.

FORILLON
TO GATINEAU

Heartstopping Beauty
Where Great Rivers Run

This is the Canada of Cartier's landfall and of broad rivers to his elusive "kingdom"—a realm that proved mightier and richer than Cartier dreamed. This great basin of the St. Lawrence and Ottawa rivers is a still largely untamed land of intricate waterways and countless lakes, and of parks part wilderness and part playground—vast parks tiny on the rugged map of eastern Canada. It is an enticing land that may frighten as it beckons, a land of heartstopping beauty, from the submerged mountains called the Thousand Islands to the infinite hills of the Laurentians and the Gaspé's defiant thrust into the Gulf of St. Lawrence. At the tip of the Gaspé, not far from where Cartier went ashore in 1534, is Forillon, one of Canada's newest (and finest) national parks. Up the broad St. Lawrence, past the mouth of the fjord-like Saguenay and the rushing Saint-Maurice, another national park has been carved from the immensity of Quebec: La Mauricie. Also in the huge basin of the St. Lawrence and the Ottawa, in the heart of Laurentian country, are three of Quebec's best-known provincial parks: La Vérendrye, Mont-Tremblant and Laurentides. Gatineau Park, neither national nor provincial, is a sanctuary and a scenic wonderland all the more appealing for its proximity to the national capital.

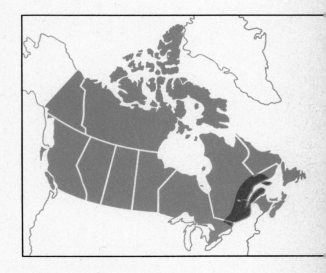

Opposite: *Autumn colors.*
Preceding pages: *The Laurentians.*

The Wild Beauty at the Outermost End of the Gaspé

Man and the land and the sea . . . these three in perfect harmony. This is the theme of wild and beautiful Forillon National Park, at the outermost end of the Gaspé.

The park, created in 1970, lies between the Gulf of St. Lawrence and the Baie de Gaspé. It takes in 92 square miles of the Gaspé Peninsula, including its narrow, five-mile-long tip, the Forillon Peninsula, and is a spectacular showcase of natural wonders. It has a rugged coastline of limestone cliffs, some shingly beaches, some sandy ones, waterfalls, rushing streams and thickly forested highlands. One of the park's many hiking trails leads to Cap de Gaspé, the farthest extension of the great peninsula.

The name Forillon has been used here since the days of New France. One explanation is that it would have derived from *pharillon*, diminutive of *phare* (lighthouse), and that the first *pharillon* was a rock off Cap de Gaspé on which fires were maintained to guide fishermen during the early 17th century. Dictionaries, on the other hand, define *pharillon* as a little stove hung on a boat; in it a fisherman lights a fire to attract fish.

The rock off Cap de Gaspé has long since collapsed into the sea, but the old name, whatever its origin, lives on, albeit with a new spelling, in the name of a peninsula and a national park.

Forillon emerges from a morning mist.

73

At Forillon we stand at one extremity of the Appalachian Mountains, a chain that under various names extends deep into the southeastern United States. With so small an area, Forillon could hardly be more hilly. One hill will be 400 feet high, its near neighbor 800. Several hills rise to 1,000 feet; others, in the southwest, to 1,500; and Forillon's proudest but unnamed summit is 1,850 feet. (Less than two hours away by car, in the Shickshock Mountains of Gaspé—another link in the Appalachian chain—some peaks are 4,000 feet.)

Terrain in the north part of the park is similar to that of the Laurentians: a gracious blending of contours smoothed by erosion. In the south the land is remarkably rugged. The effects of glaciation are much less evident in the Gaspé than throughout the rest of eastern Canada. Geologists think the Laurentian ice sheet covered the peninsula at the height of glaciation but that the topography was protected from major changes by an ice cap which had already formed there. Along the coast former strand lines up to 75 feet above sea level are represented by a succession of terraces. They define the various levels of the sea during the time when the worldwide rise of sea level, caused by the melting of ice sheets, kept pace with the local crustal rebound.

Erosion has given this shore the tortured lines we find so beautiful—the formations that will in time turn to sand. Rocks that are whipped by salt-laden waves and by sand and stones, and have been buffeted by endless bad weather and thousands of years of freezing and thawing . . . these cannot but change in shape, however imperceptibly. How else explain the countless cracks and crevices, the caves and the coves along these otherwise sheer cliffs? How else explain the great capes themselves, several now part of the park and among its most outstanding attractions?

Forillon's forest cover is mainly boreal but in many places red oak, elm and ash take over from the evergreens. Some stands of trees have reproduced here for thousands of years, tenacious reminders of an era— 4,000 to 5,000 years ago—when these parts of North America enjoyed a more moderate climate. In the valley of Anse au Griffon, open areas where once there were farms sometimes seem to explode with wild flowers. Forillon in June is marvelous, with myriads of dandelions. In July this valley lies under a snowfall of daisies. Goldenrod turns the fields yellow again in August.

Forillon boasts a rich variety of plant life. On the limestone cliffs of the east coast grow species of vigorous arctic-alpine flora—species whose presence here is not yet fully understood by botanists. Along the Baie de Gaspé coast, sheltered from the harsh weather of the Gulf, are long stretches of sandy beaches. Around Penouille is a type of vegetation usually found some

A mantle of evergreen softens a rugged fringe of the hard northeast coast of Quebec's Forillon Peninsula.

500 miles north: the forest taiga. Within a few hundred feet of the shore and its mobile sand dunes is a forest of mainly black spruce; 36 species of lichens grow on the sand among the trees. In this same southwest corner of the park are salt marshes where plants thrive on briny

water and the comings and goings of the tide. Plants that prefer fresh water embroider the streams and the few ponds and lakes to be found on the high land.

Forillon's lakes can be counted on the fingers of one hand and are so tiny as to be hardly worth mentioning (except for Lac au Renard, still exceedingly modest as lakes go). But rivers and streams—and streamlets—abound. The Anse au Griffon flows northeast across most of the center of the park. The Renard forms roughly half the park's northern boundary.

Most Forillon streams rise high in the hills—but never far from the sea—and race to the Gulf and the bay through precipitous ravines with many waterfalls.

Animals here are those found nearly everywhere in the Gaspé. Deer and moose, now "hunted" only with cameras, will surely become more numerous. Lumbering

High in the forested hills of Forillon National Park a veil of water drops toward a bed of summer buttercups.

pine, the daydreaming groundhog, the otter cavorting along the riverbank—and the red fox hunting down the hare. Beaver tirelessly patch their citadels of logs and mud, looking askance at any intruder.

Seals return to Forillon each summer, frolicking in noisy family groups on the offshore rocks. Four species frequent the waters of the Gulf. The fascinating movements of little minke and pilot whales can be observed, especially from atop the Forillon capes. The pilot whale, rarely alone, swims joyfully around Cap de Gaspé to dawdle in the calm waters off the other shore.

An estimated 220 species of birds visit the peninsula, some flying on almost immediately, some staying a while, others migrating from the Arctic to winter at Forillon. On the Gulf side, hundreds of herring gulls, kittiwakes and cormorants battle for ledges on which to nest and feed their young. Each brave bird in turn seeks food, gulls and kittiwakes at the edge of the waves, cormorants diving 15 to 20 feet into the water. What a feast for the eyes, this midair merry-go-round of soaring, wheeling birds! Gannets that nest on Bonaventure Island fish along the Forillon shore. The huge birds hover 100 feet or more above the sea, then suddenly dive vertically at their target fish.

At spawning time each spring, millions of capelin are carried in on the great tides and spill onto the Forillon beaches. No one who sees this spectacle by moonlight will ever forget it—or the summer-day sight of water near the shore suddenly aboil for no apparent reason. The sea seems to be applauding. A school of mackerel has come to spawn.

On the Baie de Gaspé side of Forillon, where life is easier, plovers nest in the tops of great pine trees and sea swallows tiptoe along the beaches with the grace of ballerinas. The black guillemot, found all around the peninsula, prefers this south shore.

At the village of Cap-des-Rosiers a side road leads to a headland dominated by a famous lighthouse, the tallest (112 feet) along the Gaspé coast. Entering the park near here, the motorist begins a scenic drive along a flat plain with mountains on his right, the Gulf of St. Lawrence on his left. At Cap-des-Rosiers-Est a secondary road leads to the spectacular Cap Bon Ami area and the main scenic road turns inland, cutting across the peninsula to the Baie de Gaspé. On the bay side is a nature trail to the village of Cap-Gaspé and Cap de Gaspé itself.

Just southwest of the park is little Baie de Penouille, part of the great Baie de Gaspé. Here the water is fine for swimming and the sandy beach a superb place to stroll—and to ponder how good life can be when man chooses to share the harmony between the land and the sea.

in years past (it now is prohibited in our national parks) had a happy side effect: it rejuvenated the forest that provides sustenance for deer and moose. The black bear and the lynx hunt in these woods, too, but not the wolf. Smaller mammals include the sauntering porcu-

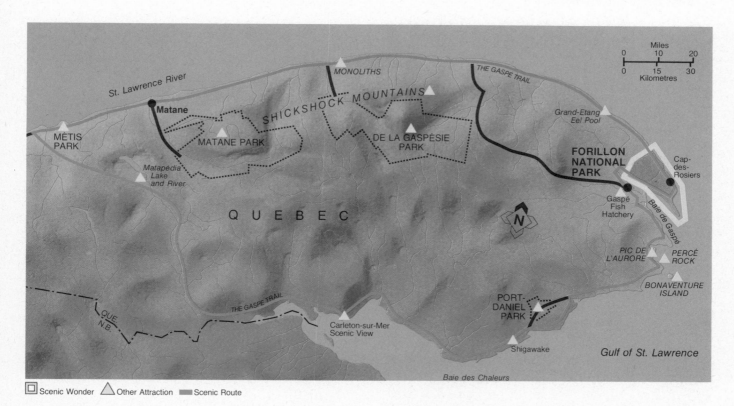

☐ Scenic Wonder △ Other Attraction ▬ Scenic Route

OTHER ATTRACTIONS

Bonaventure, Percé—and a Wriggle of Eels

Bonaventure Island North America's largest colony of gannets—35,000—lives here in summer. The 1,024-acre island, a bird sanctuary since 1919, is the home also of kittiwakes, murres, puffins, razorbills and Leach's storm-petrels. Tour boats from Percé, two miles distant, circle the island's 300-foot cliffs.

Carleton-sur-Mer Scenic View The crest of Mont Saint-Joseph (1,821 feet) offers a superb view of the Baie des Chaleurs. The New Brunswick shore is a blue smudge some 30 miles across the water.

De la Gaspésie Provincial Park The park's Mont Jacques-Cartier (4,160 feet) is the highest point in the Canadian Appalachians. It is part of the Shickshock Mountains, a rugged region inhabited by moose, deer, black bears and one of the world's last herds of shaggy woodland caribou, a species close to extinction. Ice Age glaciers that cut deep valleys did not reach the mountain tops here and alpine flora escaped harm. One of the best places to study the flowers is

Shickshock Mountains *Moody and mysterious, the Shickshock Mountains of the Gaspé are roughly parallel to the St. Lawrence River. Champlain named them the Notre Dame Mountains but they are better known as the Shickshocks, a name derived from a Micmac Indian word for steep mountains.*

77

Low tide at Percé Rock, across the Baie de Gaspé from Forillon National Park.

on Mont Albert (3,775 feet); its 12-square-mile flat top is reached by three nature trails.

Gaspé Fish Hatchery A million trout and salmon fry are hatched here each year. The 125,000 that survive the rearing period are used to stock lakes and rivers throughout Quebec. Established in 1875, the hatchery is the oldest in Quebec.

Grand-Etang Eel Pool Thousands of eels wriggle across 300-foot *portage de l'étang* (pool portage) each autumn forsaking this freshwater pool for the St. Lawrence River and the long journey to spawning grounds in the mid-Atlantic Sargasso Sea. Millions of migrating eels, forming a three-foot-wide phalanx several miles long, have been observed at sea. Young eels are about an inch long when they head north in spring. The North American eel's journey to freshwater takes roughly a year.

Matane Provincial Park The 417-square-mile park has lakes stocked with trout, rivers filled with salmon, forests that are home to moose, black bears, a few deer and the occasional caribou.

Matapédia Lake and River The longest lake in the Gaspé curves 12 miles between forest-clad hills, its waters dotted with islands, including one where loons breed.

Métis Provincial Park Some 1,500 flowers, shrubs and trees—189 species in all—grow here in the Gaspé's poor soil. Among them are exotic plants that have not been cultivated this far north anywhere else in North America.

Monoliths Wind and water and time have created two pillars of rock, 30 and 36 feet high, at Saint-Joachim-de-Tourelle.

Percé Rock The rock is 1,420 feet long and its vertical walls rise 288 feet at one end, 215 at the other. Picture this page.

Pic de l'Aurore This "Dawn Peak"—the rising sun paints the 600-foot cliff pink—is one of a series of cliffs and headlands. A path from the town of Percé reaches the peak by way of Mont Sainte-Anne (1,050 feet), revealing the vista of Percé Rock, Bonaventure Island and the Baie des Chaleurs. Inland, rugged Cap Blanc rises to 1,200 feet.

Port-Daniel Provincial Park Eighteen lakes in this 25-square-mile park are well stocked with trout. The Port-Daniel River offers salmon fishing.

Shickshock Mountains Picture preceding page.

Shigawake The village of Shigawake is above 100-foot-high shimmering red sandstone cliffs. The name is Micmac for land of the rising sun.

The Gaspé Trail The 557-mile trail encircles an area the size of Belgium. Paved since 1959, the road is still an adventure to travel, making steep climbs, sudden dips and sharp turns.

The chiton grazes over its base rock at night and, although it lacks eyes, always returns to exactly the same home spot before daylight.

The sculpin, a frequent visitor to the tide pools of Forillon Park, is difficult to spot against a background of algae-encrusted rock.

A muscular foot enables the common northern whelk to move over rocks in search of food. The whelk's main prey are bivalve mollusks.

Forillon National Park has countless tide pools, each a small marine world with its own plants and animals. High tide brings visitors. Some stay. Some are eaten. Some feed, then leave with the next tide.

This sea urchin, anchored to a mussel with some of its hundreds of sucker-tipped feet, can swivel its spines to face an attacker.

The hermit crab protects its soft body by sheltering in a snail shell. When it outgrows the shell it will move to a larger one.

This sea anemone's tentacles—which make it look more like a flower than an animal—have poisonous stingers at the tips to capture prey.

Forillon's Rocky Coast: Stepping Stone Between Land and Sea

Life between the deep water of the Gulf of St. Lawrence and the dry land of Forillon National Park is inextricably linked to the rise and fall of the tide. Along the rugged, rocky shore are three life zones: the splash zone, high on the rocks; the intertidal zone, flooded at high tide and exposed at ebb tide; and the subtidal zone, uncovered by only the lowest tides. On and near the rocks are countless communities of sea plants and animals, each specially adapted to life in its zones, illustrating the progress of life from sea to land.

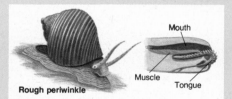

Rough periwinkle

SPLASH ZONE

Only the highest spring tides reach the splash zone. Life there relies on spray for its seawater needs and is able to withstand long periods of exposure to air. Some animals such as the rough periwinkle (left) breathe directly from the air and the young are developed, complete with shell, inside the female's shell instead of in the sea. Like other marine snails, the rough periwinkle eats minute blue-green algae, scraping them from the splash-zone rocks with an abrasive tongue called a radula. Inside the head it is coiled; when extended for feeding it is longer than the periwinkle's body. Its rows of microscopic thorns are so tough that, over many years, periwinkles can wear down rocky surfaces.

Barnacle

INTERTIDAL ZONE

Lack of moisture is no problem in the intertidal zone: it is covered with water about half the time and animals and plants retain enough to sustain them when the tide is out. But when the tide rolls in, the zone is pounded by surf. Mussels and limpets that live here must be able—more so than creatures in adjacent zones—to anchor themselves against the push and pull of the waves. Seaweeds have no roots, but the stalks have tendrils (holdfasts) with which the plants cling to rocks. Barnacle larvae spend three months in the sea before settling on a rock. Each barnacle (left) then secretes a strong adhesive and anchors itself head down to the spot it will occupy the rest of its life. The shell forms in about 12 hours. Four plates atop the shell are closed to retain moisture when the tide is out; they open underwater at high tide. The barnacle extends feathery legs to entangle plankton, then sweeps it inside to be eaten.

Starfish

SUBTIDAL ZONE

Covered by water most of the time, plants and creatures of the subtidal zone are poorly adapted to dry land. But many (such as starfish—left—sea urchins and crabs) often visit the intertidal and splash zones in search of food. Other subtidal animals, such as the sea anemone, remain anchored for most of their lives, moving only to escape danger. The starfish eats mussels, oysters and other bivalve mollusks, curving itself around each victim and pulling the shells apart with its hundreds of "suction-tube" feet. A slight opening is enough. The starfish quickly inserts its stomach into the shell and starts to digest the animal inside. A starfish can regrow a lost arm; an arm with a piece of the body attached can grow into a "new" starfish. The most abundant plants of this zone are the kelps. The fronds of these rootless plants provide moist shelters for subtidal creatures during the lowest tides.

Ancient Hills Cradle Cartier's 'Kingdom' and a Majestic River

You go north from Quebec. One scenic route hugs the St. Lawrence and you drive to Baie-Saint-Paul or Saint-Siméon before turning inland. The more direct route, through 4,000-square-mile Laurentides Provincial Park, enters Saguenay country immediately. Suddenly, only a few miles from the provincial capital, the traveler is surrounded by ancient hills that cradle some 1,500 lakes and 700 rivers—one river the mighty Saguenay itself.

The vast region of the Saguenay and Lac Saint-Jean is superlatively beautiful. In a province where so many scenic wonders bid for attention, this region stands out like a pinnacle on which nature has truly outdone itself. It is but a slice of the immense territory on which Jacques Cartier conferred the proud name "kingdom" but it is the most impressive part, the richest in contrasts.

A hundred miles west of Tadoussac (where the Saguenay meets the St. Lawrence River) is 387-square-mile Lac Saint-Jean. Around it stretch rich, fertile plains dotted with some 50 villages, and behind them, hills and mountains pile up far into the distance—a wilderness as well stocked with fish and game as any sportsman could wish. The Péribonka, most important of the rivers that cascade down from the Laurentian highlands to feed Lac Saint-Jean, is 309 miles long.

The Saguenay: half fjord, half river.

81

The Métabetchouane is 89; the Chamouchouane, 108; and the Mistassini, 179. All this tumbling water, temporarily stilled in the big lake, soon rushes to escape through two outlet channels worn in the solid rock of the Canadian Shield. Now the two become one: the seething, dizzying, torrential Saguenay.

There was a time when the great river, further swollen by tributaries below the lake, leaped and plunged for a wild 35 miles of rapids and falls to Chicoutimi, dropping more than 300 feet along the way. The drop is still there but dams have tamed the spirited waters to the service of industry. At Chicoutimi, inland seaport and chief city of the region, the Saguenay dramatically changes character. The river becomes the "fjord," an Ice Age relic by which the sea penetrates deep into the north shore of the St. Lawrence. What was the origin of the Saguenay's awful slash in the Laurentian rock? One popular story is that some apocalyptic upheaval cleaved a mountain in two. Geologists have a more plausible explanation: long before the Saguenay existed, a narrow river followed the same route to the St. Lawrence. During the last of the glacial periods, which started about a million years ago, ice covered not only the area now called Quebec but also the land that would one day be New England. The movement of this ice reshaped the land and carved the face of the Laurentians. Then a glacier, a "finger" of the ice sheet, moved slowly toward the St. Lawrence. It followed the earlier river's slash in the rock, enlarging and deepening it.

As the glacier withdrew, about 10,000 years ago, the sea invaded. Some 2,000 years later the Saguenay fjord, as we know it, was exposed. (One living—and thriving—relic of that era is the ouananiche, a salmon that the withdrawing sea entrusted to the freshwaters.)

Fjord implies salt water and for most of its length the Saguenay *is* salty. But toward Chicoutimi, seawater from the St. Lawrence pushes under fresh water coming down from Lac Saint-Jean and the Saguenay becomes a two-level river: on top it is relatively warm and only slightly saline; the lower level is icy and almost as salty as the sea itself.

The incoming tide rushes up the fjord with amazing speed: from the river mouth, at Tadoussac, to Chicoutimi, 70 miles upstream, in 45 minutes. The speed and height of the tides (especially the 20-foot equinoctial tides) create violent, unpredictable currents in the fjord. The waters smash and swirl and tear at the rocky shores. In good weather the Saguenay's conflict of motion is an impressive spectacle; in a storm it is awe-inspiring.

The Saguenay looks black in the shadow of its steep walls. But let a ray of sunlight touch it and the water's true amber is revealed.

From the river, the coniferous trees on the summit of Cap Eternité—1,150 feet high—look almost like moss.

Once, boats were often caught in the currents, like flies in a cobweb. So iron rings were fixed in the granite to which threatened craft could be temporarily secured.

The Saguenay fjord dates from the most remarkable of all glaciations on the east coast of North America. Its average depth is more than 800 feet; in one place it is 912 feet deep. To compare it to the fjords of Norway, however, is to exaggerate. Several surpass the Saguenay in length, depth and the height of surrounding mountains. (Norway's Sogne Fjord, for example, is 4,000 feet deep.) But there is an important difference: the Norwegian fjords are bays of the sea; the Saguenay is half fjord, half river. Another difference is that the Saguenay flows to the sea not directly but by way of a great river.

But what visitor dreams of faraway places when his boat is gliding between the Saguenay's cyclopean cliffs in a chasm of wind-streaked black water? Over there are the Valin and the Sainte-Marguerite mountains; there is the Tableau, an immense flat surface; and there, drawing near, is the little bay behind which tower Cap Trinité and Cap Eternité, giants whose sudden presence has an impact beyond words. They alone make the trip worthwhile. Each soars 1,150 feet and each plunges

another 800 feet *below* the water. Smoothed and polished by glaciers, the rocks of these two capes support little vegetation. But here and there—and this is true of most of the Saguenay cliffs—are patches of growth: a clump of birch, a lone spruce, a slender poplar.

Toward the summit of Cap Trinité is a statue of the Virgin, 25 feet high, yet tiny when seen from below—just as the passenger leaning over the rail of a cruise ship seems lilliputian from atop the cape. The ascent of Cap Trinité—not from the river side but from behind—is relatively easy, and the view from the heights is incomparable: eye and spirit possess a land of austere majesty. Mile after mile of ash-colored rock flanks the Saguenay. The Laurentians undulate as if to the ends of the earth, the forest giving way to an occasional house or a sudden glitter of lakes and a glimpse of rivers.

For sportsmen the Saguenay country is a region of great fishing and hunting, of forest hiking, climbing, horseback riding—even, in a "desert beside the river" at Tadoussac, sand-skiing.

But *the* great adventure is a boat trip through the fjord. Slipping between olympian walls of ancient rock, one has the impression of being where time feigns eternity. The Saguenay trip is at once a call to humility and an invitation to grandeur, a contact with the infinite.

These few hours leave an imperishable memory not only on the eyes but also on the soul.

OTHER ATTRACTIONS

Parks, Islands, Lakes Teeming With Wildlife

Bic Eight miles of mainland cliffs and coves—between Saint-Fabien-sur-Mer and Cap-au-Corbeau—and some offshore islands were earmarked in 1968 for development as a provincial park. Some 8,000 eider ducks nest on the river bank and sea otters and seals are sometimes seen sunning on the rocks. Land mammals include moose, deer and snowshoe hare.

Chibougamau Provincial Park The Chamouchouane River plunges 107 feet over Chaudière Falls and churns through a series of rapids. Canoeing is popular in the 4,250-square-mile park. Pike, trout, walleye, otter and beaver inhabit the many lakes. Marmots, wolves, moose and black bears are found in the rolling, forested hills.

Forestville Picture next page.

Hébertville-Station The Museum of Quebec Fauna has 600 stuffed specimens of birds and mammals native to the province. The surrounding country offers hunting and fishing, with ice fishing on Lac Vert in winter.

Ile aux Basques The rare Brant goose and the osprey are among birds attracted to the sanctuary on Ile aux Basques and two smaller islands. Aquatic birds that nest in the tree tops and rocky ledges of the craggy islands include great blue herons, double-crested cormorants, herring gulls and black ducks. The most common mammal on Ile aux Basques is the snowshoe hare. Dolphins are seen off the islands in spring.

Iles de Kamouraska One of North America's largest colonies of black-crowned night herons occupies the rocky ledges and reefs of these six islands. Great blue herons also nest here, and double-crested cormorants and black guillemots are regular visitors.

Lac Kénogami This glacial trough lake is 515 feet above sea level.

Les Caps From the heights of les Caps, a series of hills along the north shore of the St. Lawrence, there are great views of the river and the Laurentians.

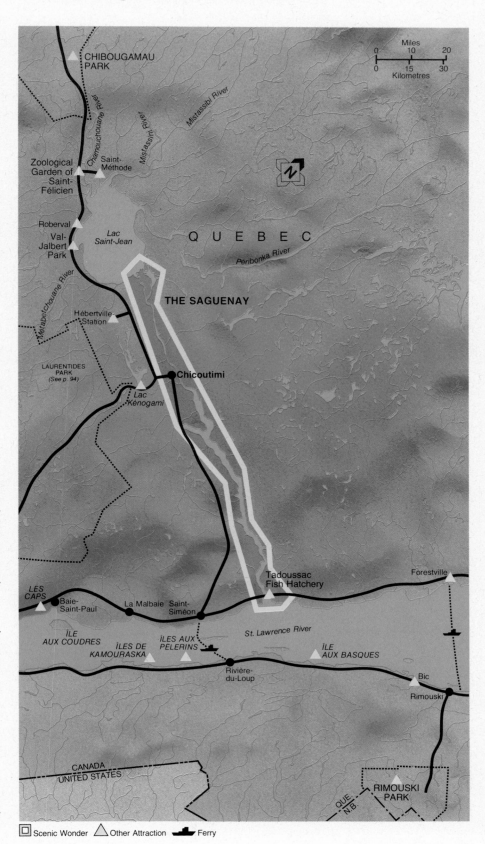

85

Forestville *Youngsters frolic on the ice of a barren stretch of the St. Lawrence River near this pulp and paper town.*

Les Pèlerins Canada's biggest colony of double-crested cormorants nests on the 150-foot-high cliffs of Grand Pèlerin. These five islands are also the home of thousands of sea and shore birds, including black guillemots, razorbills, great blue herons and black-crowned night herons.

Rimouski Provincial Park Deer are the most numerous game animals in this undulating, 300-square-mile park, but there are also moose, black bear, hare, partridge and grouse.

Roberval Sportsmen use this town as a base for hunting and fishing. Game includes moose, bears and partridge. Trout, ouananiche (landlocked salmon), pike and walleye are the most common fish.

Saint-Méthode Thousands of ducks and Canada geese stop here on spring and fall migrations. The waterfowl feed along the marshy shores of the Ticouapé River, which empties into Lac Saint-Jean.

Tadoussac Fish Hatchery From mid-May to the end of July, salmon and speckled trout are caught here on their way to spawn. About a million young fish are reared each year to be released into rivers and lakes throughout the province.

Val-Jalbert Park The Ouiatchouane River plunges 236 feet down Val-Jalbert Falls and runs for a mile between 40-foot cliffs to Lac Saint-Jean. Philomène's Cave, the largest of several potholes in the river bank, is 200 feet long but only the first 50 feet is accessible. In the rocks are the fossils of a number of marine creatures, including the trilobite, a species which resembled today's king crab and which disappeared 240 million years ago.

Zoological Garden of Saint-Félicien Of 800 mammals, birds and reptiles (both exotic and Canadian species), 450 are kept on Ile du Jardin in the Rivière aux Saumons. Every August, salmon can be seen swimming upstream to spawn. A mile away is 20-foot Chute à Michel; six miles distant is 40-foot Grande Chute à l'Ours.

Aquatic creatures from plankton to squid are plentiful where the Saguenay River joins the St. Lawrence, and it is a rich feeding ground for whales. The abundance of food is because the Saguenay is suddenly shallow at its mouth and because the deep channel that hugs the north shore of the St. Lawrence narrows here. These conditions create currents and cross-currents, some warm, some frigid. Combined with tidal action, they allow a variety of aquatic life to thrive.

The Saguenay is the home of the beluga whale, a variety of white Arctic porpoise once known as the St. Lawrence whale. Belugas are attracted by abundant shrimp and capelin (a small fish) and it is thought that beluga young are born up the Saguenay in the Baie Sainte-Marguerite area. Minke whales are frequently spotted at the mouth of the Saguenay. Nearby, along the north shore of the St. Lawrence toward Les Escoumins, there are whales by the score to be seen and heard as they surface, spout and dive. Many species have been reported: finbacks and humpbacks, blues (the largest of all), pilot and sei whales and even killer whales.

The Zoological Society of Montreal or-

Excited whale-watchers crowd the ship's rail as two finback whales surface a few yards away. When whales are sighted, an excursion ship is put on a course to intercept them. As the whales draw closer the ship's engines are shut down.

ganizes whale-watching excursions on the St. Lawrence and the Saguenay. Trips can be arranged also at Tadoussac, and Saguenay cruises provide good views of the beluga. Part of the fun of whale-watching is being able to identify the various species.

Whale-Watching Where the Saguenay Meets the St. Lawrence

Often seen in groups, belugas are one of the easiest species to identify. A beluga has no dorsal fin and the tough hide of the 15-to-18-foot adult is white.

About 30 feet long, the minke whale is blue-gray with a white underside and a white patch on the outer side of the flippers. From above, the head appears triangular.

The 25-foot pilot whale is black with a small patch of white under the chin. The flippers are long and narrow. Pilots are easily alarmed and usually are found in groups.

The blue whale weighs up to 130 tons and is as much as 100 feet long. The dorsal fin is relatively small, the head almost beak-like and the throat furrowed.

Capable of swimming 40 miles an hour, the sei whale has unusually short flippers and a large, notched dorsal fin. It is about 50 feet long and bluish black to gray.

The finback whale, light gray above and white below, is about 70 feet long. The dorsal fin is located toward the tail and the hind part of the back has a marked ridge.

Laurentian Country, Where Endless Hills Stretch to Infinity

La Mauricie National Park, in the magnificent valley of the Saint-Maurice, is 215 square miles of typical Laurentian country. Here, overladen with trees, strewn with lakes and rivers—and seeming to stretch to infinity—are rounded hills averaging 1,200 feet. Before the Ice Age they were about a thousand feet higher. Glaciers overrode them and ground them. The ice retreated, leaving smoothed peaks, creases and swellings. Thus were the Laurentian hills shaped.

The Laurentian lakes—so numerous that geographers have not named them all—were formed by the same glaciers. The ice bristled with rock and the rock in turn excavated basins in the valleys under the ice. When it melted, water was trapped in these depressions and lakes were born.

The Saint-Maurice region in which the park lies is one of wild grandeur—wilder and grander the farther north one goes. This unvarying succession of lakes and hills denies La Mauricie the dramatic look of the Gaspé or the Cape Breton Highlands or the Rockies, but it has its own *special* beauty. There are no dizzying peaks, no waterfalls to stagger the imagination, but La Mauricie unfolds a peace of the spirit, like a serenely good book. The forest echoes to the rumble of falling water, to the gurgle of the streams that link the lakes. Here life is sniffed and seen and heard. The more one tries, the

Heading north in La Mauricie.

89

more variations one senses in the perfume, the form and color, the music of nature.

La Mauricie National Park has two park neighbors—710-square-mile Mastigouche Provincial Park on the west, 617-square-mile Saint-Maurice Provincial Park across the Matawin River to the north. To the south are the flat farmlands of the St. Lawrence Valley, to the east the Saint-Maurice itself.

The fast-flowing Saint-Maurice rises about 150 miles northwest of the park in the 478-square-mile Gouin Reservoir. The river is fed by the Shawinigan and Matawin rivers and hundreds of smaller rivers in its 235-mile journey to the St. Lawrence. The area it drains is one of the biggest forest reserves in Quebec, producing much of the world's newsprint. The Saint-Maurice carries endlesss millions of logs to the mills of La Tuque, Grand-Mère, Shawinigan and Trois-Rivières.

La Mauricie has a mixed forest. Ten evergreen species in the park mingle with some 25 kinds of deciduous trees. Red and black spruce, eastern hemlock, balsam fir and eastern white pine share the hillsides and damp places with white birch, trembling aspen, sugar maple, beech, elm, ash, alder and basswood. Yellow birch is almost everywhere.

Wild flowers riot in La Mauricie from spring to the end of summer: field sorrel, hawkweed, aster and goldenrod in the open; hooded violet, false lily of the valley and bunchberry in the underbrush. Heal-all, meadow rue, fireweed and moccasin flower line the forest paths. On the lakeshores are large blue flag, pickerelweed, field horsetail, sheep laurel, Labrador tea. Grass pink orchids, leatherleaves, snakemouths, speedwells and the carnivorous pitcher plants and round-leaved sundews prosper around the many ponds and boggy areas.

Animals thrive in La Mauricie. The moose, lord of the forest, may be seen in summer, his enormous head bent to a feast of water plants at the edge of a lake. The few deer prefer the lightly wooded southeast part of the park. The black bear wanders everywhere, simply following his nose; when he comes to a lake, he plunges in with the confidence of a powerful swimmer. The crafty red fox and the even more suspicious Canada lynx are everywhere too—but seldom glimpsed. Just the opposite is the beaver. He is no showoff but his serious side compels him to toil on without interruption. The park teems with small mammals. The commonest are the

The final snowy traces of a dying winter (right) cling to the greening banks of a river in La Mauricie National Park. Below: the warm sunlight of early autumn highlights the changing of leaf colors.

red-backed vole and the woodland jumping mouse, but the meadow jumping mouse is seen too. Muskrat, raccoon, red squirrel, chipmunk, masked shrew, snowshoe hare and white-footed mouse are numerous.

La Mauricie is a bird lover's delight. The common loon, whose haunting notes vibrate across the lakes, is the park symbol. The duck sticks to Lac Antikagamac because of its marshy banks, but most other birds roam, building nests wherever the whims of mating suggest. The white-throated sparrow is happy among the conifers; the wood thrush, among the hardwood leaves. Some names conjure up bright images: the Nashville warbler and the myrtle warbler, for example; the horned lark, the chimney swift, the vesper sparrow, the wandering evening grosbeak, and the great blue heron, posing like a porcelain statue; the sad mourning dove and the solitary sandpiper; the cedar waxwing and that mimic, the mockingbird, imitating the songs of other birds. But La Mauricie is not all peace: here, ready to pounce, the sparrow hawk keeps watch . . . and the osprey . . . and the owl with its hypnotic eyes . . .

Of La Mauricie's 150 lakes, Lac Wapizagonke is the most important and virtually the soul of the park. Boxed into a narrow valley by cliffs now steep, now gentle (and averaging 250 feet high), it is 10 miles long. Folded and broken rocks of gneiss and granite form its escarpments

"There are no dizzying peaks, no waterfalls to stagger the imagination, but La Mauricie unfolds a peace of the spirit . . ."

and testify to a massive movement of the earth's crust some eight to ten miles below the surface thousands of millions of years ago. Here and there are sandy beaches, and little coves adorned by waterfalls. Also on Lac Wapizagonke, a favorite of canoeists and sailing enthusiasts, are the remains of red-ocher rock paintings done by Indian artists an estimated 2,000 years ago. Vandals have all but ruined these records of the past, already damaged by bad weather and floods. Axes, scrapers, knives and arrowheads have been found on a little island in the lake. Similar relics have been unearthed to the north of the park near the Matawin and toward Lac aux Brochets and Lac Mékinac.

A 38-mile scenic road divides La Mauricie Park into two sections. One remains in the wild state that appeals to the naturalist, the nature lover, the canoeist, the photographer and the poet. Here are footpaths, deserted beaches, islands set like jewels in lonely lakes—and that commodity so rare these days: silence. The other section is for campers less insistent on solitude. It has an interpretation center in which slide presentations of the park's flora and fauna are given by park personnel.

All superfluous recreation facilities are prohibited in La Mauricie. However acceptable (and often even necessary) they may be in some great parks, these borrowed elements of city life would rob La Mauricie of its beauty and purity. As it is, La Mauricie National Park remains a perfect mirror of the Laurentian heritage.

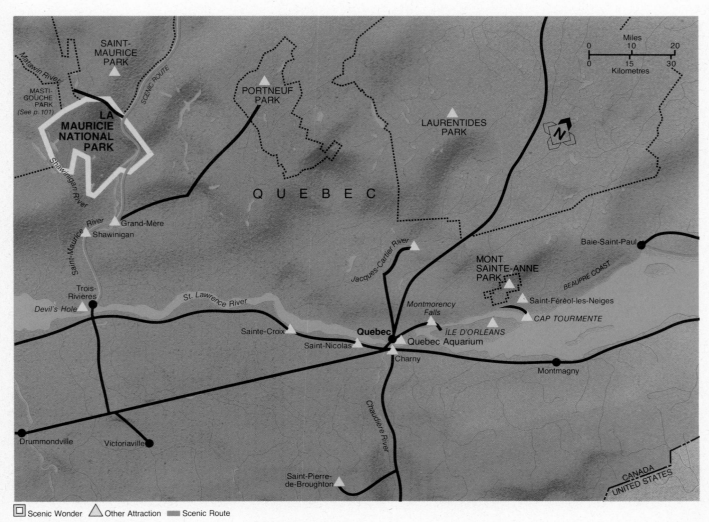

Scenic Wonder □   △ Other Attraction   ■ Scenic Route

OTHER ATTRACTIONS

Cap Tourmente and the Ice Cone at Montmorency

Beaupré Coast (Hwy 360) The route from Montmorency Falls to Baie-Saint-Paul and beyond, climbing and dipping along the rugged St. Lawrence coastline, overlooks the river, numerous small islands and bays and the Laurentians. The highway skirts the national wildlife area of Cap-Tourmente, where a nature trail leads to a cliff with a view of the river and the south shore.

Cap Tourmente Some 140,000 migrating greater snow geese and Canada geese stop at the 5,000-acre national wildlife area here and on islands in the

Sunlight and greater snow geese dapple the waters off Cap Tourmente, on the north shore of the St. Lawrence River just downstream from Ile d'Orléans.

St. Lawrence. They stay for six weeks in the fall—from late September to early November—and visit also in April and May. At low tide they feed on a type of bullrush that grows in the mudflats. An interpretation center has displays describing the history and habits of snow geese and local songbirds. There are nature trails. A ferry links Ile aux Grues and Ile aux Oies with the town of Montmagny. Picture preceding page.

Charny A waterfall near the mouth of the Chaudière River drops into a *chaudière*, a cauldron-shaped basin created by glacial action and erosion and subsequently enlarged by the waterfall.

Devil's Hole Flammable gas bubbles up through a water-filled hollow on the bank of the Saint-Maurice River.

Grand-Mère The town was named for a rock that resembles the profile of an old woman. The rock, on an island in the Saint-Maurice, was moved to a park when construction of a power dam threatened to submerge the island.

Ile d'Orléans The island offers fine views of other islands in the St. Lawrence River, communities along the north shore, and the Laurentian Mountains.

Jacques-Cartier River Picture this page.

Laurentides Provincial Park Caribou, once rare here, have been re-introduced into the 3,700-square-mile park. One of several nature trails leads to a lovely 90-foot-high waterfall on the Noire River.

Montmorency Falls This 274-foot falls on the Montmorency River is a good 100 feet higher than Niagara. An ice cone that forms in winter sometimes reaches 90 feet. Excellent views of the falls are had from the 5,700-foot Ile d'Orléans suspension bridge, from a lookout at Maison Montmorency near the top of the falls, and from Parc Montmorency, which has observation points at the base and summit of the falls. There are several walking trails on the cliff tops. Along the crest are fossils of marine life that lived in the Champlain Sea when it covered the area some 11,000 years ago.

Mont Sainte-Anne Provincial Park The 2,625-foot summit of Mont Sainte-Anne affords a magnificent view of the St. Lawrence River and the pastoral beauty of Ile d'Orléans.

Portneuf Provincial Park Several peaks in this heavily-forested, 242-square-mile park are 2,500 feet high.

Quebec Aquarium On the edge of a cliff overlooking the St. Lawrence, the aquarium has an impressive variety of exotic fishes and marine animals and reptiles, including alligators, pythons and boa constrictors.

Sainte-Croix The Petit Sault River drops 100 feet over a waterfall here as it nears the St. Lawrence.

Saint-Féréol-les-Neiges The Jean-Larose Falls tumble 192 feet here. A few miles east the Sainte-Anne du Nord River drops over Les Sept Chutes, a series of picturesque waterfalls. Also on the Sainte-Anne du Nord near here is Sainte-Anne Falls, whose three waterfalls drop into a deep pool.

Saint-Maurice Provincial Park Everywhere in this 617-square-mile wilderness park is evidence of the power of the glaciers: striated rocks, trough-shaped valleys and riverbeds gouged through rocky outcrops.

Saint-Nicolas A gallery around Saint-Nicolas Church, on a steep cliff, affords a sweeping view of the St. Lawrence.

Saint-Pierre-de-Broughton The area has more than 600 varieties of rock (including soapstone, usually found farther north).

Scenic Route Highway 155 and the Saint-Maurice River wind side by side between Trois-Rivières and La Tuque.

Shawinigan A walkway provides a closeup of a 145-foot waterfall, the highest on the Saint-Maurice River.

Jacques-Cartier River *Three main branches join in a region called Les Taureaux (The Bulls) in the southern part of Laurentides Provincial Park. Here the river deepens into a glacial valley. The Jacques-Cartier empties into the St. Lawrence at Donnacona.*

Fire! A Forest Dies— and New Life Begins

Seventy-five percent of forest fires are caused by human carelessness, the rest by lightning. Whichever the cause, a fire can be *good* for a forest—if it is overmature and clogged with underbrush and dead or unhealthy trees. New and often different plants grow in the ashes of the old, providing new food and shelter for wildlife.

Wild flowers and grasses, their seeds carried in on the wind, are the first to pioneer the new environment. They are food for mice and rabbits—which are followed by foxes and other flesh-eaters that prey on them.

Berry seeds are brought in on animals' fur or passed through their digestive systems. Bushes grow from these seeds and soon there are ripe berries to attract birds, bears and other mammals. Moose and deer arrive later, attracted by the succulent twigs of a young forest of fast-growing trees such as trembling aspen. They are trailed by a cougar or a lynx or a wolf pack, ready to pounce on the old, sick or very young.

A few pine trees sprout among the aspens—from seeds in cones that were part of a squirrel's hoard. When the aspens start to die the pines multiply until they take over the site. But they too are eventually replaced. If no fire occurs, the succession continues until the predominant trees are slow-growing and long-lived. This is a climax forest, a relatively stable association of plants and animals that could last for hundreds of years.

Fire! Trees that lived for more than 100 years will be dead in less than 24 hours. The fire will set in motion a process called sere, in which different communities of plants succeed one another over a long period of time.

The charred earth awaits regeneration. The first seeds to germinate will be light and easily borne by the wind. They must be able to grow, without protection or shade, in soil heavily mineralized by burned vegetation.

Fireweed and other wild flowers take advantage of the space created by the fire. The sun's heat makes the bare black soil too hot for the seeds of many plants. Wild flowers will be dominant for a season or two, before the next step in the succession.

Fire is necessary for regeneration of a jack pine forest. This tree prefers soil enriched by minerals deposited by burned vegetation. Its tough cones seldom burn in a fire. Heat of 57°C. (135°F.) causes cones to open, releasing seeds onto the prepared mineral soil. With no large trees to shade them, the seedlings grow rapidly. Unless another fire occurs within the next century, the jack pine forest will be incapable of reproducing and will be replaced by other trees.

Trembling aspen thrive in direct sunlight. Quick to invade a burned-over area, they often sprout from the roots of stunted aspen that existed in the understory of the forest. Aspen seeds may be blown in from a neighboring forest.

The aspens have been dominant for 70 years. Mature trees shade seedlings from the sun they need, so this forest has started to decline. It will be replaced by pine trees, a few of which have existed until now in the understory.

Autumn color and the black lakes of Mont-Tremblant Park.

MONT-TREMBLANT PROVINCIAL PARK

Wilderness and Playground in One Magnificent Setting

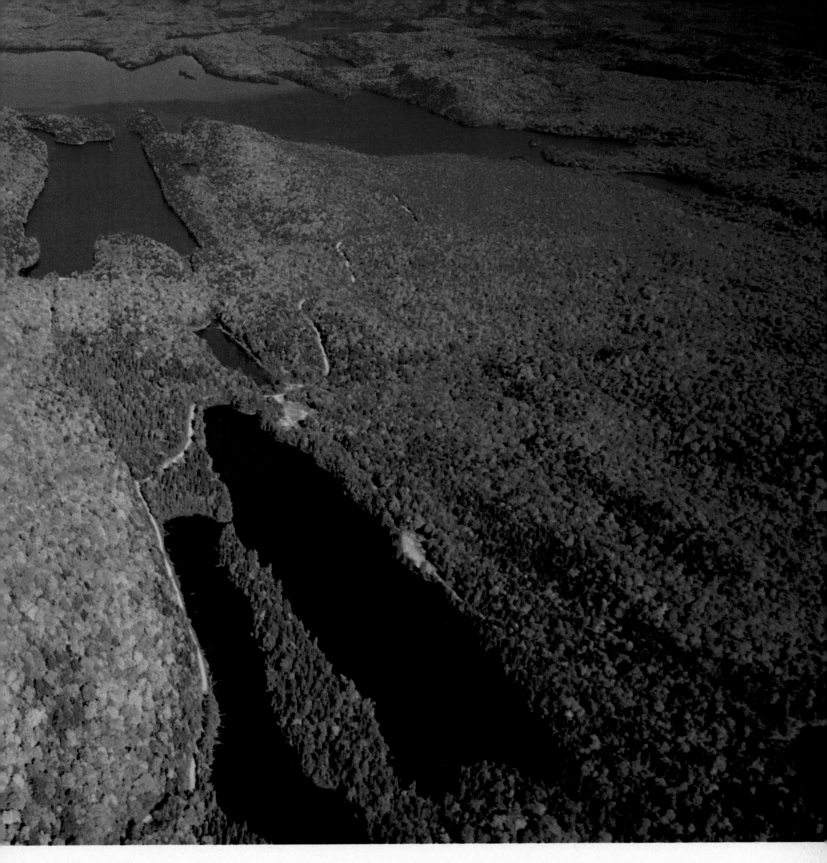

The Indians called it the trembling mountain. Sleeping on its slopes after the hunt, they said, they felt the ground move. The earth tremor sound they thought they heard comes in fact from watercourses streaming from rock to rock down into the valley. The Indians' trembling mountain is Mont Tremblant, a 3,150-foot peak that lends its name to a great lake at its foot and to a provincial park nearly 1,000 square miles in area. (But neither the mountain nor the lake is in the park.)

The park is two hours from Montreal—all but about 20 miles of the 95-mile trip is via the Laurentian Autoroute. You enter via Saint-Donat or by the principal access near Saint-Faustin. First-time visitors will almost certainly want to use the main entrance, close to Lac Monroe, for here are the park's administrative services, the welcome center and a detailed map of the Mont-Tremblant area. (There are about 250 miles of road in the park.) The main entrance is called Barrière du Diable, named for the river that rises in the park highlands and gives its name also to the valley it drains.

One characteristic of the Laurentians is the remarkable regularity of its parade of hills and valleys—and the virtual absence of any out-of-the-ordinary contours. The slow undulations are like the unbroken melodic line of the monks' plainsong. But the topography of Mont-Tremblant Park in the south is singularly uneven. Each massive hill breaks away from the next and heights vary greatly. On the flanks of exceptionally precipitous hills are bare rocks—jutting and notched. These are the roots of a mountain chain. Once far below the surface—as much as 20 miles—they were eventually exposed when the original surface rock eroded away. The vigorous shape of this southern part of the park is also partly the result of glaciation.

The center of the park is different. The tortured configuration that distinguishes the south gives way to smaller hills and to great level spaces full of lakes, ponds and swamps. This austere landscape, where everything seems repeated endlessly, is happily interrupted by an east-west group of bigger hills, some close to 2,500 feet above sea level. Beyond them is more austerity: hills that stretch to the northern limits of the park. Overall, the park's altitude varies between 740 and 3,000 feet. Most hills are 1,500 to 2,000.

Mont-Tremblant Park has almost 1,000 lakes. Here, as everywhere in the Laurentians, water seems one with the land. One principal river is the Rouge, a tributary of the Ottawa, and it drains a 1,780-square-mile basin. Its upper reaches, at the northwestern boundaries of the park, offer canoeists a 51-mile run complete with foaming rapids. The Rouge, which courses through a deep, narrow valley, has four important tributaries—the Lenoir, French, Macaza and Ruisseau Froid. In the northeast, Lac Matawin spawns a river (also called Matawin) that drains much of a central plateau, with the biggest lakes in the park, and flows to the far-off Saint-Maurice.

One river, the Diable, is of special interest because it waters the sector of greatest tourist activity. With hundreds of fishing lakes and forest roads, the northern part of the park remains a fishing and hunting preserve. The southern part, and especially the valley of the Diable, is a popular recreation zone for two reasons: it is not too far from Montreal and its natural beauties are more numerous and varied than those of the north.

The 38-mile semicircle that the main road traces from Lac Monroe to the park entrance near Saint-Donat wins over even the least impressionable visitor. The Diable

contributes to this feast for the eyes. To its many rapids it adds two falls, Chute du Diable and Chutes Croches (Crooked Falls). Everywhere there are singing little streams and deep-voiced waterfalls and at the foot of a mountain called La Roche Noire is beautiful Lac Saint-Louis. To the southeast, near the Saint-Donat gate, is Chute aux Rats (Muskrat Falls), a waterfall that races over a steep cliff cut like a staircase, an oddity that is one of the park's biggest attractions. La Corniche (The Ledge), another major feature, overlooks Lac Monroe. It is reached by a slope that puts faint hearts to the test, but from the 1,575-foot lookout is a superb view of surrounding lakes and of immense waves of green hills rolling on and on and out of sight. And if this view whets a desire for more, a path leads to still another lookout. From here the farthest folds of mountains seem part of some illusory tapestry backdrop. But there is more to do here than simply admire; one can learn. For short-term visitors and those with no liking for long walks, a nature trail (with appropriate informative signs) makes a circuit of pretty Lac des Femmes, close to the park headquarters.

Foreign visitors—most Canadian visitors too—are unaware that many parts of Mont-Tremblant Park were once still more beautiful and imposing. That old beauty was destroyed by the heavy logging of the 19th century—and since. Today, fortunately, there are efforts to reverse this degradation by planting millions of young pines in and around the park. Will logging concessions be abolished here one day? Esthetically it is hoped so but industry resists such abolition.

Like several Quebec parks, Mont-Tremblant contains a mixed forest and an already boreal forest. Taken as a whole, the forest cover is one in transition. To the south, deciduous and coniferous trees are mixed in almost equal quantities: red maple and sugar maple, sometimes silver maple, yellow and white birch and, less often, silver pine, white pine, hemlock and beech. While conifers monopolize the ridges of the hills, black spruce, cedar and ash have taken over near the lakes.

If you climb to the center of the park, you see that smaller hills attract fir, birch and black spruce, and to a slightly lesser degree white pine and trembling aspen. Cedar on the other hand prefers level ground. But now and then, probably on an island or a hilltop, you come into the presence of a great pine that has managed to escape the logger's ax. Living testimony to the past, it stands proud in its solitary majesty.

The northern part of the park is nothing but conifers. *Almost* nothing but conifers. Fishermen en route to

An early morning sun bores through mist rising from Lac Caché in the southwest part of Mont-Tremblant Provincial Park. The Laurentians (background) are swathed in low clouds.

A moose feeds at the edge of a wilderness lake in Mont-Tremblant Park. The annual hunt is rigidly controlled, keeping the moose population around 1,000.

highland lakes see stretches that power saws have denuded and where second growth is deciduous—trembling aspen, birch, willow. Thus nature adapts to changing conditions; in such areas, now exposed to the sun, a mixed forest vegetation will partly replace the stands of evergreens that fire and man have destroyed.

It is obviously not easy to say how many moose there are in a park so vast and where the forest is generally very dense, but the Mont-Tremblant moose population has been estimated at more than 1,000. The moose hunt, the only hunt permitted in Mont-Tremblant, is restricted to one three-week period and to the north section of the park.

The white-tailed deer, like the moose, prefers cutover areas because the cutting has added to the supply of its favorite food—pine and tamarack branches, the young shoots of maple and trembling aspen, and various wild fruits such as the raspberry that is to be found virtually everywhere. The deer is sensitive to cold and so usually haunts the lower part of the park. If it does venture to the north it hurries back as soon as the first snow falls.

Three seasons of the four the black bear wanders from one corner of the park to another. This is the tourist par excellence, an omnivore that finds its table always set. As autumn wanes, the bear sleeps deeply: out of the world, out of the park.

Sometimes the howl of a wolf echoes through the hills of Mont-Tremblant. Wolf, fox and lynx are numerous; their abundant prey are the varying hare and red and brown squirrels. Beaver are to be seen building and repairing and there are otter, weasel, mink, skunk, raccoon, groundhog, porcupine and smaller mammals.

How is this provincial park of so many uses to be defined? What will be its real role? It exists to conserve its fauna but nonetheless the hunt is tolerated . . . to safeguard its flora and yet logging is carried on and camping sites are allowed to proliferate. Use of the park grows at such a pace that recreation seems to have taken over as Mont-Tremblant's principal reason for being. So it is all the more important that this grand setting remain divided into two distinct zones. In the north it is a great wilderness, to be maintained intact as far as possible. In the south it is a park open eight months of the year for outdoor living and many forms of sport—but where the city dweller may also learn about the creatures and the things of the forest. Quebec's oldest provincial park (it had its beginning as a forest reserve in 1894) seems to be reconciling these twin objectives—objectives that are in line with its topography.

OTHER ATTRACTIONS

Mont Orford, the Condor Needle and Saint-Hilaire's Rare Minerals

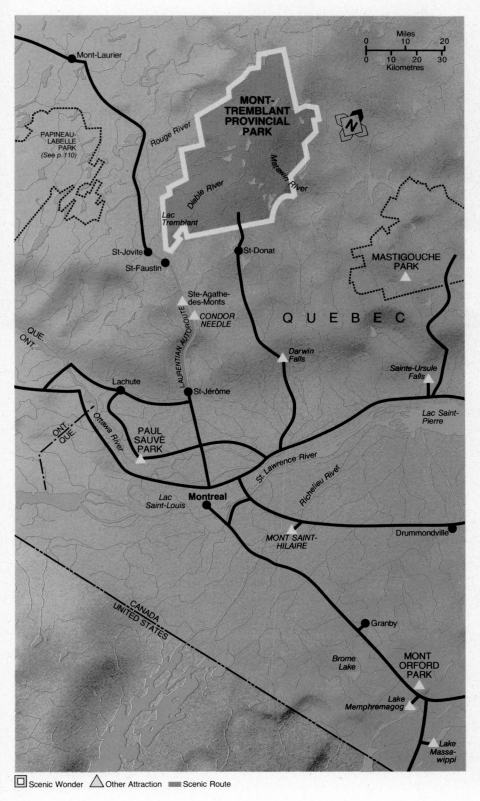

Scenic Wonder △ Other Attraction ■ Scenic Route

Condor Needle Seventy-five feet high and nearly vertical, eastern Canada's only "needle" formation stands beside Mont Condor, a 125-foot-high rock. The gap between the rock and the needle can be climbed for about 25 feet, to a point where the gap widens. Both rocks were formed of lava.

Darwin Falls In the rock face above this bubbling waterfall on the Ouareau River is the 30-inch-high likeness of an Indian head. Legend says it is the h_ad of a sorcerer who was rejected by the woman he loved. He pushed her into the falls and was turned to stone. The river drops 100 feet over a series of waterfalls.

Lake Massawippi This popular resort lake has a scenic backdrop of rolling, forested hills.

Lake Memphremagog Tour boats from Magog ply the 30-mile-long lake, which lies partly in Vermont. Panoramic lookouts from hills above the east and west shores provide views of the surrounding Eastern Townships and Mont-Orford.

Laurentian Autoroute/Hwy 117 The 50-mile Saint-Jérôme/Saint-Jovite section weaves through forest-clad hills that are resplendent with color in autumn and alive with skiers in winter.

Mastigouche Provincial Park The 700-square-mile park has limited moose hunting and fishing for ouananiche (land-locked salmon) in a setting of gently rolling hills up to 2,000 feet high. Near Les Six Chutes, a pretty waterfall on the Rivière du Loup, is the start of a 12-mile canoe route.

Mont Orford Provincial Park Four miles of nature trails wind to the 2,795-foot summit of Mont Orford and a scenic view of the 15-square-mile park. Plant and animal life typical of Quebec's Eastern Townships is abundant here.

Mont Saint-Hilaire Twenty of the 120 minerals found in a quarry near 1,350-foot Mont Saint-Hilaire have never been found elsewhere. The minerals were formed when molten rock from deep within the earth oozed up through fissures in the earth's crust and solidified just under the surface. Different rates of cooling and different chemical compositions of both the molten rock and the rock formations in which it cooled cre-

ated the unusual minerals. Near the center of Mont Saint-Hilaire is Lake Hertel, surrounded by eight peaks and a network of nature trails, all part of the Gault Estate, a conservation center and bird sanctuary owned by McGill University of Montreal. Picture this page.

Paul Sauvé Provincial Park There are nature trails throughout the forested, five-square-mile park.

Sainte-Agathe-des-Monts Each spring some 40,000 speckled trout fry are brought to a fish hatchery here. They are kept in an outdoor pool (covered to deter preying birds) until about four inches long, then released into Lac des Sables. There are daily, 12-mile boat cruises on the lake. Nearby Mont Sainte-Agathe has a chairlift to its 1,750-foot summit, where there is a scenic view of the lake and surrounding mountains.

Rainbow over Mont Saint-Hilaire, on the Richelieu River near Montreal. Once "the river of the Iroquois," the Richelieu (below, at dawn) runs through rich farmland and popular summer resort country.

Sainte-Ursule Falls The Maskinongé River tumbles over five waterfalls in a total drop of 202 feet.

Every autumn the leaves of deciduous trees across the land change color. The countryside is a riot of crimson, orange, yellow purple and brown—mingled with evergreen. But soon the spectacle is over: the leaves have fallen; maples, beeches, birches and other deciduous trees are denuded and dormant. Only the pines and other coniferous trees stay green throughout winter.

Despite their different fates, deciduous leaves and evergreen needles perform the same function, creating the food that trees need for life and growth. It is in leaves and evergreen needles that photosynthesis takes place, a process by which the energy of the sun is converted and combined with water, soil nutrients and carbon dioxide from the air to produce nourishment. A waste product of this process is oxygen, necessary to the survival of all higher forms of life. Without green plants, life on earth could not exist.

Why Leaves Change Color—and Evergreens Stay Ever Green

INSIDE A LEAF

The top side of a leaf—the cuticle—is slightly waxy to conserve moisture. Just beneath the cuticle is a layer of clear epidermis cells, and under these are chloroplasts, containing the chlorophyll that utilizes sunlight in producing food. Under the chloroplasts is a spongy layer of cells. In them are mixed carbon dioxide, which has entered through the stomata (tiny openings in the underside of the leaf) and water and nutrients, which have entered through the leaf's veins. (The veins also hold the leaf outspread so that it is exposed to as much sunlight as possible.) When sunlight strikes the chloroplasts, the chlorophyll sets off a chemical reaction in which nutrients and carbon dioxide are combined to produce glucose, a simple sugar. Chlorophyll in a leaf deteriorates as it is used, but in a healthy tree it is replaced throughout the summer. In fall, with shorter days and cooler nights, the production of chlorophyll is slowed. This exposes carotenoids, pigments which tint leaves yellow and orange. As the weather turns colder, the sugar begins to accumulate in the leaves instead of being fed back to the tree; the result is red and purple pigments called anthocyanins. These pigments, combined with each other and with tannins (waste products that turn leaves brown) give leaves their colors.

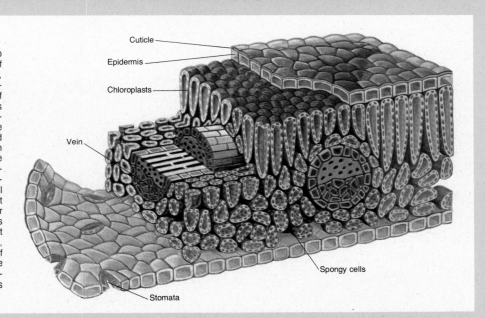

AN EVERGREEN NEEDLE

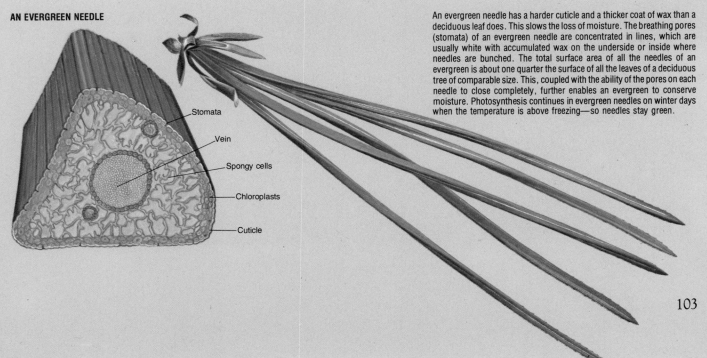

An evergreen needle has a harder cuticle and a thicker coat of wax than a deciduous leaf does. This slows the loss of moisture. The breathing pores (stomata) of an evergreen needle are concentrated in lines, which are usually white with accumulated wax on the underside or inside where needles are bunched. The total surface area of all the needles of an evergreen is about one quarter the surface of all the leaves of a deciduous tree of comparable size. This, coupled with the ability of the pores on each needle to close completely, further enables an evergreen to conserve moisture. Photosynthesis continues in evergreen needles on winter days when the temperature is above freezing—so needles stay green.

103

Timeless Rhythms of the Wilderness— at Ottawa's Doorstep

It is April. From every hillside creek comes the roar of meltwater, the music that ends the long winter silence and signals breakup in the Gatineau. The sudden excitement of spring is heard in the gabble and honk of Canada geese bound for northern breeding grounds, in the croak of wood frogs and the wild sweet music of spring peepers. Soon there is a mysterious throbbing in the air: the hills vibrate to the strangest of all woodland songs, the drumming of ruffed grouse. . . .

Gatineau Park, north of the Ottawa River in Quebec, is a wilderness within sight of Ottawa's Parliament Buildings, an 88,000-acre sanctuary for the native wild plants and animals of the Canadian Shield. Neither a national park nor a provincial park, it was established in 1938 and is administered by the National Capital Commission. The main entrance is five miles north of Ottawa on the Gatineau Parkway. This 22-mile scenic drive goes from Hull to the Champlain Lookout, the northernmost of several lookouts.

The rolling Gatineau Hills are the stumps of a mountain range that was formed perhaps a thousand million years ago. By about 500 million years ago the mountains had been worn down and a great fault occurred along the valley of the Ottawa. The land dropped, leaving the Eardley Escarpment rising hundreds of feet above

Ground fog billows among the ancient Gatineau Hills.

105

the valley floor. The giant Wisconsin Glacier, which blanketed half the continent, was the last of a series of glaciers to scour the Gatineau Hills, scraping and rounding the hilltops and gouging soil from the valleys. Glacial boulders were scattered throughout the hills and huge erratics were transported far from parent bedrock. As the glacier melted, rivers of meltwater flowed beneath the shrinking ice. A sandy esker tracing the course of one such stream cuts across the north of Gatineau Park.

About 12,000 years ago the ice finally disappeared and the land emerged, stark, bleak and devoid of life. Then began a great invasion of plants and animals that continues even today. On the rounded summit rocks of the escarpment, in the vanguard of the invasion, pioneer lichens still advance over naked bedrock, creating the first soil cover since the glaciation. Every species of living thing in the park has migrated into

The Gatineau: the simplicity of winter white against the forest's evergreen, the peace of a still lake in early autumn.

these hills during the past 12,000 years, an astonishing feat of nature when one considers such creatures as the tiny red-backed salamander or freshwater clams inching their way up the continent, century after century. The incredible moving throng still presses northward, as habitat after habitat opens up for occupation.

Indians had reached the valley of the Ottawa at least 4,000 years ago but is was not until the fur trade era, when Indians, voyageurs and coureurs de bois moved through the forests hunting and trapping for the Montreal market, that man's presence was felt in these hills in a major way. Once the beaver were depleted, the trappers moved deeper into the wilderness.

Settlers arrived in the dense pine forests of the Gatineau Hills in the middle years of the 19th century, but this, too, proved a temporary incursion. The terrain was suitable only for sheep grazing and by the turn of the century most of the settlers had left. The mountain clearings with their small log cabins were abandoned, but not before the great red and white pines had been harvested from the hills.

With the exodus of the settlers, the land reverted to wilderness. A fine northern hardwood forest of maple, beech and yellow birch has replaced the pines of the last century. Some white pines are found in the park but even the oldest are not far past the century mark.

Man invaded the hills again in the 1920s, this time for sheer enjoyment of the wooded terrain. Ski trails fanned out through the hills from the Ottawa Ski Club lodge in the valley of Fortune Creek. Many ski trails became popular hiking trails too.

In October, when the hills are splashed with the flaming colors of autumn, thousands of city folk are drawn to the park. Once the leaves are off the trees, long vistas open up. Now venturesome hikers explore the wild interior of the park, discovering unsuspected high rock lookouts, beautiful beechwood valleys and hidden ravines. If he strikes away from the traveled trails, the hiker may chance upon fresh bear tracks in the mud of a beaver dam, or glimpse an otter bounding along the bank of a stream.

The first snowfall brings a pleasant hush to the bush. In the new snow, the silent coming and going of wild creatures is recorded for all to see. There is meaning in the broad wing-sweep on the snow where the hare's tracks end, and in the sudden listening pause in the tracks of the trotting fox. Recorded, too, are the tiny scamperings of white-footed mice, the meanderings of raccoon families and, at the edge of open water, the muddy footprints of mink foraging for food. Deer tracks wander everywhere, outnumbered only by the spoor of the lively little red squirrel. But as the snows of winter deepen, fewer and fewer creatures stir.

Midwinter in the heart of Gatineau Park: the great silence and solitude that once clothed the winter forests of all Canada.

March brings ideal conditions for ranging the park on skis. Spring skiing over frozen lakes, through big hardwood valleys and along streams crisscrossed with the footprints of the wild is one of the most enjoyable ways to explore the park. To travel by map and compass through untracked country in the frosty air and the burning sun of March is exhilarating freedom, the freedom that, for many, is the real meaning of wilderness.

And then . . . breakup. The Gatineau slowly wakens and warms to another spring. The full rush of spring comes in May. Perhaps the spirit of this season is best experienced by a morning paddle into the Meach Lake marsh. Activity is the keynote, with muskrats swimming in the channels, redwings chacking and whistling from a hundred noisy nests, and great blue herons winging to fish from the beaver dams. Green frogs and leopard frogs twang and croak, swamp sparrows trill their song of love, and black ducks whir to noisy splashdowns in open patches of water. Through all the hubbub come the clear whistled notes of the olive-sided flycatcher, tossed off again and again with wild abandon. When a beaver slaps the water, there is momentary quiet. Then the sounds resume, a strange mingling of wild voices from the myriad creatures in the teeming marsh.

Gatineau Park's sphagnum bogs formed in lakes and depressions where drainage patterns were altered or blocked by glacial debris. A bog is often surrounded by a dense wood with tangled undergrowth that harbors clouds of mosquitoes—but the magnificent showy lady's-slipper grows in these boggy woods and in no other habitat. At the inner edge of the wood is a belt of black spruce surrounding the open bog; here the air is pungent with aromatic Labrador tea. In the center of the open sphagnum mat is the black water of the bog lake, slowly filling in with vegetation. To stand still on the sphagnum is to sink deeper and deeper into the cold bog water that lies beneath. Bouncing up and down on the floating mat of vegetation sways the spruce trees 20 feet away. This intriguing habitat is the home of strange and beautiful plants. The insect-trapping sundew and pitcher plant grow here, along with cotton grass, bog laurel and the beautiful wild orchid, grass pink. Other wild orchids flower in the bogs and woods and meadows of the park from May to September.

Civilization now presses close against the borders of Gatineau Park. Still the ancient wilderness cycle goes on, season after season, in an atmosphere of timelessness and permanence that only wilderness can impart. Here, within easy reach of city dwellers, is a small remnant pocket of the wildness and freedom and natural beauty that is part of our Canadian heritage.

OTHER ATTRACTIONS

Where the Shield Ends, Slate Steps Trod by Voyageurs

Almonte The Mississippi River drops a total 57 feet over Upper and Lower falls in this town.

Baskatong Reservoir The largest of many lakes in Gatineau County is 110-square-mile Baskatong Reservoir. Gamefish are plentiful in the lakes. Picture this page.

Fitzroy Provincial Park This 435-acre park, part of a pioneer homestead, occupies both banks of the Carp River, plus Butternut Island at the confluence of the Carp and the Ottawa rivers. Upstream is a 2½-mile stretch of rapids that once ended in some 23 waterfalls (Chats Falls). Although the rapids still exist, the falls were tamed by a dam.

La Vérendrye Provincial Park This 5,257-square-mile park has hundreds of lakes and rivers and 1,500 miles of canoe routes. Controlled moose hunting is allowed. Pike, walleye, smallmouth bass, lake and speckled trout are common. Picture next page.

Lièvre River The 205-mile Lièvre flows through country whose untamed appearance is enhanced by landslides, the most notorious being one that claimed 34 lives and 15 dwellings at Notre-

A misty morning on the Baskatong Reservoir, deep in Gatineau country.

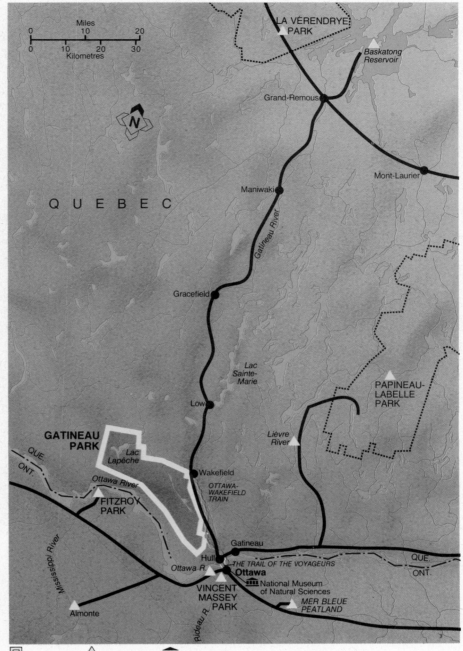

La Vérendrye Park is a vast expanse of bush, lakes and rivers—and wetlands such as this, home to a flock of ducks (center of picture).

Dame-de-la-Salette in 1908. The evidence is still there, an overgrown gash bisecting the town. The cause of the landslides is unstable Leda clay, a solid-looking substance that, when disturbed, turns into an oozy, quick-running liquid.

Mer Bleue Peatland This 6,300 acres of peat is a mecca for naturalists, drawn by its rare plants and animal life (including a species of dragonfly found nowhere else). The bog was once a channel of the Ottawa River. Fossilized pollen found in the bog provides 7,500 years of plant history.

National Museum of Natural Sciences Displays here take visitors on a 2½-billion-year journey through time. There are audio-visual displays of such things

as a volcano and of birds singing, a large model of the earth and such touchable items as a meteorite, jade, limestone and sandstone. You peer through telescopes at distant galaxies, step on a scale to find your relative weight on Jupiter and the moon, stroke water-polished jade and glacier-grooved limestone.

Ottawa River The Ottawa, in the Gatineau area, marks the southern reaches of the Canadian Shield, separating it from the gentle farmland to the south. In a few miles near Ottawa the river races through rapids such as the Chats and Deschênes and on to marshy bayous and past sandy islands east of the capital. The 7½-mile Ottawa River Parkway has bikeways and walkways.

Ottawa-Wakefield Steam Train Excursion A steam train operated by the National Capital Commission and National Museum of Science and Tech-

nology travels a scenic 20-mile route along the Gatineau River in summer.

Papineau-Labelle Provincial Park The park was created to give the public access to the many lakes within a 671-square-mile area. Main species are pike, walleye (pickerel) and trout.

The Trail of the Voyageurs This mile-long trail around the Chaudière Falls in the heart of Ottawa-Hull is one of the oldest preserved routes in Canada. Crude slate steps fashioned by the voyageurs on the north bank of the Ottawa River are still used by strollers.

Vincent Massey and Hog's Back Parks These adjoining Ottawa parks, totalling 106 acres, are thickly wooded. In Hog's Back, on the Rideau River, is 30-foot-high Prince of Wales Falls. A bicycle path that winds through Vincent Massey Park serves as a ski trail in winter.

110

Purple-fringed orchid   Ragged fringed orchid   Pink lady's-slipper   Round-leaved orchid

Showy and Shy, Orchids Adorn Woods, Bogs and Meadows

Orchids are traditionally an expensive product of steaming jungles and pampering hothouses. But they flourish wild in many places in Canada—nowhere more beautifully or in greater variety than in the woodlands, bogs and soft, wet meadows of Gatineau Park. Orchids use color and form—even fragrance—to attract insects to distribute pollen. As the insects flit from flower to flower in search of nectar, their bodies pick up and deposit the pollen necessary for cross-fertilization.

Despite their success in attracting insects, orchids are rare, mainly because of their specific environmental needs. They do not usually survive when transplanted and even in their natural setting are slow to reproduce. Although some orchids manufacture millions of seeds, only a few develop. Only if wild orchids are protected will they continue to grace the bogs and woodlands of Canada.

Orchids are amazingly diverse in structure and color. They range in appearance from the sophisticated elegance of showy lady's-slipper to the Raggedy Ann look of green adder's mouth.

Five single-blossomed fairy slippers (also called Calypso) grace a dark, wet wood. Each plant of nodding ladies' tresses, usually found in open meadows and woods of Gatineau Park, has delicate florets spiralling to the tip of the straight stem.

Exotic grass pinks cluster like butterflies against the green of the bog. Hardly exotic at all, the bedraggled Loesel's twayblade also belongs to the orchid family. Like many other Canadian orchids, the twayblade sometimes grows for years before flowering.

Arethusa was named for a Greek wood nymph who escaped from an amorous river god.

Lacking leaves and chlorophyll, spotted coralroot lives off decaying matter in soil.

In the Thousand Islands near Ivy Lea, Ont.

THOUSAND ISLANDS

The Indians' Garden of the Great Spirit, Split by the Canadian-American Border

Some are lushly forested. Some support only a few ragged pines perched precariously over the water. Some are miles long. Others are barren boulders no larger than rowboats. Some are treacherous shoals. These are the Thousand Islands, long ago part of a mountain range as majestic as the Rockies. The Thousand (perhaps 995, maybe 1,010) lie in a 35-mile stretch of the St. Lawrence River between Gananoque and Brockville. They are a popular vacationland noted for fine fishing, boating and camping, and the peace of secluded living.

The Indians called the Thousand Islands the Garden of the Great Spirit and believed the region was once a great expanse of open water. According to legend, the Great Spirit created a garden paradise along the shore in an effort to bring peace to warring tribes. Still

they fought. So he bundled paradise into a blanket and flew toward his home in the heavens. But the blanket tore. Paradise crashed into the water and broke into hundreds of islands.

There is of course a geological history too. Some 900 million years ago mountains rose where the St. Lawrence now flows. Rivers and glaciers reduced the peaks to low hills that now are islands and shoals.

The St. Lawrence, Canada's largest river by volume (the Mackenzie is second), is young by geological standards. Its relative youth and the erosion-resistant bedrock in the area have prevented the river from carving a clear channel through the Thousand Islands. In geological terms, the region is a "flooded landscape."

Water swirls through the islands at about 235,000 cubic feet a second, more than six times the flow of Churchill Falls in Labrador. It averages three knots but the speed varies with the width and depth of the river. Dams between Kingston and Montreal help regulate levels during the navigation season.

The Thousand Islands lie on a ridge of Precambrian rock that joins the Canadian Shield with the Adirondack Mountains in New York State. This strip, called the Frontenac Axis, is composed primarily of granite with a thin and irregular covering of soil.

The islands' southerly location and the moderating influence of nearby Lake Ontario make for an early spring. By late March or early April, as the ice goes and the river flows freely again, the archipelago welcomes its first visitors: ducks and geese that follow the major migration flyway that cuts across the islands.

By mid-April, when birds leave for nesting grounds in the far north, the first of millions of vacationers will have arrived. But in early spring this elegant, evergreen land belongs not to campers, cottagers and cruise boats but to creatures of the wild. Six mergansers—fish-eating diving ducks—wing low over the water in single file as if playing follow the leader. Another startled flock of birds scurries across the water and spirals rapidly upward. Their distinctive wing-whistling sound identifies them as golden-eyed ducks or "whistlers." A chickadee chirps its name from the forest.

Birds that nest in the islands include song sparrows, yellow warblers, grackles, gallinules, robins, orioles, gulls, terns, kingfishers and great blue herons.

Many animals and plants reach the limit of their Canadian range in the Frontenac Axis. A great variety of salamanders, frogs, toads, turtles and snakes thrives here. Some, such as the black rat snake, are rarely found elsewhere in Canada. About 700 plants are native to

Densely forested islands are studded with small, neat cottages, modern marinas and lavish, Victorian-style summer homes.

the region, and 200 to 300 species are normally found on any one island. Many an island supports one or more plant species found nowhere else in the area. Witch hazel, American hazelnut, downy arrow-wood, May apple and other plants typical of more southerly regions grow on the thin island soil.

On the islands are dense forests that, because of sharp temperature variations within a small area, vary considerably in their makeup. The forest cover on one island might consist of hemlock to the northeast, some mixed strands of red and white oak in the central part, and pitch pine to the southwest. Red cedar, shagbark hickory and American hickory can be found throughout the islands.

The Thousand Islands area is split lengthwise by the Canada-United States border. The seven-mile Thousand Islands International Bridge uses six islands as stepping-stones. The five-span bridge, linking Ivy Lea,

A huge boat house on Wellesley Island is framed by hardy white and pitch pines on a rocky point in the Thousand Islands. Precambrian rock formations such as this one are typical of the islands, which range from boulder size to several miles long.

Ont., with Alexandria Bay, N.Y., affords some spectacular views.

As more and more islands became cottage sites, the Canadian government decided in 1904 to set aside a 90-acre mainland area for a national park. St. Lawrence Islands National Park (at 1,000 acres Canada's smallest national park) now includes 18 islands and some 80 islets. Only its administrative headquarters at Mallorytown Landing is accessible by car. Here are 60 tent and trailer sites, a boat ramp, a beach and a children's playground. In a visitor's center, park naturalists explain the natural history of the Thousand Islands; there are films, slides and discussions.

When night descends on the islands, cottage lights and campfires wink from among the trees and cast flickering reflections across the water. The river laps rhythmically at rocky shorelines and the deep throb of a slow-moving freighter blends with the sigh of pines and the rustle of oak leaves. Before flocks of ducks and geese return to the Thousand Islands in the fall, millions of visitors will find pleasure and peace in the Garden of the Great Spirit.

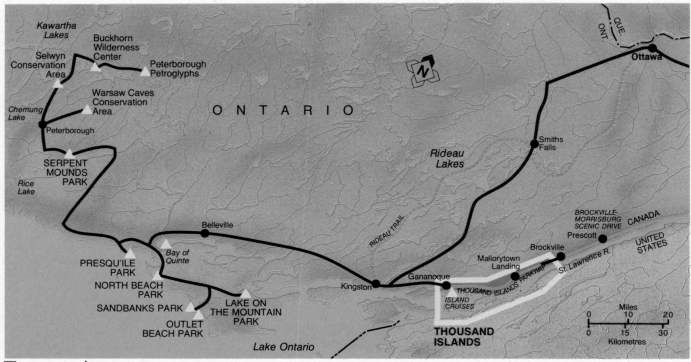

◻ Scenic Wonder △ Other Attraction ▮ Scenic Route ▮▮ Hiking Trail

OTHER ATTRACTIONS

Petroglyphs, Pictographs, Serpent Mounds, Kettles . . .

Bay of Quinte *This inlet of Lake Ontario, between the Ontario mainland and the peninsula called Prince Edward County, is 50 miles long and from six to 12 miles wide. The bay has many picturesque inlets of its own and is fed by several large rivers.*

Bay of Quinte Picture this page.

Brockville-Morrisburg Scenic Drive Highway 2 winds for 35 miles through trees and hill country, offering excellent views of the St. Lawrence.

Buckhorn Wilderness Center Hiking trails crisscross this wilderness, only 28 miles from Peterborough. It is a 1,000-acre tract of bush, forest, bogs, deep lakes and swift streams.

Island Cruises Boat tours of the Thousand Islands start at Ivy Lea, Kingston, Brockville, Rockport and Gananoque.

Lake on the Mountain Provincial Park The mile-wide, saucer-shaped lake sits on an escarpment, 170 feet above the Bay of Quinte.

North Beach Provincial Park This 75-acre sandbar park separates Lake North Bay from Lake Ontario. Seven miles away is Carrying Place, an historic Indian portage on the isthmus between Lake Ontario and the western extremity of the Bay of Quinte.

Outlet Beach Provincial Park Lake Ontario currents have built sand across the mouth of a narrow bay (now East Lake) to create 635-acre Outlet Beach Provincial Park and its two-mile shore. Cedars, junipers and bearberry bushes provide some cover.

Peterborough Petroglyphs More than 900 figures carved in crystalline limestone in Petroglyphs Provincial Park are believed the work of Algonkian Indians. The petroglyphs, estimated to be between 500 and 1,000 years old, cover a gently sloping surface 180 feet by 100. Some are barely perceptible; others are deeper, including one that is 1½ inches deep. The Petroglyph Hiking Trail leads to a good view of the carvings. Another trail leads to High Falls on Eels Creek.

Presqu'ile Provincial Park This peninsula jutting into Lake Ontario has a 1½-mile-long beach, a 2,000-acre expanse of marshes, forests and meadows and a rich assortment of plant, mammal and bird life. Thousands of migrating common terns and ring-billed gulls stop every year. Marshy areas are inhabited by minks, muskrats and star-nosed moles. Red foxes and weasels prey on hares, cottontail rabbits and smaller mammals on the drier ground. Presqu'ile Point lighthouse stands next to a museum and aquarium where naturalists lecture.

Rideau Trail This 200-mile hiking trail (between Ottawa and Kingston) passes the Carleton Forest Area, Rideau River Provincial Park, Limerick Forest, Fowley Mountain Conservation Area and Frontenac Provincial Park. Picture this page.

Sandbanks Provincial Park The park is a five-mile bar of white sand thrown across an inlet—the largest fresh water bay mouth dune in the world. Thousands of trees have been planted to prevent soil erosion.

Selwyn Conservation Area One of the last untouched sections along the Trent-Severn Waterway, these 78 acres include 1¼ miles of Chemung Lake shoreline. Some 68 species of birds have been identified here, and among the plants is the rare white cardinal flower.

Serpent Mounds Provincial Park Under Canada's best-preserved and most elaborate burial mounds lies what remains of the Point Peninsula people who occupied the region 2,000 years ago. The largest mound, 25 feet wide and six feet high, curves like a serpent for 200 feet. Eight smaller egg-shaped mounds surround it.

Thousand Islands Parkway Trees along the 24-mile parkway sometimes screen the St. Lawrence but lookouts every few miles give fine views of the river. Forty feet above the road near Brown's Bay is a half-mile-long slab of rare light gray sandstone atop the reddish granite common in this area. The largest stand of pitch pines in mainland Canada grows along this route; they are especially thick among the red and white oaks between Rockport and Ivy Lea. Great blue herons feed in roadside marshes, where also can be heard the weird pumping call of the American bittern on evenings in May and June.

Warsaw Caves Conservation Area Uncounted potholes, passages and underground streams—and a "vanishing" waterfall—have been carved in limestone here by the Indian River. On the cave walls are fossil imprints: fish, plants, snails and a nautilite, a snail-like creature that had a long, pointed shell. Temperatures in the 280-foot-long Glacière cave are just above freezing year-round. Some caves are big enough to stand in; others must be crawled through. Above ground are hundreds of potholes (called kettles), formed by boulders that were caught in river whirlpools and, constantly moving, slowly ate into the limestone. The largest pothole is 15 feet deep and tapers from seven feet across at the top to three feet at the bottom. A 15-foot waterfall dries up and reveals a stone ridge in summer when the river's reduced flow follows an underground course. Nearby is a 100-foot-deep gorge, whose sides are almost solid walls of ice in winter. Hiking and snowshoe trails lead to The Plains, 10 acres of flat rock stripped bare by water, wind and fire. Nature trails are posted in the surrounding forest.

The Rideau River, whose source is north of Kingston, flows northeast through rolling lowlands to Ottawa (below, near Carleton University). It drops over a limestone cliff at Rideau Falls in Ottawa, just before joining the Ottawa River. There are hiking trails along the Rideau.

The Ice Retreats, Mountains Become Hills, Then Islands

The Thousand Islands are on the Frontenac Axis, a granite ridge that connects the Adirondack Mountains and the Canadian Shield. Beneath the islands are rocks 900 million years old, thought to be the roots of mountains worn down by weathering. Four times in the past two million years ice sheets covered much of northern North America—and the last glaciation reached its maximum southeasterly extent at Long Island, N.Y., 18,000 years ago. Then the ice began its final retreat, signalling the eventual end of the Ice Age and setting in motion processes that would create the Thousand Islands.

14,000 YEARS AGO
The Laurentide Ice Sheet still buried the Thousand Islands region. The ice—two miles thick in places—depressed the earth's crust and deepened basins that were to become the Great Lakes. Valleys, already eroded by past glaciations, were deepened further and mountain tops were rounded.

12,500 YEARS AGO
When the retreating ice margin reached the north side of the Adirondacks, the Thousand Islands region was free of ice. Meltwaters filled the basin of early Lake Ontario and submerged the hills of the Frontenac Axis, creating Lake Iroquois. Since ice blocked the St. Lawrence lowlands, Lake Iroquois drained south, via the Mohawk Valley. Freed of its burden of ice, the land started to rise.

11,800 YEARS AGO
As the ice retreated—to where Ottawa and Quebec now stand—the land continued to rebound. The St. Lawrence Valley was now free of the ice but still below sea level. The Atlantic flooded the lowlands, creating the Champlain Sea. Early Lake Ontario poured over the Frontenac Axis. The hilltops that are the Thousand Islands appeared.

7,000 YEARS AGO
For 5,000 years the land continued to lift—to about where it is today. The Champlain Sea drained and the St. Lawrence River began to carve its channel to the sea. A 30-mile stretch of the St. Lawrence, between Gananoque and Brockville, is studded with some 1,000 islands, all bearing evidence of long and intricate geological history.

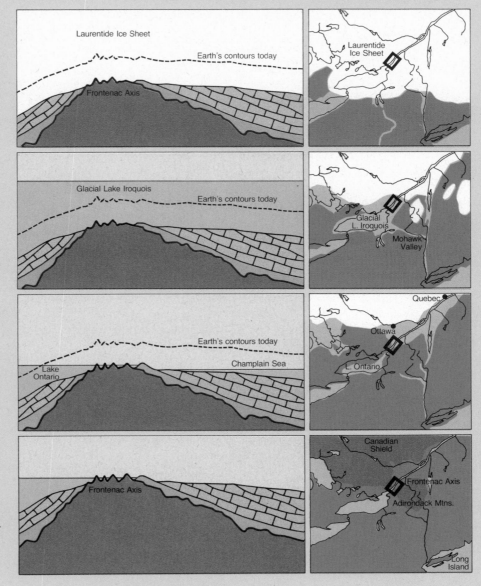

Most of the soil that covered the Thousand Islands prior to the Ice Age was scoured from the granite bedrock by ice. Today the islands are covered by soil 1 to 1½ feet deep. Rock outcrops are common.

Like rough-hewn gems, pink granite blocks adorn the shore of Aubrey Island. These rocks were formed beneath the earth's surface during a mountain building period and have endured for almost a billion years.

Along the Gordon Island shore, white pine and cedar bow gracefully over layered sandstone cliffs. The sand particles that formed these rocks were deposited in a shallow sea about 500 million years ago.

Layers of limestone on Cedar Island rest on older granite. Once the bed of an inland sea, these limestone beds were formed from the shells of marine creatures that were cemented together and turned to stone.

THE GREAT LAKES

Freshwater Seas at Mid-Continent

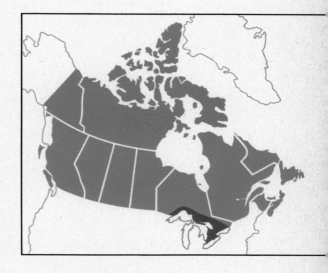

The Great Lakes, stretching from midcontinent to the mighty river that feeds them to the sea, are five of the world's 12 biggest bodies of fresh water and the center of a vast region that boasts some of Canada's finest scenic wonders. One of the lakes, 32,483-square-mile Lake Superior, is the biggest freshwater body in the world; 1,068-square-mile Manitoulin Island in Lake Huron is the world's biggest freshwater island. Canada shares Lakes Superior, Huron, Erie and Ontario with the United States; Lake Michigan is wholly in the U.S. North America's heaviest concentration of industry is around the lakes but there are also beaches and farmland and forests and dunes and, especially in the north, true wilderness. In and near the lakes are four of Canada's national parks (among them Point Pelee at the southernmost tip of the Canadian mainland and a wild jewel called Pukaskwa) and dozens of Ontario provincial parks (including such beauty spots as Rondeau, Presqu'ile and Ipperwash). Lake Huron has the rugged Bruce Peninsula and the Thirty Thousand Islands of Georgian Bay. On the Niagara River between Lake Erie and Lake Ontario is awesome Niagara Falls. And from the Lakehead to the Bruce to Niagara, from Pelee to Rondeau to Quinte's Isle, the land of the Great Lakes is a land great with the beauty and the wonder of nature.

Opposite: *Neys Provincial Park on Lake Superior.*
Preceding pages: *Wasaga Beach, Georgian Bay.*

ALGONQUIN PROVINCIAL PARK

2,500 Lakes and Countless Portages: Here You Can Paddle Your Canoe Forever

Put down your paddle. Now . . . drift. You're on a lake in the scenic wonderland of Algonquin Provincial Park. The stillness is broken only by the lapping of water against your canoe. As you listen to the wilderness you become one with it. . . .

The great park covers 2,910 square miles. A few of its 2,500 lakes are close to the well-traveled 36½ miles of Highway 60 that cross the southwestern part of the park. Most, though, are wilderness lakes, far from civilization, linked by rivers and streams and often strenuous portages. Canoeists have 23 starting points and 1,000 miles of routes. The variety possible by combining different canoe route segments is almost endless.

But Algonquin is far more than a canoeist's dream of perfect lake country. It is also a mecca for hikers, picnickers, swimmers, fishermen and campers, and for

lovers of birds, animals, rocks, trees, flowers, rugged landscape and the peaceful hush of wilderness.

This vast land of lakes, streams, spruce bogs and forests lies near the southern edge of the Canadian Shield between Georgian Bay and the Ottawa River. Created in 1893 for the "benefit, advantage and enjoyment of the people of the province," it is the oldest provincial park in Ontario and one of the largest in Canada. Algonquin has wildlife aplenty. A ban on agriculture helps to protect the wild terrain and its network of waterways.

Glaciers, sometimes two miles thick, covered the area for about a million years. The last of the ice slowly melted northward 11,000 years ago. Then life began to clothe the barren land and in a few hundred years the great forests had grown. The park's east section, in the sands left by the retreating glacier, held mostly red, white and some jack pine; the west side had a mixed

Like a flight of flying saucers or a drummer's dream of clashing brass cymbals, pond lilies lend a subtle blend of rust and gold to Algonquin Park's autumn palette. A lonesome pine, roots deep in the rocky shore, leans tall above an Algonquin lake.

forest of mature hardwoods with some pine, spruce and balsam fir. But it was the pines that dominated Algonquin; many towered 150 feet and more.

In the mid-1800s loggers came from Bytown (now Ottawa) to "hurl down the pine." They made a thorough job of it, scarring the land with slash that fed forest fires. Indians had roamed Algonquin for some 4,000 years without appreciably altering the land; in about 60 years the loggers changed it permanently.

Second growth in the western part of the park is mostly sugar maple and beech; the occasional old pine stands tall over them all, a survivor of the massacre. The area once had moose and caribou but few deer. Moose and caribou found it difficult to survive in the new forests; white-tailed deer, on the other hand, thrived for a while. But now, as the forest again matures, the number of deer is decreasing. Logging continues in Algonquin but is strictly controlled. Algonquin's popularity as a recreation area grew slowly—until 1936 when Highway 60 was opened. In 1972 some 60,000 persons camped in the interior—more than three times the number of 10 years earlier. Logging has not interfered with most vacationers because roads are kept narrow and wherever possible are built away from shorelines and portages. In summer loggers are prohibited from working near major canoe routes and from hauling after dark.

There are hundreds of places alongside Highway 60 where rockhounds examine materials that make up the park terrain. In ancient masses of rock are "flow" lines and "grain" and there are many glacial deposits of

The ice is firm but the covering blanket of snow is still not deep, so snowshoes are carried across Tona Kela Lake in Algonquin Park.

sand, gravel, silt, stones and boulders. At both park entrances and at the park museum (13 miles from the west entrance) there is literature on every aspect of the Algonquin's natural history.

Eight clearly marked walking trails lead off from Highway 60. Only one is more than two miles long but each gives some idea of what it is like in Algonquin's vast interior—and provides a close look at many aspects of park ecology. You can meander through a typical hardwood forest, get a good look at the creatures and plants of a spruce bog, watch life in a beaver colony and, at practically every turn in the path, catch a view of a lake, a river, a maple ridge.

The streams and the cold, deep lakes are the home of brook and lake trout, smallmouth bass and, in lesser numbers, splake, walleye and pike. Algonquin has many fishes, but there are remarkably few amphibians and reptiles—only nine types of toads and frogs, six of salamanders, nine of snakes (none poisonous) and four of turtles. Naturalists have recorded 218 species of birds in Algonquin. For some, such as the spruce grouse and the boreal chickadee, this is far south of their usual habitats. A few of the park's 1,000 moose are sometimes spotted from Highway 60, as are deer.

Beaver have built dams and created ponds in nearly every stream in Algonquin Park. Much more difficult to spot are such beaver pond tenants as muskrat, otter, marten and mink. The park's most famous residents, rarely seen but sometimes heard, are wolves. Algonquin is one of the few accessible places on earth where timber wolves still live. A recent estimate put their number at about 150. The wolves often respond to human imitations of their howls.

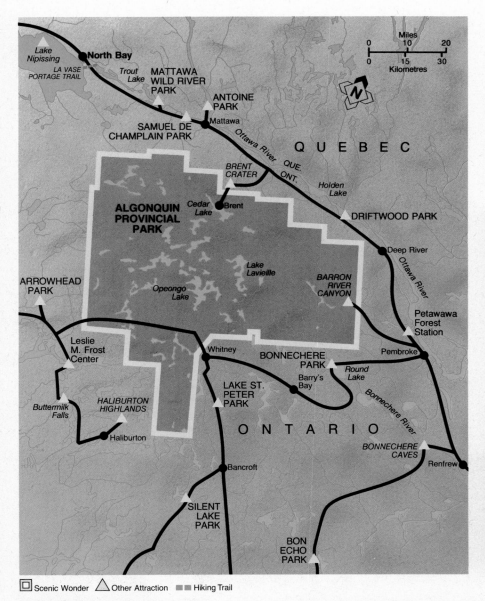

Scenic Wonder △ Other Attraction ▦ Hiking Trail

Bon Echo Provincial Park *On Bon Echo Rock, a mile-long escarpment along the east side of Lake Mazinaw, are some 135 Indian pictographs (rock paintings) of undetermined age. The "rabbit-man," a six-inch-high figure of religious significance, stands out among human and animal figures and abstract and geometric impressions*

OTHER ATTRACTIONS

A Meteorite Crater and the Highlands of Haliburton

Antoine Provincial Park This 30-acre, boulder-strewn park lies between the Ottawa River and a 600-foot-high hill to the west.

Arrowhead Provincial Park The meandering, oxbowed East River, one boundary of this park, runs with brook trout. Two lakes in the 2,400-acre park offer good fishing: bass are caught in Arrowhead Lake, brook trout in May-flower Lake. Wildlife includes moose, deer and beaver. Park naturalists provide interpretive programs, particularly for three hiking trails.

Barron River Canyon The rust-red walls of the mile-long canyon rise 300 feet. Geologists reckon that during the Ice Age the river carried about 1,000 times more water than goes over Niagara today. The encrusted saxifrage found here is a rare example of an arctic plant growing in southern Ontario.

Bon Echo Provincial Park Picture this page.

Bonnechere Caves These twisting limestone passages became accessible in 1955, with diversion of water that flowed

through from the Bonnechere River. There are hour-long guided tours. Embedded in the walls are the fossils of animals that lived in a tropical sea that covered the area 500 million years ago. Stalactites hang from the roofs. Close to the caves is the white water of the Bonnechere River's Fourth Chute. Semi-precious stones in the area include apatite, amazonite and moonstones.

Bonnechere Provincial Park On the bank of the Bonnechere river mouth at Round Lake, the 250-acre park features a good beach on the lake itself.

129

Brent Crater A hole made by a meteorite an estimated 450 million years ago is two miles wide and 500 feet deep. It is believed that the hole originally was 1,300 feet deep. But sediment from a prehistoric sea and some glacial debris atop of the sediment have filled the bottom 800 feet. Gilmour Lake, the larger of two glacial lakes, is a mile long and 80 feet deep.

Buttermilk Falls Water from Hall's Lake drops 60 feet in its quarter-mile rush to Boshkung Lake. There is an old Indian trail between the lakes.

Driftwood Provincial Park Because of flooding, after a dam altered the flow of the Ottawa River, trees were drowned and great quantities of driftwood collected on the shores of Holden Lake.

Haliburton Highlands Picture this page.

Lake Nipissing Although it is 50 miles by 35, Indians called the lake Nipissing, or little water, probably to distinguish it from Georgian Bay. Walleye (pickerel) are its most common fish, but

30-pound pike and muskellunge have been landed. Smallmouth bass are found here, unusually far north for the species. The beaches at Golden Mile, Sunset and Champlain parks are summer favorites. Several cruise boats make six-hour, 70-mile trips between North Bay and Chaudière Falls on the French River.

Lake St. Peter Provincial Park The 63-acre park and the adjacent 2,000-acre parkland preserve are the home of typical Algonquin wildlife and have an active beaver colony. A 2½-mile trail leads to a 300-foot hill overlooking the area.

La Vase Portage Trail This little-used stretch of the old voyageur canoe route links Trout Lake and Lake Nipissing.

Leslie M. Frost Natural Resources Center Established to improve public understanding of natural resource management and use, the center helps visitors develop outdoor skills and knowledge with the help of nature interpreters.

Mattawa Wild River Provincial Park Coursing through a 100-foot-high gran-

ite gorge and over two waterfalls and several rapids, the Mattawa River is a 35-mile link between the Ottawa River and Trout Lake.

Petawawa Forest Experiment Station A half-mile walk and a five-mile, tape-guided tour by automobile at Canada's oldest tree research establishment show the importance of logging to a healthy forest and teach the rudiments of soil science and geology.

Samuel de Champlain Provincial Park Some 6,290 acres of steep hills, cliffs, pine forest, lakes and rivers. The Etienne Trail, named for Etienne Brulé, is a five-hour wilderness hike.

Silent Lake Provincial Park The 1,800-acre park, whose original forest was removed by logging, is covered by a second-growth forest of white pine, hemlock, sugar maple and white birch.

Haliburton Highlands *Lakes, rivers, rapids and waterfalls riddle this 1,500-square-mile vacation area. Five-acre Skyline Park is on a high point in the town of Haliburton.*

The most distinctive call of the wild is the high-pitched, mournful wail of the wolf. The eerie howl has probably contributed more to the wolf's shabby reputation than even its two-inch fangs.

Branded as cruel and savage, wolves have been hunted to extinction in many parts of the world. Not so in Canada. Although exterminated in the Atlantic Provinces, they still are found in most of the rest of the country. In the United States, where wolves once ranged virtually the whole country, now only remnant populations exist.

But naturalists challenge the wolf's bloodthirsty image. Tales are told of "compassionate" wolves carrying food to wounded members of the pack and nursing them back to health. However, even with this softening of attitudes toward wolves, active war still is waged against them almost everywhere they are found.

Algonquin Provincial Park is one exception. The timber wolves that roam here do so unmolested and free. They are not only protected but also studied—and investigation has shown that, left alone, wolves are intelligent, placid, almost gentle, able to communicate with their fellow wolves by means of gestures and vocal patterns.

For most of the year a wolf pack or "family" has about six members. (Right: a pack in summer, before pup mortality has reduced its size.) The family is a hierarchy, most often consisting of an alpha male and female (the dominant pair), their pups, other adults and juveniles. At the bottom of this social structure is often one wolf (in some packs a male, in others a female) that is constantly chased and intimidated. This "scapegoat" (called omega) lives on the fringe of pack activities and is the last to feed. For reasons not fully understood, wolves need such an "un-

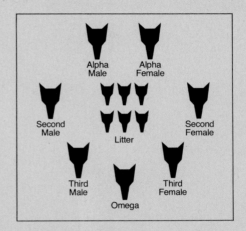

derdog." When one dies, a low-status wolf fills the vacant role. This highly structured society apparently reduces hostility and the pack benefits.

A Wilderness Hierarchy: High-Tailed Alphas and a Scapegoat Omega

The alpha male frequently exercises its dominance. Here an alpha shows its authority with a mock biting of the neck of a subordinate. The drawn-back ears and lowered head and tail of the other animal are typical of the submissive stance of low-ranking wolves.

A high tail is a sign of dominance. The alpha wolf's independent decisions—when to rest, when to hunt, whether to pursue prey—are usually followed by the other wolves. But it may change a course of action if its companions seem hesitant or fearful.

A wolf generally mates with only one partner in a season. (In fact most wolves are believed to pair for life.) It is rare for more than one pair in a pack to mate in any one year; the alpha pair produce the offspring. Wolf pups are born in spring, usually six to a litter. To feed them—they start eating meat at about six weeks—a parent often hunts far from the den. The prey—a moose perhaps, or a deer—is killed and some of its flesh is ingested and carried home, where hungry pups mouth the adult's muzzle, triggering regurgitation. The female with young is the only wolf allowed to challenge the leader.

In a ritual display of homage and affection, low-ranking wolves greet the dominant male. They surround him and each attempts to make physical contact, nuzzling the leader's fur, nipping and licking his mouth. The ceremony, which resembles the food-begging of pups, is often performed when the group awakens or when the alpha male has been away.

Wolf sounds vary with mood and condition. A female caring for her young—or pups clamoring for attention—will whimper. A low, aggressive growl is a dominant wolf's threatening warning to subordinates. Barking seems to indicate intense excitement and may be given as an alarm, a warning of the presence of trespassers in a pack's territory. Wolves howl singly and in groups, by day and by night.

Adults howl less during the pups' early development for fear of giving away the den location. Group howls are not sinister but happy, tail-wagging get-togethers that probably help serve to unite the pack. Wolves in captivity sometimes engage in long howling sessions—perhaps an expression of loneliness when separated from their companions.

131

At the brink of the Canadian Falls.

NIAGARA FALLS

'The Waters which . . . do foam and boyl'
(And the Whole World Comes to See)

This wonderful Downfal, is compounded of two great Cross-streams of Water, and two Falls, with an Isle sloping along the middle of it. The Waters which fall from this horrible Precipice, do foam and boyl . . . making an outrageous Noise, more terrible than that of Thunder; for when the Wind blows out of the South, their dismal roaring may be heard more than Fifteen Leagues off.

That was Jean Louis Hennepin's Niagara—a "vast and prodigious Cadence of Water"—in 1678. The Belgian-born missionary, explorer and writer was the first European to write an eyewitness report of the great cataract on the Niagara River. The falls have changed greatly since Hennepin's day—the crest line is constantly eaten away—but eyewitnesses have never stopped talking of Niagara in superlatives.

Some 125 years after Hennepin the overwhelmed Irish poet Thomas Moore waxed lyrical: "I have seen The Falls, and am all rapture and amazement . . . I felt as if approaching the very residence of the Deity . . . Oh! bring the atheist here, and he cannot return an atheist . . . It is impossible by pen or pencil to convey even a faint idea of their magnificence."

Many have tried, not only in prose and poetry but also with paint and brush. (Hennepin drew the first sketch of the falls.) But of the millions attracted to Niagara each year, few have done justice to this spectacle of nature, undiminished by time or erosion (although sometimes lessened by man).

The falls are near the lower end of the Niagara River, which drops 327 feet in its 35-mile course from

Lake Erie to Lake Ontario. In the mile just above the falls the drop is 51 feet. Here the river bores through rapids that create rainbows of spray.

The American Falls and the Canadian, or Horseshoe, Falls are separated by Goat Island, half a mile long and 400 yards wide and covered with brush grass and trees. The island belongs to the United States and is accessible only from the American side.

The best over-all view of both cataracts is from the Canadian side. At a lookout scant feet from the edge of the Horseshoe Falls you peer almost straight down into the mist rising from the crashing waters. It is a memorable experience—and perhaps a little frightening. Every bit as exciting is a closeup view of the Horseshoe Falls from one of three ships, each called *Maid of the Mist,* that move as close to the cataract as safety permits.

The horseshoe shape of the Canadian Falls is best seen from the air or from three observation towers up to 775 feet above the base of the falls. Note the tiny Maid of the Mist *braving the swirling waters near the foot of the cataract. For an even closer look at the falls (above) tourists in oilskins descend a spray-drenched stairway on the Canadian side.*

Of all the water allowed to flow over Niagara, more than 90 percent plunges over the Canadian Falls. They are 2,600 feet wide and 176 feet high. The American Falls are 1,000 feet wide and 184 feet high. The volume of water varies with the hour and the time of year. For the river and falls, mighty as they are, have been largely tamed by power developments on both sides of the river. A gate control system above the falls diverts much of the Niagara's water into generating stations downstream. In summer the flow is greater by day than at night: extra water is diverted at night to generate extra electricity, some of it for huge lamps that bathe the falls in multicolored light. In winter, too, more water is diverted to the power stations.

In a geological context the Niagara River and its falls are relatively young, perhaps a mere 12,500 years young. The falls were no sooner created—with the waning of the Ice Age—than they started to erode at a rapid two to seven feet a year.

The erosion is caused by the force of the water on the underlying rock structure. The rock is stratified and nearly horizontal. The upper layers are of limestone, strong and resistant; the lower layers, chiefly of shale, are weak and yielding. As the shale is worn away by the turbulent water below, the limestone is undermined, the edge projecting like a cornice. In time, it yields under its own weight and large blocks fall off. The Niagara River was an important trade route when commerce moved mostly by water. With the opening of the Welland Canal in 1829, the river lost that importance but the loss was offset by the fact that the Falls had become world famous. Soon the cities of Niagara Falls, Ont., and Niagara Falls, N.Y., were born.

Long before the hydroelectric power developments of the early 20th century (and the industrial growth they encouraged), the falls had become a great tourist attraction. With the tourists had come carpetbaggers and fast-buck artists eager to turn Niagara into a huckster's paradise. From a report published in 1873 on conditions on the Canadian side (almost all of it in the hands of

Exposed rock layers in the gorge that the falls cut in the Niagara Escarpment were once sediment at the bottom of an ancient inland sea.

land-grabbing entrepreneurs): ". . .the difficulty of escape from the organized band of cabmen, fancy and variety store keepers, guides, sight showers, picture takers, oil clothes furnishers . . . hotel keepers and runners, all working to plunder . . . has been so great as to elicit the comments of the public press . . ."

Alarmed, the Province of Ontario and the State of New York stepped in to save what they could from ruin. New York opened a park in 1885. Two years later the first provincial park in Canada was created—Queen Victoria Falls Park. Still, huckstering continued.

A curious by-product of the huckstering and the tourist trade was the arrival of the stunters, ready to risk their lives for fame and fortune—or just for the thrill of it. They came in all sizes and ages. Some made it and enjoyed public acclaim for a day or so. Others died in attempts to "conquer" Niagara.

The most sensational stunter was Blondin, a Frenchman billed as "the greatest rope walker in the world." He made his first crossing June 30, 1859. As 10,000 men, women and children cheered, he stopped above the falls to drink a bottle of water from the Niagara (symbolizing his disdain for the danger of the falls, one newspaper reported). Blondin's greatest feat came a month later. This time he determined to carry his manager, Harry Colford, on his back. Despite a strong wind, they started across. The rope swayed and Colford, frightened, tightened his grip on Blondin's throat. Colford dismounted halfway across, to give Blondin a rest, and apparently the two men quarreled. Blondin threatened to leave Colford there if he did not keep himself under control. The threat worked. Colford clambered on Blondin's back and they completed the hair-raising crossing.

But few stunters were as accomplished as Blondin. Some were killed and sometimes there were deaths in the crush of spectators too. Canada and the United States outlawed stunting in 1912.

This legislation was one more attempt to preserve the dignity of Niagara Falls. In 1880, a petition urging protection of the cataracts had been signed by some of the most notable literary men of the age, among them Thomas Carlyle, John Ruskin, Henry W. Longfellow, Ralph Waldo Emerson and Charles Dickens. Dickens perhaps had expressed the feelings of them all when once he wrote:

"Then, when I felt how near to my Creator I was standing, the first effect. . . of the tremendous spectacle was Peace. Peace of mind, tranquility, calm recollections of the Dead, great thoughts of Eternal Rest and Happiness: nothing of gloom or terror. Niagara was at once stamped upon my heart, an Image of Beauty; to remain there, changeless and indelible, until its pulses cease to beat, for ever."

OTHER ATTRACTIONS

Royal Gardens, Rugged Bluffs, and the Bongo

Beamer Memorial Park The migration of hawks can be seen closeup from a lookout atop the Niagara Escarpment. Bird watchers are almost at eye level with the hawks.

Darlington Provincial Park A half-mile nature trail follows a 50-foot-deep ravine to the shore of Lake Ontario. In the rolling, 380-acre park are 100-year-old willow trees with trunks three feet in diameter.

Elora Gorge Conservation Area Picture next page.

Iroquois Beach Provincial Park A sandy beach more than a mile long is a nesting ground for waterfowl and a feeding stopover for shorebirds. Behind the beach are 65-foot bluffs and a swampy, sandy area that is gradually being covered by vegetation.

Kortright Waterfowl Park Up to 70 species of wild and captive waterfowl nest in this 116-acre sanctuary in the city of Guelph. Among them are giant Canada geese, emperor geese and a wide variety of ducks, and the world's only whistling swans that have bred in captivity. Some birds migrate south each fall; others stay year round.

Long Point Provincial Park Long Point, a 25-mile sandspit jutting into Lake Erie, is constantly changing shape as wind and water battle the stabilizing influence of marram grass.

Luther Marsh Wildlife Management Area Twenty thousand ducks and geese, including several hundred giant Canada geese, come to Luther Marsh each spring and autumn. Other birds at the 12,000

Scarborough Bluffs One of North America's most unusual headlands stretches for nine miles along the Lake Ontario shore. The bluffs are formed of alternate layers of clay and of glacial debris, sand and clay deposited mostly during the last Ice Age glaciation.

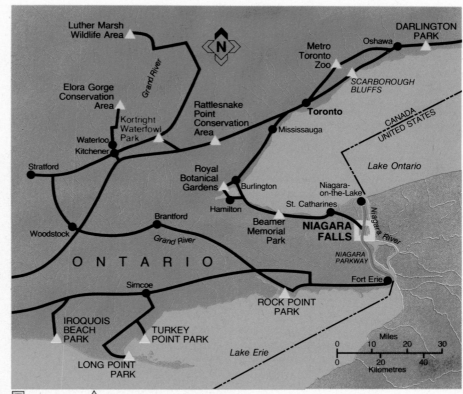

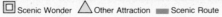
☐ Scenic Wonder   △ Other Attraction   ▬ Scenic Route

Rock Point Provincial Park *Fossils of corals an estimated 400 million years old are embedded in a water-washed limestone shelf that extends to some 1,000 feet into Lake Erie.*

Elora Gorge Conservation Area *The Grand River flows serenely along the bottom of the gorge. At one point The Cascade, a waterfall, pours over the edge of the 80-foot-high gorge walls and into the Grand. Upriver are Hole-in-the-Rock, an opening in the gorge wall, and Islet Rock, which rises about 50 feet out of swift rapids. There are nature trails on both sides of the river.*

acre sanctuary include ring-necked pheasants, mallards and herons.

Métro Toronto Zoo The 710-acre zoo, one of the world's largest, has pavilions and huge outdoor paddocks representing North America, South America, Africa, Indo-Malaya, Eurasia and Australia. In each area are mammals, birds, insects, reptiles, amphibians and vegetation native to that part of the world. Barriers, often disguised as natural surroundings and unseen by the public, separate the animals from one another and from visitors. Rare and exotic animals include the bongo (an African antelope), Siberian tiger and electric catfish.

Niagara Parkway The 35-mile route winds along the Niagara River between Fort Erie and Niagara-on-the-Lake. It passes Dufferin Islands, where the river abandons its gentle pace and begins its frantic race to Niagara Falls. Downstream from the falls and the Whirlpool Rapids Bridge the waters roar through rocky Great Gorge and twist into a whirlpool. The scenic route continues past Niagara Glen, a park with trails that descend to the edge of the river.

Rattlesnake Point Conservation Area Buffalo and elk in this 417-acre nature preserve can be seen from the Bruce Trail, which winds along the Niagara Escarpment 350 feet above their compound, and from an observation tower.

Rock Point Provincial Park Picture this page.

Royal Botanical Gardens Flowering plants are grown in forests, meadows and marshes and on the Niagara Escarpment. The Rock Garden harbors native Ontario specimens, as well as bald cypresses from Florida swamps and bottlebrush buckeye, a shrub native to Texas. Hendrie Park boasts 5,000 rose bushes and 10,000 annuals. The Spring Garden has about 250,000 iris blooms and the Arboretum has a lilac garden, as well as myriad bright wild flowers in a woodland setting. Nature trails in Cootes Paradise (woods surrounding 600 acres of marsh) pass through forests with trees and ferns.

Scarborough Bluffs Picture preceding page.

Turkey Point Provincial Park A 200-foot-high bluff overlooks Lake Erie.

Some 12,500 years ago, as the Ice Age was ending, old lakes were reborn in the wake of the retreating ice. One was Lake Erie, which first drained southwest into the Mississippi River system. But as the great thaw continued, the waters of the lake found a new, lower outlet and began to flow north, through the channel of the Niagara River, into Lake Iroquois, the forerunner of Lake Ontario. As they plunged almost 200 feet over the edge of the Niagara Escarpment, Niagara Falls was born. At that moment, the falling water started the slow process of cutting a gorge through the escarpment—a process that eventually will reduce the falls to two low waterfalls—one at Lake Erie, the other seven miles north. The existing American Falls and the Tonawanda Channel will be dry.

The cataract, now almost seven miles south of its birthplace at Queenston, retains almost its original height. This is because the escarpment is formed of layers of sedimentary rock that dip very gently to the south—soft shale and limestone overlaid by harder limestone and dolomite. Shale at the base of the falls is rapidly eroded by the impact of falling water—almost 100 million gallons a minute. As the soft rock is worn away, the more resistant limestone and dolomite jut out. But these ledges cannot support their own weight; periodically rock breaks off and crashes into the pool at the base of the falls.

If the escarpment was composed of rocks of uniform hardness or softness, the falls would recede much more slowly and would lose height with each backward move. The water would have water's usual grading effect. But the unevenness of the escarpment's resistance to erosion causes a chopping or quarrying effect. The result is Niagara Falls' rapid recession—almost four feet a year—with only a slight decrease in height.

About halfway between Lake Erie and Lake Ontario the escarpment's cap of hard rock dips south at 25 feet per mile, so there the falls will gradually get lower. Geologists calculate that, with natural erosion, this could happen in 25,000 to 50,000 years. But changes in climatic conditions and drainage patterns of the upper Great Lakes could alter the rate of erosion. The recession rate has been slowed also by hydroelectric developments that draw off great quantities of water that would otherwise plunge over the edge.

How the Falls Were Born, How They'll Likely Die

Water was diverted from the American Falls in 1969 so that the underlying structure could be examined. Rocks at the base were topmost ledges before they toppled (below).

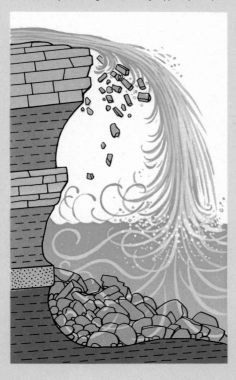

12,500 YEARS AGO
The river plunges over the edge of the Niagara Escarpment into Lake Iroquois—and the cataract is born.

Early Lake Erie

Lake Iroquois

TODAY
The falls have retreated seven miles south to their present position.

Lake Erie

Chippawa Channel

Lake Ontario

25,000 TO 50,000 YEARS FROM NOW
The American Falls and the Tonawanda Channel are dry. The Horseshoe Falls have been reduced to two low falls.

Tonawanda Channel

Falls

Gentle Climate Creates a Unique 'Way Down South

Lines as thick as the ropes of a ship are festooned from tree to tree under the dense canopy of a hardwood forest. Shrubs and undergrowth are draped with smaller, slender lianas. Beyond this matted tangle lies the swamp, a watery blackness patched with the green of duckweed. The air is humid, saturated with a heady mix of flowers and decay. Suddenly suspicious, a turtle sunning on a moss-grown log slides from its perch and disappears with a soft plop.

This is 'way down south on Point Pelee, an 11-mile-long peninsula that thrusts into Lake Erie and is the southernmost tip of the Canadian mainland, at the latitude of Rome, Barcelona and northern California. The last six square miles of the peninsula is Point Pelee National Park.

Point Pelee began to take shape some 10,000 years ago as wind and lake currents deposited sand on an underwater ridge of Devonian limestone—a ridge that today is covered by as much as 200 feet of sand. Two sandbars grew out into the lake and met nearly two miles from the shore. Generations of plants created the humus on which the present lush vegetation grows.

The land area of the park, only about one third of the total, consists of these sandbars. The eastern one is treeless and perilously narrow; the western is forested, narrow at the base but widening to half a mile where the

Point Pelee juts deep into Lake Erie.

141

two meet. A road along the middle of the western sandbar leads to a nature center, from which you can walk, bicycle, or go by trackless, pollution-free train to the tip of the point. Scattered on the wide, sandy beaches of the western sandbar are logs, branches and uprooted trees, like the bleached bones of dinosaurs.

The lagoon between the sandbars evolved into a marsh. In its four square miles are large ponds surrounded by huge areas of cattail and such other vegetation as marsh ferns, water lilies and Canada's only wild hibiscus, the pink-flowered swamp rose mallow.

Huge, moss-green carp turn lazily under the surface and glide slowly beneath the lily leaves. Foot-long specimens of their close relatives, the true goldfish, are a brilliant orange gleam through the water. Painted and spotted turtles nibble at an inexhaustible banquet of water plants, as fox snakes and water snakes wriggle across the open water. Muskrat go quietly and peacefully, eating their favorite food of cattail stems and roots, seemingly unaware that among the cattails lurks their archenemy, the mink.

From the cattail jungle come the bubbling songs of marsh wrens and swamp sparrows, the clucks and rattles and piercing whistles of red-winged blackbirds, and the loud, penetrating *witchety-witchety-witchety-witch* of yellowthroat warblers. Ducks, grebes and coots search for food in the calm water, and sora and Virginia rails may be glimpsed through the dense vegetation.

The air above the marsh is alive with twittering swallows. Yapping terns scan the water and frequently drop

A boardwalk reaches almost a mile into the Point Pelee marsh. From it, and from two towers on it, visitors have a fine view of the unique environment and its inhabitants.

like crashing planes to emerge with small, silvery fish wriggling in their beaks. There is a constant flying activity of ducks and other waterfowl. Far out in the marsh a pair of great blue herons may plane down to fish in East Cranberry Pond.

In this marsh, in the early fall of 1937, ornithologists were startled to see a scarlet ibis wading among herons and egrets. To this day it is a mystery how this tropical visitor found its way into Canada. Its close relative, the bronze-colored glossy ibis, has been spotted but must still be considered a rare visitor.

Point Pelee is one of Canada's most exciting places for bird-watching. Naturalist Dr. W. E. Saunders, in 1909, called it a place of surprises. "One never knows what to expect, but can always feel sure that there will be something doing in the bird line, and frequently that something is of unexpected and absorbing interest."

This hasn't changed, thanks to Dr. P. A. Taverner. In 1915, as Dominion Ornithologist, he recommended Point Pelee be made a national reservation because of its importance to migrating birds and because of the southern nature of its flora and fauna—the result of Lake Erie's tempering influence and the mild climate.

Through the forest on the western sandbar winds a narrow trail of soft, dark earth with fresh tracks of deer, coyote, skunk and raccoon, testifying to the rich mammalian fauna of Point Pelee National Park.

The forest reverberates with birdsong. The familiar clear, fluted compositions of the omnipresent robin blend into a great symphony with the songs of cardinal, scarlet tanager, orchard and Baltimore oriole, and indigo bunting, accompanied by an unidentifiable chorus of clucking, trilling, warbling and whistling. A catbird mews plaintively somewhere in the tangle, and the whole concert is occasionally punctuated by the hoarse cackle of a pheasant.

In this forest are such exotic birds as the tufted titmouse, yellow-breasted chat, white-eyed vireo and Carolina wren, and such jewels among birds as the prothonotary warbler, parula warbler and Kentucky warbler with its golden spectacles and black sideburns. More than 300 bird species have been reported from Point Pelee, and more than 100 species nest here.

While there is an incredibly rich fauna in the park, there are no animals dangerous to man, not even poisonous snakes. No rattlesnake has been reported since 1918. The only hazard in the woods is poison ivy. It grows underfoot and, clinging with aerial roots, it climbs the tallest trees and hangs down from the canopy. Climbers such as Virginia creeper, climbing bittersweet, Jacob's ladder and catbrier mingle with such exotic vines as fox grape, moonseed and wild potato vine.

Birds of Point Pelee, from a blue heron feeding its young (top left) to a green heron (immediately below) whose nest is high above the marsh. Marsh grasses hide the nests of a common gallinule (top center) and a least bittern and its brood of down-covered chicks (top right), but a black tern (above) builds its nest unconcealed. A sora (left) balances on a cattail, ready to snap up an insect or a snail.

143

This is one of Canada's few remaining stands of Carolinian forest. Elm, cottonwood, basswood and maple stand side by side with such southern trees as hackberry, black walnut, chestnut oak, shagbark hickory and sycamore. Most remarkable, perhaps, is the slender white sassafras which in autumn breaks into a blaze of yellow, orange and scarlet leaves around its berrylike dark blue fruits.

Hop tree and red juniper, common in the open areas,

Apparently stagnant and lifeless at first glance, Point Pelee swamps are bountiful sources of food for many of the park's wild creatures.

account for the presence of two beautiful southern butterflies, the giant swallowtail and the tiny olive hairstreak, both rare in Canada. The caterpillars of the giant swallowtail feed on the leaves of the hop tree; those of the olive hairstreak feed almost exclusively on the leaves of red juniper. A spectacular sight is a tree covered with monarch butterflies, waiting to begin the odyssey that will take them to wintering grounds around the Gulf of Mexico.

Among 600 species of plants in Point Pelee Park are flowers such as wild blue phlox, wild columbine, pink herb Robert, and yellow water buttercup. They compete for attention with flowers considered unusual in Canada: small Solomon's seal, flowering spurge, appendaged waterleaf, tall bellflower and the large-flowered pale-purple wild geranium.

The floral pride of the park is the prickly pear cactus. It grows in arid areas such as the red juniper grove behind the nature center, its bright-yellow flowers attracting hundreds of photographers and other midsummer visitors.

Extending into Lake Erie as it does, Point Pelee is vitally important to migrating birds. During the peaks of migration a single bird watcher may, in one day, see more than 100 species. He may experience the breathtaking sight of hundreds of whistling swans, thousands of geese, ducks, mergansers, loons and grebes in the marsh and in the open waters around the point. He may see tiny hummingbirds flying low over the water toward Pelee Island, often disappearing from sight in the troughs of the waves. Large hawks, eagles and vultures soar high overhead and just over the treetops are small sharp-shinned hawks.

Even after the last summer resident has left, and the last straggling migrator has reached its winter home in the warm south, Pelee Park still offers a bird watcher's treat. At the traditional Christmas bird-count, taken annually between December 20 and January 1, as many as 25,000 birds of 48 species have been observed in the park. Such visitors from the North as juncos, crossbills, northern shrikes, snow buntings and Lapland longspurs meet here with many birds on the northern edge of their wintering range, such as eastern bluebird, rufous-sided towhee, myrtle warbler, hermit thrush, robin and song sparrow.

To the Canadian bird watcher, at this time of year unaccustomed to birdsong, other than that of starling and house sparrow, the song of these winter birds at Point Pelee is unforgettable. Said Dr. George M. Stirrett, former Chief Park Naturalist of the National Parks Service: "The winter chorus is a Pelee special . . . the whistling, warbling, and twittering is astounding, musical, birdsong at its best."

OTHER ATTRACTIONS

Bluffs and a Bog: Ice-Age Leftovers

East Sister Island The uninhabited, 65-acre island supports vegetation and bird life unusual in Canada. The Kentucky coffee tree, the hackberry tree and Short's aster, a flowering herb, are the dominant vegetation. American egrets, black- and yellow-crowned night herons nest on the island.

Hawk Cliff Towering 100 feet above Lake Erie, the cliff is excellent for viewing fall bird migrations. In some periods as many as 25,000 hawks pass in a day; blue jays sometimes fly past at 500 a minute. The migrations start in August, when nighthawks and sparrows head south, and continue until late December, when snow buntings and redpolls pass. Others include peregrine falcons, turkey vultures, bald eagles, swallows, loons and Canada geese. The migrating birds do not pass Hawk Cliff in the spring, but congregate instead on the south shore of Lake Erie and disperse from there.

Jack Miner Bird Sanctuary Ducks and honking geese swarm impatiently overhead each day at 4 p.m. as corn is spread at feeding places in this 300-acre sanctuary near Kingsville. Thousands of birds stop here on migrations to and from northern breeding grounds. Other waterfowl spends the whole summer on the fields and ponds of the world-famous preserve founded in 1904 by naturalist Jack Miner. Miner's son Jasper demonstrates banding and answers questions

Kettle Point *Limestone spheres called kettles are enclosed in black shale along the Lake Huron shore in the Kettle Point Indian Reserve. The kettles average two feet in diameter and are more than 275 million years old.*

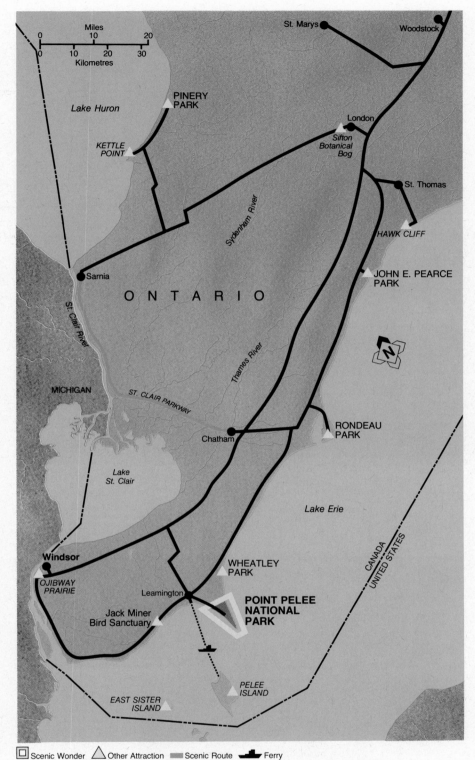

about bird migration and conservation in general. The oldest bird recorded under the Miner banding program was a 29-year-old goose shot in West Virginia.

John E. Pearce Provincial Park Hundred-foot-high cliffs are especially impressive when Lake Erie is rough and waves batter the shoreline.

Kettle Point Picture this page.

Ojibway Prairie This 250-acre field, apparently a remnant from the time 10,000 years ago when much of North America was covered with prairie grasses, supports plants now rare this far east and this far north. Prairie grasses grow as high as 10 feet and there are such plants as blaz-

Like a flurry of snow, gulls speckle the sky over the whitecapped entrance to Rondeau Bay at Rondeau Provincial Park. A 1,850-acre marsh in the park is deep enough for canoes, enabling humans to approach birds often heard but seldom seen outside the marshes: Virginia and sora rails, common gallinules and least bitterns.

ing star, sneezeweed, Culver's root, prairie dock and smooth sumac.

Pelee Island Wild flowers such as yellow water lily and pickerelweed grow in great profusion on this island eight miles off Point Pelee. (Tiny Middle Island, three miles to the south, is the only Canadian territory farther south than Pelee Island.) Thousands of monarch butterflies pause here in September and October on their way to wintering grounds around the Gulf of Mexico.

Pinery Provincial Park Four major sand dune ridges run parallel to the five-mile beach here. The ridge nearest the beach is about 10 feet high, the fourth as high as 100 feet.

Rondeau Provincial Park The 11,450-acre park has one of Ontario's last Carolinian forests (with shagbark hickory, black walnut, sassafras and tulip trees) and birds that seldom breed elsewhere in the province (white-eyed vireos, prothonotary warblers and Acadian fly-catchers). Mammals normally found much farther south include opossums and gray foxes. Migratory birds, especially ducks and shorebirds, are seen in spring and fall. The park's insects include 15 species of parasitic wasps identified as recently as 1972—10 never before reported in Canada and five never previously identified anywhere in the world. There are nature trails and a small museum. Pictures this page.

St. Clair Parkway The 50-mile parkway between Sarnia and Chatham follows the St. Clair River and passes a number of small parks.

Sifton Botanical Bog The 70-acre bog (it dates from the end of the Ice Age) has a rich variety of plants, small mammals, birds and amphibians. Masked and smoky shrews and southern bog lemmings live in the sphagnum moss; turtles and frogs inhabit the ponds, and songbirds nest in the trees. Plants include the cranberry, pitcher plant, yellow water lily and sundew, an insect-eating plant.

Wheatley Provincial Park Flowering dogwood and black gum grow atop bluffs 15 to 35 feet high. Little blue herons and bitterns nest here and migratory birds pass in spring and fall. Some migrating birds—turkey vultures, cliff swallows and ducks—stop over.

In a Tangle of Silk a Monarch Is Born

Thousands of monarch butterflies—sometimes *tens* of thousands—congregate in Point Pelee National Park each autumn before flying south to escape winter. They gather in trees to await calm weather before crossing Lake Erie. With wings closed, the monarchs resemble dried leaves. When they stretch their wings the trees appear alive with fluttering orange and black blossoms.

Monarch butterflies cannot even move when the temperature is below 4°C. (40°F.). They winter in Mexico and the southern United States and in spring the survivors set off for breeding grounds in the northern states and southern Canada.

A female may lay as many as 400 eggs, each of which she fastens to the underside of a new young milkweed leaf. The larva (caterpillar) eats only milkweed. It eats voraciously and grows so quickly that it must shed its skin four times before it enters the chrysalid stage. Leaving the milkweed, the caterpillar chooses a suitable surface—the underside of a branch, fence rail or leaf—on which to spin a tangled mat of silk. The hind legs are enmeshed in this mat and the caterpillar hangs head down, awaiting metamorphosis. After a few hours the skin splits for the last time, disclosing a chrysalis in which the larva is changing from caterpillar to butterfly.

The adult butterfly mates within a week. There are as many as four generations in one summer but most butterflies do not survive the storms, strong winds and sudden cold snaps encountered on their way south. However, enough make it to ensure that next year's milkweed crop is again a nursery for the magnificent monarch.

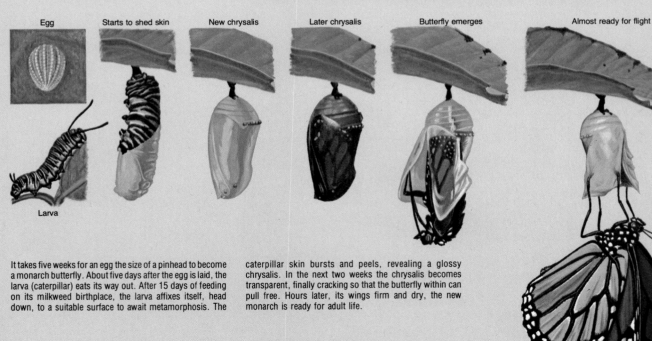

Egg | Starts to shed skin | New chrysalis | Later chrysalis | Butterfly emerges | Almost ready for flight

Larva

It takes five weeks for an egg the size of a pinhead to become a monarch butterfly. About five days after the egg is laid, the larva (caterpillar) eats its way out. After 15 days of feeding on its milkweed birthplace, the larva affixes itself, head down, to a suitable surface to await metamorphosis. The caterpillar skin bursts and peels, revealing a glossy chrysalis. In the next two weeks the chrysalis becomes transparent, finally cracking so that the butterfly within can pull free. Hours later, its wings firm and dry, the new monarch is ready for adult life.

A Huge Rock Garden of Caves and Cliffs, Ferns and Flowers

The Bruce Peninsula, which partially separates Georgian Bay from the rest of Lake Huron, is like some huge rock garden shaped by the tireless forces of nature. Ice and storm—and time—have created here an alluring blend of cliffs and beaches, of caves and underground rivers.

The peninsula called "the Bruce" is part of the Niagara Escarpment, a rocky spine that curves northwest from Lake Ontario's southern shore and reaches Manitoulin Island before arcing southwest through Michigan. The Bruce is a rough triangle, 60 miles from north to south and 23 miles wide at its base. At its northwest tip is Tobermory (locally pronounced Tubbermurray and often referred to as "the Tub"). At the west end of the triangle's base is the resort town of Southampton. At its east end is the bustling city of Owen Sound.

Gnawed by erosion, the Bruce (indeed the whole Ontario segment of the Niagara Escarpment) is gradually receding westward. The east coast of the peninsula rears out of Georgian Bay in the form of sheer limestone cliffs that are endlessly pounded and chipped by wind and waves. On a calm day it seems incredible that the waters of the bay could make a dent in, say, Cabot Head, at the northeast tip of the peninsula. Yet each year, when winter storms abate, the perpendicular 310-foot bluff wears new scars.

On the Bruce Trail, between Cabot Head and Tobermory.

149

West from the Georgian Bay cliffs the peninsula drops some 20 feet a mile and finally disappears under the waters of Lake Huron, with its alternating rocky shores and sandy beaches.

Each of the dozens of small islands in Georgian Bay seems to be a miniature of the Bruce, with a sharp limestone cliff facing east and a gentle slope to the west.

The Bruce's eastern shore has some intriguing rock formations. One is a striking limestone cliff for which the village of Lions Head is named. Along the shoreline are vast areas of flat rock polished smooth by glaciers. These formations, particularly extensive under the clear waters of Georgian Bay, are fascinating to skin divers. In the rock are grooves that form thin ridges running northeast-southwest—grooves thought to have been etched by stones embedded in receding glaciers.

Even more fascinating to skin divers are wrecked ships. Scores of broken hulls have been charted in the deep waters of western Georgian Bay and eastern Lake Huron. Other known wrecks have yet to be located.

The Bruce Peninsula owes its existence to the work of water over hundreds of millions of years. Its nearly horizontal layers of sedimentary rock were formed from mud and sand laid down on the floors of a series of prehistoric seas which covered the region 400 million years ago. Under the weight of sediment above, the lower layers solidified. The seas eventually dried and when the softer overlying and surrounding rock eroded, the escarpment

Rock-strewn caves like this one (right) are found high above the water on the Georgian Bay side of the Bruce Peninsula. Below: divers test the clear, turquoise water of Georgian Bay at Cyprus Lake Provincial Park.

was left. It contains the remains of reefs built by now-extinct aquatic animals in much the way coral reefs are formed in tropical seas today.

In Hepworth, a town near the base of the peninsula, one can often hear the faint rumble of an underground river. Seven miles northeast is Mountain Lake, which is drained by Hepworth Creek. About a mile northeast of the town, the creek disappears underground, bursting to the surface again in Spring Creek, a trout stream on the other side of Hepworth.

Gillies Lake, perched at the brow of the escarpment near Dyer Bay, was known to the Indians as Ghost Lake. (Legend says all the people of a village drowned when the ice cracked under them as they fished.) Two miles long, one mile wide and 105 feet deep, a hollow scooped out of limestone, the lake has a marbly bed that gives an eerie whiteness to the water. Gillies Lake is drained by a stream that flows through the forest for a mere 100 feet, disappears into a 300-yard subterranean channel, then breaks out and plunges down a series of cascades into Georgian Bay near Cabot Head.

The stream and falls are on the Bruce Trail (see p. 153). One of many sections of the trail, easily accessible to casual hikers, is through Cyprus Lake Provincial Park, just east of Tobermory.

Along the south shore of Colpoys Bay on the Georgian Bay side are five caves. Bruce's Cave, 50 feet deep and 30 feet high, has two openings that look like eyes staring

across the water. A narrow path to the cave is littered with limestone boulders thought to have been moved there by glaciers radiating from the Hudson Bay region during the Ice Age. The view of the bay becomes ever more spectacular as the path ascends to where Hay, White Cloud and Griffith islands are clearly visible.

Summer visitors throng the highway north to Tobermory, the jumping-off place for Flowerpot Island (a part of Georgian Bay Islands National Park) and Manitoulin Island. But few tourists seem to venture along the side roads or into the forested areas—except where these are crossed by the Bruce Trail.

The forest floor is made up of limestone slabs four and five feet across. Between them are cracks a few inches wide, deep and filled with rich soil that has a springy carpet of moss and is topped by a variety of wild flowers in spring and summer. Bird's-eye primula, dwarf iris and marsh marigold spring into bloom in May. The colors of Indian paintbrush, blue-eyed grass and twinflower are added in June. By July the bladderwort and rare ferns such as the hart's-tongue fern, wall rue fern and walking fern, cautiously emerge for their brief season in the sun, along with several varieties of wild orchids.

The ferns and the flowers, so often overlooked by visitors to the Bruce, are in a way typical of the rock-garden peninsula as a whole. Like them it deserves to be better known, for the golden beaches of Southampton, the quaint charm of Tobermory, the magnificence of Cabot Head—and all the rugged beauty that lies between the great cliffs along the bay and the sandy-rocky fringe of Lake Huron.

Like a settling flock of white birds, trilliums dot the forest floor of the Bruce Peninsula in spring.

Scenic Wonder △ Other Attraction ■■ Hiking Trail

OTHER ATTRACTIONS

Flowerpot, Mighty Manitoulin and the Thirty Thousand Islands

Flowers and shrubs grow in crevices in the two rock pillars that give Flowerpot Island its name. The island, off the tip of the Bruce Peninsula, is part of Georgian Bay Islands National Park.

Blue Mountain Scenic Caves These caves, as much as 150 feet deep, are fissures in the Niagara Escarpment, which rises 1,500 feet above the surrounding terrain. In one deep cave, accessible by ladder, are year-round ice and snow. In neighboring caves more than 150 species of ferns are found.

Boyne River Rainbow trout leave Georgian Bay, usually in April, to spawn in the Boyne and Nottawasaga rivers. A good place to see the fish is in Earl Rowe Provincial Park on the Boyne.

Bruce Trail This 430-mile hiking path follows the rocky Niagara Escarpment between Tobermory and Queenston. The trail wanders along Bruce Peninsula cliffs 300 feet above Georgian Bay, and passes caves and shale bluffs covered with 400-million-year-old fossils. The blazed trail is good for an hour's stroll, a day's walk or a longer trek. It winds through gorges, ravines and forests.

Craigleith Provincial Park Limestone terraces are embedded with fossils of marine creatures that lived in a sea that covered the area 375 million years ago. The limestone extends about 50 feet from the water's edge, each layer an inch or two higher than the one before. It stretches for almost a mile.

French River This 75-mile river between Lake Nipissing and Georgian Bay challenges canoeists with hundreds of islands, rushing rapids and portages.

Ganaraska Trail The 250-mile hiking trail runs between Port Hope and Glen Huron, where it connects with the Bruce Trail. It passes through forest, flat farmland and the Kawartha Lakes district.

Georgian Bay Islands National Park Beausoleil Island, largest of the park's 50 islands, is a refuge for the massasauga rattler, believed the last venomous snake species in eastern Canada. The rattler, up to 2½ feet long, is common in the island's swamps. White-tailed deer are plentiful and nearby Grey Island has a rookery of great blue herons. The archipelago in which the park lies was formed by postglacial flooding. Some of its rocky shoals and glacier-scraped rocks show excellent examples of folding and banding. Much of this rock is pink or pink and gray granite. Flowerpot Island, a 495-acre island off the tip of the Bruce

Peninsula and 100 miles northwest of the other islands, is named for two rock pillars, 50 and 35 feet high. Picture preceding page.

Inglis Falls Conservation Area The Sydenham River plunges over the 100-foot-high sheer rock face of the Niagara Escarpment.

Killarney Provincial Park White quartzite along the shore is in striking contrast to the pink and gray granite common elsewhere in this part of Georgian Bay. The 85,000-acre wilderness park is main-

ly boreal forest, with scattered bogs. There are waterfalls in the 1,700-foot La Cloche Mountains.

Killbear Point Provincial Park There are four miles of trails, a 1,400-foot-long sandy beach and a view of some of the Thirty Thousand Islands.

Manitoulin Island Some 500 miles of roads on the world's largest freshwater island (100 miles long, up to 40 wide) skirt a maze of clear lakes, sparkling streams and tumbling waterfalls. The East Bluff Lookout near Gore Bay gives a

view of the surrounding hills and the clear waters of the bay and North Channel of Lake Huron. The Cup and Saucer Lookout near Honora, about 500 feet above Lake Huron, has a 25-mile view in all directions. Baltimore orioles and hummingbirds are found in the Manitoulin forests, where wild flowers abound under a canopy of cranberry, boysenberry and hawthorn bushes.

Minesing Swamp The 20,000-acre swamp is along the Nottawasaga River where it is joined by Willow Creek, the Mad River and other tributaries. Six-foot levees (up to 100 feet wide) help contain the Nottawasaga and the Mad most of the year but in spring they spill over and flood about 10,000 acres, depositing sediment that continues the levee-building. Muskrats and star-nosed moles share the swamp with snapping and spotted turtles. It contains southern Ontario's largest stands of tamarack trees, a variety of orchids and some 160 species of birds. A great blue heron rookery expands by about 10 nests a year.

Mississagi Provincial Park Several canoe routes follow the shores of lakes in both the park and the Mississagi Park Reserve which surrounds it. The park and the reserve, together more than 160 square miles, have nature trails through areas where ducks, bitterns, beaver and moose are seen.

Muskoka Lakes Picture this page.

Sudbury Basin The 17-by-35-mile crater, believed formed by the impact of a meteor, contains huge nickel deposits. Parts of the landscape resembles the surface of the moon, with bleak banks of gray clay and blackened rocks stretching for miles. Nature trails in the Laurentian Lake Conservation Area lead through wooded areas to lookouts.

Thirty Thousand Islands The islands hug the east coast of Georgian Bay between Midland and Manitoulin Island. Some are craggy rocks barely able to support a single tree; others are up to five miles long and heavily wooded. Many have cliffs 30 to 35 feet above the waters. Tours of the islands include a 3½-hour trip from Midland.

Wasaga Beach Provincial Park Horseshoe-shaped dunes 150 feet high are more than a mile from Georgian Bay.

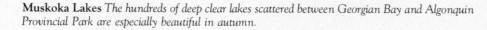

Muskoka Lakes *The hundreds of deep clear lakes scattered between Georgian Bay and Algonquin Provincial Park are especially beautiful in autumn.*

This cave at Cyprus Lake Provincial Park was once a tiny crack in the great Niagara Escarpment. Georgian Bay wave action enlarged it.

The Caves of the Bruce, Shaped by Waves and Time

Hundreds of caves riddle the Bruce Peninsula, particularly along the Niagara Escarpment overlooking Georgian Bay. Many openings in the face of the escarpment are up to 50 feet wide; some caves lead more than 100 feet into the rock.

Unlike solution caves elsewhere in Canada (such as those at Horne Lake near Port Alberni, B.C.) the caves of the Bruce have no stalactites hanging from the ceiling, no stalagmites rising from the floor, no formations created by ground water dissolving minerals and depositing them elsewhere. This solution process did start many Bruce caves, but it was the pounding waves of Georgian Bay and subsequent erosion that gave them their present form.

At the end of the Ice Age some 12,500 years ago, meltwaters penetrated the topmost layer of the Bruce Peninsula—its cap of dolomite and limestone. Each (especially limestone) is soluble in water. This dissolving of rock pockmarked much of the surface of the Bruce and, in some places, shaped small caves and networks of caves.

Meltwater and changing drainage patterns caused Georgian Bay to rise and fall dramatically. This explains why some caves are below the present water level and others are as much as 200 feet above it.

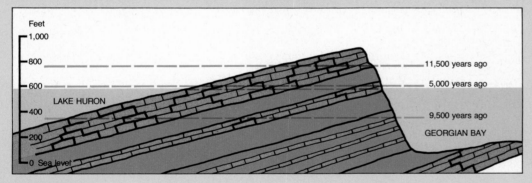

This cross-section of the Bruce Peninsula (at a point near Wiarton) shows how the level of Lake Huron and Georgian Bay has changed since the Ice Age. Vast quantities of water were released by the melting ice sheet and, as the ice retreated, new outlets for the lake were exposed. (One led to Lake Nipissing and the Ottawa River.) For a time the level dropped, reaching a low point some 9,500 years ago. But the land, relieved of the weight of the ice, started to rebound. It eventually rose more than 200 feet, tilting the lake basin south and cutting off the eastern outlets. The level rose again until the lake began draining south into Lake Erie, as it still does.

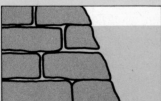

Ground water seeps through layered stone, dissolving rock particles and enlarging cracks in the escarpment under the bay.

As the level of the bay drops, waves further enlarge the solution openings, as well as fractures and other cracks.

The water level again drops, but the lower part of the cave is still pounded by waves. The ceiling starts to collapse.

The level of the bay drops well below the cave, but the ceiling continues to crumble, littering the floor with debris.

A quiet Pukaskwa cove.

A National Treasure, Lonely and Lovely: the Real Superior

West and north from Michipicoten Harbour, for 100 miles, there is no town, no village, no year-round habitation. This is perhaps the most spectacularly beautiful stretch of the Lake Superior shore—and certainly the wildest. Beyond Michipicoten, the port that serves the iron mines near Wawa, the coast runs past lonely Doré Bay, the University River, Bare Summit, Point Isacor, Floating Heart Bay, Le Petit Mort Rocks . . . Then, near Pointe La Canadienne, it swings gradually northwest toward the mouth of the Pic River and the pulp and paper town of Marathon.

Between Michipicoten Harbour and Marathon there are few signs of civilization. Here and there, tucked in the bush at the back of a bay, is a trapper's cabin or the rude shelter of commercial fishermen. But there's little more than that. At Puckaskwa Depot, where once there was a bustling logging community (which spelled Puckaskwa with a c), only crumbling buildings remain—and seven graves overgrown with evergreens. The only substantial structures along this whole shoreline—and they are abandoned for part of the year—are on Otter Island: a lodge, a lighthouse and a commercial fishery.

This wild shore and the hinterland between it and the Trans-Canada Highway, many miles inland, have long been known as the Pukaskwa Wilderness Area, after a

157

turbulent river that races to the lake at Pointe La Canadienne. In 1971, in the northwest segment of this region, Pukaskwa National Park was established, a magnificent place, without doubt a national treasure.

Pukaskwa National Park is cradled between the White River, surging down off the Canadian Shield, and the Pukaskwa River, which roars through an awesome canyon at Schist Falls. Between these wild rivers is a 50-mile stretch of splendidly intimidating shoreline, backed by 725 square miles of semi-mountainous wilderness. Forested hills range toward the park's eastern boundary, which at its farthest point is about 30 miles from the coast. The most striking hill, Tip Top Mountain, rises 2,099 feet above sea level and 1,500 feet above Lake Superior.

Pukaskwa Park lies along the high southern rim of the Canadian Shield saucer. Its hub, or central depression, is far to the north around Hudson Bay. From a line just above Lake Superior, the Shield and its rivers slope gently toward this hub. The rivers of the saucer rim, however, flow south from the height of land, most of them dropping hundreds of feet over a comparatively short distance.

Only experienced canoeists should attempt to negotiate these rivers: white water and portages pose frequent and sometimes dangerous challenges. But the wild rivers and near-mountainous backcountry seem to ensure that Pukaskwa National Park will remain a wildlife refuge. Woodland caribou still range this country. So do moose, lynx, otter, foxes and wolves.

Forested hills of Pukaskwa National Park rise sharply behind the rocky shore of Lake Superior. Wood lilies are among the flowers that adorn the Pukaskwa wilderness.

Winter storms, sweeping across 150 miles of open water, lash 40-foot waves against Pukaskwa's rock rim. For much of the year the coast is a battle zone for the thundering, pounding surf and immovable, granite palisades. Wind- and water-worn, the rock ramparts in many places have been scoured and polished to a high sheen. Islets standing out of the water are beaten smooth and swept bare of foliage.

Yet rugged headlands are interspersed with elegant little coves and bays bordered by beaches—some of sand, some of pebbles. Summer wild flowers abound. Harebells wave purple on rocky slopes. Beach pea and evening primrose garnish sandy coves. Bluebead lily and Labrador tea flourish in the forest; at waterside, cool microclimates encourage the growth of rare arctic plants far south of their normal range.

And there are birds. Loons and mergansers cruise the shoreline. Yellowlegs and sandpipers flit from beach to islet to beach. Marsh and sharp-shinned hawks nest in tall trees and great blue herons stalk the swamps.

Something of the sweep and majesty of this country can be appreciated from large boats passing well offshore. Its intimate details, however, reveal themselves only to those who pass slowly and at close range, or who go on land. The canoe is, in some ways, the ideal craft. But Lake Superior is cold even in midsummer and violent squalls sometimes strike with little warning. In colder months 20 minutes in the frigid water could be fatal. The alternative is to travel by motor craft, to ride out rough weather well clear of the inshore reefs, and to land only at safe anchorages.

Park officials are planning a trail that will roughly parallel the coastline. Branch trails will lead to various coves and bays as well as to some inland lakes. As the park is made more accessible, many persons who now race along the Trans-Canada Highway, oblivious to the magnificence of the Pukaskwa country, may come to know its rare and rugged beauty. They will hear a wolf's wail drifting down from distant hills, glimpse wildlife in the forest, contemplate the sun dying behind Pointe La Canadienne, marvel at the beauty of the northern lights, and stand in awe below bluffs which were already ancient a million years ago.

This is the real Superior—untamed, vast, powerful, a place of great beauty, a proper place to do homage to forces beyond the human scale.

Cascade Falls plunges over the southern rim of the Canadian Shield directly into Lake Superior. Scores of rivers and streams, many unnamed, wind through the hills and down the ridges of Pukaskwa National Park, all emptying into Superior.

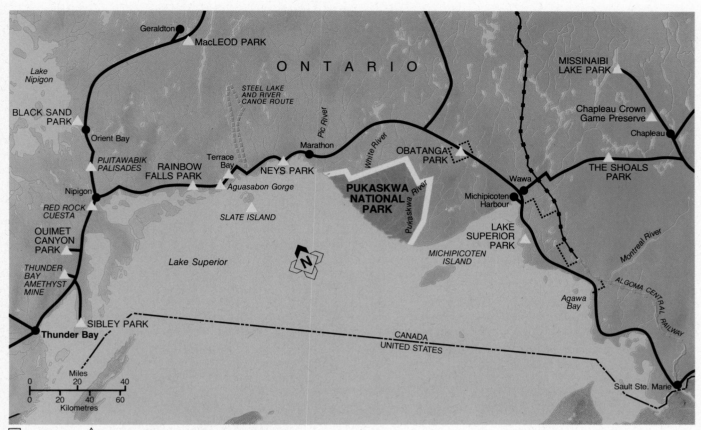

Scenic Wonder □ Other Attraction △ Canoe Route ■■ Railway ▬■▬

OTHER ATTRACTIONS

Red Rock Cuesta and the Sleeping Giant

Aguasabon Gorge The Aguasabon River makes a 90-degree turn and drops 90-feet into churning rapids.

Algoma Central Railway A 228-mile excursion from Sault Ste. Marie to Agawa Canyon and back cuts through a wilderness of massive rock formations, deep gorges and turbulent rivers. Passengers detrain for two hours at Agawa Canyon and visit Bridal Veil and Black Beaver falls. The train crosses a trestle 130 feet above the Montreal River. On non-excursion runs to Hearst, hikers and canoeists may leave or board at some 55 flagstops.

Black Sand Provincial Park A nature trail leads to a lookout that takes in a ridge of flat-topped hills called the Nipigon Palisades and Pijitawabik Bay on 1,870-square-mile Lake Nipigon.

Chapleau Crown Game Preserve Bear, moose, lynx, beaver, mink, otter and wildfowl thrive in the lakes, bogs, forests and mountains of the sanctuary.

Lake Superior Provincial Park The 600-square-mile park has deciduous and boreal (northern) forests and wildlife indigenous to both is common. Northern birds such as Arctic three-toed woodpeckers and boreal chickadees share the park with such southern birds as bobolinks, indigo buntings and scarlet tanagers. Several species of frogs are seen, as are toads and salamanders. Two non-poisonous snakes in the park seek secluded habitats and are seldom seen. There are moose, timber wolves and black bears. Nature trails pass labeled specimens of plant life and animal habitats. Sandspits and dunes are common along the beaches. The park has five canoe routes. Picture this page.

Agawa Bay in Lake Superior Provincial Park. Indian paintings in this area are thought to be more than 200 years old.

MacLeod Provincial Park This was once gold-mining country and park visitors sometimes find gold nuggets as well as agate, jasper and flint. A nature trail winds through an area devastated by fire in 1939.

Missinaibi Lake Provincial Park A herd of elk, rare in eastern Canada, lives in a clearing in this 176-square-mile park. Moose, wolf and bear are common throughout the park. On Fairy Point, 250-foot-high granite outcroppings on the shore of Lake Missinaibi, are Indian pictographs of animals and mythological creatures. Whitefish Falls is a series of rapids that descends about 60 feet in a 300-foot stretch of the Little Missinaibi River.

Neys Provincial Park Rocky hills overlook Lake Superior and a mile-long sandy beach. A small herd of woodland caribou roams the park.

Obatanga Provincial Park Pink lady's-slipper is abundant in the woods and bogs. Waterfowl nest in the marshy lakes of the park.

Ouimet Canyon Provincial Park Winter ice in depressions on the floor of Ouimet Canyon persists into summer, partly because the high walls block the sun. Air at the bottom is cooled by the ice, enabling Arctic wintergreen and species of moss and liverwort to thrive. Along the canyon floor are stunted cedar and white birch. Pussy willow, normally upright, grows horizontally, branches trailing through thick moss. A pinnacle looming out of the base of the canyon wall is named Indian Head for its resemblance to a man's profile. Picture this page.

Pijitawabik Palisades Cliffs 250 to 350 feet high flank Highway 11 for 13 miles south of Orient Bay.

Ouimet Canyon is a spectacular, tree-lined gorge, 500 feet wide, a half-mile long and 300 to 350 feet deep. Several plant species usually found only in the far North grow on the floor of the canyon, which is kept cold by winter ice that persists into summer.

Rainbow Falls Provincial Park Three-hundred-foot-high Rainbow Falls on the Selim River is reached by a picturesque nature trail.

Red Rock Cuesta A 400-foot cliff two miles long has a 50-foot-high granite base, topped by a limestone layer tinted red by a mineral called hematite. Above this is a layer of red shale, and capping the cliff is a black slab of rock called diabase.

Sibley Provincial Park The Sleeping Giant, a granite cape seven miles long and 1,000 feet high, is named for its resemblance to a prone figure (when viewed from Thunder Bay). Nearby Sea Lion Rock arches into a shape that resembles the snout of a seal. The park has several species of rare orchids, including yellow lady's-slipper, fairy slippers and spotted and striped varieties of small round-leaved orchis. The striped variety is very rare. Water snipes, ringbills, great blue herons and Bonaparte's gulls are seen here. Moose are often spotted feeding on water lilies along the shore of Joe Lake.

Slate Island The island has about 35 caribou, Canada's southernmost herd.

Steel Lake and River Canoe Route The 96-mile route follows a chain of lakes and streams. There are 19 portages.

Terrace Bay The town is built on terraces formed by the tilting and reforming of a glacial lake. As the lake level gradually lowered, deposits of sand and gravel became exposed on old shorelines.

The Shoals Provincial Park An esker five miles long and an average 70 feet high snakes through the park, then breaks down into a cluster of smaller eskers where a glacial river emptied into Little Wawa Lake. Near the lake are hundreds of steep-sided hollows called kettles, formed by the melting of glacial ice buried under glacial debris and gravel. The park was named for the numerous shoals in Little Wawa and Lower Prairie lakes.

Thunder Bay Amethyst Mine Visitors are encouraged to hunt for souvenir samples in special areas at Ontario's largest amethyst mine. They see a vein (1,000 feet long and up to three feet wide) of the transparent purple mineral.

The great horned owl (left) is the largest of Canada's nocturnal birds of prey. Among daytime predators, the osprey (above) is second in size only to the eagle. Its nest is made of branches (often as thick as a man's arm) and leaves and grass.

The Raptors: Stealthy Lords of Wilderness Skies

Most species of Canada's birds of prey are found in and around Pukaskwa National Park, from the majestic bald eagle and great horned owl to the tiny American kestrel (sparrow hawk) and the saw-whet, one of the smallest owls. The park's tall trees and high cliffs provide good breeding and nesting sites and there is abundant prey—birds, fish, insects, reptiles and amphibians and such mammals as mice and rabbits.

Birds of prey, or raptors, include eagles, ospreys, falcons and hawks. All have vision that enables them to spot prey from far off. They are masters of the stealthy approach, often flying from treetop to treetop as they stalk their victims, then relying on surprise and strength rather than speed to make their kills. Only the osprey confines itself to hunting fish. It dives headlong into the water, throwing its feet forward at the last moment to grasp its prey, often completely submerging in the process. An eagle will often steal the osprey's catch, and frequently does its own fishing.

In all raptor species the female is larger than the male and does most of the hunting and providing for the young.

The American kestrel (sparrow hawk) is the smallest hawk (9 to 12 inches long). Its call is a repeated killy-killy.

Seldom more than 8½ inches, the saw-whet is eastern Canada's smallest owl. Its call is a series of whistles.

An immature bald eagle, lacking the adult's white head and tail feathers, resembles the golden eagle.

The red-tailed hawk (19 to 24 inches long) is one of the largest hawks in Canada. A hardy bird, it remains later in autumn than many other migratory birds. Its prey includes birds as large and strong as ravens.

A long, slender tail gives the hawk owl its hawk-like appearance. Unlike most other owls this bird is active by day.

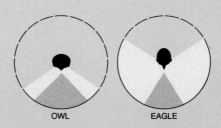

OWL   EAGLE

Most birds of prey have excellent vision. Some can distinguish details at distances eight times as great as those at which a human can. Large, frontally-placed eyes reduce an owl's field of vision to 110°, that of other birds of prey such as the eagle to 250°. Some non-raptors have fields of vision of about 335°. But a bird of prey's binocular vision (the ability to see an object with both eyes and get one image) is greater than that of most birds.

The taloned feet of this goshawk seize and hold prey. The hooked bill is used to kill and dismember the bird's victim, which may be a rodent, another bird or even a mammal as large as a marten.

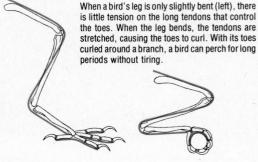

When a bird's leg is only slightly bent (left), there is little tension on the long tendons that control the toes. When the leg bends, the tendons are stretched, causing the toes to curl. With its toes curled around a branch, a bird can perch for long periods without tiring.

163

THE SHIELD

The Canadian Shield: Half a Vast Country

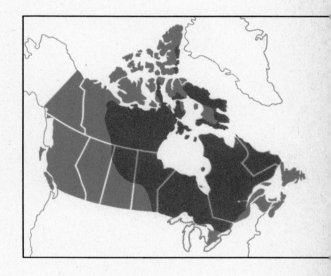

A maze of lakes and meandering rivers, an eternity of low, rounded hills and forests and huge outcrops of the world's oldest rock . . . this is the Shield, the ruggedly beautiful upland that is almost half of Canada. Taking in Labrador and most of Quebec and Ontario, the Shield sweeps north through Manitoba, Saskatchewan and Alberta before pushing into the Northwest Territories. From here, where the last twisted conifers of the boreal forest merge into the interminable tundra, it stretches all the way to Ellesmere Island. Ravaged by glaciation, the Shield inherited a legacy of more than a third of the world's fresh water. Mist-shrouded at dawn, gilded by each dying sunset, its see-through lakes and rivers were the highway of the voyageurs. The Shield is a land where the haunting cry of the loon echoes across a thousand lakes and is lost in the solitude of evening . . . where thick canopies of leafy hardwoods, incredibly resplendent in their fiery fall garb, yield to sober northern evergreens . . . where enormous pines tower sentinel-like above lichen-covered outcrops . . . where humpbacked hills roll to the horizon in mute testimony to the vastness of Canada.

Opposite: *The mighty Peace.*
Preceding pages: *Etchings of the Ice Age.*

Morning mist on Little Kashabowie Lake.

QUETICO PROVINCIAL PARK

Pink Granite and Dark Evergreens Frame a River-and-Lake Waterscape

Quetico Provincial Park is a rare and special place near the southern limit of the Canadian Shield, a wilderness with rugged Precambrian ridges, a jumble of lakes, and vestigial pockets of big red and white pine an estimated 200 years old. People come to 1,800-square-mile Quetico Park from many parts of North America, to escape from the pressures of the workaday world, to stretch sinews and harden muscles,

to *experience* the wilderness. A two-hour drive west from Thunder Bay, it is a land of winding rivers, lovely lakes and rocky outcrops of pink granite framed by the deep green of pine . . .

Toward the southern end of Kahshahpiwi Lake is a small pond created decades ago by a beaver dam that still stands firm—and seven feet high. Near the top of a cliff that looms above the pond is a small ledge distinguished only by an apparent hodgepodge of sticks. But there are design and life on the ledge for the sticks have been placed with care by a pair of bald eagles. Riding updrafts that course the cliff face, they rise high into the sky in lazy, lordly circles.

Far beneath is a vast waterscape. Quetico Park seems about half water—water lying, flowing or eddying with no discernible pattern—but only about a fifth of the park is covered by water. Its shape is the legacy of a series of glaciations which began more than a million years ago and ended about 11,000 years ago. Mile-thick glaciers—their boulder-studded bottoms much like massive rasps—ground across Quetico, tearing at the rock debris and gouging out depressions, some of them miles wide. The rock debris was dumped far to the south in what is now Minnesota and Iowa. Then the great ice sheets began to melt, their edges retreating northward. Huge glacial erratics were dropped far from where they originated. Meltwater flooded a razed and ravaged rockscape, depositing pockets and plains of sand. The gouged depressions filled with meltwater. In a twinkling of geological time they brimmed and overflowed, forming streams and rivers that tumbled from lake to lake.

It was a landscape of scoured rock, bare ridges and patches of sandy soil, a hard and barren place softened only by the intricate network of water. The softening was increased, in time, by lichens and foliage of many kinds. On the forest floor grew beds of spongy mosses, multihued mushrooms, bunchberries and ferns, a myriad of small plants.

One version of the origin of the name Quetico is that it is an abbreviation of the French phrase *la quête de la côte*—the search for the shore. Another story suggests that Quetico is short for Quebec Timber Company.

There might be an older meaning of the name. Long ago, as the oldest Indians tell it, the Ojibway borrowed the last two syllables of the word "Maymaykwaysew" from their Cree cousins. The word referred to a sort of merman whose home was within the solid rock of prominent features along shorelines. Even today the Cree and Ojibway believe that tobacco offerings to this being prevent squalls and bring good weather. And that is a far more appropriate origin of a name for a place of such great beauty.

Quetico is the rippled V of a beaver's wake . . . a black bear and her cubs ambling along on a rock ridge, pausing to feed on blueberries . . . lily pads speckling an alder-fringed pond . . . a bull moose in search of succulent lily roots, splashing through the shallows to escape the blackflies.

The grand design is forest, rock and water. Broken by beaver dams and rapids and falls, moving slowly through

Canoeists on Sturgeon Lake, part of the great waterscape of Quetico Provincial Park.

lake basins, lying almost still in reedy, marshy meadows, the water gives motion to the whole.

Quetico is well suited to canoe travel and cavalcades of paddlers have traversed these waters. Centuries ago, itinerant Ojibway, working from canoes, decorated cliff faces with paintings of their deeds and visions.

Then—for gain and glory—came the French fur trade explorers: de Noyon, La Vérendrye and many others.

rocks at Crooked Lake and Lac la Croix, pack gear across the Deux Rivieres Portage, pitch tents on sandspits and rocky shelves, drink the clean water and rest beside Chatterton and Splitfrock (Splitrock is the local name) falls. Many feel spiritual refreshment, truly re-creating themselves in an environment where the works of man give way to the soft sounds, the solitude and the challenges of a wild world.

The canoeist of the 1970s, like the voyageur of the 1770s, might see Quetico this way, starting from the foot of the great cliff at Side Lake.

He runs the rapids of the Basswood River and is barely slowed by a hailstorm on Crooked Lake. He pauses above Curtain Falls, stops at a pictograph site on Darky Lake, bucks his way upstream on the Maligne. Then comes an easy paddle across Sturgeon Lake to Jean Creek.

It is August and the creek is narrow and very shallow. There are more beaver dams to cross and, in one place, an already yellowing ash tree blocks the stream. A merganser duck and her brood skitter across a quiet pool, alerting the dozing turtles along the bank. Near Rouge Lake, a flash of rich, chocolate brown catches the paddler's eye. He pauses. A pair of brightly inquisitive eyes poke out from behind a rock. It is a young mink. Perhaps a minute passes—a frozen minute of silent, intense examination—and then the man moves. There is a final flash of brown and the mink disappears.

Now the water trail leads northwestward, through Rouge, Burntside, Little Kashabowie and Conk lakes. Seven days and roughly 90 miles pass between Side Lake and the lift-over portage joining Conk to Quetico Lake, at the north end of the park.

It is early morning, following a cold, late-August night. A heavy mist hangs over the still surface of the lake. The canoeist slips his craft into the water and paddles steadily west. Nothing breaks the silence but the soft plash of the paddle. By 9 a.m. the sun has burned the mist away, but the lake remains still, eerie. The canoe seems to hang motionless between a vast blue of sky and water.

Then, in the distance, something black rises out of the lake. As it sinks back, another rises, then a third. It is like a giant serpent. Soon the black objects lose their miragelike quality, becoming smaller and more distinct. They are otters, their sleek bodies rising high out of the water then falling back.

Evening finds the traveler camped on the north arm of Quetico Lake. During the afternoon, a light tail wind pushed him along his course, but now it has dropped and the lake is still once more. Warm evening light glows pink on the red pines . . .

Later still came Henry, Harmon, Mackenzie, Fraser and Thompson, with crews of voyageurs, the human engines of the trading companies. For most of the 18th century and much of the 19th, the exploitive thrust of the fur trade colored Quetico country. The two main canoe routes between the Great Lakes and the *pays d'en haut* (upper country) north and west of Lake Winnipeg passed through the present park.

Thousands of canoeists thread the rivers and lakes each year. They test their skills in the rapids of the Maligne and Basswood rivers, pause beneath the picture

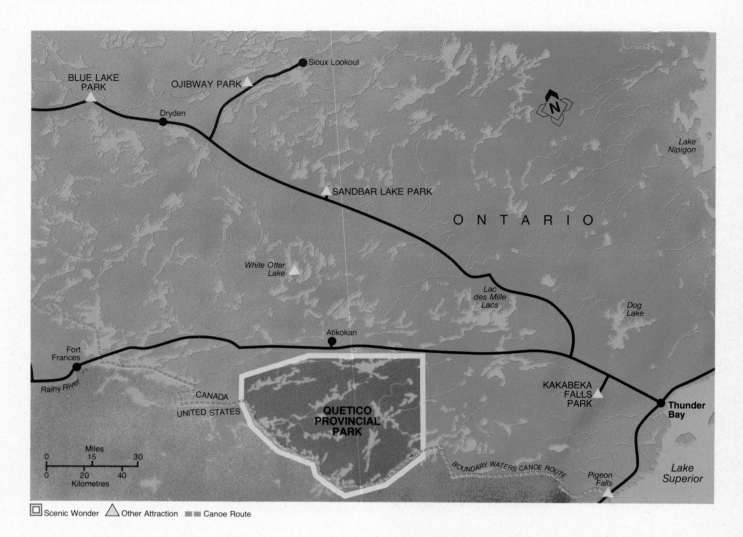

Scenic Wonder △ Other Attraction ▪▪ Canoe Route

OTHER ATTRACTIONS

Shield Parks and an International Canoe Area

Blue Lake Provincial Park Jack pines that dominate the forest all date from a 1910 fire.

Boundary Waters Fur Trade Canoe Route Hundreds of lakes and streams form a continuous 325-mile route between Kenora on Lake of the Woods and Grand Portage, Minn., on Lake Superior. It passes through Quetico Provincial Park—which adjoins the United States' 1,660-square-mile Boundary Waters Canoe Area. It is a region of spectacular granite cliffs and sandy beaches and is rich in wildlife. A canoeist may spot a lone bull moose feeding, a bear and her cubs ambling through blueberry patches or a bald eagle soaring high overhead. Hundreds of animals—timber wolves, ospreys, painted turtles and non-poisonous snakes, to name just

a few—are seen and heard in adjoining forests and bogs and along the canoe route itself.

Kakabeka Falls Provincial Park The falls, a swirling curtain of white on the Kaministikwia River, are 108 feet high and 326 feet wide. Below the falls are rapids hemmed in by towering black rock walls. A bridge about 100 yards upriver from the cascade provides an impressive view of the falls and the rapids. About 1,000 feet below the falls, the wind whispers eerily into the narrow entrance to the "Cave of the Winds."

Ojibway Provincial Park The 6,130-acre park hugs the rocky shores of Little Vermilion Lake, named for the bright orange lichens along its shoreline. One trail leads to a lookout over the lake.

Pigeon Falls The Pigeon River plunges 100 feet over Pigeon Falls (locally called High Falls), then continues in a series of rapids in its rush to Lake Superior. The 150-foot-wide waterfall is near the edge of Middle Falls Provincial Park, named for another (25-foot-wide) waterfall upstream on the Pigeon.

Sandbar Lake Provincial Park Rock-strewn rapids interrupted by lacy waterfalls connect Sandbar and Indian lakes. Along the north shore of shallow Sandbar Lake is a 1½-mile sandy beach. Wild ginger, rare this far north, has been found in the park.

White Otter Lake The shores of the lake are heavily forested and have huge rock outcrops. There are beaver dams on streams that empty into the lake.

Winter: A Hard Time for Some Animals— Others Sleep It Away

Although its luxuriant forests provide abundant food and shelter in spring and summer, Quetico Provincial Park is inhospitable for much of the rest of the year. Quetico has only 120 frost-free days. Snow carpets the forest floor for nearly eight months. Temperatures sometimes drop to −45°C. (−50°F.).

Some creatures, such as the red-winged blackbird and the common loon, quit Quetico each fall to escape its long, harsh winters. Those that remain must adapt—or die of freezing or starvation. Bodies must change to withstand the bitter cold, appetites must adjust to dwindling food supplies. Like creatures of similar habitats, Quetico animals have evolved to ensure that winter survival, if not a sure thing, is at least probable.

Long, slender legs enable moose to wander through snow as much as three feet deep. In deeper snow, like deer, moose concentrate in easily accessible areas with abundant food. These "yards" have forest overstories which reduce snow and provide protection from storms. Standing on four-foot hind legs, moose strip aspen bark that is 12 feet off the ground.

The snowshoe hare (also called varying hare) is so named for its stiff-haired hind feet that glide easily over snow. It is well camouflaged year round, a dark summer coat giving way to white in September.

Bud-eating ruffed grouse find ample food in winter but have few defenses against the cold. This grouse shelters in a shallow depression hollowed in fluffy new snow that acts as an insulator, trapping air and slowing down the escape of heat from the soil. Grouse are endangered by lack of adequate snowfall and by sub-freezing temperatures that encrust the protective snow cover.

The red squirrel, one of the forest's most industrious creatures, passes warm days collecting cones, mushrooms and nuts and storing them, singly or in clusters. One hideaway may contain as much as 10 bushels of food.

A red squirrel's food cache—under a log or a rock or at the base of a tree—may contain (left to right) beaked hazelnuts and bur oak acorns, fly mushrooms, and black spruce and jack pine cones (containing seeds that are a staple in Quetico). In midsummer, red squirrels busily strip trees of their cones, burying them in moist ground to keep the seeds from scattering. Cones sometimes are piled in middens, heaps as high as three feet and as much as 30 feet across.

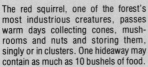

One answer to winter is hibernation, a slowing down of body processes to conserve energy and eliminate the need for food. Chipmunks do not hibernate but retreat to burrows to pass the winter in a semi-dormant state. They awaken often to feed on stored nuts and seeds. Chipmunks frequently use the same burrow year after year, renovating and adding rooms until a single network extends 30 feet. The maze of a seasoned chipmunk has pantries, escape routes, a toilet and one deep chamber, lined with dried leaves, that is used as a nest in spring. The winter temperature in a burrow may be considerably higher than on the surface.

The meadow jumping mouse hibernates. During autumn, its weight increases by a third; most of it is excess fat to be burned during a 6-to-8 month fast. The mouse curls up in a burrow and its temperature falls to 4°C. (39°F.) Respiration is irregular and as slow as once every two minutes. If body temperature falls to a level at which organs and tissues cannot survive, shivering restores heat to the animal. The hibernation response is believed controlled by the brain and triggered by temperature and light.

On an Inland Sea, a Magnificent Maze of Myriad Islands

Lake of the Woods is a vast inland sea dotted with almost 15,000 islands. Some are mere reefs, humpbacked and bald. Others span hundreds of acres, reaching high out of the water, with crowns of magnificent spruce, pine and aspen. At water level—the canoeist's level—the lake is geographical confusion: Labyrinth Bay, Quandary Bay, Infernal Point, Zig Zag Island, Corkscrew Island, Cul de Sac Lake . . . Except for these names, conferred by bewildered white men, parts of the huge lake are little changed from the days of the Indian birchbarks.

Fish brought the first nomads to Lake of the Woods—Cree and Ojibway from the north, Sioux from the south. While Plains Indians geared their lives to the ever-moving buffalo herds, the Lake of the Woods people feasted on a never-ending supply of pike, pickerel (walleye), lake trout, whitefish, sturgeon and muskellunge. Explorers told of Indians fishing with nets, hooks and lines, spears, even clubs.

Living with nature and revering its bounty—as their religion taught—the Indians were one with the majestic lake they called Min-es-tic (Lake of the Islands). By that name or Lac des Bois (from which came Lake of the Woods), or any other, it is one of central North America's biggest waterways, 65 miles from north to south and 55 miles wide. It is a major lake in the giant

The land of La Vérendrye.

175

Rainy River system, taking three-fourths of its flow, then spilling it into the Winnipeg River and on to Lake Winnipeg.

The landscape is a legacy of Ice Age glaciers that ground and gouged the rock and left deposits of till. As the last glacier retreated, its meltwaters filled the lake basin. But traces of much earlier volcanic action survive. Lava flow and ash deposits are preserved on many outcrops. Pillow lava—bun-shaped globs of lava rock which fit together to form a beveled surface—is a feature of the shoreline.

Lake of the Woods, sprawled across parts of Manitoba, Ontario and Minnesota, is the natural habitat of the canoe. Anthropologists have not discovered how this frail craft evolved, but here on the Precambrian Shield its development was as significant as that of the wheel. Birchbarks took Indian families from mainland camps to summer fishing grounds, to far-off islands laden with berries. Many a canoe was light enough for one man to hoist over his head and carry over a rocky portage; its buoyancy carried him through rapids; strong arms could propel it into the lee of an island when a sudden summer storm whipped the lake water into whitecaps.

Lake of the Woods' permanent population of 21,000 doubles when summer cottagers arrive, but this is still Indian country. The 2,000 native people have 10 reserves, work as hunters and guides, and reap the lake's wild rice, a delicacy whose annual harvest sells for up to $500,000.

Old Indian paintings and carvings have been found on rocks at 19 sites, and offerings of clothing, tobacco and prayer sticks are still left nearby to enlist the aid of the spirits against sickness or trouble. Most of the aboriginal art is on vertical rock faces close enough to the lake to have been created from canoes or low footholds. The paintings, rusty orange to dull red, have withstood centuries of weathering. Some scientists believe iron oxide, sturgeon oil and egg fluid were used in the paint but the formula, alas, cannot now be duplicated.

A common humanlike outline with outstretched arms is thought to represent the medicine man-artist. Many sites have handprints and deer, moose and serpentine forms. Those in Whitefish Bay on Painted Rock Island and in Devil's Bay are well preserved and not difficult to reach. The most accessible site is three miles from Sioux Narrows. Paintings and carvings there show indications of contact with European explorers—an impression of a fort, a boat with a flag.

The first white man to press this far west of Lake

Forests reach almost to the rocky waterline of islands in Whitefish Bay on Lake of the Woods. On several islands in the bay are Indian rock paintings.

176

The setting sun over Lake of the Woods tints land, water and sky. The lake abounds in fish and the surrounding forests are rich in wildlife.

Superior—in 1688—was Jacques de Noyon, but little is known of his expedition.

The most important explorer of Lake of the Woods was Pierre de La Vérendrye. On Magnuson Island, at the mouth of the Northwest Angle Inlet, he built Fort St. Charles, one of a chain of forts that stretched from Lake Erie to the Saskatchewan River, near the north end of Lake Winnipeg. Massacre Island, also at the mouth of Northwest Angle Inlet, was so named because it is believed a band of Sioux murdered 21 whites there, including La Vérendrye's son, Jean-Baptiste, and the Rev. Jean-Pierre Aulneau.

The first white men into Lake of the Woods sought not the beauty that now makes it a prime vacation area but, instead, wealth and power. Explorers, voyageurs and traders pushed big trade canoes west from Lake Superior to harvest what seemed an inexhaustible sup-ply of furs. They sought mink, marten and otter but chiefly beaver for the hats of the rich and aristocratic Europeans.

Nor did the great lake pleasure the next wave of white men. To surveyors and engineers it was an accursed accident of nature athwart the trade routes of a burgeoning nation. To them the picturesque rock-girt bays meant only millions of yards of ballast—for a railway that they had to swing north of the lake.

Now visitors come to sun, sail and fish, or to pitch a tent on one of the 14,632 islands—all but about 40 are in Canada. Canoeists and sailboaters know that just around every rocky point is a new vista. Tourist facilities range from ultramodern motels on the Trans-Canada Highway and Ontario Highway 71, which skirt the north and east shores, to fly-in camps, island hideaways, public campgrounds and lake cruises. The lakeside resorts of Kenora, Sioux Narrows and Nestor Falls are points of departure for those who want to enjoy the scenic sights of this land of La Vérendrye.

178

OTHER ATTRACTIONS

A Meteor's Lake, an Ice-Age Esker

Alf Hole Wild Goose Sanctuary As many as a thousand geese at a time—Canada geese, giant Canada geese and lesser snow geese—are seen at this sanctuary on the eastern prairie flyway migration path. At a center overlooking the feeding area are mounted specimens of geese, maps of migration routes and films. A game-bird refuge surrounds the waterfowl sanctuary. Both are in Whiteshell Provincial Park.

Argyle Boat Tours An 18-mile cruise out of Kenora weaves past many of Lake of the Woods' 14,632 islands.

Assiniboine Park Zoo Thirty-five endangered species, including the parma wallaby (indigenous to Australia, New Zealand and New Guinea), are among more than 300 species in the 100-acre zoo. Some of the zoo's rare creatures are the wisent (European bison) and Père David's deer (both extinct in the wild), the North China leopard, the red-fronted lemur and the Barren Grounds grizzly of northern Canada. Pumas, polar bears, Siberian tigers and Darwin's rheas, the rarest of large flightless birds, live in enclosures landscaped to resemble their natural environment.

Belair Provincial Forest One of several nature trails in the 185,000-acre forest leads to a fire tower which provides a magnificent view of the countryside.

Birds Hill Provincial Park The park is on an esker, a ridge of sand and gravel deposited by a glacier.

Cooks Creek Picture next page.

Grand Beach Provincial Park This 1½-mile-long beach on Lake Winnipeg is backed by constantly shifting dunes.

Lake Winnipeg *The 176-foot Lord Selkirk II makes two- and five-day cruises of Lake Winnipeg (at 9,417 square miles the world's 13th largest lake). The only stop on the weekend trip is at Berens River; the five-day cruise—from Selkirk—includes stops at Grand Rapids, Berens River and Gimli.*

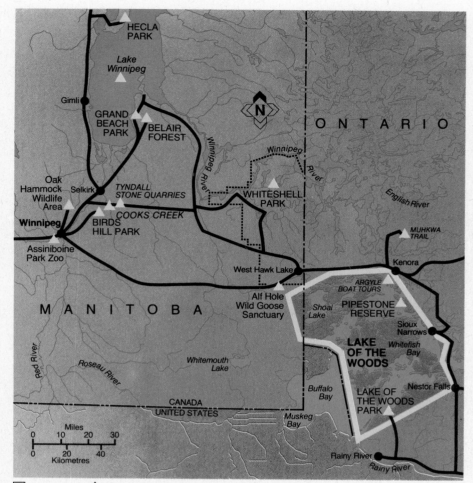

☐ Scenic Wonder △ Other Attraction

Cooks Creek *Like a desert fortress, these cliffs of compressed sand and gravel (conglomerate) are in the Cooks Creek pits between Cooks Creek and Birds Hill, north of Winnipeg. Ice Age glaciers deposited huge amounts of sand and gravel in many places on the western plains.*

Yellow and white lilies on dark green pads decorate Lily Pond in Whiteshell Provincial Park. A cliff nearby consists of alternate layers of sedimentary and volcanic rock.

Hecla Provincial Park Ducks and geese nest in the marshes of this island park in Lake Winnipeg. Timber wolves, bobcats, weasels, lynx and snowshoe hares are found here.

Lake of the Woods Provincial Park A high rock lookout gives a 40-mile view across Lake of the Woods and its islands. One of Ontario's northernmost colonies of pelicans—some 200 birds—nests in the 2,700-acre park.

Lake Winnipeg Picture preceding page.

Muhkwa Trail The 10-mile trail winds through forest and along the rugged shores of a dozen lakes.

Oak Hammock Wildlife Management Area Some 250,000 ducks and Canada, snow and blue geese gather here before their migration south each fall. The 8,000-acre area has marshland, some uplands and a little cropland. The area is only 10 miles north of Winnipeg, unusually close to a major urban center for a waterfowl staging area.

Pipestone Provincial Reserve A 3,560-acre wilderness, the reserve is accessible only by hiking from Highway 71 or by taking a boat into Andrew Bay.

Tyndall Stone Quarries Tyndall limestone is quarried at Garson, from one of the world's oldest sedimentary rock formations. Formed some 400 million years ago when much of North America was covered by warm seas, the limestone has been used extensively on many Canadian buildings, including the Parliament Buildings in Ottawa. Embedded in the rock are fossils of creatures that lived some 250 million years before the first dinosaur appeared on earth.

Whiteshell Provincial Park Rock formations along the Winnipeg River have been dated at more than 2½ billion years, among the oldest rocks on earth. The rocky outcrops are thought to be the roots of ancient mountains, exposed by ice caps that carved away the surrounding soft rock. The 1,066-square-mile park harbors a variety of animals and its more than 130 lakes and rivers provide excellent fishing. West Hawk Lake, formed by a meteor 150 million years ago, is three miles by two and 365 feet deep, Manitoba's deepest. Picture this page.

Nature's Web of Life: Milfoil to Mammals

Lake of the Woods supports an infinite variety of living forms in its 1,485 square miles. All are caught up in an intricate web of dependence on the earth and on one another. At the base of this finely balanced network are green plants—from complex, multicelled milfoil to phytoplankton, microscopic plants that range in size from 1/5,000 to 1/30 of an inch. The plants, having absorbed minerals that seep from rocks and nutrients that fungi and bacteria release from organic remains, provide nourishment for tiny, weak-swimming animals called zooplankton. These are eaten by fish and insects and other small creatures—which in turn are sustenance for birds that get most or all of their food from the lake, and for certain mammals, such as muskrats. Most of these are preyed on by other creatures.

Plankton (such as in the first four of these five photographs) are minute plant and animal life and larvae, the indispensable base of the food chain. Diatoms and desmids (above), plants encased in silica or cellulose, exist in myriad designs. Their shapes and their shells help keep them afloat and close to the sun.

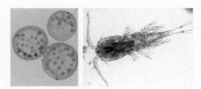

The many-celled volvox (left), both plant and animal, uses two whip-like projections to propel itself through water. The cyclops (right), probably the world's most abundant animal, breeds after two weeks of life.

Some fish and insects, such as the phantom midge (left), are planktonic only in their larval stage. Fuzzy white hairs on a tiger fish barb (right) are not plankton but a fungus that causes decay. Decomposers are essential to the food chain for they recycle nutrients and reduce debris.

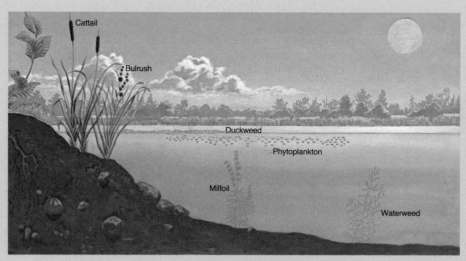

Green plants manufacture their own food. In a chemical reaction called photosynthesis, they use the sun's energy to combine hydrogen (from water) and carbon dioxide (from the air). This produces oxygen and materials such as carbohydrates used by all other living things for growth, repair and reproduction. The abundant phytoplankton, the smallest plants, are usually found near the surface, absorbing the sun's energy.

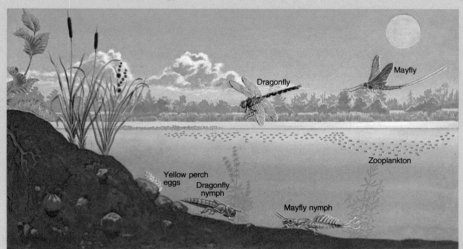

Nourished by plants, zooplankton are consumed by such fish fry as newly-hatched yellow perch, which wriggle out of eggs attached to the underside of rocks. The dragonfly nymph may moult 8 to 15 times before emerging from its nymphal skin as a winged adult. During this two-year larval stage it feeds on plankton and even small fish.

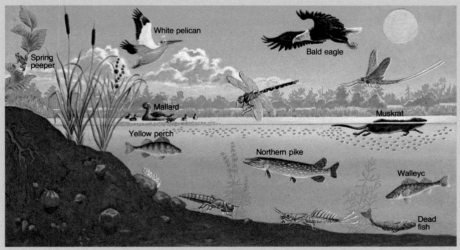

Fish large and small feed on plankton, insects and one another. Lake of the Woods' most common species, yellow perch, is taken by white pelicans and by larger fish such as walleye, which also favors mayflies. Plant-eating mallard ducklings are easy prey for the greedy northern pike, which in turn may be eaten by a bald eagle. On the lake bottom the cycle is perpetuated by tiny decomposers which extract vital elements from the dead and dying—returning their nutrients to the waters and to the next generation of life.

Drinking Falls on the Upper Churchill River.

THE UPPER CHURCHILL

Wild and Wonderful, Not So Much a River as an Endlessness of Lakes, Rivers and Falls

No river in Canada—in the world, perhaps—is like the wild and wonderful Saskatchewan section of the mighty Churchill. This upper part (the rest of the 1,000-mile Churchill wanders through northern Manitoba and empties into Hudson Bay) is less a river than a seemingly endless series of lakes, big and small, connected by rapids and roaring waterfalls. Rivers and lakes on both its flanks form a vast network of channels known as the Churchill system.

Some streams that feed the great river are said to rise in the snowfields of the Rockies and the remote Barren Grounds. But in truth the Churchill begins in northern Saskatchewan at Lac La Loche, near the Alberta border. In the days of the voyageurs and early explorers, this was the crossroads of the continent.

La Loche was the end of navigation on the Churchill

and the site of the most important portage in the northwest. Portage La Loche, also called Methy Portage, crossed the Arctic divide, giving access to the Athabasca, Mackenzie and Peace rivers and routes to the Pacific and the Arctic oceans. Over the arduous 14-mile mountain trail passed the first men to cross Canada, all the supplies for the Peace River settlement and all the furs from the great Athabasca region.

Men clambering up and down the rocky slopes of the portage somehow had time for the beauties of the landscape. Some waxed lyrical about the little Clearwater River, especially the awe-inspiring view of its valley when approached from the Churchill. It is a sight reserved for the hardiest canoeists or for sportsmen traveling by bush plane.

Most trips to the headwaters of the Churchill begin at Ile-à-la-Crosse, but the most popular approach to the river is at Lac La Ronge Provincial Park, with its campsites, guides, outfitters and all kinds of rental equipment.

The Lac La Ronge highway reaches the Churchill at Otter Rapids, the only place where the main stem of the river is bridged. It is one of the great beauty spots of the Canadian Shield: wild river, draining thousands of square miles of watershed, pours through a rocky gorge into the calm waters of Otter Lake. Eighteen miles southeast, at the end of the lake, is Stanley Mission, where Saskatchewan's first Anglican church, with stained-glass windows brought by ship and canoe from England in 1860, still stands.

The Upper Churchill is in no sense settled or civilized. It was the highway of the fur trade, the heart of Saskatchewan before it became a province. But as great ranches and cities grew up in the south and the fur trade dwindled and died, the river went back to a handful of Indians. Today it is almost as truly wilderness as in 1778 when Peter Pond discovered Portage La Loche and the route to the Athabasca country.

By way of the Great Lakes, Lake Winnipeg and the Churchill, Montreal fur traders penetrated inland almost 3,000 miles to establish a fort and trading post at Ile-à-la-Crosse in the spring of 1776. Here, and at other points along the northwest river network, they could intercept Indians taking furs to York Factory on Hudson Bay. This helped to initiate the great trade war—frequently accompanied by bloodshed—between the North West and Hudson's Bay companies.

The HBC built its own post at Ile-à-la-Crosse and, to get its share of the furs, traded in rum like the Nor' Westers. For years the Indians refused to give beaver pelts for anything but spirits until, according to HBC records, 50,000 *gallons* were traded in 1820. The next year, when the companies amalgamated, the liquor trade declined to 10,000 gallons. The names of Keg

Much of the Upper Churchill (left, a stretch near Lac La Ronge) consists of lakes connected by streams. Above: Pelicans on Dipper Lake.

Lake, Drinking Lake and similar places along the Churchill recall those colorful days.

Along the Upper Churchill are countless arms and dead ends winding off through blue and purple bedrock. Lining the river are great banks of pink granite, black basalt and gray metamorphic rock formed two billion years ago and exposed by the weathering of the earth's primal crust. Metamorphic rock was twisted, deformed and changed by great pressure and heat. Hot solutions welled up through cracks and fissures, depositing green quartzite and veining it like marble. Ice Age glaciers then polished the rock, hollowed some lakes, disrupted the drainage pattern to form other lakes, and then, a mere 8,000 years ago, melted. The Churchill began to flow as it does today.

For most of its length the Churchill cuts across the Canadian Shield; the exposed part of the ancient continental rock core of North America. But it rises on the Shield's western edge, and skirts it on the south until well past Lac Ile-à-la-Crosse.

To the north, where the Churchill leaves Ile-à-la-Crosse and the boreal moss, spruce forest and sphagnum bog are laced with great outcroppings of bedrock. Hogbacks and ledges and rounded treeless hills rise everywhere against the sky. The lakes are full of islands, the biggest only seven or eight square miles, the smallest merely bare rocks. Such a maze of islands and waterways confronts the visitor that he wonders how the voyageurs managed.

A trip on the Churchill is still a test of stamina. Between Ile-à-la-Crosse and Otter Lake—240 miles— are 19 rapids and falls that should be portaged downstream as well as up, and several others that can be shot only by experts and even so need towing or lining. The modern voyageur finds it difficult to believe that HBC

Governor George Simpson, in 1828, averaged 53 miles a day, *upriver*, traveling from Trade Lake to Ile-à-la-Crosse in 5½ days. The modern canoeist, making the same run *downriver*, takes two weeks.

East of Trade Lake the Churchill is joined by the Reindeer River, which runs south for 200 miles from the head of Reindeer Lake. Below here the Churchill becomes even wilder, flowing through country so broken that HBC traders abandoned this route as too difficult. The modern traveler can see a small part of it by going north from the Hanson Lake Road through Pelican Narrows to Sandy Bay. For about half its length this road parallels the voyageur trail that was the principal link between Cumberland House on the Saskatchewan and Frog Portage on the Churchill.

From the Churchill's chain of scenic delights it is difficult to select any one lake or falls or cataract for special mention. A one-day trip upstream from Otter Rapids takes you past Devil Rapids and through Nipew Lake to Lake of the Dead. There Alexander Mackenzie found the bones of Indians who had died in the great smallpox epidemic of 1781-82. The route then goes past rapids, small lakes and waterfalls into Trout Lake.

A one-day trip in the other direction from Otter Rapids goes to Stanley Mission through Otter Lake and Mountain Lake. Spruce forests, domed islands and vast granite outcroppings make it a spectacular region.

The picturesque Upper Churchill near Island Falls, west of the Manitoba border.

Many other stretches of the river are equally beautiful. Everywhere are wading birds, gulls, terns, mallards, ospreys, eagles and the Churchill's specialty: vast flocks of huge white pelicans. Big game is rarely seen along the well-traveled shores of the river but its creeks and tributaries lead to the haunts of moose, woodland caribou and bear. Beaver, once almost exterminated, are plentiful again, as are otter and mink.

Along the banks are boulders buried in great splashes of orange lichens. This spectacular pioneer plant, thriving on naked rock, is killed by even a trace of sulphur dioxide and so is found only in true wilderness.

Government camping parks at Buffalo Narrows, Ile-à-la-Crosse, Otter Rapids and Otter Lake are mainly for motorists. The Churchill has so many excellent natural campsites that no boating party would think of using a serviced campground. If you spend a night or two anywhere on the southern bank, there's an excellent chance you'll see a spectacle of northern lights across the water.

The Churchill is one of the last great wilderness rivers of Canada. Not a city is built anywhere on its watershed. The few tiny settlements on its banks are mere villages, lost in the immensity of the great northland. Its silt-free waters cascade over clean bedrock with a sense of immense power, but at only one point—Island Falls—is there a modest hydroelectric development. It is still a free river, singing under the silent stars, the only great river of Canada that is still largely untamed and can also be reached easily by the average traveler wearied with pavements and hungry for wilderness.

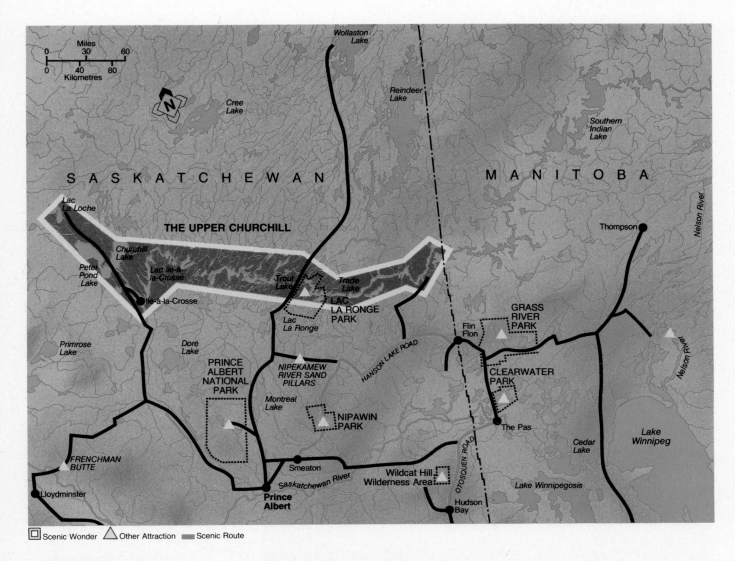

Miles
0   30   60
0   40   80
Kilometres

SASKATCHEWAN

MANITOBA

THE UPPER CHURCHILL

Wollaston Lake

Reindeer Lake

Cree Lake

Southern Indian Lake

Lac La Loche

Churchill Lake

Thompson

Peter Pond Lake

Lac Ile-à-la-Crosse

Trout Lake

Trade Lake

Nelson River

Île-à-la-Crosse

Lac La Ronge

LAC LA RONGE PARK

GRASS RIVER PARK

Flin Flon

Primrose Lake

Doré Lake

Lac La Ronge

Nelson River

PRINCE ALBERT NATIONAL PARK

NIPEKAMEW RIVER SAND PILLARS

HANSON LAKE ROAD

CLEARWATER PARK

Montreal Lake

NIPAWIN PARK

The Pas

Lake Winnipeg

FRENCHMAN BUTTE

Smeaton

Saskatchewan River

Wildcat Hill Wilderness Area

Cedar Lake

OTOSQUEN ROAD

Lloydminster

Prince Albert

Lake Winnipegosis

Hudson Bay

☐ Scenic Wonder   △ Other Attraction   ▬ Scenic Route

OTHER ATTRACTIONS

Sand Pillars and a Wilderness Where Cougars Roam

Clearwater Provincial Park The lake, which is half of the 230-square-mile park, is noted for its astonishingly clear water. The lake bed, part of a limestone formation between the Saskatchewan River plains and the Precambrian Shield, is smooth and reflects light well. Little silt is washed into the lake and the limestone turns the water alkaline, discouraging the growth of some algae.

Frenchman Butte This 100-foot hill, in the midst of rolling grasslands, provides a view of the North Saskatchewan River and the surrounding countryside.

Tall trees grow in patches near the Nelson River, thriving where frost heaves have left layers of thick soil atop the permafrost.

187

Clear and cold, the lakes of Prince Albert National Park are favored by fishermen for their trout, walleye, pike, yellow perch, whitefish and tullibee.

Grass River Provincial Park Many of the park's 154 lakes are linked by the Grass River and other rivers and streams. A canoe route (80 miles of it within the park) connects with the Churchill River.

Hanson Lake Road In the 225 miles between Smeaton, Sask., and Flin Flon, Man., the Hanson Lake Road (Highway 106) passes no settlement. Along the lonely, lovely route are dense forests, glimmering lakes and patches of muskeg.

Lac La Ronge Provincial Park Wild and remote, the park covers some 600 square miles between Lac La Ronge and the Churchill River. The Rapid River runs through rapids, drops over Nistowiak Falls, then races into Nistowiak Lake, a part of the Churchill River system. There are canoe routes through the park.

Nelson River On its wild descent from Lake Winnipeg to Hudson Bay, the Nelson races through limestone chasms, sometimes 200 feet deep, and through rolling country blanketed with thick evergreen forests. At places along the 410-mile river are slow-growing evergreens an estimated 150 years old but with only six-inch-thick trunks. Round kettles in the riverbank rock are holes created by stones that were trapped in crevices and whirled around by the water. The fast-flowing Nelson (which drops 712 feet) is cold and its only abundant fish is sturgeon. Picture preceding page.

Nipawin Provincial Park On a clear day you can see up to 20 miles from atop an Ice Age esker that rises 200 feet above the plains. The 3½-mile esker is a narrow ridge of sand and gravel deposited by a stream that flowed under a glacier. Bald eagles, ospreys, great blue herons, elk and woodland caribou are found in the park. There are nature trails.

Nipekamew River Sand Pillars Pillars of silica and sand rise to more than 100 feet along the south shore of the river. They are three quarters of a mile from Highway 165.

Otosquen Road These 76 miles of Highway 109 wind from Hudson Bay, Sask., past the Pasquia Hills to the Manitoba border. There the road joins Manitoba Highway 283, which leads to The Pas. Several nature trails crisscross the wilderness on both sides of the Otosquen Road.

Prince Albert National Park The southern part of the 1,500-square-mile park is dominated by trembling aspen, and the commonest mammals are badgers and ground squirrels. Where prairie plants give way to aspen parkland, elk are common, and gray wolves prowl in the boreal forest of the extreme north. Among almost 200 bird species recorded in the park are the bald eagle, osprey and blue-winged teal. White pelicans nest on an island in Lavallée Lake. There are two scenic drives—one along the south shore of Waskesiu Lake, one along the north shore. The park has nature trails and a canoe route, and a small herd of buffalo is in a paddock at the southern end. Picture this page.

Wildcat Hill Wilderness Area The 70-square-mile area is accessible only by air or by hiking west from the Otosquen Road. The reserve is named for cougars believed to inhabit the area.

The Shimmering Spectacular in the Northern Skies

The shifting, weaving patterns of glowing light known as aurora borealis occur from 40 to 120 miles above the earth, where the atmosphere is extremely thin. Canoeists along such northern rivers as the Churchill have a ringside seat for these spectacular Northern Lights—ranging from huge arcs sweeping across the sky to barely visible patches of shimmering light rising like waves from low in the sky.

The spectacle is created in much the same way as neon lighting: electrically charged particles pass through rarefied (thin) gases. In a neon light, particles strike and excite neon molecules, causing them to glow. In the case of the Northern Lights the rarefied gas is the upper atmosphere and the charged particles (A) are protons and electrons (the solar wind) caused by storms on the sun. Most particles never reach the atmosphere but are deflected by Earth's magnetic field (B), the 40,000-mile-thick barrier of magnetism that surrounds the planet.

Some particles are trapped in the magnetic field and begin to spiral back and forth along north-south magnetic lines of force (C). (The magnetic poles—D—are not true north and south but magnetic concentrations to which compass needles point.) Above the areas surrounding the magnetic poles there is less protection from radiation. It is here that some particles trapped in the magnetic field escape into the earth's atmosphere. They strike molecules in the atmosphere and excite them, causing them to glow and creating the auroras.

Although the Northern Lights usually appear white, they are often bright enough for colors to be distinguished. As the pressure and composition of the atmosphere varies according to altitude, so do the colors of the lights. At extremely high altitudes, where atmospheric pressure is low, oxygen molecules produce a reddish glow when excited by the sun's charged particles. At lower altitudes, excited oxygen creates the more common auroral green. This green sometimes has a reddish lower border, caused by nitrogen molecules being struck by the charged particles.

A place of surpassing beauty.

PEACE-ATHABASCA DELTA

A Major North American Wetland, Vital to Migrating Waterfowl

The Peace-Athabasca Delta in Alberta's northeast corner is one of the world's great deltas, a place of surpassing beauty comparable to the Florida Everglades and the delta of the Nile. It is one of North America's few remaining great areas of undisturbed grass meadow and sedge and a key intersection among the continent's four major migratory bird flyways. Most of the delta—a vast summertime expanse of green broken by patches of water and shrub—is in 17,300-square-mile Wood Buffalo National Park, the largest national park in the world and the home of 8,000 buffalo, the biggest herd anywhere.

The delta, a complex that covers 1.5 million acres, is really three deltas—those of the Peace, Athabasca and Birch rivers. The largest, the Athabasca Delta, has filled the west end of Lake Athabasca and continues to en-

croach on it. The delta of the Birch River is expanding into Lake Claire, which in turn empties into Lake Athabasca. Only the Peace Delta is relatively inactive; that river is contained within the delta banks except at floodtime.

Lake Athabasca, 200 miles long, is one of the largest lakes in the Mackenzie River system. Into it empty the Athabasca River, originating deep in the Rocky Mountains, and the Fond du Lac River, which rises in Saskatchewan's Wollaston Lake, near the Manitoba

Whistling swans arrive in the Peace-Athabasca Delta in May, as do such ducks as blue-winged teals (right). Some swans and ducks nest in the delta; others go farther north to breed.

border. The Rivière des Rochers and the smaller Chenal des Quatre Fourches flow out of Lake Athabasca and join the Peace. The Slave River is born where the Rivière des Rochers meets the Peace. The Slave flows north to Great Slave Lake, the source of the Mackenzie as it starts its epic 1,120-mile run to the Arctic Ocean.

Life on the delta follows the rise and fall of all the

rivers, great and small, that empty into Lake Athabasca (and of their tributaries). Floodtime is in June or July when all of the delta channels and basins are filled by the waters of swollen Lake Athabasca. By late summer the levels drop. Minimum levels are reached in March and the delta again awaits flooding and runoff.

The delta has taken shape (and has constantly changed shape) during the past 10,000 years. As river waters lost speed (and the slope of the riverbed became more gentle) near Lake Athabasca, they dropped silt and sand to the bottom and on the banks. Gradually the bottom built to the surface, forming a delta. Bars, islands and peninsulas were formed, dividing the river into channels coursing through the newly-formed delta plain. Plants grew on the exposed surfaces and their presence in turn helped increase the accumulation of sediment. The process goes on: as the Athabasca continues to fill the west end of Lake Athabasca, it may eventually flow directly into the Slave River.

The delta is a wetland, a complex and dynamic system of rivers, creeks, oxbows, potholes and lakes, interspersed with forested levees, sedge, grass meadow and granitic Precambrian outcrops. It is home to 45 species of mammals, among them muskrat, timber wolf, black bear, moose, mink, fox, beaver and otter. The 18 fish species in delta waters include goldeye, walleye, northern pike, whitefish and lake trout.

The delta is of major importance as a nesting and moulting ground, a giant staging area for migrating birds. The delta and surrounding area are an important feeding and breeding habitat for some 215 species of birds, ranging from 15 kinds of ducks to four kinds of geese, the whistling swan, the endangered peregrine falcon and the bald eagle. They come here from the Pacific, Central, Atlantic and Mississippi flyways and in spring the marshes teem with birds resting and feeding on their journey north to nest. This movement begins in late April with the arrival of Canada geese, just as the ice breakup starts and the first water appears.

During the first three weeks of May, as many as 400,000 ducks and about 145,000 geese and swans may stop to rest and feed. The birds seek the mud flats and the immature meadow. Although many move north, a large number remain on the delta to breed and raise their young. By midsummer, they are joined by ducks and geese that have bred elsewhere but have come to the delta for moulting. By late August, the southward migration is in full force as thousands arrive to join those already there—to rest and feed before moving on. A recent estimate was that 1,200,000 ducks and 165,000 geese moved through on their way south.

Summers on the delta are short and cool, winters long and cold. But the expanse of water has a moderat-

193

ing influence and there is a longer frost-free growing season—about 100 days—than in areas just beyond the delta. Five categories of plant life—aquatic, shore, meadow, shrub and forest—are imperceptibly but constantly changing, one to the next, according to the cycle of flooding.

The people of the Lake Athabasca region total some 5,000—Chipewyans, Crees, Métis and a handful of whites. The biggest of five communities (and the closest to the delta) is Fort Chipewyan, with a population of 1,500 Indians. Many of them, because of their isolation, speak only their native tongue. There have been gradual changes in their life-styles recently, with hunting, fishing and trapping giving way to lumbering, commercial fishing and government jobs.

The country is beautiful but harsh and the delta likely never will be a major tourist attraction. But it can be visited—by plane from Fort Smith, Fort McMurray and Edmonton to Fort Chipewyan on Lake Athabasca and from there by boat. (Aircraft are not permitted to land in the park.) The delta could remain a virtual wilderness.

Periodic flooding of the delta ensures that the forest will not invade and destroy the wetlands.

But its very existence has been threatened, as in 1967 when the W.A.C. Bennett Dam in British Columbia, 700 miles from the delta, tamed the mighty Peace. This meant the river flowed steadily year round. No longer were there annual spring floods followed by low water—the ebb and flow essential to the special character of the delta.

If no counteraction had been taken, the delta might have dried up and the effects on migrating wildfowl might have been disastrous. But a series of dams was planned to control the level of Lake Athabasca. Periodic flooding was still possible.

More than a million ducks populate the delta in summer. Toward the end of summer they are joined on the delta by other ducks migrating south from the Arctic and by geese, swans and other birds.

One of the most important functions of the delta is to serve as a retreat in years of drought. As prairie wetland conditions deteriorate, more and more waterfowl move north to breed (although when a prairie wetland improves, the waterfowl return).

So there is a growing need to preserve and improve the wetlands in the North. The effect of loss of the delta would be considerable. There is little doubt that the wetlands are necessary for waterfowl to survive.

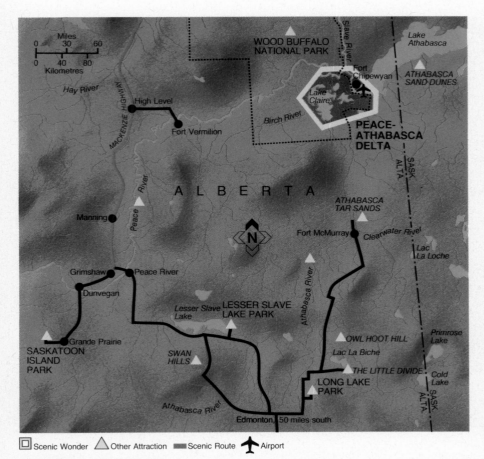

Scenic Wonder △ Other Attraction ▬ Scenic Route ✈ Airport

OTHER ATTRACTIONS

Dunes, Tar Sands, Our Biggest Park

Athabasca River Some 375 miles from its outlet at Lake Athabasca the river is placid. But it soon changes. It runs through the Pelican and Stony rapids and the Rapides du Joli Fou. Then, about 80 miles upriver from Fort McMurray, at Grand Rapids, it drops 54 feet in less than a quarter mile. At Brule Rapids, 15 miles farther on, the Athabasca froths with natural gas bubbling to the surface. Near Fort McMurray, as the river cuts through the Athabasca Tar Sands, its banks become black and oily.

Athabasca Sand Dunes The largest dune area in Canada not stabilized by vegetation, the Athabasca Sand Dunes cover some 115 square miles south of Lake Athabasca. There are two sections. In the larger—some 90 square miles between William River and Ennuyeuse Creek—are the seif dunes (which run parallel to the direction of the winds that build them). Picture next page.

Athabasca Tar Sands This biggest of Alberta's tar sand deposits, a potential source of huge amounts of crude oil, covers some 9,000 square miles around Fort McMurray. Some of the sands are 2,000 feet down, others are near the surface.

Long Lake Provincial Park The park is in a hilly valley mostly covered with aspen and poplar. Several species of ducks and grebes nest on the lakeshore.

Mackenzie Highway The Alberta section of the Mackenzie Highway—which ultimately will reach the Arctic Ocean at Tuktoyaktuk—covers 289 miles between Grimshaw and Cameron Hills on the Northwest Territories border. North of Grimshaw is Lac Cardinal, then typical Peace River country. In the lovely valley of the Notikewin River is the settlement of Manning.

Lesser Slave Lake Provincial Park This park at the east end of Alberta's second largest lake has extensive sand dunes

Peace River A 90,000-square-mile region on both sides of the Peace River between Grande Prairie/Valleyview and High Level/Fort Vermilion is famous for rich soil that produces fine barley and rapeseed and huge fruits and vegetables despite a short growing season. The vast plateaux of the Peace River country are some 1,000 feet above the floor of the river valley. Left: Typical Peace River country not far from Dunvegan, Alta.

The salt plains, near the eastern border of Wood Buffalo National Park, are open areas with salt streams and salt springs and some soil so alkaline that there is little or no vegetation. Evaporation in places has created salt mounds 50 feet by 70 and up to three feet high.

Some of the Athabasca Sand Dunes are seif dunes, with a sharp ridge, unlike rolling beach dunes. The Athabasca dunes are about one-half mile apart and as high as 100 feet.

doing constant battle with adjacent trees and bushes.

Owl Hoot Hill Millions of mauve crocuses cloak this 300-foot sand hill in spring. In summer it is covered with wild roses, in autumn with blueberries and cranberries.

Peace River Picture preceding page.

Saskatoon Island Provincial Park Saskatoon berry bushes cover most of the 252-acre, horseshoe-shaped island park.

Swan Hills Deer are common along roads that wind through these pine-clad hills some 4,000 feet above sea level. Grizzlies are sometimes seen.

"The Little Divide" This modest cousin of the great Continental Divide, the lofty spine of the Rockies, is a 100-foot-high ridge between Beaver Lake and Lac La Biche. Streams flowing from Beaver Lake join waterways that drain into Hudson Bay. Water from Lac La Biche joins a system that empties into the Arctic Ocean. Birds that nest on the nearly 100 islands in Lac La Biche include white pelicans, great blue herons, western grebes and loons.

Wood Buffalo National Park Two thirds of 17,300-square-mile Wood Buffalo, the world's largest national park, lies in Alberta, the rest in the Northwest Territories. Established in 1922 to protect some 1,500 wood bison—North America's last remaining herd—the park later received some 6,600 of the smaller plains bison. Now most of the park's 8,000 buffalo are hybrids. The park is generally a land of poor drainage, meandering streams and shallow lakes and bogs. It contains some two thirds of the Peace-Athabasca Delta (see pp. 190-194). In several places are enormous sinkholes, where underlying soft rock has been dissolved by sub-surface runoff and the surface terrain has collapsed into the resulting cavity. One sinkhole is 120 feet across and 80 feet deep. Pine Lake, near the eastern border of the park, was created when several sinkholes overlapped and filled with water. It is three miles long and some 70 feet deep. The park is the only breeding ground of the nearly extinct whooping crane, and it harbors North America's northernmost colony of white pelicans. Picture this page.

The first birds to arrive in the Peace-Athabasca Delta every spring are Canada geese. Tens of thousands fly in as soon as there is open water, usually in late April. They are joined by snow, white-fronted and Ross's geese and by whistling swans and 15 species of ducks. All rest in the delta; most then wing on to more northerly regions.

Many have flown from wintering grounds as far south as Chile, some 6,000 miles from the delta, and go hundreds of miles farther to nesting areas on the Barren Grounds and Arctic Islands. Across northern Canada, within 500 miles of the North Pole, 31 species of waterfowl are summer inhabitants of marshes, lakes and ponds. Ample food and long days help birds hatched in the north to mature in time for the autumn trip south.

North America's four main migration routes (flyways) intersect over the Peace-Athabasca Delta (boxed area on map) and it is used spring and fall by migrating birds. Some birds stay in the delta to breed, establishing territories in early May. Many waterfowl that breed elsewhere return to the delta in midsummer to molt. On open water where the shore access is protected by vegetation, the birds may safely lose their flight feathers

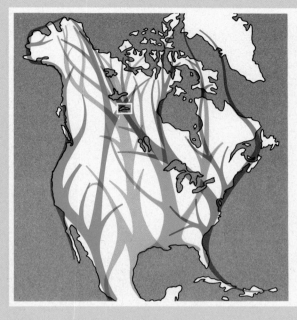

Not all birds follow only one of the four major North American flyways. Nor do birds necessarily fly the full length of any one flyway. For instance, some pintails winter in Mexico every year, others in the Queen Charlotte Islands.

■ PACIFIC FLYWAY
Autumn rains, melting snow and a warm climate make the Sacramento and San Joaquin valleys in California a principal center for wintering birds.

■ CENTRAL FLYWAY
The north end of the flyway has millions of water-filled potholes, prime duck habitats. Two million geese and ducks winter in southeast Texas.

■ MISSISSIPPI FLYWAY
The floodplains of the Mississippi River—from Missouri to the Gulf of Mexico—and the marshes of Louisiana are the principal wintering grounds.

■ ATLANTIC FLYWAY
With more than 7,000 miles of irregular coastline, this route provides hundreds of islands, bays, estuaries and tidal flats ideal for waterfowl.

and wait for new ones to grow. By late October all the migrating birds are gone.

They will know when the time is right to return. In spring again, from southern ponds and lakes and coasts, they will appear over the delta, guided by the sun and the stars, riding the winds, pressed by an instinct that calls them home.

The Delta—Crossroads for Millions of Migratory Birds

Ducks such as the mallard (1), shoveler (2) and pintail (3 female, 4 male) live in the shallows of ponds and marshes and feed on crustaceans, insects and aquatic plants. The bobbing birds are a male (center) and a female mallard.

Lake Athabasca and nearby Lake Richardson to the south are frequented by such diving birds as lesser scaup and redheads. Unlike dabblers, these birds can swim underwater and dive down to 12 feet in search of food.

In early August the blue-winged teal begins its migration to South America. One teal once flew 3,800 miles in a month, one of the longest recorded flights for a duck.

Ross's goose, the smallest Arctic nesting goose, stops in the delta on its 4,600-mile round trip between nesting areas in the Northwest Territories and wintering grounds in California. They numbered only 2,000 in 1949; there now are 36,000.

The majestic whistling swan migrates from breeding areas in Canada's low Arctic and Alaska, crossing the Rockies at altitudes of up to 12,000 feet. After resting on the delta, it heads for wintering grounds in California's Sacramento and San Joaquin valleys.

Hordes of Canada geese take off from the Peace-Athabasca Delta in fall—dispersing into the major flyways, assuming the familiar V formation of all Canada geese in flight. Young geese remain with their parents until they return north the next spring.

THE PRAIRIES

Scenic Variety Fills the 'Empty' Prairies

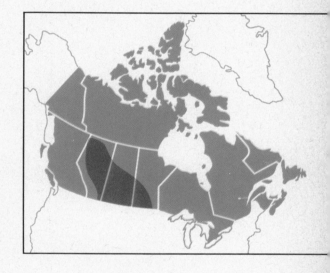

The sun blazes high in an expanse of cobalt blue as vast as any mid-ocean sky. Few trees or landforms interrupt the far, faint line where the great sky dips and yields to the land. A sudden lazy breeze skitters over the tall prairie grasses and there is momentary relief from the scorching heat. Amid the incessant, insistent buzz of insects a meadowlark warbles its proud territorial claim. . . . The prairies stretch some 900 miles from the Canadian Shield in eastern Manitoba across Saskatchewan to the rolling Alberta foothills in the sunset shadow of the Rockies, from the border north to the boreal forests. In these 239,000 square miles is some of the world's richest land, where in late summer phalanxes of harvesting machines mobilize against rippling, ripened wheat. But the prairies are more than crop-clad flatlands. For those who forsake the main east-west highways and stop awhile, there are scenic nuggets for the taking: crystal lakes hidden in groves of aspen, meandering rivers nestled in the embrace of pastoral valleys far below the prairie floor, badlands filled with the strange shapes of erosion, huge sand dune areas not quite dry enough to be called deserts, mini-mountains whose wildlife seems to belong elsewhere. . . . The "empty" prairies abound with scenic interest—for those who stop and look.

Opposite: *In the valley of the Red Deer River.*
Preceding pages: *A march-past of prairie clouds.*

A Wedge of Green in Giant Silhouette Above the Plains

Riding Mountain—not really a mountain but part of an escarpment—rises from the flat plains of middle Manitoba, a giant green wedge silhouetted against the prairie sky. The thin edge is the southern end of Riding Mountain National Park; the thick edge, along the park's northern and eastern borders, drops to a Joseph's coat of colorful crops—the brown of oats and barley, the green and gold of wheat, the blue of flax, the yellow of rapeseed, the earthy tones of intermittent blocks of summer fallow.

Riding Mountain is seen in all its massiveness only from Highway 5 between McCreary and Ste. Rose du Lac. But most visitors come to the 1,150-square-mile park another way, from the south, on Highway 10. Some wonder where the mountain is: The highway winds through gently rolling farmland and the change in elevation is hardly noticeable. Even near the park gates the road goes up only a small hill, then flattens as it enters Wasagaming, the park headquarters and its only community.

But the mountain is there, and visitors who forsake Wasagaming's comfortable lodges and motels have only to continue 30 miles north along Highway 10 (called Riding Mountain Parkway through the park) to reach the brow of the escarpment. The view from the edge— 1,500 feet above the prairie—is superb.

A meadow near Lake Audy.

203

Almost all of this tree-clad "mountain"-on-the-plains is in the national park. It is a section of the Manitoba Escarpment, an interrupted ridge stretching more than 800 miles from North Dakota northwest through Manitoba and into Saskatchewan.

The elk is the symbol of Riding Mountain National Park. This elk's dark beige color blends with the muted fall tones of the park underbrush. It holds its head high and horizontal, as it does when walking or running, a trait it shares with the camel.

From along the escarpment can be seen Lake Manitoba (40 miles east), Lake Dauphin (15 miles northwest), and the bustling city of Dauphin (12 miles north). But there is more than a magnificent view. Spread out here is evidence of the geological history of this part of central North America.

Salty inland seas covered the area several times. When the last of these was gone it left a flat land barely above

sea level. Part of the surface was gently uplifted, forming the escarpment; it then was cut in several places by rivers tumbling over it. The last Ice Age glacier ground enormous quantities of shale from the highlands and dumped them in the valleys.

Farms that checkerboard north and east of the escarpment are on the bed of Lake Agassiz, formed when the glacier melted. Some 8,000 years ago the freshwater lake drained off to Hudson Bay, leaving behind fertile plains, sparkling lakes and the cool highlands that form Riding Mountain National Park.

Variations of terrain give Riding Mountain its abundance of plant and wildlife species. Starting from the boggy lowlands you can move up 1,000 feet through grassland, meadows, thick stands of birch and aspen, hardwood forests and, finally, the evergreen woods of the highlands. There are 233 bird species, 60 kinds of mammals, at least 10 kinds of reptiles and amphibians, and more than 500 kinds of trees, shrubs and flowering plants.

Fragrant prairie flora exists side by side with forest flowers; pocket gophers and ground squirrels are the unlikely neighbors of bear and moose; bald eagles, ravens, ospreys and turkey vultures soar silently in the azure sky while geese, ducks, grebes and loons nest on the quiet waters below. The variety of birds seems endless, from the majestic golden eagle to the busy and noisy black-backed three-toed woodpecker, and his cousin, the northern three-toed woodpecker.

In a grassy enclosure on the shore of Lake Audy wanders a herd of buffalo; one of Canada's largest herds of elk roams the park. Here you can find western gray tree frogs, red-bellied snakes and western painted turtles. On Riding Mountain are all the shrew species known to exist in Manitoba, along with the northern grasshopper mouse, northern bog lemming, mule deer, least weasel, Canada lynx and ermine.

Riding Mountain is thought to be the dividing line of the satyrid butterfly's range. These insects exhibit intriguing and unexplained behavior; they are seen fluttering *west* of here only in odd-numbered years. In even-numbered years they are seen only *east* of Riding Mountain.

Exquisite wild flowers worth watching for are the round-leaved orchis, bishop's-cap, stemless raspberry, gaywings, bearberry and the one-flowered wintergreen.

Every summer, park naturalists conduct wolf-howl excursions in remote sections of Riding Mountain. Between 10 p.m. and 2 a.m. groups of people imitate wolf howls and are often rewarded with spine-tingling replies from the park's wolves.

Wasagaming, the park headquarters, is on the south shore of nine-square-mile Clear Lake, the park's largest.

Roads and more than 100 miles of backpacking, riding and nature trails lead from Wasagaming to the more than 50 lakes in the park. Boat-loading ramps are provided at some of the larger lakes and there are many campgrounds.

The view from Escarpment Lookout, the highest point in Riding Mountain National Park: it stretches to distant prairie farmland, far beyond the 1,500-foot-high escarpment that defines the park's eastern and northern boundaries.

Baldy Lake is one of dozens in Riding Mountain National Park with only hiking trails leading into them. Most of the park's 50-odd cool clear lakes offer eastern brook trout, rainbow and lake trout, pike, yellow walleye and yellow perch. Reptiles and crustaceans along the shores are a rich source of food for diving and wading birds.

Cree and Assiniboine Indians controlled this territory when Pierre de La Vérendrye and his sons explored and traded on the surrounding plains two centuries ago. Their name for Riding Mountain translated as "hill of the buffalo chase." The Cree and Assiniboine moved west in the wake of the dwindling buffalo herds and were replaced by the Ojibwa, forced from the eastern woodlands by civilization. The trading post of Fort Dauphin was established in 1741 just north of the present park, and the highlands became Dauphin (or Fort Dauphin) Mountain. The settlers' best way across was by horse. Thus Riding Mountain.

Late in the 19th century Riding Mountain was withdrawn from settlement and in 1906 it was designated a forest reserve. The first permits to lease land and build cottages were issued in 1916, and 14 years later Riding Mountain National Park was established.

OTHER ATTRACTIONS

Prairie Peaks and a Marsh Full of Birds

Asessippi Provincial Park Scattered through the 5,000-acre park are several eskers—long, narrow ridges of sand and gravel, remnants of the Ice Age.

Delta Marsh Thousands of ducks and other migratory birds summer in this 36,000-acre marsh, separated from Lake Manitoba by a long sandy ridge. Nesting among the sloughs and bays and channels are mallard, pintail, canvasback, shoveller, bufflehead, goldeneye and several other species of ducks. Other birds are belted kingfishers, white pelicans and several kinds of geese. There are large stands of a tall yellow reed commonly called queen of the prairie. At a waterfowl research station on the marsh are laboratories, pens and a hatchery where annually 2,000 ducks of 18 species are hatched.

Duck Mountain Provincial Park One of Canada's few turkey vulture coveys nests in the 315,000-acre park. The Duck Mountains, a part of the Manitoba Escarpment, are major nesting grounds for great blue herons. Cormorants, great horned owls and several hawk and duck species are also found. Elk and mule deer graze on the park's ranges, which include

Souris Agate Pit *Treasures such as this fossilized shell of a creature that lived millions of years ago have been found in a 12-acre pit near Souris. The pit is open to the public. Also found have been fist-sized multicolored pebbles, agates, pieces of jasper and petrified wood ranging in color from red to brown.*

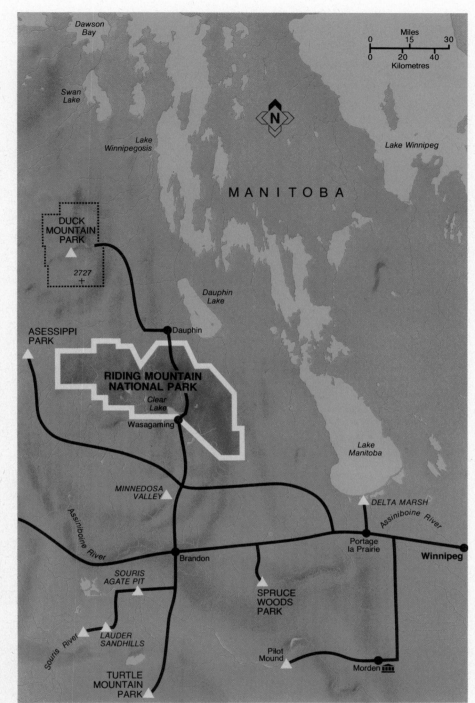

Scenic Wonder △ Other Attraction ▥ Museum

2,727-foot Baldy Mountain, the highest in Manitoba.

Lauder Sandhills Wildlife Area Some 8,000 acres of sand dunes are the wintering grounds of large numbers of white-tailed deer.

Minnedosa Valley Picture next page.

Morden Museum It displays fossils of birds and reptiles that thrived in a shallow inland sea here some 70 million years ago. Most of the fossils were preserved by shale and a fine volcanic ash. Among them are almost complete skeletons of a mosasaur (the largest of these was about 40 feet long), and of a plesiosaur, a 10-foot-long swimming creature with a long neck.

Pilot Mound An estimated 500,000 blue and snow geese stop in fields in this area on their migrations.

207

Spruce Woods Provincial Park *Sand dunes blanket much of this 90-square-mile park, the only place in Manitoba where the lizard called northern prairie skink is found. Biologists speculate that skinks burrowed deep into the sand here to avoid the worst effects of the Ice Age. White spruce, rare in this region, also survived here because of the sandy soil. It retains enough moisture for the tree to survive with less rainfall than it normally needs. Other plant life not common to the region but found in the park are tamarack and pincushion cactus.*

Souris Agate Pit Picture preceding page.

Souris River Near the town of Souris the river swirls through a series of 100-foot-deep gorges. In the rolling hinterland are owls, hawks, Canada geese, swans, great blue herons and green-winged teal. A good view of the river can be had from the 582-foot-long suspension bridge in Souris (the longest foot bridge in Canada).

Spruce Woods Park Picture this page.

Turtle Mountain Provincial Park Dotted with sloughs and small lakes, this 47,000-acre park is a stopover for about 250 species of migratory birds. The park contains the Canadian part of the International Peace Garden (the rest is in North Dakota). The 2,433-acre park has spillways, an 18-foot-wide floral clock and a sunken garden with a cloverleaf pool and 2,000 rose bushes.

Minnedosa Valley *Trees almost obscure the Minnedosa River as it winds along the floor of the pastoral valley.*

High and dry inside the lodge, a beaver nurses her kits (left). They are weaned at about a month but even before that they have begun to eat green plants. Right: A kit is given a helpful nudge up into the lodge.

Once Upon an Ice Age, Beaver Was King Rat

Before and during the Ice Age—which ended some 10,000 years ago—the beaver was King Rat. The ancestor of the shy, four-foot-long creature we know today was a nine-foot giant weighing about 800 pounds. Today adult beavers are 40 to 60 pounds, with an occasional heavyweight of 100 pounds.

A beaver family usually consists of two adults, three or four yearlings and the latest litter of kits. The living chamber of their lodge is usually less than two feet high; the diameter depends on family size. The exterior of the lodge is constantly being repaired and expanded, and when more space is needed inside, the beavers gnaw out the chamber walls. Bedding is dry, shredded wood, more practical than grass or moss, which would probably rot after being immersed in water.

The beaver is well adapted to its aquatic habitat. Guard hairs almost three inches long cover the luxuriant undercoat, and regular grooming with a glandular oil waterproofs the fur. As a beaver enters the water, its mouth, nose and ears are closed tightly and protective transparent membranes slide over the eyes. It can stay submerged for as long as 15 minutes without coming up for air. Beavers remain active when their pond is iced over. In mild winter weather, air holes in the ice are kept open by constant use. In colder weather, oxygen for long underwater trips may be found in bubbles of air trapped under the ice—air that may have been exhaled by the beaver during a previous swim and re-oxygenated by the water.

The beaver's gnawing teeth are kept sharp by being ground against each other. The chisel shape of the ends is retained as the outer surface is harder than the inner.

A beaver can close its mouth behind its gnawing teeth (incisors), enabling it to gnaw wood without swallowing splinters or water.

The beaver's small but extremely supple forepaws grasp and hold almost like human hands. Strong, curved claws help to dig burrows or dredge up mud.

Large webbed hind feet propel the beaver through the water with ease. Two toes on each foot have double claws which are used like pincers to clean and groom fur.

The first thing beavers build is a dam. To make the base, branches are stuck lengthwise in the stream bed, the thickest ends pointing upstream. Other branches and sticks are then heaped on top. Mud is plastered on the upstream side and, together with sediment and debris being swept downstream, is forced into holes in the dam, giving it a strong, leak-free foundation. An island lodge is made by building a solid mound of sticks and branches, then gnawing out passages from the base up.

The living cavity of the lodge is always above the waterline. The final touch is a coat of mud. For ventilation the top of the lodge is left free of mud. Beavers also dig burrows in the stream bank, and sometimes the lodge itself is built into the bank. Winter food is provided by an underwater cache near the lodge—a pile of saplings and branches so high that it often breaks the surface of the water.

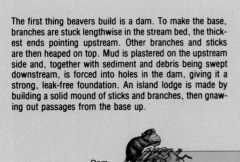

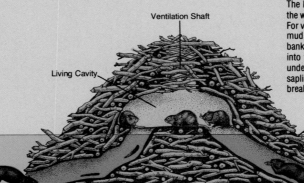

Ventilation Shaft

Living Cavity

Dam

Food Cache

Echoes of a Legend Enhance Tranquillity Along 'Calling River'

You don't see the valley of the Qu'Appelle until you're almost into it. Then, suddenly, dramatically, it is there, a giant crease across the prairie, as much as 448 feet deep and up to 1½ miles wide, separating the flat plains from the rolling parklands to the north. Down in the valley is the Qu'Appelle River, widening once into Buffalo Pound Lake, another time to form The Fishing Lakes, later to become Crooked Lake and Round Lake.

The Qu'Appelle and its lakes were part of the fur traders' main canoe route between Fort Garry (Winnipeg) and the northwest. The valley was briefly a refuge for Sitting Bull in 1881 after the Battle of the Little Big Horn in Montana, and troops detrained at the town of Qu'Appelle for the march north and west to put down Louis Riel's rebellion in 1885. But the valley is best known as a verdant farmland and a well-endowed recreation area—and for its legend.

That story, told on a marker near the village of Lebret (and in a poem by E. Pauline Johnson), is of an Indian on his way to see his bride-to-be. Someone calls his name. *"Qu'appelle?"* (Who calls?) he shouts. There is no reply—only the valley echoing his own voice.

He later comes to believe he had somehow heard his faraway sweetheart, calling for him just before she died. Whatever the truth behind the legend, the Qu'Appelle

The Qu'Appelle Valley west of Crooked Lake.

211

is known for the remarkably strong echo to be heard at many places along its 250-mile length.

Meltwaters from a retreating glacier etched this valley into the plains some 11,000 to 12,000 years ago. The peaceful Qu'Appelle (but it is capable of destructive flooding) wanders east from Lake Diefenbaker, near Elbow in western Saskatchewan, to join the Assiniboine seven miles inside Manitoba, near St. Lazare.

The valley is the habitat of a splendid variety of songbirds, migratory birds, small mammals and wild flowers. Prairie orchid and spotted touch-me-not sway to a Qu'Appelle symphony of birds and crickets and grass-hoppers and the rustle of prairie grass. Dainty fairy bells, fleabane daisies, prairie lilies, fireweeds, scarlet paint-brush, goldenrod and two-leaved Solomon's seal are a vivid backdrop to this concert.

Bird lovers along the valley can see white pelicans, and sandhill cranes and rookeries of great blue herons, and watch ruby-throated hummingbirds draw nectar from honeysuckle. Ruffed grouse can be heard drum-ming in the spring and thrashers and shrikes rear their young in the seclusion of thorny buffalo berry and haw-thorn clumps. In hardwood groves are cuckoos, catbirds, finches, flycatchers, warblers and woodpeckers. In bluffs along the river are six species of hawk: Swainson's, Cooper's, red-tailed, sparrow, sharp-shinned and broad-winged. Any day during the spring migration even a novice may sight birds of as many as 100 of the 325 species known to frequent the valley.

Some wooded ravines near the river and the lakes have never felt the plow and remain the preserve of deer, fox, porcupine, badger and skunk. Here too are thirteen-lined and Franklin's ground squirrels. Berries such as the chokecherry, pin cherry, gooseberry and black currant abound in the valley.

Along the valley slopes in springtime the sweet scent of wolf willow fills the air. Roses, snowberry, various willows and mauve bergamot ring the aspen poplar clumps that favor the north slopes. On the dry, sun-baked south slopes are prickly pear and ball cactus, as well as scarlet mallow and crocus anemone. Manitoba maple and green ash fill the ravines and thrive along the riverbanks. Hardier than other trees, perhaps, the aspen poplars flourish even in times of drought, when their roots force out hundreds of saplings, thus multiplying without seed.

Settlement along the Qu'Appelle started in the late 19th century. Most settlers chose high ground back of the river—free from flood and less vulnerable to Indian attack but close enough to the valley for timber, grass and water. Some settlements wove their own threads

Canada geese assume their familiar V formation after lifting off from a Qu'Appelle Valley field.

into the ethnic tapestry of southeastern Saskatchewan: Scots at Wapella; Hungarians at Esterhazy; Scandina-vians at Stockholm; Icelanders near Churchbridge; Germans near Langenburg. Near Wapella, in the 1880s, Russian and Bessarabian pioneers formed western Canada's first all-Jewish settlement.

Now the almost hidden valley is a vacationer's de-

light. The sudden descent into the Qu'Appelle can be an impressive descent into tranquillity. In and near the valley are four provincial parks. Two are Buffalo Pound, on Buffalo Pound Lake north of Moose Jaw, and Rowan's Ravine, west of Bulyea on Last Mountain Lake (which drains into the Qu'Appelle River). The other parks, Katepwa and Echo Valley, are near Fort Qu'Appelle and, like The Fishing Lakes, make that part of the valley a recreational bonanza. Here the legend seems strongest. "When the moonrise tips the distant hill" (as Pauline Johnson wrote in *The Legend of Qu'Appelle Valley*) one seems to hear the echo of the voice of the heartbroken Indian brave:

> *The paleface loves the haunted lakes they say,*
> *And journeys far to watch their beauty spread*
> *Before his vision; but to me the day,*
> *The night, the hour, the seasons are all dead.*
> *I listen heartsick, while the hunters tell*
> *Why white men named the valley The Qu'Appelle.*

213

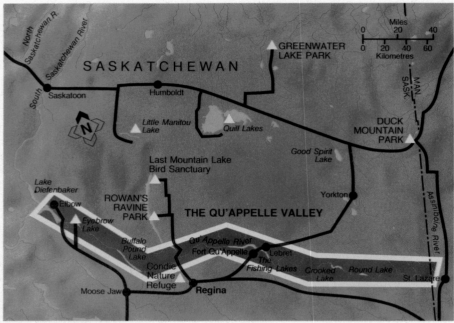

☐ Scenic Wonder △ Other Attraction

OTHER ATTRACTIONS

Mineral Lakes and Bird Sanctuaries

Quill Lakes *Big Quill Lake (above) reflects the changing blue of the prairie sky. Big and Little Quill are shallow and neither has a steady intake; come summer, their water evaporates, leaving dazzling white alkaline flats. Middle Quill, smaller than the others, is fed by the fresh water of Milligan Creek but is still alkaline. Migrating birds, notably sandhill cranes, stop over on the lakes.*

Condie Nature Refuge Hundreds of Canada geese, pintails, mallards and grebes nest in marshland around Condie Reservoir. Great blue herons often feed but do not nest here. The sanctuary has grassland and parkland.

Duck Mountain Provincial Park A trail winds up aspen-covered hills that rise 700 feet. This is one of Saskatchewan's few turkey vulture habitats.

Eyebrow Lake Nine hundred wing-clipped Canada geese live on this marshy lake, the captive nucleus of a provincial government project to increase Saskatchewan's goose population. Project Nisk'u (Nisk'u is Plains Cree for big goose) was started in 1969; its target is 15,000 goslings by 1985. Each year's brood is distributed among lakes in the province just before the goslings learn to fly, for geese normally return to where they first take wing. The main Nisk'u area is 3,500 acres at the east end of the four-mile-long lake and visitors can drive through it on dikes.

Greenwater Lake Provincial Park A colony of great blue herons inhabits three-mile-long Marine Lake. The park is also home to moose, elk, deer, black bear, coyote, the odd timber wolf and the rare turkey vulture. A nature trail follows a creek into highland timber country.

Last Mountain Lake Bird Sanctuary Birds from the tiny last surviving flock of whooping cranes stop here or in the vicinity as they migrate between Texas and the Northwest Territories. This sanctuary, at the north end of Last Mountain Lake, was established in 1887 and is the oldest in North America. Its 2,500 acres form part of a 20,000-acre wildlife management area. Sandhill cranes, swans, double-crested cormorants and gulls are seen.

Little Manitou Lake The 12-mile-long lake, fed by groundwater that picks up mineral salts, has greater salinity than the ocean. There is no outlet, and constant evaporation increases the salt content year by year.

Quill Lakes Picture this page.

Rowan's Ravine Provincial Park The ravine in this 720-acre park is 20 feet deep and more than a mile long.

Colors, Scents Vital in Reproduction Cycle

From early spring to late fall, the Qu'Appelle Valley is filled with the vivid colors and heady scents of its splendid native wild flowers. But the blossoms and perfumes of wild flowers are more than mere spectacle: they are vital to the survival of the species.

Just as inbreeding weakens an animal species, plant species would be adversely affected if they pollinated themselves. So most flowers have ingenious devices to prevent self-pollination. The transfer of pollen from the male stamens of one plant to the female pistil of another plant (guaranteeing healthy, adaptable offspring) is most often accomplished by an insect or bird seeking a flower's sweet nectar. Pollen sticks to the insect or bird when it touches the flower's stamens. When it visits another plant of the same species, some of the pollen grains shake loose or brush onto the pistil, thus fertilizing the plant.

Honeybees are well suited to helping most flowers reproduce. Pronged claws (1) enable a honeybee worker to cling to flowers while sipping nectar through its proboscis (2). Nectar is carried in the honey stomach and emptied at the hive, where it is converted to honey. Pollen grains, which serve as food for newly hatched bees, are caught by the worker bee's hairy body (3), then brushed by the rear and middle legs (4) into the pollen basket (5) for transportation to the hive.

Typical of flowers that honeybees use, wild meadowsweet is round and heavily scented and has landing platforms and nectar guides.

IRRESISTIBLE GUIDES

Violet

Toadflax

Honeysuckle

To ensure that animals play their role properly, flowers have evolved colors, odors and signposts that lead pollinators in. The Canada violet has stripes on its petals, pointing to nectar and pollen. The toadflax has petals with patches of color that taper at the nectar source. The night-blooming honeysuckle entices moths with an overwhelming perfume.

GENTLE SEDUCTION

The complicated milkweed is so constructed that it cannot pollinate itself. Orange milkweed petals are turned down and topped by a crown of five hoods containing nectar. An insect must perch in order to feed; its legs slip between the hoods into masses of pollen.

PLAYING HARD TO GET

Few insects can get inside the tightly-closed petals of this blue gentian. But the bumblebee, larger and stronger than the honeybee, has little trouble reaching the sweet nectar, receiving and depositing pollen in the process.

SWEET LURE

The hummingbird's long bill and tongue reach deep nectar in flowers such as this penstemon. It attracts the bird with its shape and color. The ruby-throated hummingbird beats its wings 55 times a second when hovering. To compensate for such expenditure of energy it must feed every 15 to 20 minutes. A hummingbird never alights on a flower but gathers all its food in flight. But its forehead is dusted with pollen as it sips nectar.

SETTING TRAPS

Bees attracted by the lower lip of the yellow lady slipper orchid are trapped in the smooth, bulbous petal. Fine hairs guide the bee to its only avenue of escape, a slit at the base of the petal. As it gets away, the bee brushes against grains of pollen.

NIGHT BLOOMERS

Night-blooming flowers require no bright colors or nectar guides but they are lightly tinted so as to be visible in the dark. The western yellow evening primrose emits a strong scent to attract nocturnal insects such as the twin-spotted sphinx. It uses its two-inch tongue to reach nectar.

A Lonesome Badland Where Once Rustlers Hid From the Law

The Big Muddy is solitude, spectacular scenery and a silence sometimes almost frightening. Two miles wide, this badland of eroded earth and sandstone is a 35-mile-long gash on the face of the flat Saskatchewan prairie. In its multicolored coulee walls, as high as 500 feet, is the saga of how the earth's crust was formed. One chapter per layer.

Near the valley floor is the white and gray Whitemud Formation, laid down 65 million years ago. Above it is the gray-green-yellow Ravenscrag, with coal seams up to 10 feet thick. Near the top is the quartzite gravel of the Wood Mountain Formation, a mere five million years old. Here is part of the saga of the structuring of the earth, so clearly defined that it seems to have been recorded especially for the geologist—and the artist, the student and the tourist.

Before the Ice Age—until about a million years ago—the Big Muddy was no more than a slight depression in the plains, a grassy land with shallow freshwater lakes. Lilies grew in the ponds; ferns bordered the swamps and rivers. Magnolias and sycamores flourished in dense marshes. Grapevines and fig trees and stands of oak, beech and walnut covered the hillsides. Fossils of all of these are found in the Big Muddy.

Water erosion slowly enlarged the depression. Then came the mile-thick ice of the Ice Age, gouging the

The layered walls of the Big Muddy Valley testify to its geological past.

217

valley deeper. As the ice sheet began to wane 10,000 years ago, meltwater formed such lakes as Old Wives Lake and watercourses such as Big Muddy Creek, today a tiny stream in the huge valley.

Creek and valley wind southeast from near Willow Bunch to Big Muddy Lake—where the badland itself ends—then south into Montana where the creek flows into a tributary of the Missouri River.

For the visitor approaching the Big Muddy from the north—from Bengough—the first sign of this strange land is Castle Butte, a 200-foot-high outcrop of compressed clay rising abruptly from the prairie. In the Big Muddy proper are many more buttes, flat-topped hills with almost vertical sides. Many rise 100 to 200 feet above the valley floor; some are 600 feet high.

Despite the spectacular buttes, the weathered sandstone hills and the peace and beauty of the Big Muddy, relatively few persons visit this remote part of Saskatchewan. But it is a mecca for scientists and travelers who desert the blacktop, take to the cattle trails and discover the spell of the strange valley.

I t is almost as lonely as in the days of Dutch Henry, a turn-of-the-century rascal, horse thief, smuggler and cattle rustler whose hideout was in the Big Muddy. Dutch, chased out of Dodge City, Kans., in the late 1880s, migrated to Montana, then settled for the desolation of the wild valley just a gallop across the border.

In a hillside near Peaked Butte he and his rustler pal Tom Owens carved two caves, one large enough for horses, the other for men. Fitted with a stovepipe, the cave-home provided seclusion between rustling raids

Gullies that slice into a wall of the Big Muddy Valley have created a spur ridge (right). A resistant piece of sandstone (below) has protected part of the softer rock layer beneath it; the result is another of the hoodoos that dot the strange, remote valley in southern Saskatchewan.

into Montana. (The caves, 15 miles southeast of Big Beaver, can be visited.) Nearby was a year-round source of fresh water and from the top of Peaked Butte the rustlers had an uninterrupted view of both the Canadian and the U.S. approaches to their refuge.

Henry and Owens were two main reasons the North West Mounted Police established a post in the Big Muddy in 1902. Two years later the detachment was expanded from two men to six because of "horse thieves whose depredations to the south of us have made them the terror of the community." Dutch Henry was shot to death in Roseau, Minn., in 1906. The following year, significantly, the Mounties' Big Muddy detachment was cut to three men.

Then came settlement. Soon the Big Muddy was ringed by small towns: Bengough to the north, Big Beaver to the south, Harptree to the northwest, Minton to the east. But even today the isolation that attracted Dutch Henry has changed little.

This may once have been buffalo country. On a ranch near Minton are 1½-foot stone cairns 10 to 12 feet apart,

The Valley of the Big Muddy grows as gullies eat into adjacent uplands. Steep ridges between gullies will ultimately become hoodoos, which will finally disappear.

forming lines several miles long and converging on a cliff overlooking the valley: apparently a buffalo jump built by Indians. No buffalo is seen here now but the Big Muddy's solitude has helped preserve other mammals. The pronghorn antelope, the coyote and the mule deer all thrive, virtually unaffected by man and his machines. Smaller mammals include Nuttall's cottontail, white-tailed rabbit, jackrabbit, Richardson's ground squirrel and striped skunk. Big brown bats have been collected from hillside caves.

Hawk watchers find the Big Muddy particularly rewarding. Soaring on thermals uplifted by valley contours are such species as the ferruginous hawk, Cooper's hawk, marsh hawk, Swainson's hawk, pigeon hawk, sparrow hawk, prairie falcon and golden eagle. Plains garter snake, bull snake and smooth green snake have been collected in lowland marshes.

A day in the Big Muddy is like a day stepping back in time. You run your hand over a fossilized turtle that 65 *million years ago* swam in a sea that covered this land. You find inside a cracked stone a 50-million-year-old fossilized fern leaf. You sense the mystery and the glory of creation in the silence, the overwhelming silence, of the Big Muddy.

Scenic Wonder △ Other Attraction ⬛ Museum

OTHER ATTRACTIONS

Waterfowl Near a Provincial Legislature

Halbrite Badlands Picture next page.

Isle of Bays Wildfowl Sanctuary Because alkaline Old Wives Lake has no fish, the 800 white pelicans that nest here fly some 40 miles for food—all the way to the Qu'Appelle River and Buffalo Pound Lake. Back at their island in Old Wives Lake, they regurgitate food for their young. The sanctuary also has ring-billed and California gulls, double-crested cormorants and black-crowned night herons.

Moose Mountain Provincial Park The mile-long Blue Heron Nature Trail slices through aspen poplar forests and skirts several lakes. The heavily forested, 154-square-mile park is dominated by Moose Mountain, which rises some 500 feet above the plain.

Roche Percée Picture this page.

St. Victor In the hills just north of this village is an impressive outcropping that forms a 60-foot cliff. In the soft sandstone are Indian petroglyphs depicting human heads, hands and feet. The carvings are unusual in that they are on a horizontal slope. (Most Indian petro-

Roche Percée *Near this town are sandstone outcroppings such as this "petrified lizard." The town is named for another outcropping, 25 feet high, that once formed a long arch.*

glyphs are on vertical rock faces.) One head has teeth; the only other known toothed-head petroglyph east of the Rockies is at Lake of the Woods in On-

tario. There is a small park at the base of the cliff. A dirt road winds to the cliff top, from which there is a spectacular view of the plains.

221

Halbrite Badlands *About eight miles by five, this hilly region along Roughbark Creek is dotted with clumps of sagebrush, chokecherry, saskatoon berry and maple trees. There are coulees and bluffs and boulders.*

Saskatchewan Museum of Natural History Twenty-four life-size dioramas depict Canadian mammals and birds in a variety of Saskatchewan landscapes, portraying the relationship between the animals and their environment. The displays show some of the province's various regions: the grasslands of the south, aspen grove, mixed woodland, the coniferous forests, and the sub-arctic. Texts provide insight into various aspects of the dioramas and the creatures' lives. Among the scenes are timber wolves on the trail of a moose, geese gathering to feed in flooded grain fields during a migration stopover, and beaver cutting saplings in front of their dam and lodge. Other displays show records of millions of years of life preserved in geological deposits. Marine reptiles dating from millions of years ago when much of Saskatchewan was covered by seas, and land mammals such as the mammoth, musk-ox and titanothere (that had a branched horn on its snout and resembled the rhinoceros of today) are among the fossil skeleton exhibits.

Wascana Waterfowl Park Some 360 acres of marsh along shallow Wascana Lake near the Saskatchewan legislature are nesting grounds for Canada geese, wild ducks and songbirds. Muskrat, mink, weasel and other small mammals also are found on the marsh. Among waterfowl in the sanctuary are mallard, pintail, canvasback, blue-winged teal, whistling swan, mute swan and western grebe. Hot water from a power plant keeps about an acre of the lake from freezing. This and a feeding program encourage migratory waterfowl to stay in the park year-round. About 75 birds of different species found on the marsh are kept at one end of the waterfowl park, so that visitors can see them and their habitat at close range.

Wild Animal Regional Park Buffalo, phronghorn antelope and elk roam in this 300-acre Moose Jaw park. Some 200 other animals, including timber wolves, lions, yaks, monkeys, deer, bears and raccoons are in cages. There are also several Canada geese, sandhill cranes, swans, eagles and a variety of wild ducks.

Eerie but nonetheless exquisite, the scarred faces of Canada's badlands have been shaped by erosion, the gradual wearing down of the land by one or more of nature's sculpturing agents—water, wind and ice. Water is the chief architect of the badlands of Alberta and Saskatchewan, eating away at rock that has been millions of years in the making, fashioning coulees, steep slopes and hoodoos.

Erosion is a never-ending process. The fluted bluffs and graceful spires that adorn valleys such as those along Big Muddy Creek and Alberta's Red Deer River (*see* p. 233) will one day disappear. But for centuries to come they will continue to lend their stark beauty to the rugged badlands of Canada.

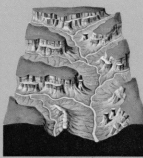

Gullies are predominant in all badlands. Streams and rain carve these miniature valleys in soft rock formations that lack a protective cover of absorbent soil and plants.

A main watercourse and its tributaries excavate steep-sided gullies. The channels steadily grow, creating canyons and oddly-shaped masses of eroded rock—mesas, buttes and hoodoos.

As streams approach a region's base level (the lowest level to which water will cut), the area is leveled. Isolated landforms are worn away. The valley now may widen but will not deepen.

Water Is Chief Architect of the Badlands' Eerie Beauty

Materials that form badlands are soft and easily eroded. But various rocks resist the forces of erosion at different rates. **Shale,** one of the most abundant rocks on the earth's surface, occurs in both hard and soft forms. When wet, soft shale decomposes into mud. Its fine-grained appearance reflects its vulnerability to runoff and erosion. **Sandstone** is formed of sand grains held together by natural cement. Much water is absorbed into "pores" between the grains so fewer grains are washed away. This porosity and the nature of the cement—usually calcium carbonate, silica or iron oxide—made sandstone more erosion-resistant than shale.

In the dry climate of the badlands, with little soil or vegetation to absorb water, the bare rock is an easy target for erosion.

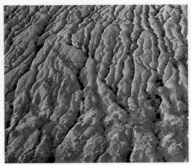

Rainfall in arid and semiarid regions is scarce but often torrential. Etched by fast-running water, this rock face at Halbrite, Sask., is a network of rills, some of which are several feet deep.

The channels on a Big Muddy cliffside resemble the pipes of some giant organ. Behind them are vertical tunnels that carry away rock fragments and water.

Hoodoos sculpted by rain have slow-yielding top layers of rock that protect the softer strata underneath.

Unlike the steep-sided remnant in the background, this shale mound has been stripped of its protective cap, making it more vulnerable to the erosive power of water.

A towering hoodoo of soft shale on the floor of the Red Deer Valley. A sandstone cap has saved it from collapse.

223

Adams Lake in Cypress Hills Provincial Forest.

CYPRESS HILLS

This Lofty 'Island' in the Great Plains Was Once Surrounded by a Sea of Ice

224

Twenty miles south of the Trans-Canada Highway and astride the Saskatchewan-Alberta border is the geological accident called the Cypress Hills. One summit, Head of the Mountain, 4,810 feet above sea level and 2,000 feet higher than the surrounding plain, is the highest land between Labrador and the Rockies. This peak was at the center of an 80-square-mile Ice Age "island," the only part of western Canada left uncovered by a mile-thick sheet of ice between the Rockies and the Laurentians.

In this string of hills the incongruous is common. Wild flowers and songbirds once believed native only to the Rockies proliferate in the Hills. Scorpions and horned toads exist nearby, more than 1,000 miles north of others of their kind. Hognose snakes and kangaroo rats still slither and bounce through the grasslands. Petrified

figs and locusts found around the Hills also attest to an earlier, warmer clime. You see desert cactus in the lowlands, orchids beside a still pond on the heights only three miles away.

Eons ago the hills were part of a tropical swamp inhabited by dinosaurs, rhinoceros and other prehistoric giants. When the last Ice Age glacier inched its way through the lowlands here, the remains of early specimens were ground away. But fossils of dozens of prehistoric species have been uncovered in the Hills. Some were ancestral cousins of the deer and some were clearly exotic, such as tiny camels and a distant forerunner of the saber-toothed tiger.

Rising in Saskatchewan near Eastend, the Cypress Hills roll gently westward into southeastern Alberta. They are 60 miles from east to west, 20 to 25 miles from north to south. Little creeks that chuckle away on parallel courses in the high country have different objectives, for this is a major watershed. One will head southeast to the Gulf of Mexico while its neighbor takes off for Hudson Bay.

From the air the Hills are a series of green-black undulations, their evergreen heights dark against the beige of the surrounding rangeland. Few fields are plowed in these flatlands: this is short-grass country, kept semi-arid by an average of only seven inches of rainfall each summer.

But there is adequate rain in the Hills and atop them is a flat plain (the Bench to ranchers, a dissected plateau to the geologists) on which cattle wander in luxuriant, shoulder-high grass. On the flat the grass is called prairie wool—low, brown, unattractive. On the Bench, 1,800 feet higher, the dominant species is a bunchgrass called rough fescue which flourishes with only 18 inches of precipitation annually.

The first white men to visit the Cypress Hills were most likely Peter Fidler, chief surveyor for the Hudson's Bay Company, and his voyageurs. They came in 1800 to gather spruce gum to mend their canoes and among them may have been some who spoke French and who thought the lodgepole pines of the Hills were *cyprès*, jack pines. *Montagne du Cyprès* was poorly translated as the Cypress Hills.

Capt. John Palliser tells in his journals of a visit to the Cypress Hills in 1859 and how he killed buffalo and rested after his two-year exploration of the plains, foothills and mountains. He described the Hills as an oasis.

The road (left) between the Saskatchewan Cypress Hills park and a forest preserve on the Alberta border provides some lovely views of the Hills. Right: A conglomerate outcropping, consisting of naturally cemented gravel.

Settlers found them an oasis indeed; here were fish, fowl, deer and buffalo for the table, feed for livestock, water year round. As a bonus, no one had to chop firewood—they could dig chunks of long-burning lignite from the hillsides.

HBC agent Isaac Cowie built a trading post at the east end of the Hills in 1871. By company policy he could sell no whiskey. Others who could, and did, cornered the market for trade goods. But one season was long enough for Cowie to ship out the hides of 750 grizzly bears and 1,500 elk.

In May 1873 came the Cypress Hills Massacre. Drunken Assiniboine Indians got into an argument with Montana wolf hunters, also drunk, over stolen horses. Shooting followed. The whites, armed with deadly repeating rifles, repulsed the Indians, raided their village and reportedly killed 30 men, women and children.

The tragedy hastened the establishment of the North West Mounted Police and in 1875, a year after the first Mounties went west, Fort Walsh was built in the Cypress Hills. Its walls, stockade and roofs were built of poles cut

The Rock Pile, about 100 huge stones laid out as if they were once part of a wall, are in the Cypress Hills near the replica of Fort Walsh, a historic North West Mounted Police post. Some stones weigh many tons. Geologists say it is likely they did not get there naturally so they might have been collected by man. One fanciful suggestion is that this was once an outpost of the Mayas or Aztecs.

from nearby hillsides. Fort Walsh was abandoned in 1883 after the CPR reached Maple Creek, a few miles north, and later was dismantled.

Bird watchers in the Hills can expect to see red cross-bills, pine siskins, red-breasted nuthatches, Swainson's hawks and such warblers as Audubon's, MacGillivray's and common yellowthroats. In all, 207 species of birds have been sighted in the Hills. Under the campground's electric lights you witness a dramatic sight—the evening spectacular of moths, including such beauties as ribbed underwing, mountain beauty and barred sallow.

Botanists have recorded 669 species and subspecies of plants, including 99 species of mosses, 14 orchids and nine liverworts. Terrain and elevation sort out the tree growth in specific areas. Above 4,200 feet is lodgepole pine, so named because the Indians used it in tepees and lodges. In cool, moist areas and on north-facing slopes is white spruce. Also on north slopes, immediately under the lodgepole pine, are long, narrow belts of aspen. High on the western plateau are the fescue grasslands. At the east end of the Hills, on the drier, south-facing slopes, are mixed-grass prairies.

Buffalo have been extinct in the Hills since the 1890s. Gone too are mountain lions and black and grizzly bears. Still here are lynx, bobcat, coyote, red fox, elk, moose, white-tailed deer and pronghorn antelope.

Tourist, camp and recreation areas in the Hills include Saskatchewan's 17-square-mile Cypress Hills Provincial Park, just north of Cypress Lake. In Alberta is a 70-square-mile park around Elkwater Lake.

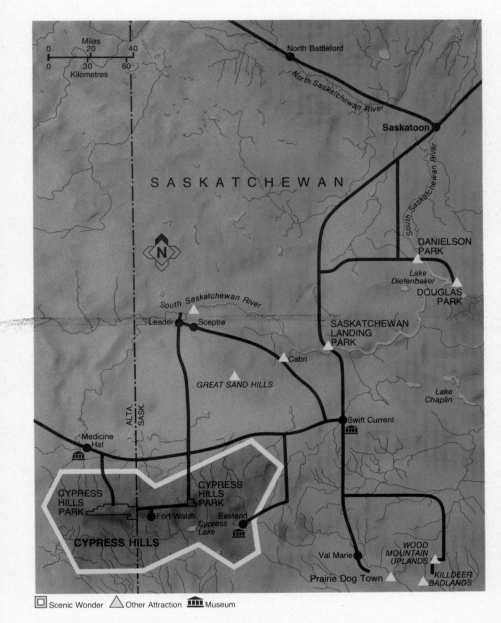

Scenic Wonder △ Other Attraction ⊞ Museum

OTHER ATTRACTIONS
Prairie Dogs and Pronghorn

Cabri The name of this town is Indian for pronghorn antelope. Hundreds of pronghorns roam southwestern Saskatchewan and southeastern Alberta in herds of 30 to 40. These shy animals, the fastest mammals in North America, are not easily spotted, but local ranchers usually know where they can be seen.

Danielson Provincial Park Construction of the Gardiner Dam (210 feet high, 16,700 feet long and one of the largest earth-fill dams in the world) is changing the face of southwestern Saskatchewan. Lake Diefenbaker provides water for irrigation, hydropower and recreation.

Douglas Provincial Park One tenth of this naturally forested 10,000-acre park is covered with sand dunes. Some sand is stabilized by scrub brush but a substantial amount is perpetually shifting.

Eastend High School Museum The three-foot skull of a triceratops, a 20-to 25-foot reptile common in southern Saskatchewan millions of years ago, is among prehistoric bones and fossils displayed in this museum.

Great Sand Hills Picture next page.

Killdeer Badlands Picture next page.

Medicine Hat Historical and Museum Foundation On display are the fossilized teeth of sawfish that swam in an inland sea that covered Alberta 75 million years ago. Other exhibits include fossilized bones and teeth of prehistoric dinosaurs, bison, reindeer, beavers, camels and horses, and fragments of hide from prehistoric crocodiles. The teeth of mammoths (hairy forerunners of the elephant) might have been swept down from Alaska in glacial gravel. A 100-pound ammonite shell has whorls that give it the appearance of a ram's horn.

Prairie Dog Town Prairie dogs once burrowed in the plains in the millions. Ranchers poisoned most of them, claiming horses and cattle were in constant danger of breaking legs in the myriad burrow entrances. Soon the dogs—

South Saskatchewan River *Parts of the valley of the South Saskatchewan—like this section north of Sceptre, Sask.—are almost desert-like. This is a prairie wilderness, up to two miles wide and some 300 feet deep, with rolling sagebrush-dotted hills along the valley.*

229

Killdeer Badlands *Eroded clay hills that support no vegetation dot the badlands southwest of Killdeer. Some "dobbies" are circular, up to 300 feet in diameter and 200 feet high.*

foot-long rodents—were threatened by extinction. Help came from the Saskatchewan Natural History Society, which leased 160 acres of prairie, 14 miles southeast of Val Marie, as a sanctuary for one of the last prairie dog colonies. Amid cactus and scrub brush, with pronghorn antelopes and burrowing owls as neighbors, the amiable residents of Prairie Dog Town have become a tourist attraction. They always keep near their burrows. These drop almost vertically for six or seven feet, then extend horizontally as much as 80 feet.

Saskatchewan Landing Provincial Park The South Saskatchewan River has cut as deep as 600 feet into the prairie, with rugged results that contrast with the surrounding flat farming country. A 1,400-foot beach nestles under a stand of cottonwoods. Burial mounds and 265 tepee rings are evidence of Cree Indian use of the land.

South Saskatchewan River Picture preceding page.

Swift Current Natural History Museum Displays of animal habitats found in southwestern Saskatchewan include those of prairie dogs, mule deer, buffalo and pronghorn antelopes. There are mounted specimens of the sandhill crane, golden eagle, snowy owl and (extinct) passenger pigeon.

Wood Mountain Uplands Rising 3,200 feet above the prairie, these uplands were once part of an ancient plateau. The Ice Age and subsequent erosion wore down the surrounding area, leaving the 30-mile-long, semi-arid uplands. There are numerous steep-sided coulees throughout the area.

Great Sand Hills *These rippled dunes stretch from just north of Maple Creek north 200 miles toward the valley of the South Saskatchewan River. The hills cover 4,000 square miles and are home to many pronghorn antelopes. Sand in some parts has been stabilized by sagebrush, buck brush and hay grass.*

Ever alert to danger, a family of pronghorn antelope rests after grazing on sagebrush. Found only in North America, pronghorn once numbered several millions. Severe winters, disease and man have reduced them to about 250,000.

The Art of Animal Survival: Adapt or Die

The Great Sand Hills, a semi-arid expanse of dunes, grass, cactus and sagebrush, stretch from the Cypress Hills 200 miles north to the South Saskatchewan River. It is inhospitable country in which animals have to adapt to survive. They must tolerate scorching summer heat, winter temperatures that drop far below freezing, and a meager eight inches of rainfall. They must also elude predators on terrain that offers little or no cover.

Pronghorn use their exceptional eyesight and sense of smell to locate coyotes, and their speed to keep at a safe distance. Oversized lungs, heart and windpipe enable healthy pronghorn to sprint at up to 60 miles an hour, making them the fastest mammal native to North America. Other creatures too have learned to survive in the perilous sand hills.

Pronghorn see objects a mile away. (Some experts say several miles.) When danger threatens, white hairs on a pronghorn's rump stand erect, creating a flash that other pronghorn can spot at great distances. The muscles that move the rump hairs also activate glands which emit a musky odor. Thus, pronghorn who because of the lie of the land cannot see the warning flash are alerted by the scent.

The kangaroo rat manufactures its own water supply. As its body breaks down reserves of fat, water is produced; unlike most animals, it utilizes this water. It can also absorb water from its bladder, moisture that would otherwise be sloughed off as waste. It conserves moisture by not sweating or panting, as other animals do to release excess body heat. Instead, the kangaroo rat avoids the heat of summer by staying in burrows during the day and foraging for food only at night. It can propel itself six feet in the air with a flick of its powerful tail—a necessary maneuver in eluding owls and snakes.

The white-tailed jackrabbit depends on speed and agility to survive. It can run at 45 miles an hour and, using its powerful hind legs only, bound 20 feet. It can jump over six-foot obstacles and change direction without slowing down. The position of its eyes enables the jackrabbit to spot danger on all sides. Its large ears, which pick up the slightest sound, are important to the animal's survival in hot weather: blood flowing through the ears loses heat easily. Jackrabbits do not burrow, but rest in shallow depressions during the day, emerging at night to forage for cactus and sage.

Where vegetation is sparse, many animals live underground. Richardson's pocket gopher, with strong forepaws for digging, can excavate a network of chambers that may extend over an acre. A rodent, this gopher is active at night, stuffing its cheek pouches with food for storage underground.

Closely related to the wolf, the coyote eats almost anything: rodents, badgers, rabbits, insects, fruit, young antelope, deer—and livestock. In the past this lack of discrimination made the coyote a target for farmers and cattlemen. But despite traps, poison and hunters (some using planes and snowmobiles), coyotes have survived and have even extended their range. Only recently has the coyote's importance in the balance of nature been recognized.

Common in dry, sandy regions, the harmless western hognose snake is so thick-bodied that fleeing from danger is seldom possible. When faced by, say, an owl, the snake strikes a fearsome pose to frighten off the predator. If that doesn't work, the snake, with its mouth open, appears to lose strength, contorts its body and flops on its back, apparently dead—but alert for any opportunity to flee. It plays dead even if it is picked up on the chance of escaping later.

Lacking the internal temperature controls and sweat glands of birds and mammals, cold-blooded reptiles regulate body heat by alternating between sun and shade. To avoid temperature extremes, this short-horned lizard uses its limbs and sharply pointed head scales to dig a furrow in the sand, taking refuge three to four inches beneath the surface. Its scaly body prevents moisture loss, and water in its body tissue can be used in times of drought. This slow-moving insect-eater spurts blood from the corner of its eye to frighten predators.

Spadefoot toads breed only after a rainstorm, an infrequent occurrence in the sand hills. It is only after a storm that the female has a puddle in which to lay her eggs. If the puddle does not evaporate too quickly, the tadpoles hatch and develop into adults in 30 to 40 days. A spadefoot spends most of the year in a dormant state, lying in a burrow that it digs with sharp, horny projections on the bottom of its hind feet.

Coulees, Canyons and Hoodoos Mark This Burial Ground of Prehistoric Life

Wheat and poplars and chokecherry trees grow right to the edge. There the black-topped roads start their long, curving descent to the valley floor 400 feet below. Now the greens and browns of ripening crops give way to terraced cliffs almost devoid of vegetation. At the bottom is the now blue, now muddy Red Deer River, contrasting with the pinks and grays and golds of canyon walls. This is the mile-wide Red Deer Badlands, a great eroded valley of grotesque hoodoos and dinosaur skeletons. A. Y. Jackson called it "the most paintable valley in western Canada."

This deep-cut section of the Red Deer—the 200-mile stretch between the city of Red Deer and Brooks—is also a treasure-house of prehistory, a vast graveyard in which scientists can read the story of a time when much of southern Alberta was a swampy delta alongside an inland sea. Not only dinosaur remains are found but also the fossils of crocodiles, turtles, fishes, oyster shells and of trees that once flourished here—redwood, swamp cypress, plane tree and the subtropical ginkgo.

The erosion that shaped the valley has created strange geological formations. There are scores of steep, isolated hills called buttes, and of hoodoos, pillars of glacial till (clay, sand, gravel, boulders) that resist erosion and reach as much as 75 feet into the badlands sky.

Dinosaur skeletons, however, are probably the most

Horseshoe Canyon, near Drumheller.

233

fascinating of the valley's treasures. The giant reptiles of the Cretaceous period, which started 135 million years ago and lasted 65 million years, thrived here. Almost 400 major dinosaur discoveries have been made along the Red Deer since Joseph B. Tyrrell, one of Canada's foremost geologists, found the first skull in 1884. Remains dug from this "Valley of the Dinosaurs" are displayed in museums in Toronto, Ottawa, New York, London and other European cities.

But some of the more impressive remains lie where they were found, in what now is Dinosaur Provincial Park, roughly 70 miles southeast of Drumheller, 30 miles northeast of Brooks. The 22,000-acre park, in a water-eroded, windblown wilderness that supports little veg-

Cactus flowers (top left) daub beauty into drab corners of the semiarid Red Deer Badlands and stubborn rusty lichens brighten a piece of petrified wood. It has created its own pedestal by shielding the underlying soft sandstone from the rain. Centuries of water erosion created the flowing forms of a badlands coulee (left).

etation, is perhaps the world's richest burial ground of prehistoric creatures. Huts have been built around the remains of three dinosaurs.

Of the eight dinosaur families whose remains have been retrieved in the badlands, duck-billed plant eaters were the most numerous. In 1912, six miles east of Drumheller at Michichi Creek, Dr. Charles H. Sternberg found the first complete dinosaur skeleton to be mounted in Canada. It now is in the National Museum of Natural Science in Ottawa. The skeleton of a duck-billed dinosaur, 30 feet long and eight feet high, is shown in the Drumheller Dinosaur and Fossil Museum.

Other dinosaurs of the Red Deer were swamp dwellers and plant eaters like the duck-billed but were markedly different in appearance. The armored dinosaur resembled a tank in both outline and protective covering. Its 15-foot-long body was encased in bony plates and its principal weapon was an armored tail, the end of it almost solid, fashioned of plates fused together. *Triceratops,* a horned dinosaur, had the largest head of any reptile, any time, anywhere. For protection, it developed a bony crest that ran from the skull back over the neck and shoulders. Horned and armored dinosaurs walked on all four legs. They needed only crouch with lowered heads to be almost invulnerable.

The smaller dome-headed plant eaters and others that resembled today's ostrich were all preyed upon by still another dinosaur family, the flesh eaters. One flesh eater, *Albertosaurus,* was eight to ten feet high, with 30-foot-long body, three-foot jaws and four-inch teeth. It dined (and breakfasted and lunched) for millions of years on its swamp-dwelling contemporaries.

Layered like a giant cake, the walls of the valley of the Red Deer are a record of eons of land building. Muddy silts and sands eroded from higher elevations to the west were carried here by streams that met and formed the Mowry Sea—which once covered all of central North America. As each sedimentary layer was overlaid by the next it became a storehouse for the dead plant, animal and marine life of its age.

In time the primordial mud turned to rock. Volcanic ash drifted in on wind and water, forming deposits of bentonite, now a distinctive feature of these colorful layers. During the millions of years that the Mowry Sea existed the northern part of North America was rising. This tipping united the Mowry and the Gulf of Mexico, and brought north such life forms as clams, snails and ammonites, whose shells had rippled whorls suggestive of ram's horns. Periodically flooded lowlands became the site of huge oyster beds.

The end of the Cretaceous period was marked by high geological drama: in a series of uplifting spasms the Rocky Mountains were formed, directing the Red Deer River and its tributaries eastward. Their waters finally cut into the sedimentary rocks and—with the assistance of glaciation, wind, rain and frost—laid bare these valley walls and exposed the story of their formation. This endless erosion continues today.

In Drumheller, at the heart of the Valley of the Dinosaurs, an 18-foot-high replica of the dinosaur *Tyrannosaurus* guards the south bank of the Red Deer River. The 30-mile Dinosaur Trail leads out of Drumheller on the east side of the Red Deer and returns to the city along the west side. It first climbs to a lookout at the edge of Horsethief Canyon, affectionately known as "the little Grand Canyon."

From here are seen sandstone outcrops, hoodoos, multicolored layers of rock. Now the trail drops again, then skirts oil and wheat country. The river crossing is on the tiny Munson car ferry, formerly called the Blériot ferry after a farmer who was breaking sod here while his famous brother Louis Blériot was piloting the first aircraft over the English Channel in July 1909. Near Drumheller, toward the end of the trail, is Prehistoric Parks, where 20 steel-and-concrete life-size dinosaur replicas are displayed.

Man's fascination with the Age of the Dinosaurs continues as each new generation seeks to add to its knowledge of the long-ago. In the Valley of the Dinosaurs, in the beautiful Red Deer Badlands, this generation has a superb opportunity to do that.

The flowing lines of weathered sandstone in the Red Deer Badlands: left—a grotesque hoodoo near Willow Creek; right—a rounded ridge snaking along the valley floor.

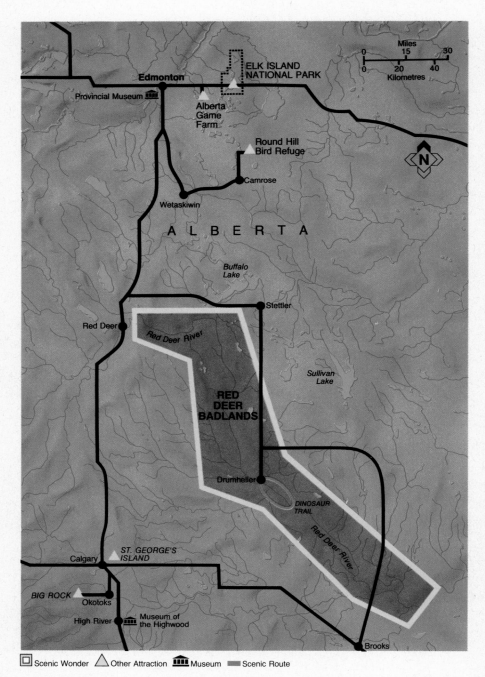

Scenic Wonder △ Other Attraction 🏛 Museum ▬ Scenic Route

OTHER ATTRACTIONS

Yaks and a Train of Erratics

Alberta Game Farm Grizzly bears from the Swan Hills of northern Alberta, believed descended from the long-extinct plains grizzly, are among the rare creatures at this farm near Edmonton. Others include a pair of Przewalski's horses (once thought extinct) and some of the few hundred remaining Père David's deer. Also among the more than 4,000 mammals in the 1,500-acre sanctuary are Chinese water deer, mountain gorillas, purebred Chilean vicunas, Tibetan yaks, white rhinoceros, giraffes, Siberian tigers and cheetahs. The farm is run by Al Oeming, a zoologist renowned for his work with animals and the introduction of foreign species to Alberta. There are rolling meadows, bush, muskeg, ponds, and a 1½-mile-long lake (with freshwater seals from Russia's Lake Baikal).

Animals threatened with extinction in their own parts of the world have adjusted to the often harsh Alberta climate despite being kept in unheated (though insulated) shelters.

Big Rock This giant, as big as an ocean freighter, juts from the prairie five miles west of Okotoks—the biggest rock among thousands in a 400-mile chain called the Foothills Erratics Train. According to one theory, the train was caused by a rock slide onto a moving glacier; as it melted, the rocks dropped in its wake. Although this train in the shadow of the Rockies is at least 10,000 years old, it is gradually losing its distinctive identity. Weathering and erosion have split Big Rock; other erratics have been buried or shattered in the course of construction projects.

Elk Island National Park Wood bison, a buffalo species once close to extinction, can be seen in an isolated area of the 75-square-mile park. Some 400 plains bison and 500 elk also graze on the undulating terrain. Waterfowl and migrating songbirds nest in sloughs and marshes.

Museum of the Highwood In this one time railway station at High River is an exhibit that records the geological history of the area. Rocks, fossils, petrified wood, coal, the tooth of a mammoth and parts of a dinosaur skeleton are arranged in time sequence.

Provincial Museum Embedded in the Tyndall, Man., limestone of its exterior walls are fossils of creatures that lived some 445 million years ago in a shallow sea in what is now southern Manitoba. In the museum's natural history section are Alberta birds, mammals, minerals, fossils and plants.

Round Hill Bird Refuge Canada geese and mallard ducks nest here. This privately-owned, 640-acre refuge and a small museum are open to the public.

St. George's Island Forty-six life-size statues of dinosaurs common in the area millions of years ago are scattered in lifelike settings throughout Dinosaur Park. One is of a 32-foot-high brontosaurus which weighed 120 tons. The fossils and bones of these creatures are exhibited at two small museums. The nearby Calgary Zoo has more than 350 animal species.

Dinosaur fossils are usually found in terrain such as the Red Deer Badlands. The Red Deer River and its tributaries created the 400-foot-deep valley, exposing the multicolored rock layers and their fossil treasures.

During a period that started some 80 million years ago—and lasted some 17 million years—the interior plains of North America rose and sank several times as tremendous geological forces moved the entire continent. During most of this period an inland sea stretched from the Arctic Ocean to the Gulf of Mexico. Along its ever-changing shores were wet lowlands and subtropical forests. Here dinosaurs thrived.

Monsters That Roamed the Subtropical West

Where now there are rolling foothills and plains just east of the Rockies, there once were low coastal plains and vast swampy deltas at the edge of a shallow inland sea. Rivers and streams that flowed east from the still-forming Rockies dumped countless billions of tons of sediment onto the plains and swamps and into the sea.

The subtropical climate of these times (more than 63 million years ago) fostered North America's first flowering plants and supported giant redwoods, cypresses, cycads (palm-like trees) and ferns. The lush vegetation nurtured great plant-eating dinosaurs,

which in turn were food for their fearsome flesh-eating cousins.

The steep bluffs and furrowed gullies of the Red Deer River valley are what remain of one part of that flooded land—the eroded beds of ancient lakes, lagoons and floodplains, long since turned to rock. Fossil remains of prehistoric creatures preserved within these ancient formations enable scientists to describe accurately what many of the dinosaur species looked like.

Albertosaurus was a ferocious meat-eater with three-foot jaws and four-inch teeth. It attacked smaller dinosaurs.

The finding of this skull enabled scientists to determine what **Pachyrhinosaurus** looked like. One of the least-known horned dinosaurs, this 10-to-12-ton monster had a huge bone along its nose, probably covered with thick hide. The bone was used as a battering ram and for pushing trees while feeding.

The skin imprint immediately below is possibly that of **Chasmosaurus.** It was first preserved in mud that later turned to ironstone. Bottom: Duck-billed dinosaur tracks found along the Peace River in Alberta are 25 inches long and 25 inches wide.

Hadrosaurs (also called duck-billed dinosaurs because of their snouts) were the most common dinosaurs in the area where the Red Deer now flows. The skeleton of one duckbill, **Edmontosaurus** (right), is 8 feet high and 30 feet long and weighs one ton. It probably supported a four-to-five-ton body (above), about the size of a bus.

This skeleton (left) of **Lambeosaurus** (a duck-billed dinosaur) was discovered near Manyberries, Alta. The plant eater's carcass was covered by soft sediments before the skeleton could be damaged. The hollow crest on its head (illustration below) might have increased the creature's sense of smell or hearing or served as a sounding chamber, enabling it to project its voice.

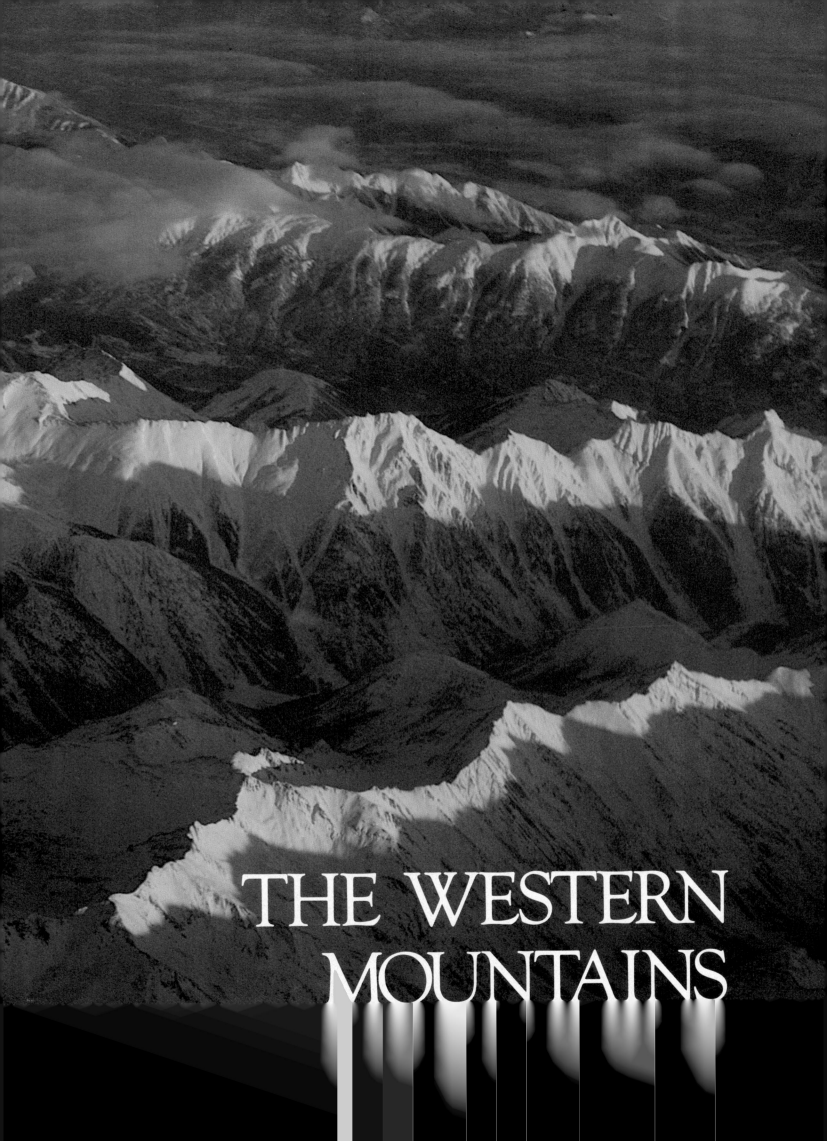

THE WESTERN MOUNTAINS

The Mighty Barrier, Aloof and Majestic

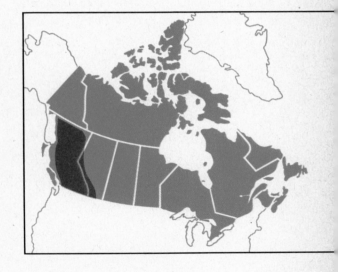

Few regions on earth match Canada's Western Mountains in magnificence, variety and wild extremes. In this mighty barrier between the Prairies and the Pacific are some of the country's wettest and driest regions, some of the coldest and some of the hottest. To many Canadians the Western Mountains are simply the Rockies. But other great chains combine with the Rockies to form a *world* of mountains that stretches some 1,500 miles northwest from the United States border and is as much as 400 miles wide. The Columbia Mountains, the Skeenas, the Ominecas, the Cassiars, the Coast Mountains . . . in and among them are deep canyons, broad valleys, dense forests, major rivers. There are huge ice fields and glaciers and the ranchland of the Cariboo and Chilcotin plateaus. There are dry regions of cactus and sagebrush such as those along the Similkameen River. Visiting the Western Mountains is sometimes not easy, for the mountain barrier is formidable and most highways and railway tracks follow the great river and valley systems. But engineers often have been forced to drape their miniscule ribbons of asphalt and steel along mountain flanks exposed to avalanche and rockslide. And sometimes, as if to remind man of his frailty, a mountain has shrugged and a highway or a rail line or a town has been obliterated. Man, in his own little way, exploits and marvels. The mountains, in all their aloof majesty, remain dominant.

Opposite: *Yoho National Park.*
Preceding pages: *A "land of shining mountains."*

Shining Mountains, Deep, Narrow Lakes Are Nature's Record of a Violent History

In less than half a mile the slow, rolling hills of the prairie give way to glittering mountains whose peaks soar to 8,000 and 9,000 feet. Here, slung along the eastern slope of the Rockies in the southwest corner of Alberta, is Waterton Lakes National Park, a 203-square-mile sanctuary for huge old spruce and fir—and one of Canada's most splendid collections of wildlife.

This "land of shining mountains" is thought to have been inhabited almost continuously for 10,000 years. Mild winters, broad grasslands, nearby passes and—at one time—huge herds of buffalo made it a pleasant land for Indian and white man alike. Until relatively recent times it was a stronghold of the Blackfoot. Whites have named many of its features: Hellroaring Creek, Lost Horse Creek, Ruby Ridge . . .

Traces of oil were found in 1886 in Lineham Creek, near the present town of Waterton Park. Alberta's first oil well, with a daily output of 300 barrels, was drilled there a few years later. In 1895, as settlers became numerous, the area was preserved and protected as a national park. In 1932 it was linked to Glacier National Park in Montana to create Waterton-Glacier International Peace Park.

The valley of the Waterton Lakes has some 60 ar-

Waterton Park townsite, at Bosporus Strait.

245

cheological sites; a tributary valley, the Blakiston Valley, has an estimated 200. All date back thousands of years to when Kutenai and Flathead Indians hunted with spears and bows and arrows. Today, within the park, hunting is banned and the relatively few settlers live in the picturesque town of Waterton Park, built on a fan-shaped delta deposited by Cameron Creek.

The town seems incongruous. Surrounded by an awesome wilderness and mountains millions of years old, it rises as a symbol of modernization, with hotels, motels, cabins, camping grounds and an abundance of recreational facilities. The steamer *International* takes tourists down the seven-mile length of Upper Waterton Lake—which straddles the Canada-U.S. border—to

Alberta and Montana Rotary clubs proposed in 1931 that Waterton and Glacier national parks be joined. The following year they became the world's first international peace park.

Goathaunt Ranger Station in Glacier Park. The three Waterton Lakes, which separate the Lewis and Clark mountain ranges, are linked by straits called Bosporus and Dardanelles. Upper Waterton, the largest lake, is

nearly 500 feet deep in places. To the north are Middle and Lower Waterton Lakes.

Vimy Peak (7,825 feet), opposite the town, dominates the surrounding landscape. Its mass, like many mountains in this region, is a complex configuration of gray, red, green and purplish hues. Vimy is an "upside-down" mountain, built by a great overthrust fault that affected the eastern slopes of the Continental Divide. It folded some mountains so that older sedimentary rocks overrode more recent formations. Mount Crandell (7,812 feet), north of the town, is similar.

The area around the Waterton Lakes has a violent geological history. More than a billion years ago it was covered by a vast inland sea. Layers of sediment more than a mile thick were thrust upward 900 million years later, sculpted by the elements and colored by the passing of time. The sharp peaks, narrow ridges and interlocked U-shaped valleys are the result of water erosion followed by glaciation. Cirques, tarns, waterfalls and hanging valleys are other marks of the glaciers.

The highest peak is in the northwest section of the park: Mount Blakiston (9,600 feet), named after Lt. Thomas Blakiston, said to have discovered the lakes while with the Palliser Expedition in 1858.

The area has changed little since then. It is a land of profound, elemental silence disturbed only, perhaps, by the haunting call of a loon or the quicksilver passage of a trout in the moonlight.

Because it embraces both prairie and mountain, Waterton Lakes National Park is alive with a fascinating range of plant life. The lowlands are carpeted with large-flowered gaillardiae, pasqueflowers and double windflowers and wild roses and geraniums of brilliant pinks and purples. The lower mountain levels are ablaze with false hellebores, yellow columbines, avalanche lilies, Jacob's ladder, white asters—and an assortment of bearberry, silverberry, dogwood, juniper, Saskatoon and chokecherry.

Most trees are evergreens. Engelmann spruce, alpine fir and mountain ash are common in the higher reaches; at lower altitudes are Douglas fir, lodgepole pine, limber pine and white spruce. A hybrid of Engelmann spruce and white spruce is found throughout the park. Near the prairie region are trembling aspen, paper birch, cottonwood, willow, Douglas maple and Sitka alder.

Like the plants, the animals and birds have adapted themselves to the demands and opportunities of the region. They are found principally in habitats most suitable to their survival. White-tailed deer, wary of cougars and coyotes, move stealthily across open grasslands. Beaver, muskrat and mink live around the shores of the lakes, as do marsh birds, waders and shorebirds, and herons spearing for food, swans gliding sedately.

A 1½-mile self-guiding nature trail leads through Red Rock Canyon in the northwestern part of Waterton Park.

During migration in spring and fall, there are flocks of geese and ducks.

The park waters teem with fish. Pike are found in the shallow, warmer waters of lakes; whitefish may be caught in the Waterton Lakes and the Waterton River; and several species of trout populate cold, swift-flowing waters in the area.

Many animals, preferring a combination of sun and shade, have settled near the tree line—at about 7,500 feet. Hikers watch a band of bighorn sheep on a sunny slope, or see ptarmigan, marmot, pika and ground squirrel avail themselves of profuse vegetation. Rocky Mountain goats may be spotted against the dark rock walls that provide their favorite haunts. Overhead a golden eagle watches for its food.

Some large mammals usually prefer the shade and protection offered at middle elevations by the evergreen forests. These include grizzly and black bears—which graze on lush green avalanche slopes—and moose, mule deer, elk and bighorn sheep. The community is completed by tree squirrels, ground squirrels and their natural enemies—the marten, weasel and hawk.

Toward the upper reaches of the mountains, particularly in high basins, the visitor may come upon the broken tip of a horn belonging to the bighorn ram. At mating time the rams—some weighing as much as 350 pounds—crash horns in ritualized battle. Higher still, near the snowcapped peaks, there is a calm simplicity. Animals are fewer but there is a better chance of seeing mountain goats. Tiny forget-me-nots dot the landscape and lichens and mosses cling to rock faces. High in the sky, golden eagles fly a seemingly endless patrol. Occasionally a fierce peregrine falcon makes a sudden dive at 180 miles an hour.

In winter, when violent winds sweep the snow from the ground, herds of wapiti (elk) and mule deer descend into the lower regions to feed on exposed shrubs and grasses. On cold winter evenings and during early morning, it is not unusual to see hundreds of wapiti foraging through the aspen forests along the eastern slopes of the mountains.

Most visitors follow Alberta highways 5 and 6 and enter the park from the north and east, passing a small herd of buffalo on the northern route. The buffalo are protected by law—a symbol, it seems, of determination to preserve areas such as Waterton Lakes National Park for future generations.

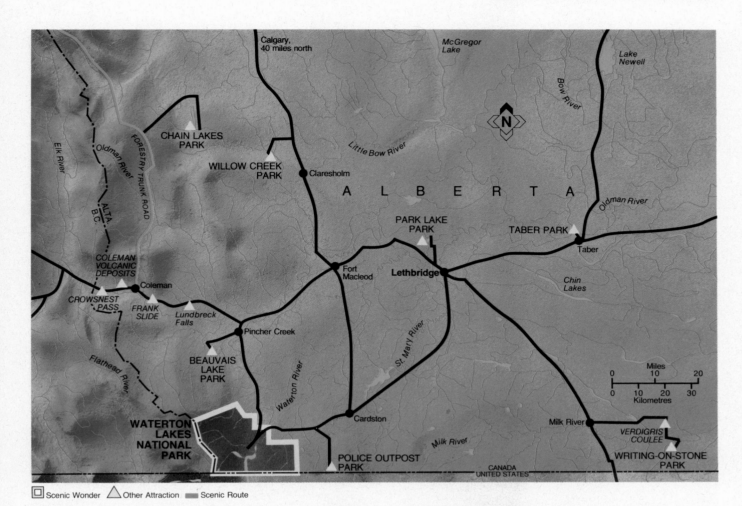

□ Scenic Wonder △ Other Attraction ▬ Scenic Route

OTHER ATTRACTIONS

The Crowsnest, the Frank Slide and Writing-On-Stone

Beauvais Lake Provincial Park Foothills merge with mountains here and the park has animals and plants common to both.

Chain Lakes Provincial Park The Rockies and the Porcupine Hills rim seven-mile-long Chain Lakes Reservoir.

Coleman Volcanic Deposits The ashes and cinders of Alberta's only major volcanic deposits are believed 100 million years old—older than the eastern ranges of the Rockies.

Crowsnest Pass This pass through the Rockies rises to 4,450 feet. Fortresslike Crowsnest Mountain (9,000 feet) guards its north side. Picture next page.

Writing-On-Stone Provincial Park is named for Indian carvings in soft sandstone formations.

Crowsnest Mountain stands in splendid isolation northwest of Coleman, Alta., and some seven miles north of the eastern end of the Crowsnest Pass. Crowsnest Lake is nearby.

Forestry Trunk Road Knifing through mainly evergreen forests, this gravel road stretches for 620 miles between the Crowsnest Pass and Goodwin, Alta. Mountain sheep and goats, moose, elk, deer and bears are common in the adjacent Rocky Mountains Forest Reserve. About 25 miles north of Coleman, in the Livingstone Mountain Range, is The Gap, a narrow gorge through which the Oldman River crashes in its wild descent to the foothills. Livingstone Falls, a quarter-mile-long rapids, is on Livingstone Creek. Plateau Mountain, its 8,200-foot summit well above the tree line, has vegetation similar to that of the Arctic tundra. Dwarf alpine flowers here, uncommon this far south, include alpine bluebell and alpine oxytrope.

Frank Slide A square-mile scar of limestone rubble in the Oldman River valley marks the Frank Slide of April 29, 1903. Some 90 million tons of rock cascaded down the slopes of Turtle Mountain in 100 seconds, killing 70 persons and covering much of the town of Frank. There is a striking view of the debris from the 3,000-foot summit.

Lundbreck Falls This 60-foot waterfall on the Crowsnest River marks the east end of the Crowsnest Pass.

Park Lake Provincial Park Park Lake, an irrigation reservoir, is a nesting area for ring-necked pheasants and Hungarian partridges. Migrating Canada geese, swans and mallards stop here.

Police Outpost Provincial Park Alberta's southernmost provincial park, the site of a North West Mounted Police post, has excellent trout fishing.

Taber Provincial Park More than 10 species of birds, including mourning doves, great horned owls and Baltimore orioles, nest in towering cottonwoods and other trees.

Verdigris Coulee A 3,000-foot-high plateau overlooks the coulee, which gets its name from a green crystalline substance along its banks.

Willow Creek Provincial Park White-tailed and mule deer, cougars, elk and moose inhabit rolling hills and coulees here.

Writing-On-Stone Provincial Park Sandstone cliffs and sentinellike hoodoos along the alkaline Milk River give much of the 1,000-acre park the look of a badland. Some 200 species of prairie flowers and grasses and several species of cactuses grow in the park. Picture preceding page.

From icy peaks to dry prairie, Waterton Lakes National Park abounds with life, each species adapted to site and climate. Above the treeline (7,300-8,800 feet) are tundra, snow and ice—and flowers vividly colored to attract the few insects at such altitudes. Heavily waxed leaves help flowers retain moisture and herbs such as moss campion huddle close to the ground, out of the wind. Some animals in this rocky zone have cloven hooves; most are thick-furred for retaining body heat. Evergreens flourish in the Hudsonian Zone's cold, dry air. Wax-coated needles minimize

water loss and since leaves are not shed there is no loss of nutrients. Trees are often stunted and twisted, battered by high winds. The heavily forested Canadian Zone provides plenty of food and cover for fur-bearing animals. Lodgepole pine and white spruce are prevalent and such broad-leaved trees as Douglas maple grow along riverbanks. Grasses predominate at Waterton's lowest levels and where grasslands give way to foothills there are stands of trembling aspen. Most animals are burrowers but mammals from higher altitudes take refuge here in winter.

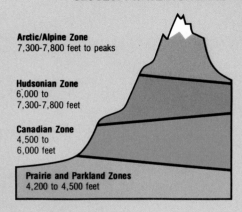

CLOSEUP: WATERTON LAKES

Arctic/Alpine Zone
7,300-7,800 feet to peaks

Hudsonian Zone
6,000 to
7,300-7,800 feet

Canadian Zone
4,500 to
6,000 feet

Prairie and Parkland Zones
4,200 to 4,500 feet

Waterton's Life Zones: From Icy Peaks to Dry Prairie

ARCTIC/ALPINE ZONE

Hoary Marmot | Mountain Goat | Golden Eagle | Arctic Poppy | Moss Campion | Lichens

HUDSONIAN ZONE

Wolverine | Moose | Bighorn Sheep | Spring Beauty | Beargrass | Alpine Larch | Engelmann Spruce | Alpine Fir

CANADIAN ZONE

Mountain Lion (Cougar) | Wapiti (Elk) | Black Bear | Queenscup | Buffalo Berry | Lupine (blue) | Douglas Maple | White Spruce | Lodgepole Pine

PRAIRIE AND PARKLAND ZONES

Meadow Vole | Columbian Ground Squirrel | Rough Fescue (grass) | Blue Grama (grass) | Indian Paintbrush | Pasque Flower (Crocus Anemone) | Trembling Aspen

251

The west side of the Creston Valley.

CRESTON VALLEY

A Green Oasis Between the Mountains, the Lovely Land Along the Kootenay

The Creston Valley, lush and lovely, nestles between the 7,000-foot peaks of the Selkirk and Purcell mountains in southeastern British Columbia. It is a cluster of neat towns, a patchwork of grainfields and orchards, an expanse of lakes and sloughs and marshes—and a key corridor on the great Pacific flyway. It is a bird watcher's delight, a main route spring and fall for thousands of geese and swans and tens of thousands of ducks. The 16,000-acre Creston Valley Wildlife Management Area—about one quarter of the valley—is one of Canada's biggest conservation areas, administered by the British Columbia Fish and Wildlife Branch and the Canadian Wildlife Service.

The watery valley, named after the town of Creston, is 20 miles long and 3 to 5 miles across, one of the few wide, flat trenches in the British Columbia interior.

Along its length wanders the Kootenay River, flowing up from the United States and into Kootenay Lake.

Waterfowl have followed the Kootenay for thousands of years, some pausing but a few days, others remaining to nest and breed in this pleasant valley. Each spring flocks of goldeneyes and teals and flights of swans and geese break formation high above the Kootenay and settle slowly into the Creston wetlands.

At the north end of the management area, abutting Kootenay Lake, are Six Mile Slough (between the west and east branches of the Kootenay River) and Duck Lake (between the east branch and Highway 3A). South of the great slough are Leach Lake and, astride Highway 3, Corn Creek Marsh. Marshes on Indian reserves south of Creston are part of the management area. So is Dale Marsh near the U.S. border.

Highway 3 crosses the valley. (Highway 3A, skirting the east side of Kootenay Lake, approaches from the north. Highway 21 is the valley's link with the United States.) The Highway 3 approach from the west—out of the Selkirks—is through one of the highest mountain passes in Canada, the 5,820-foot Kootenay Summit. Then the road follows Summit Creek as it races to the valley bottom. It goes through Corn Creek Marsh and farmland bordering the Kootenay River, then—east of the river—to Creston.

Seeing the Creston Valley bottom land as a boater or canoeist is an unforgettable experience. Six Mile Slough, Leach Lake, the Kootenay and old river channels offer adventure, day after day. Power boats are banned from Duck Lake and some shallow sloughs, but visitors can take "voyageur canoe rides" arranged by the Creston Valley Wildlife Centre, located in Corn Creek Marsh.

The valley has 58 miles of dikes. Many can be driven, others are used as walkways by hikers, naturalists, hunters, fishermen and photographers.

An observation tower overlooks 3,800-acre Duck Lake, of which 850 acres have been turned into a marsh. Water levels are controlled by dikes and pumps and the acres teem with life. An estimated 900 muskrats inhabit the Duck Lake marshes. Wood ducks occupy only 20 percent of the 450 nesting boxes erected for them; the rest have attracted everything from flickers to sparrow hawks and starlings. Wildlife in Six Mile Slough includes some 25 nesting pairs of ospreys.

The Leach Lake area is made up of a wide mud flat and shallow water surrounded by sedge and willow. Snow and Canada geese and whistling swans are seen during

Duck Lake, at the north end of the Creston management area. Visitors may spot any of 23 species of ducks, 5 of geese and 190 of other birds. On rare occasions a white pelican or a trumpeter swan is seen.

Snow geese and white whistling swans, flying a corridor of the Pacific flyway, return year after year to the Creston Valley.

the spring and fall migrations. The swans come in the thousands but only rest here before flying to nesting grounds in the Far North.

A three-mile hiking trail leads from the Summit Creek campground, eight miles west of Creston and near the edge of the management area, to a suspension bridge across the creek, and then along portions of the old Dewdney Trail to a spot overlooking Leach Lake and the valley. In August and September brilliant red Kokanee salmon ascend Summit Creek to spawn and die.

Wildlife abounds on the mountains and in the valley. On the slopes are elk, moose, bear, deer and upland game birds. White-tailed deer are common in the bottom land, often slipping along the edges of cover to feed in the surrounding farm fields, not far from the valley's ducks and geese.

The birds return year after year even though nature and man long made the valley a harsh place. Spring floodwaters again and again destroyed nests and young. Skunks and coyotes devoured eggs and killed adult birds. Nest-building materials and cover from predators were sometimes scarce because of overgrazing by cattle.

Attempts to drain the Creston plain for agriculture go back to the 1880s but it was not until the 1930s that the first successful reclamation program was started. Sixteen thousand acres were set aside for waterfowl in 1965 and three years later legislation was passed setting up the management and development area. Now marshland water levels are controlled, the cattle population is decreasing in the management area and new nesting sites are cropping up everywhere.

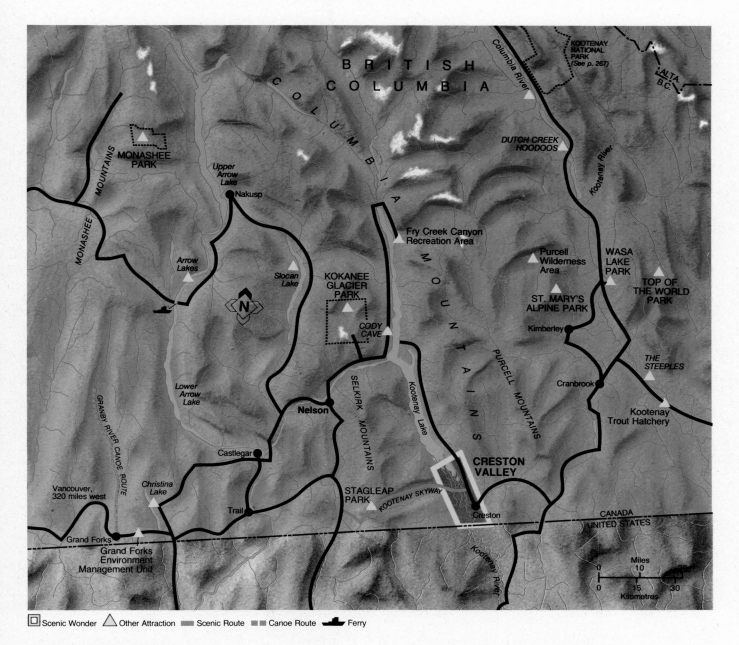

□ Scenic Wonder △ Other Attraction ▬ Scenic Route ▬ Canoe Route 🛥 Ferry

OTHER ATTRACTIONS

A Spectacular Throne Room and the Mighty Columbia

Arrow Lakes Flanked by the spectacular Selkirk and Monashee mountains, these two widenings of the Columbia River (Upper and Lower Arrow lakes) stretch 115 miles but are seldom wider than 2 miles. St. Leon Falls tumbles 20 feet into Upper Arrow Lake from St. Leon Creek. About a mile south, on the opposite side of the lake, is 100-foot-high Fosthall Creek Falls. Across the lake from the town of Deer Park a 150-foot ridge of stone forms a 60-foot-high natural bridge.

Christina Lake This alpine lake extends for 16 miles through the Christina Range of the Rocky Mountains.

Cody Cave Some 1,500 feet of passages have been charted in this cave in the Selkirk Mountains. The spectacular Throne Room has stalactites, stalagmites, calcite columns and thin, hollow formations known as soda straws. The cave was formed as Cody Creek eroded Kootenay Arch, a 150-mile-long underground limestone formation.

Columbia River From Lake Columbia in the Rockies, the Columbia winds for 1,250 miles before draining into the Pacific. In its 500 miles in Canada the river falls 1,360 feet. White water makes much of the river impassable but there are several canoe routes in the Canadian section. The Columbia is the second longest North American river draining into the Pacific (after the Yukon).

Dutch Creek Hoodoos Picture next page.

257

Dutch Creek Hoodoos *About 250 feet above Dutch Creek, these pillars of clay, sand, gravel and boulders are on private property.*

Fry Creek Canyon Recreation Area A six-mile hiking trail skirts the canyon rim, providing a breathtaking view of Fry Creek 100 feet below.

Granby River Canoe Route The 20-mile route, with some rapids, eddies and short drops, is generally safe. It passes through canyons and between the Christina and Midway ranges.

Grand Forks Environment Management Unit This 17,000-acre wildlife preserve, established to protect herds of

mule and white-tailed deer, is grazed also by cattle from nearby ranches.

Kokanee Glacier Provincial Park Half of the 100-square-mile wilderness is higher than 7,000 feet, and Kokanee Peak reaches 9,100 feet. Kokanee Glacier provides summer skiing. Cutthroat trout are caught in 400-foot-deep Kokanee Lake.

Kootenay Skyway The 42-mile highway, Canada's highest major road, reaches 5,820 feet in Stagleap Provincial

Park. It connects highways 6 and 3A (linking Creston and Salmo) and has spectacular views of the Selkirk Mountains, Kootenay Lake and Bridal Lake.

Kootenay Trout Hatchery It produces some four million rainbow, cutthroat and brook trout, char and Kokanee salmon fry each year. There are four aquariums, a model of a spawning pond and an exhibit showing fish eggs from the unfertilized stage to the hatching stage.

Monashee Provincial Park Caribou, deer, grizzly and black bear inhabit this wilderness park, accessible only by two hiking trails, each eight miles long.

Purcell Wilderness Conservancy Area Eight glaciers meet in an ice front that ends in Lake of the Hanging Glacier and pieces breaking off the 70-to-100-foot-thick wall become icebergs. The lake drains into Horsethief Creek, which has a 300-foot-high waterfall.

St. Mary's Alpine Provincial Park This 35-square-mile park has 32 lakes, four waterfalls 400 to 500 feet high and four others at least 100 feet high.

Slocan Lake A fire tower atop 7,479-foot Idaho Peak provides a view of the 22-mile-long lake.

Stagleap Provincial Park Woodland caribou can be seen in the Selkirk Mountains here.

The Steeples These six Purcell Mountain peaks are all more than 8,000 feet high. Snowcapped at the summit, forested on lower slopes, the pinnacles are inhabited by Rocky Mountain sheep and goats, elk and white-tailed deer.

Top of the World Provincial Park This park, on a 6,000-foot plateau in the Kootenay Ranges, has a variety of alpine flowers and mammals. Meadow cinquefoil, golden fleabane and Lyall's aplopappus grow in abundance; mountain goats, Rocky Mountain sheep are found and elk and mule deer are common. Limestone beds contain 500-million-year-old fossils, and a translucent rock called chert, once used by Indians in making arrowheads.

Wasa Lake Provincial Park The lake lies between the Purcell Mountains and the Hughes Range.

A bird nest may be a hastily scratched trough in the ground or an intricately woven pouch suspended by plant fibers or animal hair from a slender branch. It may be a tunnel in a cliffside or a hole in a dead tree. It may be on a narrow ledge high on a mountain, or it may float on a lake, exposed to winds and waves and rain. Nest types are almost as diverse as bird species—and birds build virtually anywhere, but especially in such multi-habitat places as the Creston Valley. Its lakes, marshes, fields, woodlands and mountains attract some 215 species.

In all species either the male or the female chooses a site for the nest. (Sometimes both make the choice.) But in most species it is usually the female that builds it. Some birds use only natural materials such as twigs, animal hair and grass; others use string, paper, plastic bags. The female instinctively follows a precise sequence, each step of the building triggering the next until the nest is complete. The simple nests of some ground-nesting species are finished in a few minutes or a few hours; the elaborate nests of other species take weeks. Because nests become infested

with parasitic mites and other insects, small birds normally construct new ones every breeding season. But such birds as ospreys and eagles use their huge nests for several years, steadily adding material until a nest may weigh several hundred pounds.

The four or five nests that a pair of wrens may build are slept in by the male. The female perches. But at mating time she selects the best nest and provides it with a soft lining of down. Some marsh wrens build extra nests—to decoy predators away from the actual nesting site.

Birds Build Almost Anywhere, With Almost Anything

The female rufous hummingbird builds a delicate nest of cottony fluff from willow tree seeds and green moss cemented with spiderweb. It is decorated with bits of leaves, bark and lichens.

Like other woodpeckers, the yellow-bellied sapsucker nests in holes in trees. It drills an opening about 1½ inches in diameter leading to a cavity about 14 inches deep and 5 inches wide. The nest is lined with wood chips.

The nest of this long-billed marsh wren—a mass of woven grass and reeds—is securely suspended among rough-textured stalks of bulrush. It is sometimes plastered with mud. The nest has a side, rather than a top, entrance.

Apparently unaware that he is a foster father, a male yellow warbler feeds a brown-headed cowbird that has hatched in the warbler's thick-walled nest of plant fibers, down, fine grasses and shredded bark. Cowbirds make no nests of their own: females lay eggs in thrush, finch, vireo and warbler nests. Unwitting foster parents often incubate the eggs and raise the cowbirds as their own.

Cliff swallows build gourd-like nests of straw-reinforced mud on cliff faces or the walls of stone or brick buildings. The narrow entrance leads to a chamber lined with dried grass and feathers.

Bank swallows bore tunnels 15 inches to 8 feet long in steep clay embankments. At the end of each tunnel, in a chamber about five inches in diameter, is a nest of straw, weed stalks and grass.

The nest of the common loon is usually a mass of decaying vegetation and is often built on a small island in a lake or marsh or atop a muskrat house. Sometimes, as in this picture, the nest is built by piling a mound of material in shallow water.

259

Peaks and Meadows, Glaciers and Lakes In Our First Park (and Most Famous)

The first and most famous of Canada's national parks is an incomparable combination of towering peaks and flower-strewn meadows, multihued lakes, massive glaciers and keen mountain air. These—and sulphur hot springs—have made Banff one of North America's most exhilarating and spectacular resort areas.

The hot springs, emerging from what now is called Sulphur Mountain, first drew Banff to national and world attention. In the winter of 1883, CPR workmen noticed wisps of what appeared to be smoke or steam rising from a hole in the ground on the south side of the Bow Valley. A light dropped down the hole revealed a cavern with a pool of steaming, sulphurous water. Filing a claim, two workmen constructed a small bathing pool for their fellows to soak in. Only when one of the two secretly sold his share to a third party and legal complications arose did the springs—and their presumed healthful properties—come to the notice of the then Department of the Interior. The upshot, in June 1887, was an Act of Parliament designating 260 square miles around the springs as "Rocky Mountains Park." It was the birth of Canada's national parks system.

But the real story of the park—now 2,564 square miles and spanning the eastern slope of the Continental Divide for 150 miles—begins much earlier. Once cov-

Bow Lake in Banff National Park.

261

ered by a vast but shallow inland sea, the area gradually underwent dramatic changes some 70 million years ago. Enormous pressures beneath the earth's crust began lifting and buckling the massive sedimentary layers that made up the old sea bottom. Like folds in a crinkling blanket mountains began to emerge from the ancient sea. Then the erosive forces of wind, water and, much later, ice carved them to their present shape.

Comparatively young, the mountains are a geologist's delight. Layer upon layer of sedimentary rock can be distinguished in the mountains that flank the roadside. Fossils are abundant in parts of the park. Geological oddities ranging from hoodoos to hanging valleys are found within a few miles of the Banff townsite.

But by far the most striking and visible of the forces that have shaped the mountains of Banff are the glaciers

that cling to the peaks and poke their tongues into the valleys. Lake Louise owes its astonishing milky-emerald color to rock flour—minute particles of suspended glacial debris. Chateau Lake Louise stands on a giant glacial moraine ridge that dams the waters in their place.

Climb the trail from the west end of Lake Louise and you can approach the Victoria Glacier itself, almost one square mile in area, up to 500 feet thick and creeping

along at the rate of 4½ inches a day in the center (less than half that speed at the edges). Take the steep but manageable trail to Lake Agnes (at 6,685 feet, about 1,100 feet above Lake Louise) and note the glacial striations in the surface of this cirque (basin), scratched and gouged by rocks or pebbles gripped in the massive bulk of passing ice.

For no less dramatic evidence of the awesome powers of glaciation, drive the seven miles to Moraine Lake, cradled in breathtaking beauty by the Valley of the Ten Peaks. Dug by glacial activity, the lake is backed by an outwash of glacial debris from the glacier on Wenkchemna Peak. Great cones of gravellike debris, or scree, pried loose by the freezing and thawing of the ice, flank the lake's southeast side. (The gigantic rock pile that dams the lake is now, however, believed by geologists to be the remains of two massive rock slides from the 7,590-foot Tower of Babel above.)

As befits Canada's oldest park, Banff offers perhaps the greatest variety of ways to reach its natural splendors. In addition to hardtop highways, more than 700 miles of trails and 2,500 campsites serve hikers and backpackers. You can raft down the churning Bow River or join a horseback trail ride for anything from one hour to several days. A gondola lift whisks you 1,300 feet up Mount Norquay or 2,300 feet up Sulphur Mountain to altitudes of more than 8,000 feet, while the Whitehorn Gondola offers a stunning view of Lake Louise, the Victoria Glacier and the Continental Divide, including Mount Assiniboine to the south—at 11,870 feet the highest mountain in the parks.

For hardier types, experienced mountain guides are available in the townsite. But park officials insist that all those venturing into the "backcountry" check in and out of wardens' offices or self-registration stations.

Whatever your bent, the natural starting place is Banff townsite itself, a bright and bustling community of some 3,200 permanent residents who—thanks to the skiing boom—now serve a year-round tourist population. Here are an information center, a museum of natural history, an archive and the park administration staff, all ready to help you orient yourself. Split by the Bow River, surrounded by its own superb mountain panorama, the townsite is no ugly duckling.

Within a mile of the Bow River bridge stands the park's most impressive human structure, the Banff Springs Hotel, gazing out on what must surely be one of the most perfectly framed scenes confronting any hostelry on earth. Far below, the glinting blue of the Bow River winds its way through a green valley, past the great

Like the buttresses of some great white cathedral, the jagged side of Mount Temple near Lake Louise.

limestone walls of Tunnel Mountain (5,500 feet) and Mount Rundle (9,838 feet).

The hot springs, which first drew tourists to the original hotel and the town, appear in six places in the Banff area, five of them on Sulphur Mountain. They can be seen—and used, for there are both warm freshwater pools and hotter mineral and steam baths—to best advantage at the Cave and Basin, one mile from the Administration Building, and the Upper Hot Springs, 2½ miles away on the slope of Sulphur Mountain.

As you venture up into the mountains of Banff—whether by car or gondola or on horseback or on foot—three distinct ecological zones unfold before you.

First is the *montane* zone, thickly clad with aspen, lodgepole pine, Douglas fir and white spruce. As you advance through the second, *subalpine* zone, the grasses give way to a dense carpet of lichens and mosses, the forest to Engelmann spruce, alpine fir, larch and whitebark pine. Now, near the timberline, the trees dwindle to stunted and twisted skeletons—the elfinwood or Krummholz. Finally, in the *alpine* zone, scoured by winter winds as harsh as in the Arctic, hardy perennials and low shrubs and patchworks of moss and lichen struggle to compete with the bare rock and the snow of the summit.

But nature has its way of enlivening even the harshest

Peyto Lake, fed by Peyto Glacier, is sky-blue in spring, then a glorious green in summer when the glacial flow is greatest.

scene. The mountain roads are alive with color—red Indian paintbrush, magenta fireweed, blue clematis and yellow columbine—and in August wild strawberries and blueberries are found along the forest trails. Turn a corner as you struggle panting up a timbered mountainside and suddenly a subalpine meadow opens out before you, soft and green, glowing with bluebells, wintergreen and mountain heather.

The mountain fauna is no less diverse than the flora. Sixty species of mammals and 225 species of birds make

their homes in the park. You are unlikely to see the park's most formidable resident, the grizzly, but black bears do visit campgrounds and garbage dumps in search of food. Stern warnings about approaching or feeding them are at every hand. A sharp eye may sight moose, elk, deer, beaver, porcupines, and marmots.

Luckiest of all Banff visitors are those who catch a glimpse of the park's handsomest and most statuesque inhabitant, the Rocky Mountain sheep. Though these bighorns habitually retreat to the high pastures in summer, they can occasionally be seen from the Trans-Canada Highway, the Mount Norquay road, or Highway 1A west of Banff.

The natural route to follow through the park is northward to Lake Louise, then up the 143-mile Icefields Parkway to Jasper. Surely one of the world's great scenic routes, the highway follows the Bow River which sets much of the character of the park's southern half and winds past Mount Eisenhower, one of Banff's most distinctive peaks. Once called Castle Mountain because of its fortresslike aspect, Mount Eisenhower rises to 9,030 feet in a series of castellated layers, culminating in a file of formidable gray peaks and towers.

At Lake Louise, 36 miles north of Banff, the Trans-Canada Highway breaks toward Field, B.C., and Yoho National Park. To get away from the trailers and tour buses that now jam Lake Louise, drive eight miles into Yoho to the fire-road leading to Lake O'Hara, "Gem of the Rockies." There you must leave your car in favor of a bus that bounces and rattles up a picturesque, steep gravel road to Lake O'Hara Lodge and a vista as majestic as anything the Rockies can offer. Utterly still, the blue-green lake and its thick collar of evergreens, more than 6,000 feet up, are surrounded by gargantuan ice-topped peaks. On trails leading out from the lake you can take a simple stroll or hike 12 grueling miles over Abbot Pass (9,558 feet) and back over the Continental Divide to the Plain of the Six Glaciers and Lake Louise.

The Icefields Parkway, now Highway 93, forges northward to the stupendous Columbia Icefield, which straddles the boundary between Banff and Jasper national parks. Up to 3,000 feet thick in places and 120 square miles in area, the ice mass acts as a giant air-conditioning unit and the air is decidedly chilly as you climb toward Sunwapta Pass.

Here you are at the very apex of the Continental Divide and a crucial point in the geology of North America. For, at the Snow Dome in the ice fields where Banff and Jasper meet, the meltwaters begin their long journey to three different oceans—the Columbia River to the Pacific; the Athabasca River to the Mackenzie and thence the Arctic; the North Saskatchewan to Lake Winnipeg, Hudson Bay and the Atlantic.

265

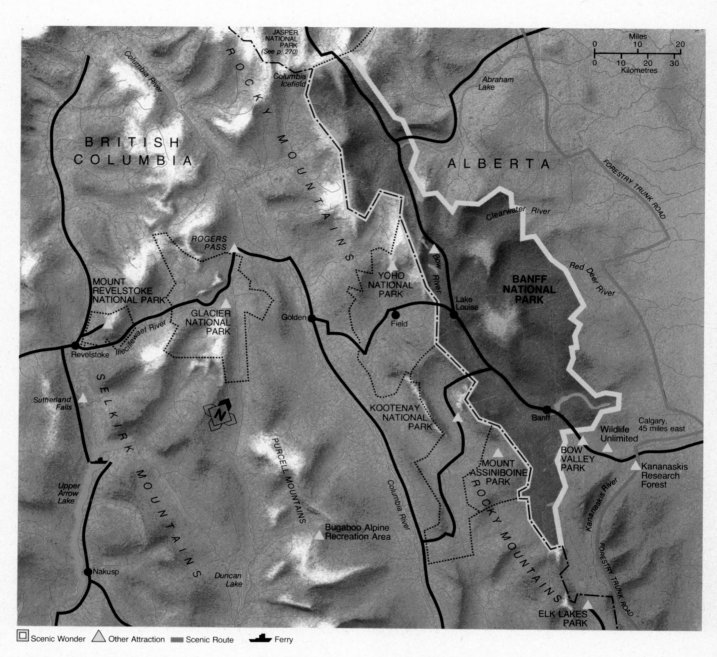

Scenic Wonder △ Other Attraction ■ Scenic Route 🚢 Ferry

OTHER ATTRACTIONS

Exciting Trails Through Mountains and Foothills

Bow River It flows for 365 miles through mountains, foothills and prairies. The river rises at 6,787-foot Bow Pass—the highest point on the Icefields Parkway between Banff and Jasper parks.

Bow Valley Provincial Park Moraines and eskers—ridges of earth and stone deposited by the last Ice Age glacier to cover the foothills—can be seen from Highway 1A that runs through the spruce- and pine-covered park.

Bugaboo Alpine Recreation Area Snafflehound, Howser and Crescent spires and Osprey Peak are among more than 20 summits higher than 9,000 feet that challenge mountain climbers in this 96-square-mile area in the northern Purcell Mountains. Access to the area is through 1½-square-mile Bugaboo Glacier Provincial Park. Hikers can take a steep, three-mile trail skirting Bugaboo Glacier to a base camp used by mountaineers.

Elk Lakes Provincial Park Meltwaters from three glaciers have formed Upper and Lower Elk lakes, good for boating and fishing for cutthroat trout and whitefish. Elk, mountain goats and grizzly bears are sometimes seen in the backcountry of this 21-square-mile park in the Front Ranges.

Forestry Trunk Road Bighorn sheep and mountain goats can be seen on ridges above Highwood Pass, the south-

ern end of the 241-mile Banff section. The road is the only continuous north-south road through Alberta's western forests. A 30-mile stretch north of High-wood Pass follows an Indian trail along the Kananaskis River. Dense pine forests blanket the lower slopes of the Kana-naskis Range to the west and the Fisher Range to the east. Eighty miles north of the Trans-Canada Highway intersection is Corkscrew Mountain, named for the zigzag path the road follows. Some 50 miles north of the mountain is the town of Nordegg, the end of the Banff section of the road. Picture this page.

Glacier National Park More than 100 glaciers crown the summits of the Purcell and Selkirk mountains, whose 105-million-year-old rocks are tens of millions of years older than the Rocky Mountain ranges to the east. Meltwaters from the glaciers spawn hundreds of alpine lakes, rivers and waterfalls. Thick forests and meadows covered with lush grasses and bright flowers are also part of the stunning scenery in the 521-square-mile park. One of several hiking trails provides spectacular views of Ille-cillewaet and Asulkan glaciers and surrounding peaks.

Kananaskis Research Forest Lodgepole pines predominate in this 23-square-mile federal experimental zone along the Kananaskis River south of Seebe. Interpretative trails show the processes of scientific forest management.

Kootenay National Park The 65-mile Banff-Windermere Parkway provides dramatic views of the snowcapped Rockies. It passes through Sinclair Canyon, whose sheer walls rise 200 feet above the highway, and 4,875-foot Sinclair Pass. The road through the 543-square-mile park skirts the Rock Wall, the almost-vertical face of the Vermilion Valley. A 70-foot waterfall at the head of Marble Canyon is fed by glacial meltwater; rock particles ground by the ice give the cascade a milky color. The canyon follows a fault in the limestone and marble rock, which has been eroded as deeply as 120 feet by Tokumm Creek. The Paint Pots, not far from the parkway, are three ponds stained bright red and yellow by large quantities of iron oxide in the springs that feed them. The waters of Radium Hot Springs seep through fissures in the earth's crust, are heated by masses of molten rock and rise to near the surface as steam. It condenses as it cools and emerges as hot water 45°C. (113°F.). Picture this page.

Mount Assiniboine Provincial Park Resembling a pyramid, 11,780-foot Mount Assiniboine dominates this 150-square-mile wilderness of mountains, glaciers, alpine meadows and lakes. Mount Assiniboine was sculptured by glacial ice that carved depressions (cirques) in its flanks. The distinctive shape—called a horn—was revealed when the glaciers melted. The mountain is known as Canada's Matterhorn. Four other peaks in the park are at least two miles above sea level, and 20 others are more than 9,000 feet high. Wapiti (elk) and golden eagles inhabit the park.

Mount Revelstoke National Park Erosion and glaciation have relentlessly chipped and carved the landscape in this 100-square-mile national park in the Selkirk Mountains. The Mountain Meadows Trail, one of several nature trails, leads past the "icebox," a permanent patch of ice protected from melting by the rock walls around it. This trail also crosses a meadow filled with such alpine flowers as Indian paintbrush, blue lupine, yellow arnica and white valerian. The turquoise water of Upper and Lower Jade lakes contrasts with the glaciers on the mountain slopes. Eva Lake appears to rest on a ledge—a few feet beyond its shore the land drops several hundred feet to a valley below.

Rogers Pass The 92-mile section of the Trans-Canada Highway between Revelstoke and Golden traverses one of the most famous mountain passes in Canada. East from Revelstoke the road winds through Mount Revelstoke National Park, following the Illecillewaet River to Glacier National Park and the highest point in the pass at 4,354 feet. Flanking the highway are the 10,000-foot peaks of the Selkirk Mountains. The average annual snowfall in the pass is 370 inches, creating huge drifts on lee slopes. The drifts often break loose, creating avalanches that strip the slopes of trees and bury sections of the road. (Concrete snowsheds cover four key sections of the highway.) Earthen dams catch or redirect smaller avalanches; rubble mounds in a checkerboard pattern dissipate the force of the tumbling tons of snow. A howitzer is often used to trigger avalanches before they become too large. Parts of the highway are closed during these dangerous periods. Summit Mountain Viewpoint, near the top of the pass, affords a splendid view of the rugged scenery of the Selkirk Mountains.

Sutherland Falls These spectacular falls in 600-acre Blanket Creek Provincial Park, 16 miles south of Revelstoke, drop a total of some 500 feet. The longest single drop is about 40 feet.

Wildlife Unlimited This 350-acre wildlife park in the pine-spruce country of the Rocky Mountain foothills has about 50 animal species—some normally seen only in the more remote areas of the mountains. Bears, Arctic and gray wolves, elk, Arctic foxes and a variety of birds of prey are kept in large enclosures.

Yoho National Park Hundreds of varieties of alpine and subalpine flowers heighten the beauty of this 507-square-mile park in the heart of the Rockies. Takakkaw Falls, 1,248 feet, is created by meltwater from the Daly Glacier. The Trans-Canada Highway through the park offers superb views of Yoho's peaks—28 of which are more than 10,000 feet. Lovely Emerald Lake, named for its deep green color, is surrounded by several snowcapped peaks. Hoodoos, 30-to-50-foot-high columns of glacial till, rise up the steep wall of Hoodoo Valley. The Kicking Horse River has carved a hole in a wall of sedimentary rock, leaving a 50-foot natural bridge. The Yoho River, milky gray with silt from Yoho Glacier, crashes into the clear Kicking Horse River.

Sinclair Canyon, barely wide enough for Sinclair Creek (which carved it) and the Banff-Windermere Parkway, is in Kootenay National Park. It forms the eastern approach to Radium Hot Springs.

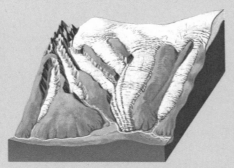

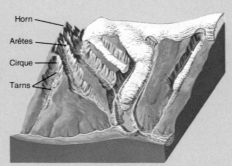

Horn
Arêtes
Cirque
Tarns

Before glaciation (left): the Rockies are rounded and scored by narrow, V-shaped, river-carved valleys. During glaciation (center): weathering and small glaciers carve cirques, depressions with vertical sides thousands of feet deep; lakes form in basins dammed by ice; lateral moraines (rock

debris) accumulate at glacier edges; as glaciers join, so do lateral moraines, becoming center (medial) moraines. After glaciation (right): valleys are U-shaped; expanded cirques have reduced the mountain peak to a sharp **horn;** other **cirques** intersect to form jagged **arêtes;** in some cirque

basins are lakes called **tarns;** tributary valleys hang above main valleys, their streams often cascading in spectacular waterfalls; lateral moraines become ridges; and an end moraine—debris deposited by the foot of a glacier—blocks a valley and creates a lake.

The Rivers of Ice That Helped Shape the Rockies

High in the mountains of Alberta, British Columbia and the Yukon are vast permanent ice fields that spawn glaciers—rivers of ice that creep (or sometimes gallop) down through the valleys, bulldozing everything

in their path. The best known and most accessible ice field in the Canadian Rockies is the 150-square-mile Columbia Icefield. It feeds the Athabasca, Saskatchewan and Columbia glaciers, as well as several smaller

tongues of ice. Glaciers, nature's most powerful tools of erosion, helped mold the Rockies into the massifs of incomparable beauty they are today. Even now they continue to alter the mountain landscapes.

The Rockies show the handiwork of many glaciers: carved peaks, jagged ridges and deeply scoured valleys.

Nurtured by the Columbia Icefield, the Athabasca Glacier is six miles long and up to 2,000 feet thick. The 250-foot-high ridge to the left of the glacier is a lateral moraine.

The summit of 11,780-foot Mount Assiniboine, Canada's "Matterhorn," was sculpted by expanding glacial cirques, which left only this semi-pyramidal tower.

Lake Louise fills a depression carved by ice that once extended the length of the valley. When the Victoria Glacier retreated it left an end moraine which dammed the meltwater from the shrinking ice.

Rock ground to a fine powder by Peyto Glacier clouds Peyto Lake in summer, giving the water its emerald-green color. Gravel and sand washed from the glacier created the delta at the head of the lake.

Takakkaw Falls plunges 1,248 feet in British Columbia's Yoho National Park. The stream that feeds the waterfall originates in the Daly Glacier and courses through a U-shaped hanging valley.

400 Miles of Trails In a Beauteous Land Along the Great Continental Divide

The summer day begins and massive wings of ice on 11,033-foot Mount Edith Cavell are tinged with the sun's scarlet. Angel Glacier seems to hover free of the dark cirque that bore it thousands of years ago and still holds it, a slowly fading prisoner of the living rock.

As the light grows stronger, pink clouds float above the teahouse below the glacier and over green alp lands sprinkled with yellow alpine buttercups and white anemones. Ranks of spruce march down through swirling mists to the brawling Astoria River, soon to be subdued in the milky Athabasca, flowing on to the Mackenzie and the Arctic Ocean.

Frost sharpens the silver profile of the mountain. At the head of the Tonquin Valley trail leading to Amethyst Lakes, it is a sparkling mantle on a packhorse. It nips the district warden's fingers as he readies his outfit for a patrol to the west boundary of Jasper National Park. But the sun warms. Frost melts to shiny dewdrops that suddenly cascade from leaf to leaf.

Mount Edith Cavell, the image of its snow-powdered head shining up from Cavell Lake, is one jewel in a mountain diadem crowning Jasper National Park. Created in 1907 at the advent of a transcontinental railway that would make it accessible to tourists, Jasper

Jasper's mountain diadem.

271

Park is 4,200 square miles of mountains, glaciers, lakes, wild rivers and some of North America's finest back-country trails.

Adjoining Banff National Park at the Columbia Icefield, Jasper Park sweeps northwest along the Continental Divide that separates Alberta and British Columbia. It is a ragged rectangle some 130 miles long and close to 54 miles across at its widest. From east to west, gradually loftier ranges rear up from the foothills of Alberta to the glacier-hung monarchs of the divide.

Jasper Lake, north of the town of Jasper, is a widening of the Athabasca River. Around it are beaches of sand and silt that were covered by water when the lake was much larger.

These mountains once formed a seabed and it is as if the great sea had heaved itself up on edge to create a more turbulent ocean of ice-capped stone.

The rivers that bisect this ancient uplift have hauntingly evocative names. They speak of an Indian culture that survived here (according to some researchers) from 10,000 years ago until the turn of the century: Athabasca (where there are reeds), Sunwapta (turbulent river), Poboktan (owl)...

Each of three entrances to the national park is guarded by sentinel mountains. The most spectacular is in Sunwapta Pass (6,675 feet) on the Icefields Parkway, 69 miles south of the town of Jasper. A wide green meadow suddenly opens on the left to a view of ice-topped Mount Athabasca and the tongue of the six-mile-long glacier below it.

Leaving the Icefields Chalet at 7,000 feet, the parkway winds down in the next four miles to the valley of the Sunwapta River, 1,500 feet lower. At Summit Viewpoint, three miles north of the ice field, forested ridges make colossal window frames for the hanging glaciers of Mount Kitchener (11,500 feet) and the Stutfield Glacier. The scenery is often enhanced by the sight of a bearded white mountain goat or a bighorn ram foraging beside the road.

Thirty-five miles from Jasper, the green Sunwapta is divided by a small pine-clad island. Swiftly the two arms are reunited in a headlong plunge through the two canyons of Sunwapta Falls. In another mile the Sunwapta adds its weight to the mighty Athabasca and 19 miles farther on the combined waters hurtle 75 feet over Athabasca Falls. The river cascades over the rainbow-hung brink and leaves the canyon in a scene like a Chinese painting, past limestone promontories, under misty ledges where lime-green moss and small evergreens cling, then down between smooth portals of stone that open on the widening flood below.

Farther north, 3.5 miles from Jasper, an aerial tramway on The Whistlers (8,085 feet) carries travelers to a stunning view of the townsite and some 40 lakes that dot the broad valley of the Athabasca River.

Jasper, the park headquarters, is a town of 4,000 permanent residents. It is on the CN main line and the Yellowhead Highway; the nearest commercial airport is at Hinton, 40 miles east. Near Jasper is The Whistlers Campground, the biggest of 11 campgrounds in the park. It has spaces for more than 500 tents and some 250 trailers. From Jasper it is a 50-mile drive to the highest peak in the Canadian Rockies, 12,972-foot Mount Robson. Twenty-eight miles southeast of Jasper is emerald-green Maligne Lake, surrounded by six 10,000-foot peaks. A launch makes a nine-mile trip up the lake, stopping at a viewpoint on Spirit Island.

Hikers and backpackers take to the wilderness for days or weeks at a time on Jasper Park's more than 400 miles of trails. There are horses and pony guides for day and overnight trips, and mountaineering guides for hikers who want to get off the trails. Climbers and overnight trippers must register, to ensure that the warden rescue team has vital information when people are lost or injured in the mountains.

Animals, many of which are seen along the highway in spring and fall, are a main Jasper Park attraction, to be

An aerial tramway on The Whistlers (8,085 feet) carries sightseers to this stunning view of Jasper town and the broad valley of the Athabasca River.

seen and photographed but not fed. Mule deer feed among jack pine and poplar in the montane zone of the major valleys. Moose are sometimes observed in the shallow waters of Medicine Lake, 13 miles from Jasper on the Maligne Lake road. Wapiti (elk) are at home in mule-deer country and in the subalpine meadows favored by bighorn sheep. The sheep share their range's upper limits with mountain goats, but are left below when the goats climb to thin ledges shared only with eagles. Rarest of all sights in the park is a glimpse of mountain caribou. A small herd ranges the headwaters of Maligne Lake in high alpine country.

Grizzly and black bears roam the backcountry. Some

273

The three peaks at the center of this picture are those of Mount Fryatt, 11,026 feet at its highest. On the right is 9,550-foot Whirlpool Peak.

are occasionally seen along the highway and in the campgrounds, where they can be a menace to anyone foolish enough to feed them. The grizzly is the true monarch of the mountains. A distant sight of a mature "silvertip" playing with her cubs in a high meadow is a rare but cherished memory for lucky backpackers.

The chipmunk is a frequent camp visitor. So is the Canada jay or *wisagat-chak*—that white men call whiskey jack. If a gray phantom steals from your table and flies up into a pine to cackle about it, that will be the jay.

Columbian ground squirrels, mistakenly called gophers, will struggle into an open rucksack for what's left of your lunch. Keep it out of their reach—for the sake of the squirrels' precarious metabolism. High-

country travelers see and hear the hoary marmot, a badger-sized yellow rodent with a distinctive call like a policeman's whistle.

The music of Jasper Park in spring is the hollow drumming of a male grouse dusting his fancy feathers. As the sun gets warmer, and avalanches high on the mountainsides testify to the weakening grip of the snow, hummingbirds thrum the flower-scented air with iridescent wings, and robins, nuthatches and chickadees celebrate the season. Autumn's wildest music is the far-off bugling of bull elk rounding up their hinds for the autumn rut. In winter, when evergreens hang heavy in the snowy shadow of Mount Edith Cavell, coyotes raise their high-pitched howl and wolves their deeper chorus. Season after season, year after year, Jasper National Park echoes to the sounds of wild creatures, a song that is their endless celebration of survival.

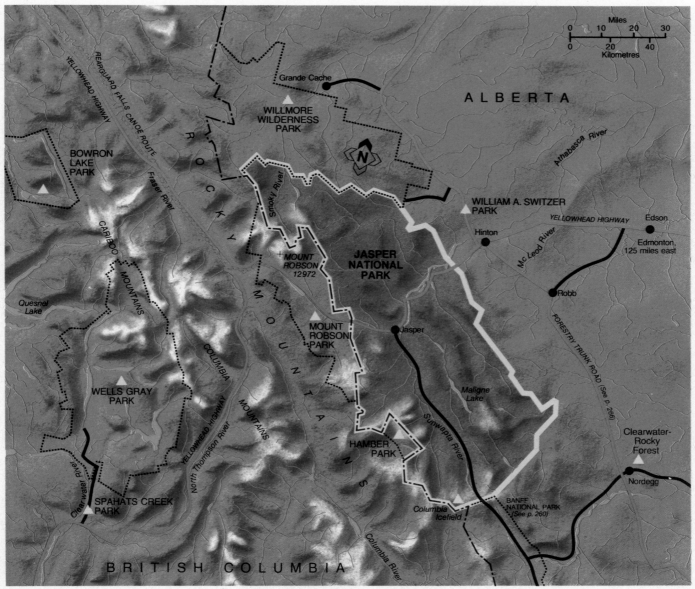

Scenic Wonder ▲ Other Attraction ■■ Scenic Route ■ ■ Hiking Trail or Canoe Route

OTHER ATTRACTIONS

The Columbia Icefield and the Rockies' Highest Peak

Bowron Lake Provincial Park A 73-mile canoe route—along six lakes and two rivers—follows the roughly rectangular perimeter of this 304,000-acre park in the Cariboo Mountains.

Clearwater-Rocky Forest Some 100 wild horses, thought to be the descendants of tame runaways, roam the 6,837-square-mile forest.

Columbia Icefield Straddling the Continental Divide, the icefield feeds river systems that flow into three oceans—the Athabasca to the Arctic, the Columbia to the Pacific and the North Saskatchewan to the Atlantic via Hudson Bay. The most accessible of the many glaciers that jut from the main body of the icefield is the Athabasca Glacier, which can be reached from the Icefields Parkway. Snowmobile tours on the glacier (that would be discontinued if ice conditions deteriorated) give visitors a close look at mill holes (deep, circular holes) and crevasses (long, nearly vertical

fissures). Athabasca Glacier, receding at about 24 feet a year, may begin to advance by 1990, scientists estimate.

Hamber Provincial Park A 14-mile trail from Sunwapta Falls in Jasper National Park is the only access to these 60,000 acres of mountain woodland. It has wilderness camping.

Mount Robson Provincial Park Here are the highest peak in the Canadian Rockies, the source of British Colum-

Lake McArthur, in Yoho National Park (see p. 268) in British Columbia, is fed by a glacier flowing off 10,878-foot Mount Biddle.

bia's longest river, and the deepest cave in Canada. A 14-mile trail runs from the Yellowhead Highway through the Valley of a Thousand Falls to Berg Lake at the base of 12,972-foot Mount Robson. At the southern tip of the 848-square-mile park are the headwaters of the Fraser River. Arctomys Cave, surveyed at a depth of 1,715 feet, lies in a valley east of Mount Robson. The 8,000-foot-long passage to the bottom is difficult even for experienced cavers.

Rearguard Falls Canoe Route More than 800 miles from the mouth of the Fraser, Rearguard Falls is the farthest east that Pacific salmon spawn. The 280-mile downstream trip to Prince George takes seven days.

Spahats Creek Provincial Park Slicing through an ancient lava flow, Spahats Creek has created a narrow canyon 400 feet deep.

Wells Gray Provincial Park Among many waterfalls in the 2,000-square-mile park are 450-foot Helmcken Falls and 70-foot Canim Falls. Trails lead to lava beds at Kostal Lake and the alpine meadows of Battle Mountain. A branch from an eight-mile trail along the Murtle River leads to the top of an extinct volcano. Clearwater and Azure lakes are connected by the Clearwater River and form a 64-mile canoe route.

William A. Switzer Provincial Park Five lakes linked by Jarvis Creek provide almost 20 miles of canoeing interrupted by only two portages.

Willmore Wilderness Park Alberta's largest wilderness area (1,075 square miles) is accessible from logging roads.

Yellowhead Highway The 1,867-mile highway is named for Tête Jaune (Yellow Head), an Indian trapper and guide whose real name was Pierre Hatsinaton. It extends from Portage la Prairie, Man., into British Columbia, splitting at Tête Jaune Cache. One branch leads southwest to Kamloops, the other west and north to Prince Rupert. The highway reaches its highest point—3,675 feet—in the Yellowhead Pass on the B.C.-Alberta border.

Ripples in the bed of an ancient inland sea became ripples of sediment when the shallow water slowly dried up—then ripples of rock as, over millions of years, the sediment turned to stone. Thrust upward by the emerging Rockies, the seabed is now atop a mountain in Jasper Park.

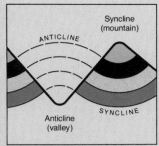

Layers of sedimentary rock folded like a ∪ are called synclines; those like a ∩ are termed anticlines. Synclines tend to form mountains. Anticlines, because the rock at the top of the fold is stretched and cracked, are easily eroded to create valleys. Cascade Mountain in Banff National Park shows both.

From an Ancient Seabed, the Lofty Peaks of the Rockies

150 MILLION YEARS AGO

Where now the Rockies tower there was a vast trough and a great inland sea in which sediment had been accumulating for 500 million years. The weight of the sedimentary layers depressed the sea floor—but no faster than the sediment buildup, so the sea was always shallow. Eventually, the flat layers solidified into rock.

105 MILLION YEARS AGO

Buckling, fracturing and metamorphism (compacting) of rocks was accompanied by volcanic activity in what now is coastal British Columbia. As this mountain-building "belt" pushed east, some strata in the Rockies folded and broke—and some of the oldest were thrust up over younger rock, finally to be eroded and to form the main (western) ranges of the Rockies. Rivers carried debris east from the eroding highland and deposited it on broad plains and swamps.

50 MILLION YEARS AGO

Millions of years of erosion had continued to reshape the land. The sea had once more submerged the plains to the east. Now, with new pressure from the west, the already-built main ranges were pushed east across the underlying resistant "basement." Layers of sedimentary rock to the east were compressed and folded. Many were bent and broken and pushed upward along steep, west-dipping faults. Some layers on the west side rode over the younger rocks to the east.

2 MILLION YEARS AGO

Starting about 10 million years ago, extensive regional uplift of the land gave streams steeper gradients. River erosion and weathering became more active, carving greater relief into the landscape. The "modern" relief was further modified by Ice Age glaciers (p. 269), up to about 10,000 years ago.

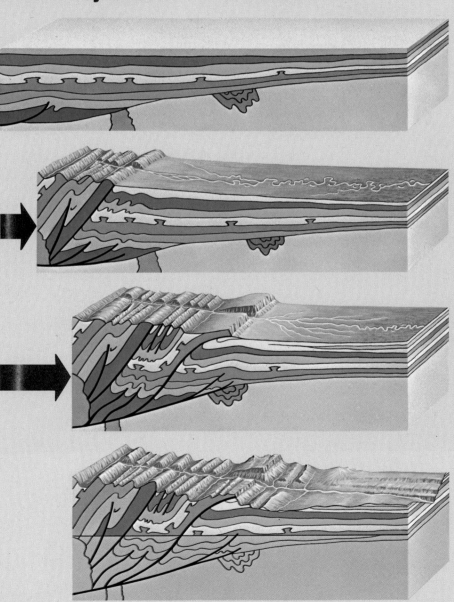

277

The Spectrum Range.

MOUNT EDZIZA PROVINCIAL PARK

Lava and Cinder a Mile Thick
In a Unique Volcanic Wilderness

A great volcanic peak, part of a spectacular mountain range, is the showpiece of Mount Edziza Provincial Park in northwestern British Columbia. Mount Edziza (9,143 feet) is surrounded by lava and cinder a mile thick—and by huge cinder cones and extensive pumice fields. The rest of the Spectrum Range is deeply eroded and richly stained by mineral salt: the mountains are splashed with orange and red and

yellow, and tinted with gray and tan and mauve.

The 900-square-mile park, south of the Stikine River and west of the Stewart-Cassiar Road (Highway 37), was established in 1972 to preserve a unique volcanic wilderness. Geologists estimate that volcanic action started here four million years ago. Mount Edziza, born probably one million years ago, has erupted at roughly thousand-year intervals ever since.

The shattered surface of a debris-covered glacier on Mount Edziza resembles an eerie mountain landscape when photographed through a telephoto lens. But the "peaks" are only two or three feet high.

The latest eruption in the area was of Eve Cone, north of Mount Edziza, perhaps less than 200 years ago. At about the turn of the century, an old Tahltan Indian said she remembered a time of thunder louder than a thousand thunderstorms, a time when the earth shook,

the skies turned red and clouds of ash blotted out the sun. This was probably an eruption of Eve Cone.

Mount Edziza reigns some 4,000 feet above the Tahltan Highland that it created, a rugged wasteland of lava and cinder 25 miles long, 10 miles across. Its main, two-mile-wide crater holds a melting snowfield.

The volcanic veneer that spills over the plateau is virtually unchanged since Edziza's latest eruption. Only

mosses and lichens grow on the lava plains that surround the peak.

The cinder cones around the peak were formed by eruption on the plateau itself. Eve Cone is 500 feet high, the rim of its rust-colored 1,300-foot-wide crater almost perfectly circular. To the south are Cocoa Crater (500 feet high) and the slightly bigger Coffee Crater.

Mount Edziza, relatively young, has not been sub-

jected to the glacial erosion that shaped the older mountains in the Spectrum Range. They lie south of Raspberry Pass, which crosses the middle of the park. There the steep mountainsides seem awash in watercolors, a blend of the bright and the subdued, the pale and the vivid. At the valley bottoms all these colors of the Spectrums fade into the greens of stunted trees that are nourished by meltwaters from the mountain crests.

Deep valleys flank the park on the west and the north. Mess Creek, the western boundary, once discharged glacial ice. It cut as much as 2,500 feet down into the volcanic residue, exposing clues to the geological history of the plateau. Water action through the centuries has gouged out the Grand Canyon of the Stikine River, part of which marks the northern boundary of the park. The canyon walls in places are 600 feet high.

The lichen-covered West Escarpment, south of the barren terrain surrounding Eve Cone, supports such large mammals as Stone sheep, caribou and mountain goats. In the boreal forest on the fringe of the Tahltan Highland are grizzly bears, timber wolves and moose. Lakes along the east side of the park—Mowdade, Kakiddi and Nuttlude—and Buckley Lake in the north all contain rainbow trout.

One of the two roads that approach the park (none enters it) is along the northern edge of the Stikine canyon—the unpaved road that winds, climbs and dips for some 60 miles between Dease Lake and Telegraph Creek. The other is the Stewart-Cassiar Road (Highway 37), well to the east of the park.

With no road access to Edziza, visitors must enter the park on foot (or fly in by plane or helicopter from Eddontenajon, Dease Lake or Telegraph Creek). There are only two trails. From the settlement of Iskut, the Telegraph Trail runs west through Raspberry Pass to Mess Creek, then north to Telegraph Creek. The other trail, about 40 miles long, runs east from Telegraph Creek across the north part of the park to Buckley Lake and then along the Klastline River. Neither trail approaches the park's most spectacular sights. The most brilliantly hued of the Spectrums rise 8 to 10 miles south of the Telegraph Trail. Mount Edziza is 16 miles north of it. Neither trail is suitable for any but experienced outdoorsmen.

Erosion shaped these spires from rock spewed by the Edziza volcano. Pillow lavas (below) were lava globs that cooled in water. Crusts formed, then cooled and cracked; molten lava escaped, creating pillow lavas. Slower cooling inside the globs caused the bands seen here.

Most of the relatively few persons who have invaded the Mount Edziza wilderness have been not vacationers but geologists, volcanologists and survey and mapping crews.

Among the first were the men who in 1899-1901—at the time of the Klondike gold rush—built a telegraph line that linked New Westminster, B.C., and Dawson in the Yukon. The line was in operation until 1940. Some traces of the telegraph right-of-way still exist along the Telegraph Trail and the trail up the east side of Mess Creek.

Protected by its very remoteness, Mount Edziza Provincial Park seems likely to remain largely inaccessible for many years to come, its wild beauty preserved in a setting little altered since the forces of nature created it one million years ago.

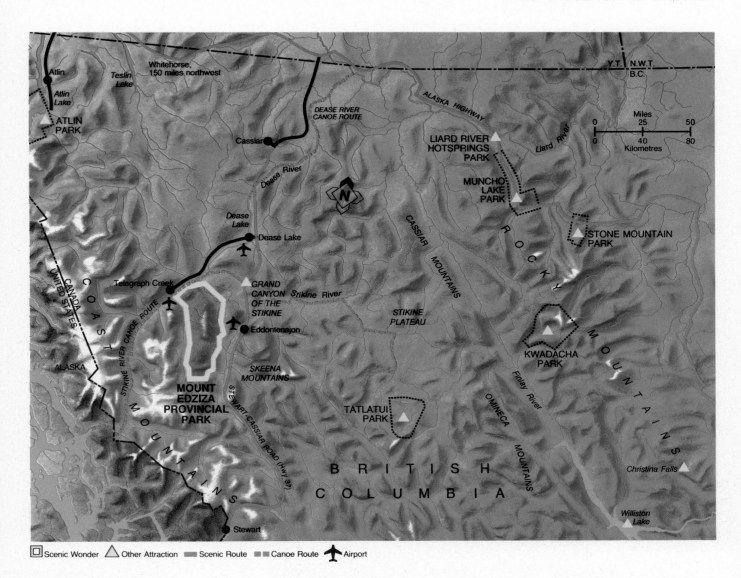

□ Scenic Wonder △ Other Attraction ▬ Scenic Route ▬ Canoe Route ✈ Airport

OTHER ATTRACTIONS

Roads to the North—and a Teetering Rock

Alaska Highway This rugged 1,523-mile route (all but 302 miles are in Canada) runs between Dawson Creek, B.C., (Mile '0') and Fairbanks, Alaska, crossing the British Columbia-Yukon border five times. At Mile 147 is Pink Mountain, where rocks are tinged pink by traces of iron. The mountain has several hiking and climbing trails. Trutch Mountain (Mile 190) gives an excellent view of the Rockies and the Minaker River valley. Steamboat Mountain (Mile 353) and Indian Head Mountain, eight miles farther, were named for their distinctive shapes. Nearby is Teetering

Muncho Lake, 730 feet deep, is surrounded by 7,000-foot Rocky Mountain peaks.

Rock, a rock (about a city block square and about as high as a three-storey building) that appears about to fall from its smaller eroded base. Tour buses make two-day trips from Dawson Creek to Whitehorse (Mile 918). In Canada, less than 400 miles of the all-weather, year-round highway is paved.

Atlin Provincial Park In the rugged southwest of the park are peaks of the Coast and Boundary ranges and glacier-filled valleys and *nunataks*— isolated peaks surrounded by glacial ice. Picture this page.

Christina Falls A narrow, 220-foot cataract on the Graham River.

Dease River Canoe Route Only two portages interrupt the 165-mile canoe journey between Dease Lake and the Liard River. For about 100 miles the 7,000-foot peaks of the Cassiar Mountains tower over the Dease. Then it bends to cross the Liard Plain lowlands.

Grand Canyon of the Stikine The Stikine River gouged this spectacular, 60-mile-long canyon through the Stikine Plateau. The canyon is between

the Stewart-Cassiar Road bridge across the Stikine River and a point about five miles upstream from the settlement of Telegraph Creek. The steep walls of the rugged canyon are tinted gray, green, pink and purple by various minerals in the rock walls.

Kwadacha Provincial Park Straddling the Continental Divide, the park is surrounded by the towering peaks of the Rockies, including 9,550-foot Mount Lloyd George. The Kwadacha River drains the Lloyd George Icefield, the largest in the northern Rockies.

Liard River Hotsprings Provincial Park Six hot springs that bubble through the ground in a swampy area are reached by a boardwalk. Temperatures reach 49°C. (120°F.) in a large mineral pool that has been outfitted to allow bathing. Luxuriant vegetation—monkey flowers, bog spruce and goldenrod—wreathes the swamp.

Muncho Lake Provincial Park Stone sheep, caribou, goats and moose frequent a small area where minerals such as calcium and magnesium are exposed in loamy soil. The animals can be photo-

graphed at short range. Muncho Lake picture preceding page.

Stewart-Cassiar Road (Hwy 37) This 350-mile road crosses mainly wilderness country between Stewart and Cassiar. Passing through only two small settlements—Eddontenajon and Dease Lake—the route provides magnificent views of the Coast Mountains and the Stikine Plateau. It skirts the edge of Bear Glacier (part of the 300-square-mile Cambria Icefield) and follows the Bell-Irving River for 30 miles. There are campsites along the route.

Stikine River Canoe Route The start of this 285-mile route to Wrangell, Alaska—with five portages—is at Tuaton Lake and is accessible only by float plane, although there are places along the route where it can be reached by canoe. The Stikine flows through barren country laced with huge rock outcrops until it reaches the Chukachida River, where there is an excellent view of Mount McNamara (8,278 feet) and Mount Albert Dease (7,670 feet). Below the Pitman River is Goat Canyon, half a mile long with vertical, 120-foot walls. At the Stewart-Cassiar Road bridge, canoes must be taken from the water and transported 58 miles to Telegraph Creek. The last 115 miles of the route provide spectacular views of the Coast Mountains. Glacial features such as moraines and eskers are common along the shores of the river in this region.

Stone Mountain Provincial Park Pillar-like stone formations near Summit Lake, where the Alaska Highway reaches its highest point (4,218 feet).

Tatlatui Provincial Park The modest peaks and ridges of the Tatlatui Range of the Skeena Mountains are good for hiking. Melanistic Peak (7,710 feet) is the park's highest, while Mount Hoy (7,075) is the lovely backdrop for Hoy Lake. Within the park are the headwaters of the Finlay River, a major tributary of the Mackenzie.

Williston Lake This 668-square-mile lake created by the W.A.C. Bennett Dam at Hudson's Hope is British Columbia's biggest. There are two-day excursions aboard "wilderboats"— vessels specially designed to cope with the floating debris and high winds prevalent on the lake.

Llewellyn Glacier (below) and Willison Glacier together cover more than one third of 900-square-mile Atlin Provincial Park.

Some mountains and mountain chains are volcanic in origin, formed of raw materials that came from deep in the earth's interior. Mount Edziza (9,143 feet), towering 5,000 feet above the surrounding plain, evolved through a series of eruptions that started 10 million years ago and ended perhaps as recently as 300 years ago. It is one of the few volcanoes in Canada to have erupted in recent geological time.

No two volcanoes are identical in magnitude or behavior. But all volcanoes have one basic ingredient: magma, molten rock formed deep inside the earth. Scientists believe it comes from the earth's upper mantle, a 125-mile-deep zone directly under the earth's crust.

The crust forms the continents (as much as 30 miles thick) and the ocean floor (up to three miles thick). Its weight exerts tremendous pressure on the mantle—more than 100 tons per square inch at depths of up to 30 miles. But when pressure is reduced—because of cracks or fissures in the crust—rocks in the mantle liquefy into magma. Melted and very hot rocks—982° to 1,093°C. (1,800° to 2,000°F.)—are combined with gases and escape toward the surface through fissures or vents. Existing volcanoes erupt anew or new volcanoes are created.

Edziza: A Landscape Born of Molten Rock and Fiery Ash

Some volcanoes erupt violently, with a force comparable to that of several atom bombs. If molten material is viscous (thick), it rises slowly and has a tendency to harden, making it difficult for accompanying gases to escape. When the contained gases build up enough pressure there is a tremendous explosion. The crater at Mount Edziza's peak was the result of such a build-up.

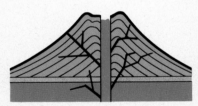

Shield volcanoes are formed when lava (magma that has reached the surface) gently rises through long fissures in the ground. The lava eventually builds a high, thick cone with gently sloping sides. The 25-by-10-mile plateau that surrounds Mount Edziza was built up in this way. In some places the accumulation of lava is a mile thick.

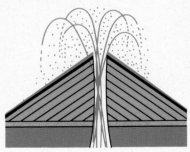

In a hot ash or cinder eruption, fiery dust or pebble-sized rocks are expelled by rapidly escaping gases, forming cinder cones such as those for which Mount Edziza Park is known. Cinder activity frequently alternates with lava eruptions. There are 30 such cones on Mount Edziza's slopes in various stages of reduction by erosion.

Along the West Escarpment of the Edziza plateau, water has carved gullies through extensive layers of volcanic ash. In the background, Mess Creek has cut a 2,500-foot-deep valley through the volcanic ash and lava.

Eve Cone, on Mount Edziza's northwest flank, is almost symmetrical. It rises 500 feet above the lava plain.

A small glacier flows down the west slope of the two-mile-wide crater at Mount Edziza's summit.

This Spectrum Range peak is a volcanic dome. Domes form when thick, molten lava, instead of flowing, piles up in great blisters, usually in a shape resembling a mushroom cap. This dome has been altered by erosion.

Fields of light-colored pumice such as this are common on the Edziza landscape. Pumice is formed when moisture in thick lava creates a honeycomb of steam bubbles. After it solidifies, the rock is so light it will float on water.

285

The Coast Mountains, along the western boundary of Tweedsmuir Park.

TWEEDSMUIR PROVINCIAL PARK

Rain Forest, Mountain Peaks, Plateau— This Biggest of B.C. Parks Has Them All

On the west are Douglas fir and hemlock, forming a dense green canopy over the dimly lit floor of the coastal rain forest. On the east are lodgepole pine, Engelmann spruce and trembling aspen, spilling onto the semi-arid Fraser Plateau of central British Columbia. In between are glacier-clad mountain peaks and alpine valleys and, far below, rivers racing to the Pacific.

It is hard to conceive of Tweedsmuir Provincial Park as an entity, so great is the variety of landforms in its nearly 4,000 square miles. Between the lakes that bound it on the north and the rugged glaciers of 11,590-foot Monarch Mountain—140 miles to the south—lie great granite cliffs and jumbled masses of rock, deep canyons and rolling meadows, eternal snowpacks, vast marshes—and a variety of microclimates. This diversity

287

Summer along the Rainbow Range: rust-colored streaks of minerals on the upper slopes contrast with skirtings of evergreens—and with lingering patches of snow.

provides habitats for a profusion of wildlife and makes Tweedsmuir one of British Columbia's most intriguing parks (as well as its biggest).

Most of it is pristine wilderness, little changed since 1793 when Alexander Mackenzie camped here on his historic journey to the Pacific. Tweedsmuir, nearly 200 years after Mackenzie, is for those who enjoy primitive travel with few amenities but nature's. There have been trail improvements but today's backpackers follow paths trod centuries ago by Indians moving to and from ancestral fishing and hunting grounds.

Automobile access to the park is limited to a 40-mile stretch of Highway 20, a 300-mile gravel road that connects the town of Williams Lake and the fishing community of Bella Coola. The road, carved out of the mountainsides, is one of the park's most exciting attractions. From 5,000 feet at the west end of Heckman Pass the narrow, switchback route falls away to nearly sea level in only 12 traveled miles. In this short distance it passes from semi-open, subalpine forest through transitional timber types to the giant trees of the coastal valley. Each twist in the road offers a breathtaking new view of serrated peaks and massive snowfields.

On the eastern edge of the park and to the north of the road is the Rainbow Range, dominated by Tsitsutl Peak. The round-topped mountains were built up through volcanic action that piled lava and fragmented rock as high as 7,000 and 8,000 feet above the plateau.

In the Mackenzie valley, a shallow subalpine basin that sweeps gently up the sides of the Rainbows, is a profusion of colorful wild flowers (mountain valerian, louseworts and marsh marigolds), shrubs and grasses. Mountain caribou in and above the valley feed on grasses and ground lichens. Grizzly bears root and graze along the exposed slopes in spring and early summer before invading the marmot colonies and the berry patches for the main courses of their midsummer diet. Moose browse along the marshes and watercourses where weeds, dwarf willows and scrub birch are abundant. Wolverines range from the rock rubble, where industrious little pikas busily cache winter food, to the willow thickets and their ptarmigans and mice. Occasionally a small band of mountain goats is sighted grazing on bunchgrass above the valley and the attentive and lucky observer may glimpse black bears, lynxes and wolves.

The grassy basins between mountains are a mass of blue-purple lupins, bright crimson Indian paintbrush, vivid yellow western buttercups and mountain dandelions and red-purple fireweed. Red heather and white moss that cover stretches of open mountainside may be accompanied by trailing azalea, whose tiny pink bell-like flowers look too fragile to withstand the rigors of an alpine habitat. Springs and snow-fed rivulets encourage the growth of yellow-blossomed glacier lilies and mimulus and their white cohabitants, valerians and grasses of Parnassus.

A traveler isolated in this plateau country experiences an exhilaration peculiar to such a mountain fastness. The intermittent rumbling of the shifting ice pack among the crags of Thunder Mountain, on the western boundary of the park, is an awesome sound. Brawling brooks tumble down the heights, spill over precipices, and linger in the meadows or rest in clear lakes that reflect the snowfields of their birth, before moving on to join the rivers that take them to the sea. Incessant winds murmur and moan among the subalpine trees—and whine and scream as they wheel around the highest pinnacles.

The road through the park parallels boisterous Young Creek as it descends from the plateau. It eases onto the valley floor (and into the Atnarko River) and seems to relax, as if relieved to be finished with the frantic race

Hunlen Falls, where the waters of Turner Lake plunge 1,150 feet between vertical canyon walls, is a Tweedsmuir Park showpiece. It is North America's fifth highest waterfall.

that has brought it from the mountain heights to the tranquil valley bottom.

From this campsite a good trail leads 10 miles up the valley of the Atnarko to 1,150-foot Hunlen Falls. Its wild and spectacular leap contrasts with the generally placid lakes of the Turner Lake chain behind the falls. They offer almost ideal flat water canoeing through a forested plateau edged by mountains. To transport a canoe into this wilderness is a formidable chore but canoes and accommodations may be rented at a park concession on the west shore of Turner Lake.

East of Turner Lake, nestled in the Atnarko Valley 1,500 feet below, is six-mile-long Lonesome Lake, home of a flock of trumpeter swans. The 400 huge white birds that winter here receive supplemental feeding through a program sponsored by the Canadian Wildlife Service. The flock is estimated to be 20 percent of the world's trumpeter swan population. On the east side of the lake, towering above this "valley of the swans," is 7,362-foot Trumpeter Mountain.

The Atnarko River sparkles amid the cathedral-like atmosphere of the coast forest in Tweedsmuir Provincial Park.

Fed by snowpacks and glaciers and surrounded by forests that help prevent flash floods, the Atnarko is a near-perfect habitat for fish. Grizzlies and black bears come down into the valley from the higher reaches of the park in the fall and feed on spawning salmon. Bald eagles work the banks along the redds, cleaning up spawned-out salmon that are washed ashore, while ospreys and kingfishers dive into the clear pools for smaller fish. The productivity of the river also assures abundant food for otter and mink.

Although these sights and activities are all relatively accessible to the automobile traveler, many of the charms of Tweedsmuir Park are reserved for those whose time and ability permit them access to the more remote regions. Primitive and unsullied, the park beckons the self-sufficient and experienced wilderness wanderer.

Following a visit in 1937, Lord Tweedsmuir, the 15th Governor-General of Canada, wrote: "I have now travelled over most of Canada and have seen many wonderful things, but I have seen nothing more beautiful and more wonderful than the great park which British Columbia has done me the honour to call by my name."

Basalt Cliffs *Columnar cliffs of basalt (volcanic rock) south of Alexandria, B.C., are an estimated 15 million years old. Some basalt cliffs in this part of B.C. are 100 feet high.*

OTHER ATTRACTIONS

The Twin Falls at Glacier Gulch

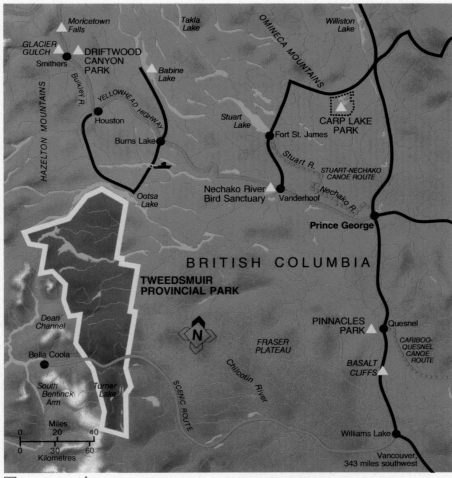

Scenic Wonder △ Other Attraction ▬ Scenic Route ▬▬ Canoe Route ⬛ Ferry

Babine Lake Sockeye salmon, which turn reddish as they return to Babine Lake to spawn, are seen by the thousands each fall. The lake has 380 miles of shoreline in the shadow of Babine Range peaks as high as 8,000 feet. There are Indian pictographs on rock formations along the eastern shoreline.

Basalt Cliffs Picture this page.

Cariboo-Quesnel Canoe Route A canyon 1½ miles long with sheer 400-foot walls is a main attraction of the Cariboo River section of this 108-mile route, but the canyon must be portaged. Along the swift upper Cariboo are good views of horns, cirques and taluses—sharp peaks, bowl-shaped depressions and slopes formed by rock debris. A second canyon near where the Cariboo flows into the Quesnel River also must be portaged. From there it is about 50 miles to the Quesnel's confluence with the Fraser River.

Carp Lake Provincial Park The terrain of this 75-square-mile park was moulded by Ice Age glaciers that covered the area about one million years ago. The lake's north shore is a sandy beach as wide as 1,000 feet; the south shore is littered with boulders and other glacial debris. The lake, laced with islands and ideal for canoeing, is linked to War Lake, five miles away, by the McLeod River.

Driftwood Canyon Provincial Park Fossils up to 70 million years old are embedded in the rock of the 75-foot-deep canyon, thought to have been the basin of a prehistoric lake. There are fish, insect and plant fossils, the most prevalent being the Metasequoia, a redwood. Beavers have dammed Driftwood Creek in several places.

Glacier Gulch Two narrow waterfalls pour over the wall of this mile-long gully. One falls 300 feet, the other 100. Kathlyn Glacier, 2 miles long, 1½ miles across and 400 feet thick, feeds Glacier Creek and Twin Falls. Hudson Bay Mountain (8,700 feet) and other peaks of the Hazelton Mountains form the impressive backdrop to the rugged gulch.

Moricetown Falls The Bulkley River narrows into a 50-foot-wide canyon, then thunders over a drop of more than 200 feet on the Moricetown Indian Reserve. Salmon fight up the turbulent

Jagged sandstone formations are in Pinnacles Provincial Park near Quesnel.

river each autumn, climbing the falls with the aid of fish ladders. A campground overlooks the falls.

Nechako River Bird Sanctuary As many as 100,000 migratory birds—mostly Canada geese—stop every spring on the sandbars of a three-mile stretch of the Nechako. They are attracted by newly-sprouted wheat in nearby fields. Only a few of the birds stop here during the autumn migration.

Pinnacles Provincial Park Twenty-foot pillars of eroded sandstone stand below an escarpment that parallels Baker Creek about four miles west of Quesnel. Picture this page.

Scenic Route Highway 20 between Williams Lake and Bella Coola traverses the arid Interior Plateau, winds through spectacular snowcapped mountains and then drops down into the valley of the Bella Coola River. From Williams Lake the 300-mile route crosses the Fraser River, then follows the Chilcotin River across a part of the Interior Plateau known as the Chilcotin Plateau. It winds beneath the peaks of the Coast Mountains before entering forests of moss-festooned trees and giant ferns. Because of steep grades and switchbacks, trailers cannot be towed on the 40-mile section of the highway that is in Tweedsmuir Provincial Park.

Stuart-Nechako Canoe Route This 120-mile route is between Stuart Lake, where the Stuart River begins, and Prince George, where the Nechako River empties into the Fraser. Surrounded by high sand cliffs at the confluence of the Stuart and the Nechako is a campsite on the former site of a Carrier Indian village. The Nechako flows 1,000 feet below the Interior Plateau, through a trench believed to have been carved by a glacial lake.

Yellowhead Highway This scenic part of the Yellowhead passes the Cariboo Mountains, skirts many lakes and gives access to several canoe routes. West of Hazelton the road climbs and dips among the peaks and valleys of the Hazelton and Coast mountains. A glacier on 8,700-foot Hudson Bay Mountain can be seen from the road.

The egg-shaped female cones of the black spruce (above), about an inch long, are purple when immature or first ripe, and later turn brown. They open at intervals, releasing seeds gradually, retaining some for years; the cones themselves are not shed. Eastern hemlock cones (right, enlarged) are less than an inch long. Seeds are shed during the winter, cones the following spring.

Not Really Flowers, Not All 'Pine Cones' Either

Some of the most colorful "flowers" of the forest—the cones of evergreen trees—grow high up and are often obscured by lower branches. After they have fallen, cones become brittle and drab. (Laymen tend to call them *all* "pine cones.") But while still on the trees they can be as attractive as the true flowers on the forest floor.

Just as the seeds of most other plants are reproduced by their flowers, so the seeds of the more than 30 species of "flowering" native evergreens in Canada come from their cones. These vary from the familiar woody, brown pine cones to fleshy red, yellow and purple "berries."

Male cones produce pollen; female cones, seeds. Except for a few such species as junipers, each tree bears both male and female cones, on different parts of the tree. Female "flowers," larger than the male and usually on upper or outer branches, are upright during pollination; each of many overlapping scales bears two immature seeds. Each scale of the less conspicuous male cone contains two pollen cases; the cone hangs down when pollen is released.

Each seed in the female cone secretes sticky resin. Wind-carried male pollen from another tree sticks to the female resin and germinates, developing a tube that carries male germ cells down to the immature seed. (Only a tiny fraction of the pollen grains released by a tree ever reaches female cones.)

Fertilization takes from several weeks to more than a year. Male cones develop in one season, shed their clouds of yellow pollen, then wither. Female cones may need two years to mature and may stay on a tree long after they have dropped their seeds.

Lodgepole pine cones can be short and cylindrical or oval. Mature cones usually remain closed but they sometimes open in autumn to release seeds.

The female cone of a Douglas fir, the giant of western Canadian forests, is about four inches long. Three-pointed bracts (petals) stick out between the scales.

The largest of the spruces (often 175 feet), the Sitka spruce bears cylindrical cones up to four inches long. They fall during late autumn and winter.

Grand, Black, Wild: An Anarchy of Rock, a Jungle of Cliffs and a Roiling River

To Simon Fraser, the stubborn Scot who gave it this name, the canyon was a horror. "I have... never seen anything equal to this country..." he wrote in his understated journal in 1808. "We had to pass where no human being should venture." Novelist Hugh MacLennan, more than a century and a half later, described it as "the most exciting country in Canada.... Its beauty makes you catch your breath."

The Fraser has been called the Black Canyon and the Grand Canyon. Although neither as unremittingly black nor as inspiringly grand as other rock-ribbed valleys in North America, this canyon is uniquely remarkable, a jarring anarchy of rock, a jungle of cliffs that contain one of the wickedest rivers on the continent.

The Fraser River carved the canyon out of the Coast Mountains and provided a gash through those mountains where man could hang the Trans-Canada Highway and the main Canadian National and Canadian Pacific rail lines. But every mile of road and track was won painfully. The canyon resisted, as it had always done. Simon Fraser was amazed to find Indian trails in the canyon: "...there is a regular footpath impressed, or rather indented, by frequent traveling upon the very rocks. And besides this, steps which are formed like a ladder, or the shrouds of a ship, by poles hanging to one another and crossed at certain distances with twigs and

The Fraser, near Lillooet.

295

[tree boughs], suspended from the top to the foot of precipices, and fastened at both ends to stones and trees...." The chaos of the canyon has also tested modern contractors: in one 27-mile stretch of the Trans-Canada between Yale and Boston Bar they were forced to build two bridges and blast seven tunnels.

The Fraser Canyon has been thoroughly explored, and marked on countless maps, but disagreement lingers as to where exactly it begins and ends. Some chroniclers suggest its southern end is the town of Hope, 95 miles east of Vancouver; but most geographers put the southern limit at Yale, 16 miles north of Hope. While its northern limit is generally considered to be Lillooet, 96 miles by road from Yale, the canyon in fact extends beyond there. But by the time the river reaches Soda Creek, 120 miles beyond Lillooet, its walls are no longer high enough or defined enough to be considered canyon cliffs.

Geologists also debate when the canyon was begun; it offers no neat layering of rocks to read. They do know it was chiseled by streams dating at least to 70 million years ago. Bruce Hutchison in *The Fraser* quotes geologist John F. Walker: "When one drives through the Fraser Canyon one gets the impression of a gorgelike valley, a youthful valley, something quite young. This is true only in part. The upland slopes, away from the valley, are those of a mature valley. The great gorge itself is old. It is only the canyon in the very bottom of the gorge that is young. The canyon would not appear as young were it not for the hard granitic rocks which have confined the river in its lower reaches above Hope."

Sheds carry falling rocks, snow slides and spring runoff water over a rail line (left) that hugs the Fraser near Lytton. Above: the view from a lookout on Jackass Mountain.

Driving up the canyon, being constantly distracted by the cliffs and deceived by the contortions of the highway, it can seem difficult to make sense of the Fraser's channel through the Coast Mountains. Between Vancouver and Hope, the river has been a sedate east-west waterway, brown with silt, free to stretch wide

across the rich countryside. At Hope you round a bend, leaving the flat farmland, and find the Fraser rushing from north to south between the canyon's pincers. The water rages at its confinement, and the sides of the canyon are slippery with the foam and mist of the river's roiling.

Sixteen miles upriver, at Yale, the mountain walls loom menacingly above the Fraser. It was one mile south of here, at Hills Bar on the south bank, that six Califor-

nia miners found gold in 1858. Their discovery launched a rush of fortune hunters who turned Yale into a town of 20,000, including 3,000 prospectors who worked $2,000,000 worth of gold out of the sandbar. To service the miners, steamboats came upriver, their paddles churning as they fought the torrent as far as Yale. Beyond there, the canyon constricts the river so tightly that big boats could not survive.

When the miners descended upon the Fraser, follow-

The Fraser: sometimes sedate, sometimes—as at Hells Gate (right)—racing past at 25 feet a second.

ing it up to the Cariboo goldfields, the British colonial governor, James Douglas, decided a wagon road had to be built to the interior. But the canyon seemed impossible to conquer. In 1861 Douglas rode a horse out of Yale to seek a practical route; the diary of his trip is still an accurate description of the canyon:

"Grades here and there rather steep. Scenery grand beyond description. Mountains rising to the skies on either side of the narrow pass, and at our foot the Fraser is frantically tearing its way in foaming whirls. Neither is the pass destitute of softer features, every spot of earth is prolific of vegetation and the mountainsides are covered with beautiful flowers...." Douglas rode through fir forests, across cliffs splashed with the small, violet-petaled beardtongue and scented with the blossoms of wild currant and Saskatoon shrubs.

He did determine that a trail could be built and directed a company of Royal Engineers from England to design a road that tunneled and bridged and inched its way along and across and above the mighty river. It took

298

two years and $1,250,000 to manage the 400 miles from Yale to Alexandria, but the Cariboo Road was so well chosen that the men who built the Trans-Canada a century later had no option but to follow it through the canyon. A plaque alongside the Trans-Canada four miles north of Yale commemorates the Royal Engineers' astonishing job; nearby is a strip of the original wagon road.

North of Yale the modern highway runs through two tunnels to the community of Spuzzum, then another mile to the 1,610-foot-long Alexandra Bridge across the canyon. A 13-mile drive up the road and a hike down a steep 600-foot slope lead to a series of fish ladders at the most dramatic site in the canyon: Hells Gate, a cauldron of water that bursts through a rocky gap only 120 feet wide (but up to 175 feet deep during floods). It once had been much broader, but in 1914 the builders of the Canadian Northern Railway mistakenly dynamited a mountainside down into the water and reduced the river to a narrow deluge.

Hells Gate was a great sight, but it was an all but insurmountable hurdle for sockeye salmon struggling upriver to spawn. During the three decades after the accidental dynamiting, British Columbia lost perhaps half a billion dollars in salmon. Leaping, lunging, flinging themselves against a current gushing at 25 feet a second, millions of salmon died below Hells Gate without spawning, without producing a new crop.

In 1946 the International Pacific Salmon Fisheries

Commission built fish ladders, actually concrete tunnels fitted with baffles that control the current and create steps of pools that allow the fish to climb the gap. Even with the ladders it will be many more years for the salmon to complete their comeback. But now, in good years, gill-netters and seiners catch 15 million salmon from the Fraser River run.

Eight miles upstream the canyon is crossed by an aerial ferry that links Boston Bar and North Bend. The ferry car is suspended from 1,208 feet of cables. The 40 passengers (or one three-ton vehicle) are only 30 feet above the river at high water.

Now the highway traveler is near two viewpoints that reveal stunning vistas of the canyon. Fifteen miles north of Boston Bar looms Jackass Mountain, named for a gold prospector's mule; overburdened on its journey up the Cariboo Road, it bucked and slipped to its death down the cliff. Four miles farther on the motorist overlooks the sweep of the canyon, its mountain backdrop and two railway bridges that span it near Cisco.

Lytton, three miles north of Cisco, was the site of a flourishing Indian village that Simon Fraser happened across in 1808. It became a busy mining town—not surprisingly, because here the Fraser meets the Thompson, another lusty river that was ripe with gold. Their union is great natural theater: the turquoise water of the Thompson smashes a path into the dirty brown Fraser, which gulps it down completely within a scant hundred yards.

The Fraser Canyon at Lytton has donned a different cloak. The pine of the southern mountains survives, but dogwood and maple have yielded to the sagebrush of the dry belt that scars the interior of British Columbia. In summer Lytton becomes a bake oven, regularly reporting the highest temperatures in Canada, searing the landscape.

Northwestward lies Lillooet, 40 miles up the corkscrewing Lytton Road, where the canyon is surrounded by semidesert irrigated in places to produce hay for the cattle of this ranch country. The Lillooet mountains, Bruce Hutchison has written, "at dawn or in the evening dusk, have the texture and the wonder of a dream. They hang like draperies of soft, flimsy stuff, almost transparent and deep azure. Woven through this cloth is the gleaming thread of the river."

This is almost the final flourish of the Fraser Canyon. Between here and Soda Creek, in remote countryside few Canadians ever see, the cliffs begin to lose their sharp form and the canyon proper disappears. Elsewhere it is lofty, sculptured, starkly beautiful, well deserving its nickname, the Grand Canyon. But even today it is also the Black Canyon, dark, wild and threatening—just as it was to its 19th-century explorer, Simon Fraser.

299

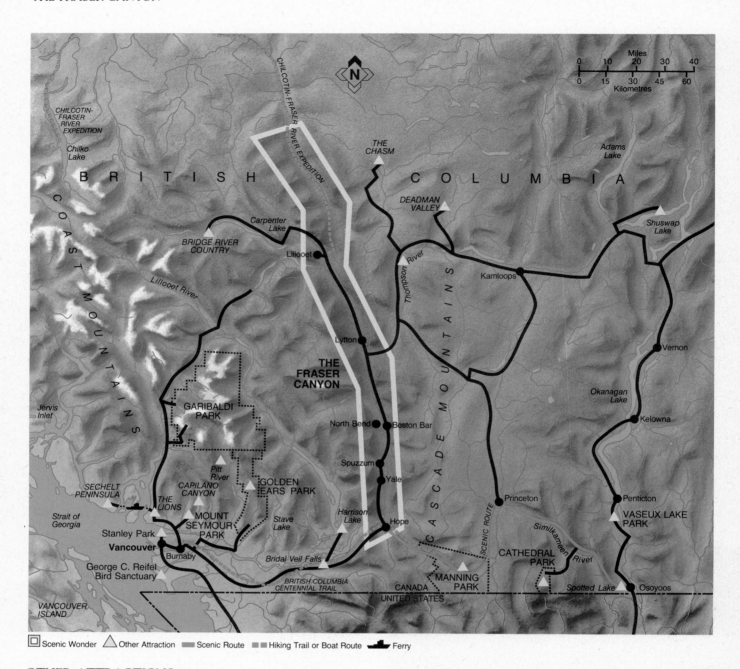

☐ Scenic Wonder △ Other Attraction ▬ Scenic Route ▰▰ Hiking Trail or Boat Route ⛴ Ferry

OTHER ATTRACTIONS

Stone City, Spotted Lake and The Lions

Bridal Veil Falls A lacy spray tumbles over an 80-foot cliff on Bridal Creek.

Bridge River Country Fed by a glacier, the Bridge River twists through narrow gorges before emptying into the Fraser River above Lillooet. Gun Lake, nestled among rolling, forested hills, provides fine boating, swimming and fishing.

British Columbia Centennial Trail The trail stretches 200 miles between Bur-

naby and Cathedral Provincial Park. Much of the route parallels the Fraser River, and along some sections Sumas Mountain and Mount Vedder can be seen. South of Chilliwack the trail enters dense rain forests of cedar, hemlock and Douglas fir. Cyclists can use parts of the trail.

Capilano Canyon A footbridge 450 feet long swings 230 feet above the Capilano River gorge.

Cathedral Provincial Park A quartzite formation called Stone City has been eroded by the wind and resembles a cluster of small buildings. Other formations include the Giant Cleft, an 8-foot-wide gash in a 1,000-foot-high cliff called the Ramparts, and a jumble of rocks called the Devil's Woodpile.

Chilcotin-Fraser River Expedition A 200-mile white-water excursion down the Chilcotin and Fraser rivers in spe-

cially outfitted rafts begins at Chilko Lake and ends at Lillooet. It passes through rapids on the Chilcotin and the rapids of Moran Canyon on the Fraser.

Deadman Valley Cactus and hoodoos—sand and gravel pillars about 35 feet high—dot the 40-mile-long valley. The hoodoos are capped with boulders which protect the soft columns from erosion. At Mile 29 of the Deadman-Vidette Road, the eroded valley wall resembles a castle more than 200 feet high. Deadman Falls, a 150-foot-high torrent of white water in spring, is divided into three strands in autumn as the level of the Deadman River drops. Summer temperatures in the valley reach 43°C. (110°F.) in the shade.

Garibaldi Provincial Park Volcanic rock formations are found throughout this 756-square-mile wilderness park, which is dominated by 8,787-foot Mount Garibaldi. Atop 7,598-foot Black Tusk mountain is a basalt formation, the eroded remains of a volcanic core that "plugged" an ancient volcano when it cooled. The Barrier, a lava flow a mile long and up to a mile thick, towers 1,500 feet above the west side of Garibaldi Lake—which is 900 feet deep. Erosion created strange shapes in The Gargoyles. Picture this page.

George C. Reifel Migratory Bird Sanctuary Canada's largest winter population of waterfowl is found in this marshland on a Fraser River estuary. Visitors walk

The highest of Garibaldi Provincial Park's magnificent mountains is Mount Garibaldi, named for Giuseppe Garibaldi, the Italian patriot, soldier and statesman.

along dikes and climb a tower to observe birds that use the 850-acre sanctuary. Among the 180 species that nest here are bushtits, European widgeons, gyrfalcons, whimbrels and black-bellied plovers. Great blue herons are often seen. Many of the birds can be hand-fed.

Golden Ears Provincial Park The 215-square-mile park is separated from Garibaldi Provincial Park by a formidable ridge of the Coast Mountains. One of several trails leads to the summit of 5,598-foot Golden Ears mountain.

Harrison Lake Water from sulphur and potash hot springs is cooled to 37°C. (99°F.)—normal human body temperature—and piped to a public pool.

Manning Provincial Park Thickly forested slopes rise above pristine lakes in this 275-square-mile wilderness park. The Monument 78 Trail winds through the park for 6½ miles before connecting with the American Pacific Crest Trail.

Mount Seymour Provincial Park Only nine miles from Vancouver, the park is a popular ski and snowshoe area in winter. An access road has three lookouts over the Strait of Georgia, the Gulf Islands and Vancouver Island. A trail climbs five miles to the 4,766-foot summit of Mount Seymour.

Pitt River From its headwaters near the peak of 8,787-foot Mount Garibaldi, the Pitt River tumbles for 39 miles through rugged and dangerous country before flowing into 18-mile-long Pitt Lake. The lower Pitt, however, is placid in its 14-mile trip to the Fraser.

Scenic Route (Hwy 3) This highway follows the Dewdney Trail that was completed in 1865 from Hope to goldfields deep in the B.C. interior. The 440-mile trail ended at Wild Horse Creek, near present-day Cranbrook, but the highway continues to the Crowsnest Pass at the Alberta border. The route winds through the Cascade Mountains and passes the Hope Slide, where in 1965 two miles of highway was buried to a depth of 260 feet. At nearby Rhododendron Flats a mile-long trail meanders among thousands of pink-mauve rhododendrons. The highway crosses Manning Provincial Park, climbing to 4,400 feet through Allison Pass. Near Princeton it crosses the Similkameen Valley, where there are some 20 Indian rock painting sites.

Sechelt Peninsula Sharply indented bays and inlets along the Strait of Georgia give way to the forested slopes of the Coast Mountains.

Shuswap Lake In peak years, as many as 10 million sockeye salmon surge up the Adams River (connecting Shuswap Lake to Adams Lake) to spawn. Each October the spawning salmon turn a distinctive crimson color, often making the narrow river appear red. A viewing platform provides a close look at the spectacle. Indian rock paintings at 11 sites around Shuswap Lake date from before 1860. Most are visible only from the water.

Spotted Lake The water of the 40-acre lake has one of the world's heaviest concentrations of minerals, arranged in multicolored circular "spots."

Stanley Park Deer are still found in giant stands of Douglas fir, hemlock and cedar in Vancouver's lovely 1,000-acre park. Twenty-two miles of trails weave among the trees, across rolling lawns and around lily-padded Beaver Lake and Lost Lagoon. At the Vancouver Aquarium are 595 aquatic species housed in displays which take visitors on simulated trips from the open Pacific through the Strait of Georgia and coastal inlets into freshwater rivers and lakes. A whale pool with underwater viewing areas has two killer whales and a Pacific striped dolphin. In other pools are beluga whales, sea otters, sea turtles, piranha, lemon sharks, moray eels and octopuses. Among the 570 species at the Stanley Park Zoo are polar bears, monkeys, seals, Arctic wolves, kinkajous, opossums and chinchillas. The zoo has one of the world's finest king penguin collections.

The Chasm A mile long and up to 400 feet deep, The Chasm was formed at the end of the Ice Age, some 10,000 years ago, by streams of glacial meltwater.

The Lions Two rocky outcrops almost 5,000 feet high resemble crouched lions. Hiking trails lead to The Lions and to lookouts over Howe Sound.

Thompson River To the north of the North Thompson are the Cariboo Mountains and the Quesnel Highland; south of the South Thompson are the Monashee Mountains and the Shuswap Highland. Below Kamloops, where the two branches meet, the Thompson flows between the Fraser Plateau to the north, the Thompson Plateau to the south. Picture this page.

Vaseux Lake Provincial Park Canada geese, trumpeter swans, white-headed woodpeckers and lazuli buntings are among birds found at a sanctuary in the park. A hot, dry climate enables sagebrush, cactus and bitterroot to thrive here. Rattlesnakes and western painted turtles are common.

This semi-desert terrain is near Cache Creek, B.C., north of the big bend of the Thompson River. The North and South Thompson merge at Kamloops to become the Thompson.

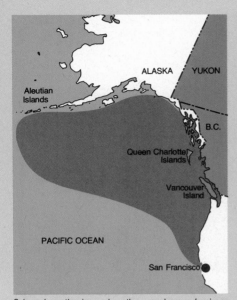

Salmon leave the rivers where they were born and swim as far as 1,000 miles into the Pacific. They stay for two to five years before returning to spawn.

During spawning runs, most salmon change from steely blue to red or pink. They also stop eating and live on body fat and protein. Males undergo several changes in form, varying according to species. Jaws may become hooked, fins ragged and backs humped.

The Incredible Odyssey of the Pacific Salmon

One of North America's last great examples of abundance, Pacific salmon by the millions leave the sea in summer and autumn to spawn in more than 1,300 rivers and streams along the British Columbia coast. In none are their numbers greater than in the Fraser River and its tributaries.

The five species that occur off the B.C. coast—sockeye, pink, coho, spring and chum—are seen twice a year, like a red army at war with the Fraser and with time. Following one of the strongest instincts in nature, they seek the stream of their birth. Most find it. Some don't, dying of exhaustion in rapids or in trying to leap up a falls.

As incredible as the salmon's determination and strength is the fact that they make it back to the river at all. Guided mainly by a highly developed sense of smell, some start their journey home from as far as 1,000 miles at sea.

In the Fraser they travel up to 30 miles a day, often in schools. But once they reach home waters males especially become territorial and aggressive. Adults usually die within a few days of spawning.

The salmon eggs hatch into alevins, which then develop into fry. The following spring the fry leave their gravelly birth sites, some heading for the sea almost immediately, swimming by night and hiding by day. Others stay in fresh water for as long as two years before making for salt water. Once in the sea they eat voraciously (spring salmon often reach 60 pounds). At the onset of sexual maturity in the last year of their life cycle (two to five years according to species) they begin the epic journey home to perpetuate their kind—then die.

Traveling up to 30 miles a day, some species of salmon go to their birthplace in a school (left). Each female lays thousands of eggs in a gravel bed that she digs with her tail. The nest—called a redd—is up to 1½ feet deep. Over it, the spawning fish wriggle vigorously (center) and the male fertilizes the eggs. Several males may spawn with one female. She covers the eggs with gravel and guards the site until her death, usually within a few days. Bottom left: Eggs hatch into alevins which grow rapidly under the gravel, emerging after several months as fry which feed on plankton and small insects.

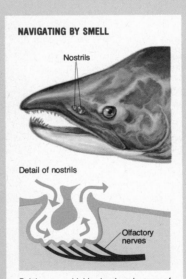

NAVIGATING BY SMELL

Nostrils

Detail of nostrils

Olfactory nerves

Relying on a highly developed sense of smell, the salmon "memorizes" the odor of its home stream. Water flows into its front nostrils and past smell receptors, linked by nerves to the brain, before going out rear nostrils.

303

THE PACIFIC COAST

An Alluring Complex of Sea and Mountains

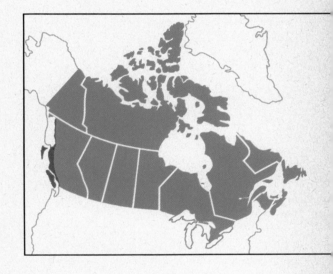

The coast of British Columbia is a winding and a twisting of waterways, a confusion of islands, bays, inlets and fjords, a towering of great mountains whose flanks slip sharply into the sea. This 4,400-mile coastline is one of the most complex in the world—and one of the most alluring, a fascinating blend of restless surf, rugged cliffs, forest-clad peaks and sandy beaches of white, gray, even black. Perhaps the loveliest is Long Beach, the showpiece of Pacific Rim National Park on Vancouver Island. But the adventure and excitement of the coast can be enjoyed at many places. The Sechelt Peninsula, called the Sunshine Coast, is easily reached from Vancouver. Ferries in the Strait of Georgia thread their way among the Gulf and Coast islands. The Island Highway connects Victoria with Kelsey Bay far up on Vancouver Island. From Kelsey Bay a ferry plies the Inside Passage—protected from the open sea by a string of islands—all the way to Prince Rupert. The mist-shrouded Queen Charlotte Islands, despite boat and air service, are still remote—and the more attractive for it. Echoes of the Haida, the Kwakiutl, the Coast Salish and other Indian tribes—and of their mystic rapport with the land and sea—are everywhere. Most of the Pacific Coast is still wild and lonely. And enchanting.

Opposite: *Cathedral Grove, near Port Alberni.*
Preceding pages: *The Gulf Islands.*

307

Long Beach.

Long Beach, the Broken Group Islands and a Rugged Trail at the Sea's Edge

On the rugged, wind-lashed west coast of Vancouver Island is Pacific Rim National Park, a nature's treasury of rocky islands and surf-swept headlands, of thick forests and tranquil lakes, all against a backdrop of blue-tinted mountains. The three regions of the 250-square-mile park—Long Beach, the Broken Group Islands and the West Coast Trail—attract some 200,000 persons a year. They share one of the richest and most varied funds of nature in Canada.

More than 200 species of birds sing in the woodlands and feed from the sea and shore. There are about 20 types of mammals—some seldom seen because they are either nocturnal or attuned to the dense, often almost impenetrable forest. And Pacific Rim has more than 100 species of plant life. In the sea are more than 300 types of fishes and 20 kinds of marine mammals, from salmon, herring and haddock to whales, seals and sea lions. The ocean's invertebrates include sea gooseberries, pink-tipped sea anemones and sand dollars.

Heavy rain, prolonged cloudiness and moderate temperatures produce fog that dominates the Pacific Rim landscape, draping the forests and the sea in low, gray mist and bestowing a quality of deep mystery.

Eighteenth-century Nootka Indians, great hunters, set off through the fog in tiny boats in pursuit of the gray whale, and harpooned seals and sea lions on the rocks. Capt. James Cook visited the area in 1778 and bought otter pelts. A century later loggers and miners arrived. Soon there were permanent white settlements, some trading in furs and fish. Rumors of gold drew more settlers. In 1910 a road was begun between the two nearby towns—Ucluelet ("good landing place" in Nootka), and Tofino, which had been named in 1792 after a Spanish admiral.

The geological history of Pacific Rim National Park is similar to that of Vancouver Island in general. Some 200 million years ago a chain of underwater volcanoes stretched along the west coast of North America. They released unimaginable quantities of molten lava beneath the sea, then became inactive. Aquatic plants and animals occupied the region and over millions of years their bodies created a limestone cap on the older rocks. When the volcanoes exploded anew, the molten lava piled high enough to rise above the sea—and Vancouver Island was born.

The most northern phase of the park, the 48-square-mile Long Beach area, has a seven-mile crescent of almost white sand facing the open Pacific. The beach is the domain of gooseneck barnacles, big blue California mussels, green sea anemones and common purple starfish, among many more. Flocks of sandpipers and plovers dart to and fro with the rhythm of the waves. Overhead, bald eagles patrol the beach in search of cast-up fish, and ospreys soar on the wind, seeking flatfish and perch in shallow waters. Herds of imperious, dark-brown sea lions weave and shuffle over the rocks in sheltered coves, or slide through the ocean like water-born cavalrymen.

Also in the Long Beach sector are dense rain forests against a background of mountains rising in places to 6,000 feet—and vast, rich tidal mud flats in the Grice Bay area, where eelgrass and algae provide food for migrating waterfowl. In April and October flocks of black brants, pintails and mallards stop here to feed and

As the mist lifts in Pacific Rim National Park, Long Beach comes alive with beachcombers, clam diggers and strollers.

rest; during October and November the flats are a feeding ground for an estimated 10,000 Canada geese.

Between the flats and the beach is a thick belt of trees and bushes. Most of the trees are Sitka spruce, which thrive in summer fog and winter salt spray, but there are salal, black twinberry, salmonberry and stunted spruce. Western red cedar, western hemlock and amabalis fir abound and among these the sweet songs of the fox sparrow and winter wren may be heard. In tall, wild ryegrass, where the wind whips the sand into deep dunes, and elsewhere in the park, the familiar song sparrow makes his home.

Farther south, in the mouth of Alberni Inlet, are the nearly 100 forested islands and rocky islets known as the Broken Group Islands, flanked by the icy fingers of Loudoun and Imperial Eagle channels. The islands' sheltered lagoons offer safe anchorage for boaters—and fine fishing. Chinook and coho salmon are intercepted here as they head for their spawning grounds—and trawlers scoop shrimps from the depths.

The west coast of Vancouver Island is "the graveyard of the Pacific." In the past 100 years, more than 50 vessels have sunk along the coast near the Broken Group Islands—one a mile. Today they are the targets of adventurous scuba divers looking for treasure.

Animal life on and around the islands is abundant.

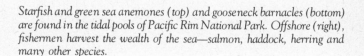

Starfish and green sea anemones (top) and gooseneck barnacles (bottom) are found in the tidal pools of Pacific Rim National Park. Offshore (right), fishermen harvest the wealth of the sea—salmon, haddock, herring and many other species.

Northwestern crows, ravens and more than 170 pairs of bald eagles find an unlimited supply of food there. Eleven-foot, one-ton northern sea lions are seen in the open waters. On some large islands there are stable populations of raccoon and mink which feed on crabs they catch or that are washed up by the sea.

The West Coast Trail area is along 50 miles of coast between Bamfield in the north and Port Renfrew in the south. The trail itself winds through 45 miles of dense vegetation nurtured by 180 inches of rain a year. Often shrouded in fog, the forests are lined with a carpet of moss and are alive with birds—Steller's jays, brown creepers, red crossbills and chickadees. Where the trail meets the sea, red-throated loons, pelagic cormorants and black oyster catchers are seen hunting.

The broad beach, the many islands, the long rugged trail... these are the rim of the Pacific, the superb elements of a great park in which there is special magic at a summer dusk. Sea lions majestic on their rocks are backlit by a red sun soon lost beyond the ocean's distant edge. The sea is calm, the birds are still. Now nature heightens the beauty of this west coast jewel: in from the Pacific comes a veil of soft mist. Long Beach, the Broken Group Islands and the West Coast Trail are wrapped anew in their own deep mystery.

OTHER ATTRACTIONS

Killer Whales and Coastal Cactus

Butchart Gardens Thousands of flowering plants, shrubs and trees—illuminated at night—occupy a 25-acre former quarry. There are an English rose garden and an Italian garden with finely manicured shrubbery. A Japanese garden has flowering cherry trees, a secluded waterfall and a sunken garden.

Cleland Island More than 10,000 petrels, mainly Leach's storm-petrels, nest on a grassy knoll atop this small, treeless island. Black oyster catchers, rhinoceros auklets and tufted puffins also nest here.

Cowichan Valley Forest Museum Forester's Walk takes visitors along a nature trail where 25 species of trees are found, including 300-year-old Douglas firs. A 15-acre forest depicts various stages in a tree's growth.

Goldstream Provincial Park Some 5,000 coho and chum salmon that spawn in the Goldstream River each November are easily seen in the clear, shallow water. Douglas firs and western red cedars grow throughout the park and flowering dogwood is found on some ridges.

Gulf Islands Several dozen small islets and 15 comparatively large islands have been curiously molded by the wind and sea. Lacework patterns have been carved on rocky headlands and bluffs, and undercutting waters have created hollows and even caves at the shoreline. One formation, Galiano Gallery on Gabriola Island, is a 300-foot-long sandstone roof hanging out over the water. A 100-foot cliff about four miles south has been so slashed by surf and eaten by salt that it is a mass of eroded formations—some holes only a foot square, some with huge hollows and ledges. Three peaks in Mount Maxwell Provincial Park on 70-square-mile Saltspring Island (the largest of the Gulf Islands) are higher than 1,900 feet. They provide excellent views of southern Vancouver Island, the Gulf Islands and the British Columbia mainland. Killer whales are often seen in the waters around the islands. Picture next page.

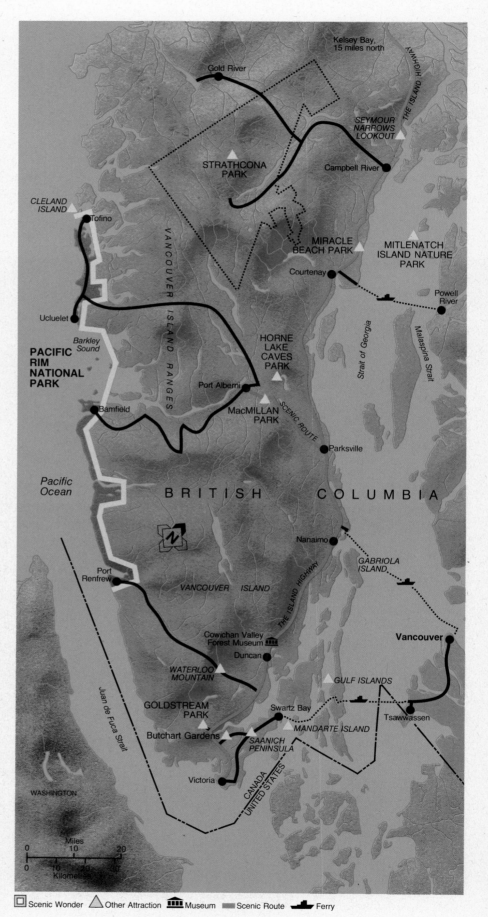

Scenic Wonder △ Other Attraction ▥ Museum ▬ Scenic Route ⛴ Ferry

314

A killer whale leaps clear of the water off one of the Gulf Islands. Several pods of killer whales roam the waters around Vancouver Island and are regularly sighted by boaters and from land. Below: A picturesque waterfall in Little Qualicum Falls Provincial Park west of Parksville.

Horne Lake Caves Provincial Park Four large caves and several smaller ones dot the rolling hills of this 71-acre park. The longest—Euclataws (1,740 feet)—is barred to all but groups gathering scientific information. Horne Lake Main Cave and Lower Cave (450 feet and 250 feet) are open to the public. Euclataws has rooms 60 feet high filled with stalagmites and twiglike lateral projections called helictites. Stalactites and stalagmites meet in several places, forming huge white columns.

MacMillan Provincial Park Hundreds of giant Douglas firs, some more than 600 years old, grow in Cathedral Grove. Many are more than 200 feet tall and 5 feet in diameter. One is 9½ feet in diameter (more than 30 feet in circumference) and 244 feet high. Mount Arrowsmith (5,962 feet) is surrounded by forests inhabited by cougar and deer.

Mandarte Island More than 2,000 pairs of glaucous-winged gulls nest on this small, barren island. Wild roses and chocolate flowers bloom in the spring.

Miracle Beach Provincial Park Hair seals and porpoises are common off the mouth of Black Creek and killer whales are often spotted farther out in the Strait of Georgia. Several species of crabs and seabirds inhabit the shorelines and 195 plant species have been identified. A museum has photographs and information on plant and animal life.

Mitlenatch Island Nature Park Harbor seals are common and sea lions are sometimes spotted in the waters off this small, craggy island. Colonies of red sea urchins blanket the rocky shorelines, and garter snakes visit the tidal pools to feed on blennies, sculpins and clingfish at low tide. Thousands of seabirds, including black oyster catchers, glaucous-winged gulls and pelagic cormorants, nest on the rocky ledges. To protect the nesting birds, park naturalists escort visitors on nature walks. The brittle prickly-pear cactus, the only cactus found on the British Columbia coast, blooms in the hot, dry days of June.

Golden Hinde in Strathcona Provincial Park is Vancouver Island's highest peak at 7,219 feet. It was named for Sir Francis Drake's ship.

Saanich Peninsula Mount Newton, the highest of several hills at the north end of the peninsula that reach almost 1,000 feet, gives a beautiful view of the sea, the Gulf Islands, the Olympic Mountains in Washington and the mountainous peninsula. The peninsula is the only place in North America where the skylark may be seen. Japanese cherry blossoms, tulips and other flowers are abundant in the spring.

Scenic Route The 29-mile highway between Parksville and Port Alberni lies in the shadow of Mount Arrowsmith. Much of the forested terrain was scarred by a fire in 1967 and the effects are still visible. The Englishman River tumbles about 120 feet in two separate drops through a rocky gorge at Englishman River Provincial Park. Another two-level waterfall drops 200 feet at Little

Qualicum Falls Provincial Park. Park picture preceding page.

Seymour Narrows Lookout Vertical rock walls, in many places more than 200 feet high, line the deep, blue waters of Seymour Narrows. The cliffs on the west side of the two-mile-wide narrows are part of Vancouver Island; most of those on the east side are on Quadra Island. The narrows are more than 500 feet deep.

Strathcona Provincial Park Snow-capped mountain peaks loom above this heavily forested, 560,000-acre wildlife sanctuary. Glaciers cover some slopes; snow on others lingers into July. Western red cedar, Douglas fir and hemlock dominate the valleys, giving way to myriad bright wild flowers on higher slopes, including those of 7,219-foot Golden Hinde. Della Falls, Canada's highest waterfall, plummets 1,443 feet over three spectacular chutes. Wolverine, cougar, deer, wolf and some of

the last remaining elk on Vancouver Island inhabit the park. Picture this page.

The Island Highway This 214-mile route between Victoria and Kelsey Bay hugs the east coast of Vancouver Island, providing unsurpassed views of the Gulf Islands and the Strait of Georgia. Twelve miles north of Victoria, on the Malahat Drive, is a lookout with a striking view of the snowcapped Olympic Mountains in Washington. From the lookout, 1,200 feet above the shoreline, visitors see the entire Saanich Peninsula. The Coast Mountains on the mainland can be seen from several vantage points along the route. Elk Falls, at the junction of the Elk and Quinsam rivers, drops 90 feet into a rocky gorge.

Waterloo Mountain A plaque points out a Douglas fir that may be Canada's oldest living tree. The giant fir, one of several trees here more than 1,000 years old, was a seedling in A.D. 650.

Headland, Arch and Sea Stack: The Carving of a Coastline

The waves of the sea destroy—and they create, too. Through centuries of battering and caressing they can reduce a cliff to a series of craggy headlands—but with gentle beaches tucked in between. Waves can ultimately transform long stretches of once rocky coast into a coast of extensive beaches.

The power of waves is greater when they contain erosive matter such as sand. Breaking waves that deposited such material on gently sloping terraces built Long Beach (below) in Pacific Rim National Park.

The handiwork of the pounding Pacific is evident along much of the rugged west coast of Vancouver Island. Learning to "read" coastal formations leads to greater understanding of the power of waves.

Three stages in the erosion of a coastal cliff are illustrated here: a headland (bottom), an arch and a sea stack (top). The erosion of weak rocks leaves the more durable rocks of a headland jutting into the sea. But crosscurrents formed by the headland erode it from behind, finally cutting a hole and creating an arch. When the arch collapses, the end of the headland is a sea stack cut off from the shore and subject to assault by the sea from all sides. Ultimately it will be reduced to a small rock, then disappear beneath the waves.

Waves are formed by winds, tides and ocean currents. The combined effect of these forces far out at sea is a gradual, undefined swell. But near shore their motion is altered. As the ocean becomes shallower, the movement of the swells is slowed, causing them to crowd together. The water "backs up," the swells become higher and steeper, and finally they topple forward as breakers. The foamy crest of the wave, called swash, rides up the beach, depositing sand at the top of the beach, called the berm. The spent wave—backwash—is pulled back by gravity.

At sea the wavelength is 20 times the wave height.

A wave starts to peak when the wavelength is twice the depth.

A wave breaks when its height is ¾ of the water's depth.

Dune

Berm

Swash

Misty and Moody, a Giant Waterway Where Klondikers and Haida Sailed

The Inside Passage, one of Canada's great scenic waterways, is 330 miles of wandering channels flanked by spectacular fjords and mist-shrouded mountains—a lovely, moody route sheltered from Pacific storms by a string of hundreds of islands.

Haida warriors paddled south through these waters to raid and to trade in the region of Washington State's Puget Sound. Gold seekers, loggers, fishermen and adventurers steamed north to Prince Rupert, the Queen Charlotte Islands, the Klondike and Alaska. Now tiny tugs tow huge barges through the passage with logs and wood chips for pulp and paper plants. Pleasure boats from many a Pacific coast port travel the passage, as does the B.C. car ferry *Queen of Prince Rupert*, which makes a 330-mile run between Kelsey Bay and Prince Rupert, linking the coastal islands in southern British Columbia with those in the north of the province.

Only traces of the passage's romantic past are visible today. But the scenery is as the Haida and the Klondikers saw it. Some islands are mere brown rocks, perhaps topped by a single tree or a salal bush. Some are low, their green trees shading away to a distant purple horizon. Always the ultimate backdrop is rank on rank of mountains, some velvety green, some topped with snow, some populated with giant trees on the lower slopes but turning to sheer rock decorated with sheets of

The Inside Passage, near Prince Rupert.

319

ageless ice. Here and there, like a silver thread in the mountain distance, is a glimpse of plunging river, disappearing into the green as if into a deep sponge.

Scattered along the shore, half hidden in protective coves, are fragments of history: fish camps that lie in ruins, victims of time and refrigeration and radar and sonar ... the hulks of a few big ships, etched with rust ... scores of boats on their sides in the mud....

The coast of British Columbia has two main moods, two distinct textures. And nowhere are they more apparent than along the Inside Passage.

One is the texture of the coast in bright sunlight, when everything is unmistakable geographical reality. Islands are islands: Hunter Island, Roy Island, Price Island, Swindle Island.... Trees are trees: fir, cedar, spruce, hemlock.... Mount Buxton on Calvert Island is identifiable. So is Mount Palmerston just north of Kelsey Bay. Inlets that open to view one after another can be pointed out as Seymour Inlet, Rivers Inlet, Kwatna Inlet.... The sun shines on such places as Ripple Passage, Caamaño Sound, Laredo Channel.... Over there is Alert Bay. The next one north is Port Hardy. At night there is a starry sky, and the lights of Bella Coola, Klemtu and Butedale are bright against the black velvet of one of the world's largest forest areas.

But there is the other texture, when all the world seems cloaked in ethereal fog. There are no islands, only glimpses of trees entangled in mist that may drift off to expose a black reef—but only for a moment. The whiteness shifts again and the reef is gone and the world is a surround of giant trees like an army of mute monsters on a mythical shore.

Then the milky shadow may rise, exposing a precipitous ravine filled with ice—or was it water? Whichever, it had no name for it departed from reality as it had come. And there, between those islands, was it a dock? A house? A boat? And who lives there? How do they get their food? Mail? Are there children?

A seabird is created out of the mist for a second, then plunges back into the primordial, timeless world of the unseen. And was that an old weather-beaten cedar snag surrounded by driftwood or was it a totem pole and a group of Haida Indians?...

On both sides of the Inside Passage, whether the sun shines or the mist is swirling, is a world that is no part of the passing of man, no part of the search for gold or the catching of fish or the hauling of logs. It is the dark, damp rain forest of fir, cedar and hemlock—where old

Fog near the entrance to Kelsey Bay, the port in northern Vancouver Island from which the cruise ship Queen of Prince Rupert *sails up the Inside Passage.*

giants die, then stand dead for centuries while fungi, ants and termites laboriously weaken the great trees. Then ... one snowflake too many or an extra caress of wind brings a giant down in a thundering crash, to lie prone now for centuries. The final agony is violent: As the old tree falls, so do all the dead and living trees in its path—and in their paths too.

Now the sun again has access to earth for a moment in time and on the giant's decaying carcass life starts anew. Another seed starts its long journey to an encounter-in-death with a snowflake or a breeze.

Fallen tree upon fallen tree, decay upon decay, cover the forest floor. Living trees in all sizes stand shoulder to shoulder, stretching on tiptoe to reach the life-giving sun above the velvety green treetops.

But there is life on the ground, an underworld of animals, each in frantic pursuit of the continuation of life. This is a world of hunters that are not hunted—grizzly, black bear, wolf, cougar, wolverine. Here also are those that hunt and are hunted—otter, mink, ermine, fox, raccoon, fisher, marten. And those that are just hunted—deer, beaver, squirrel, porcupine.

Many a man, through the years, has axed his way into the rain forest that lines the shore of the Inside Passage. The trails are mostly gone now, covered with fallen logs and branches. Some cabins are still there but, having been made from it, they have no immunity from the forest. They soon sag as ants and termites eat the walls. Salal and berry bushes grow from the roofs. Steller's jays inspect the interiors for leftovers.

An old cabin sets the new intruder to wondering. Who was here? Perhaps a prospector. For gold? Copper? Where is he now?

Under a decayed bed is a pop bottle. What could have been the occasion? One bottle of soda pop by ship up the passage, then carried for miles....

But man was here long before the prospector.

A mile back in the deep green is an enormous cedar stump. Lying out from the stump, where it fell after being cut down, is the tree, looking like a partially completed dugout canoe. Growing out of the center of the canoe is a hemlock about 30 years old. The unfinished canoe is 30 feet long—and a mile from water.

When the texture of the coast is bright sunlight, the reality of the Inside Passage is what is seen from the ship: the islands, the mountains, the fields of ice—and the following gulls, the great bald eagles sweeping the sky, the pods of whales, the herds of sea lions. But when the texture is mist and the mood is mystery, in the passage itself the traveler may sense the presence of Haida and their dugouts, prospectors and their broken dreams, dead giants crashing into the chaos of the rain forest....

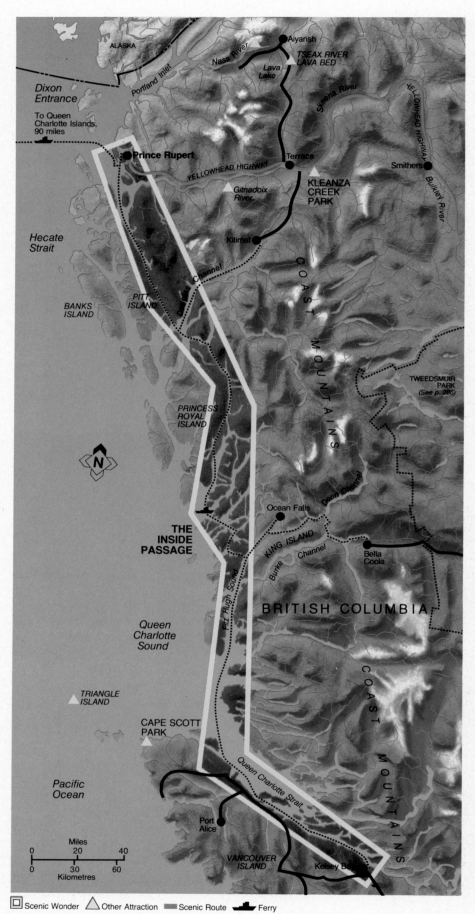

OTHER ATTRACTIONS

A Fish You Eat— Or Use for Light

Cape Scott Provincial Park Thousands of seabirds nest along a wild, 40-mile Pacific shoreline of craggy headlands and long, sandy beaches.

Gitnadoix River This 15-mile river flows from Alastair Lake, through a valley bordered by mountains up to 6,000 feet high, to the Skeena River.

Kleanza Creek Provincial Park Kleanza Creek rushes through a small canyon with sheer rock walls 35 feet high.

Nass River Thousands of *oolichans* (candlefish) spawn each March in the Nass River some 50 miles northeast of Prince Rupert. In their 10-to-15-mile ascent from the sea they are often pursued by gulls, bald eagles and seals. *Oolichans*, prized for their flesh and oil, are also dried and, with wicks inserted, used as candles.

Triangle Island Thousands of seabirds jam the narrow ledges and steep, grassy slopes of this treeless, 211-acre island. Black oyster catchers, pigeon guillemots, common murres and pelagic cormorants live at the lower levels. Tufted puffins and rhinoceros auklets burrow in the slopes and Cassin's auklets and storm petrels nest on the cliff tops.

Tseax River Lava Bed Rocks and boulders strewn over 15 desolate square miles are evidence of two volcanic eruptions some 300 years ago. The first eruption from a now-dormant volcano (eight miles southeast of Aiyansh on the banks of the Tseax River) left a crater 1,200 feet wide. The second eruption (from within the first crater) created a 75-foot-deep crater surrounded by a cone some 300 feet high and 250 feet across. Alder Peak (7,282 feet), part of the Nass Ranges, forms a rugged backdrop to the lava bed.

Yellowhead Highway The Skeena River and the snowcapped Coast Mountains (averaging 5,000 feet) flank the 95-mile stretch of the Yellowhead Highway between Prince Rupert and Terrace.

Up-and-Down Air and the West Coast's Shattered Climate

The part of British Columbia along the Pacific coast is one of the world's wettest regions. Yet while some parts receive almost 300 inches of rain and snow every year, others get little more than 20 inches. It is what meteorologists call a shattered climate. The extremes are the result of warm, moist air that blows off the Pacific being manipulated by the coastal fjords, valleys and mountains.

The air has absorbed great amounts of moisture on a long journey around the Pacific. The North Equatorial Current, moving west across the ocean, is turned north at the Philippines and becomes the Kuroshio (Japan Current). That in turn becomes the North Pacific Current, heading east toward North America.

As the moisture-saturated air confronts the mountains of British Columbia, it is forced upward. It cools, lessening the amount of moisture it can carry: the excess vapor condenses and falls as rain or snow. Up the faces of the first ranges, precipitation increases steadily from about 100 inches to 200 inches a year. Certain fjords cause even heavier rainfall in limited areas. They compress rain clouds in a funneling effect and drive them suddenly upward at the ends of the fjords.

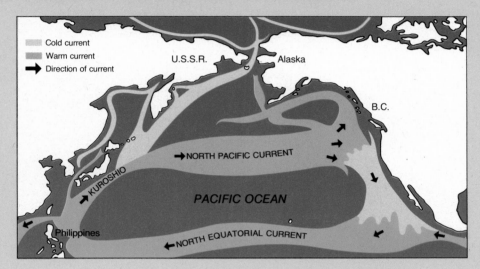

When air masses descend the eastern slopes of the mountains they become warmer. Again they are capable of holding more moisture. The result often is a dramatic reduction in rainfall within a few miles. This "rain shadow" effect continues until the air starts to ascend the next series of ranges. By the time it crosses the eastern slopes of the Rock-

ies and the Alberta foothills the air has lost most of the moisture that creates the great rain forests along the Pacific Coast. Were it not for the western mountains, the air blowing off the Pacific Ocean would distribute its precipitation more evenly not only across the dry Prairies but across the North American continent as a whole.

Moisture-laden air flowing east from the Pacific Ocean is forced upward as it meets British Columbia's Coast Mountains. As the air rises it cools, greatly reducing its ability to retain moisture. This results in heavy rainfall, which in turn creates the lush coastal rain forests on the mountains' western slopes (below).

After crossing the mountains, air masses descend. The air warms, increasing its ability to retain moisture. Hence there is much less rainfall on the eastern slopes (the "rain shadow" of the mountains), creating semi-arid conditions such as those along the Fraser River near Big Bar Creek (below).

Enticing, Isolated, a Mysterious Region Ruled By Wild Nature

A sea lion sweeps through a school of herring in the light-green waters of Skidegate Inlet—herring that suddenly attract a confusion of diving loons and gulls and cormorants and mergansers. Now harlequin ducks move in, and goldeneyes, scaups, scoters and pigeon guillemots. Now a pod of harbor porpoises rolls toward the herring.

As a ribbon of trumpeter swans clears trees that rim the bay, two skeins of black brants wing low and silent to a splashdown and a feed of eelgrass. A great blue heron poses, peering into a pool uncovered by the ebbing tide. Bald eagles clutch high, seaward branches, waiting, watching. A pair of ravens patrol the beach.

This is the Queen Charlotte Islands—as they are less than half a mile from the airport at Sandspit.

West of Skidegate Inlet is Skidegate Channel, which separates the two main islands of the Queen Charlottes—Graham Island to the north, Moresby Island to the south. The 26-foot tide in the inlet is the highest on Canada's Pacific coast. Tides run to 14 feet at the west end of Skidegate Channel and water sluices through the channel at up to seven knots.

Graham, Moresby and about 150 other islands, part of a submerged mountain range, form a triangular, 4,000-square-mile archipelago, the ancient home of the Haida. It is about 150 miles long and 50 wide at its north

Seabirds off Langara Island.

325

end. "The Charlottes," as they are called by their 5,000-odd people (who inhabit only six of the islands), are a strange and mysterious land of rugged mountains and fjord-like inlets, abandoned whaling stations and ancient totem poles rotting in humid rain forests. Although the islands are at the latitude of James Bay, winters here are mild, summers cool, and seasons moderated to an annual average of 8°C. (46°F.) by a countercurrent of the great Kuroshio (Japan Current). The weather includes brutal winds exceeding 100 knots and rainfall of more than 7½ inches in a 24-hour period.

Geologists read a long history of violence in the Queen Charlottes' eroded, glaciated rocks. Altered volcanic rocks are faulted, uplifted, intruded and folded—looking like marble cake frosted with a thick layer of lava. Coal and soft, lustrous black argillite—not duplicated anywhere—formed in the Slatechuck Mountain area of Graham Island. Carbonized portions of trees, and fossils of tiny clams, leaves and ammonites are exposed on eroded shores.

The Charlottes are on the edge of the continental shelf, a ridge that extends west from the British Columbia mainland. It runs under Hecate Strait (50 to 300 feet deep) and climbs to the heights of the Queen Charlotte Ranges. Then, on the west side of the archipelago—the very edge—the shelf plunges steeply into the sea. The seabed levels off at about 10,000 feet some 100 miles from the Charlottes' west coast.

The craggy Queen Charlotte Ranges, none more than 3,700 feet, run virtually the entire length of the archipelago. Midway down Moresby Island the mountains begin to taper into a single staggered ridge before dropping undersea at the last of the Kerouard Islands.

Scientists are intrigued by these isolated islands. The luxuriant vegetation of the Northwest Coast region is nowhere more highly developed than on the Queen Charlottes.

Among their 450 mosses and liverworts are one known previously only in Japan, two others known only in western Europe and five found only in the Charlottes. Subspecies of the saw-whet owl, hairy woodpecker and Steller's jay are restricted to these islands. The owl and jay are larger and all are duskier than their mainland cousins.

The Charlottes have only seven native land mammals: two species of deer mice, a shrew, an ermine, a marten, a river otter and a black bear. An eighth native, the dwarfed, mouse-gray Dawson caribou, became extinct during the past half century. Other animals have been introduced. The abundant black-tailed deer tends to dwarf. Beaver, raccoon, muskrat and squirrel expand their range each year. The elk is seldom seen. There are no snakes.

The Haida Indians were the islands' first known residents, a sea-oriented people who lived in harmony with a wild and bountiful nature. Perhaps 8,000 Haida lived in 18 villages scattered around the rim of the archipelago. From massive cedar logs—easily hewn and split, slow to rot—they built sturdy longhouses and seagoing canoes up to 70 feet long. The Haida's needs were limited, their hunting and fishing primitive. They could not deplete a fecund nature.

Totems, many fallen, are found in abandoned villages throughout the islands. Petroglyphs decorate tidal rocks on Lena Island and at Yaku and Kiusta on Graham Island.

Soon after the first Europeans arrived in 1774, the Haida had means and incentive to take more than they needed. Sea otters and seals were slaughtered almost to extinction in only 40 years. The Haida, in turn, were nearly annihilated by the white man's diseases.

Trade in sea otter furs brought Capt. George Dixon to the North Pacific in the British ship *Queen Charlotte* in 1787. He named the archipelago Queen Charlotte's Islands in honor of the consort of George III.

Most modern visitors arrive in the Charlottes at Sandspit Airport on Moresby Island, then go by road, along a beach strewn with glacier-deposited boulders, to Alliford Bay. A ferry crosses Skidegate Inlet to Skidegate on Graham Island.

Graham, the largest island, has four-fifths of the islands' population. There are seven road-connected settlements. Masset, Queen Charlotte City and Port Clements have stores, cafés, and lodging, as does Sandspit. Haida and Skidegate Mission are Haida villages. Juskatla is a logging company headquarters and Tlell is the center of a ranching district.

In addition to the 89 miles of asphalt public roads—most follow the shoreline—hundreds of miles of hard-packed private logging roads have been punched into the interior. They are available to the public after working hours and on weekends, some wending through forests with spruce trees as big as 14 feet in diameter and along purling streams where campers may relax.

West of Port Clements, on Masset Inlet near the center of Graham Island, a trail leads into a parklike rain forest. One tall and stately tree of gold looms from the dark green forest. The Golden Spruce, a unique tree, more than 300 years old and 165 feet tall, that is a mystery to foresters. Its seeds produce only green boughed seedlings. Fifteen miles inland from the Golden Spruce is an area of extinct volcanoes.

Like miniature mountains these tree-capped pinnacles loom out of the mist off the east beach of Cox Island. The island is in Cloak Bay on Langara Island.

At Masset, at the north end of Graham Island, is the Delkatla Wildlife Sanctuary, where sandhill cranes, trumpeter swans and Canada geese and other waterfowl may be photographed while they rest and feed during migration.

A gravel road leads from Masset to Naikoon Provincial Park, which occupies the low, nearly featureless northeast corner of Graham Island. At a picnic site on McIntyre Bay, a footpath leads to the top of 500-foot Tow Hill. On a clear day Langara Island can be seen 50 miles to the west. North, across Dixon Entrance, are Alaska's Dall and Prince of Wales islands. At the end of a seven-mile hard-packed sand beach is Rose Point, the northeastern tip of the Charlottes. Naikoon Park's nearly 60 miles of beaches are loaded with razor clams. Beyond the breakers of Dixon Entrance and Hecate Strait fishermen trap dungeness crabs. Backpackers continue around Rose Point and south along Hecate Strait, to Tlell, at the south end of the park.

Sunny summer days, 18 hours long, are the time to enjoy the Charlottes by boat or float plane. Rocky-shored islands indented by coves and hidden bays form a labyrinth of meandering waterways, enticing boaters and kayakers to Moresby's east coast. Snorkel and scuba divers peer through crystal water at rocks and sandy bottoms alive with rock scallops, pinto abalone, starfish, bêche-de-mer, varicolored sea urchins and darting fish.

The Queen Charlottes are by far the most active earthquake area in Canada and many a steep shoreline is scarred by a jumble of rocks and broken trees, the result of earth slides initiated by seismic activity. Along this east coast of Moresby Island and on other islands there are jumbles, too, of decaying buildings and rusting equipment. Sixty years ago prospectors and miners, loggers, whalers, fishermen and cannerymen, trappers, traders, and wireless operators challenged this wild land. Few stayed. Alders rushed in to cover the scars.

Today logging companies move in and clear-cut, replant, then move to greener hillsides. Scientifically managed, fast-growing uniform-sized trees will reach maturity in 100 years. Meanwhile, deer have good browse, a variety of small birds and blue grouse have good cover, sportsmen enjoy excellent hunting, and hikers follow old roads and trails.

The Charlottes' finest and largest collection of totems is in the derelict village of Ninstints on Anthony Island, near the southern end of the archipelago. Around a tiny bay is an uneven arc of 20 to 25 tottering heraldic and

Northern sea lions congregate on a wave-lashed rock at Cone Head on Graham Island. Right: A male peregrine falcon brings food to its young. The nest is on a ledge near the top of a cliff on Langara Island, the northernmost island in the Queen Charlottes.

mortuary totems, abandoned for nearly a century. Blotched with lichens and gray with age, these Haida totems are balanced and artistic creations of eagles, ravens, killer whales, bears and other animals. Excavations edged with mouldering, moss-covered cedar logs are all that remains of communal longhouses. A path cleared generations ago for hauling dugouts to tidewater is still usable.

At the southernmost tip are the tiny Kerouard Islands, low and surrounded by turbulent seas, where gulls, cormorants and other seabirds nest. One islet is a pupping ground for hundreds of Steller's sea lions. Half of the estimated 5,000 sea lions along the British Columbia coast live in the Charlottes.

Graham Island's west coast is edged with jutting reefs and rows of breakers pounding beaches of silvery sand caught between fingers of sharp lava. Short streams gush through gravel banks sparkling with carnelians, jaspers and agates. Wind-toppled trees are everywhere and the hulls of ships and boats lie on and near this coast where beauty and violence marry.

Bright-billed tufted puffins, knob-billed rhinoceros auklets and Cassin's auklets nest in burrows along the west and north coasts, as do small ancient murrelets (the Queen Charlottes are their only Canadian breeding ground). These alcids spend most of their lives at sea, feeding in large flocks and thriving in the turbulent

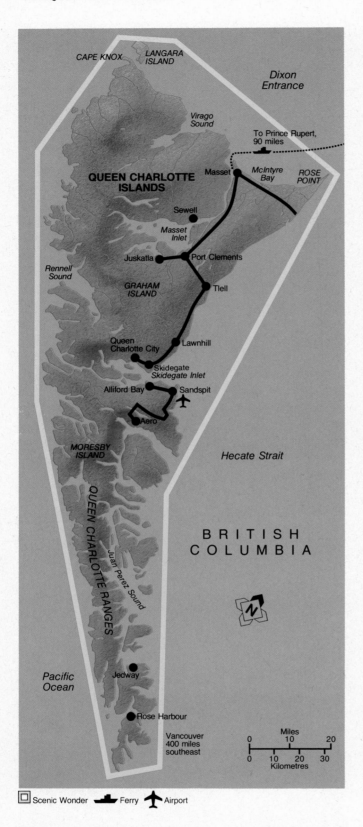

QUEEN CHARLOTTE ISLANDS

CAPE KNOX
LANGARA ISLAND
Dixon Entrance
Virago Sound
To Prince Rupert, 90 miles
Masset
McIntyre Bay
ROSE POINT
Sewell
Masset Inlet
Juskatla
Port Clements
Rennell Sound
GRAHAM ISLAND
Tlell
Queen Charlotte City
Lawnhill
Skidegate
Skidegate Inlet
Alliford Bay
Sandspit
Aero
MORESBY ISLAND
Hecate Strait
QUEEN CHARLOTTE RANGES
Juan Perez Sound
BRITISH COLUMBIA
Pacific Ocean
Jedway
Rose Harbour
Vancouver 400 miles southeast

Miles
0   10   20
0 10 20 30
Kilometres

☐ Scenic Wonder   ⛴ Ferry   ✈ Airport

fish-rich waters. They, in turn, are easy prey for peregrine falcons nesting on cliffside shelves overlooking their food market.

A pair of falcons are secure in their aerie atop Pillar Rock, a column of conglomerate and sandstone that rises 95 feet above a tidal shelf on the northwest shore of Graham Island. Other rock formations, shaped to grotesque figures by wind and sea, are to be seen, but none so spectacular.

The sea around the Charlottes may be almost mill-pond flat in summer and winter but it is rarely so in spring and fall. Gentle swells quickly boil into steep waves whipped by winds gusting to 100 knots. Crests are slashed off and the spume is driven in horizontal sheets—or swirled upward more than 100 feet as sea dust. Williwaws sometimes cascade down steep western slopes, striking as sledgehammer downwinds.

Gray whales migrate through the waters of the archipelago. Sperm whales feed along offshore reefs. Humpbacks come into bays to rub their snouts and flippers against sheer rocks and scratch off parasitic barnacles. Killer whales, always on the move and usually in packs, rush into an inlet with high dorsal fins cleaving the water; they catch an unwary seal or porpoise and are gone. On rare occasions a 2½-ton northern elephant seal is sighted poking his inflatable snout above the water.

Laysan and black-footed albatross glide effortlessly, rising and dipping with each six- to eight-foot swell. Smaller sooty shearwaters also scour the sea for food. Noisy black oyster catchers leap from their nests on offshore rocks, flashing long red bills and pink legs.

Rafts of hundreds of thousands of vellela, a sail jellyfish 2½ to 3½ inches long, are sometimes encountered, moving in great blue-green windrows. Sun jellyfish are often seen, looking like great raw eggs two or three feet across.

As August showers turn to September downpours, frisky salmon school up near the stream of their origin, slapping the water as they leap in excitement. They are losing their silvery beauty, changing to somber colors. Upstream, after escaping man, bears and birds, each female deposits hundreds of bright red eggs. As she drifts away, a male fertilizes the eggs. A new generation is assured. Old life nearly spent, the pair swim away.

There comes a heavy overnight rain and the streams overflow. Spawned-out salmon are flushed onto the valley floor. Bears come to feed, to fatten for hibernation. Birds gorge. It is a time of feasting, a time to prepare for winter.

As rains wash the Charlottes, the music of migrating geese signals winter's approach. Lethargic bears amble into their dens. Squirrels add a few more lodgepole pine cones to their already abundant supply.

The enticing, exciting Charlottes are isolated by distance, weather and style. They continue to demand a distinctive way of life—as they did of the Haida—a life attuned to and frequently regulated by a wild nature.

Where It's 10,000 Feet to the Ocean Floor

Along most of Canada's 150,000 miles of coastline the land that dips beneath the sea quickly levels off underwater to become the continental shelf. This shelf usually extends several miles from shore, sometimes hundreds of miles. Its edge is a cliff that plunges to the ocean's depths.

Off the coast of mainland British Columbia the shelf is about 50 miles wide. But the Queen Charlotte Islands, separated from the mainland by the 300-foot-deep Hecate Strait, are poised on the very brink of the shelf. The islands' west coast is the top of a great cliff that plummets almost 10,000 feet to the floor of the Pacific Ocean.

Millions of years of volcanic eruptions and of folding and faulting of the earth's crust in this area have given the islands three distinct regions. The Queen Charlotte Lowlands, mostly flat muskeg, were once part of the floor of Hecate Strait. The ridges and flat-topped hills of the Skidegate Plateau form the central part of the island group. To the west are the Queen Charlotte Ranges, the old volcanic backbone of the islands. These mountains are steep and rugged and more impressive than their 3,000-to-4,000-foot heights suggest. Their western flanks are the steep cliffs that drop into the sea.

The islands are in Canada's most active earthquake area. They are on a shear, an extension of the Denali fault. (Shears and faults are cracks in the earth's crust and a sudden slip of the crust along a shear or a fault is what causes an earthquake.) Since 1921, seventeen quakes have shaken the Queen Charlotte Islands but there has been no loss of life. The map at right locates the epicenters, the points on the earth's crust directly above the focuses of the quakes.

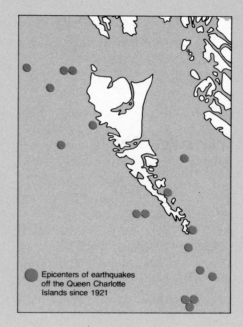

Epicenters of earthquakes off the Queen Charlotte Islands since 1921

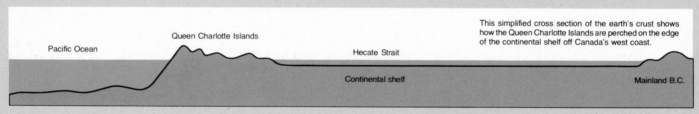

Pacific Ocean

Queen Charlotte Islands

Hecate Strait

Continental shelf

Mainland B.C.

This simplified cross section of the earth's crust shows how the Queen Charlotte Islands are perched on the edge of the continental shelf off Canada's west coast.

Cliffs on the west coast of Moresby Island fall steeply to the sea, then almost straight down to the ocean floor some 10,000 feet below.

THE NORTH

A Last Great Frontier of Surpassing Beauty

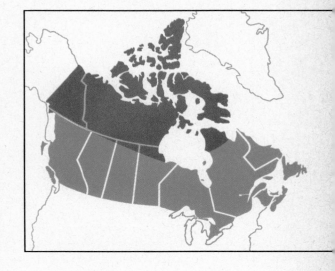

An inhospitable, windswept wasteland it sometimes is, beset by numbing cold, howling winds and wearying blizzards. But the North, our last great frontier, is a land of delightful surprises and unexpected beauty. It is a land where, in places, long months of total darkness give way to blissful months of uninterrupted daylight. Here live wondrous creatures that most Canadians have never seen—the narwhal, walrus, musk-ox, seal, polar bear, lemming, beluga whale, caribou and gyrfalcon. Here, in the realm of mystery and legend that is Nahanni National Park, hot springs bubble to the surface and rivers rage between towering canyon walls. Among the dizzying summits of remote Kluane National Park is 19,524-foot Mount Logan—Canada's highest peak. In vivid contrast to the mountains, the flat Barren Grounds sprawl across almost half a million square miles—an incredible collage of animal and plant life. The broad Mackenzie, Canada's greatest river, makes its epic 1,070-mile journey through the North to the Arctic Ocean, collapsing into 20,000 lakes at its own delta. In Auyuittuq National Park, the world's first national park north of the Arctic Circle, are teeming bird colonies perched on the sheer sides of spectacular fjords, and massive glaciers which have been snaking down lonely mountainsides since the Ice Age. The North, enticing and misunderstood, is a land apart—but a part of the essence of Canada.

Opposite: *Kluane Lake.*
Preceding pages: *Polar bear on Baffin Bay.*

Mount Logan, highest of the highest.

KLUANE NATIONAL PARK

Azure Lakes in the Shadow of Canada's Highest Peaks

336

Kluane. The name stretches. Kloo-aw-nee. The vowels are long and lingering, like the breadth and sweep of the land itself. The word is Indian for big fish, and Arctic grayling and kokanee salmon do grow large in Kluane's translucent lakes. But in almost every way this corner of the Yukon—east of Alaska and north of British Columbia—is a place of superlatives.

Kluane is 8,500 square miles (almost four Prince Ed-ward Islands) and second in size among Canadian national parks. (Only Wood Buffalo, 17,300 square miles and the biggest national park in the world, is larger.) All but a thousand square miles is unrelieved rock and ice. Canada's highest mountain, 19,524-foot Mount Logan, looms here, amid Canada's loftiest range, the St. Elias Mountains, with eight peaks over 15,000 feet. Kluane's ice fields are among the world's largest. Its Steele

Glacier, no classic slow-moving river of ice, has been known to gallop close to half a mile in one month. Wolves prowl along 184-square-mile Kluane Lake, the Yukon's biggest lake, and throughout the region roam Dall sheep, caribou and grizzlies—a grouping of animals found in no other national park. Kluane was declared a national park reserve in 1942 and the following year was designated a game sanctuary in which hunting and trapping were banned. But mining was allowed—it had gone on since 1903—and in and near the park are remnants of gold-miners' camps. In Silver City, alongside the Alaska Highway, 10 sod-and-log cabins stand in disrepair and you may happen on rusting gold pans and rotting sluice boxes.

Gold and copper mining continue beside the park (created in 1972), and the side of one mountain visible to motorists is scarred by a miners' road. Yet man has made little lasting mark on Kluane. Mountaineers have climbed many of its peaks, but to speak of *conquering* such immensity seems presumptuous. Mount Logan's imposing summit was first scaled in 1925. The remote Centennial Range was climbed in 1967 by an expedition of 250 persons. They named 12 of the mountains for the provinces and territories, reserving the title of Centennial Peak for the highest (12,320 feet). Hundreds of other peaks remain unclimbed.

The Kluane Ranges are the first mountain barrier on the northeastern boundary of the park. To the southwest, above a valley called the Duke Depression, are the St. Elias Mountains, which include the Icefield Ranges, with ice that survives from the Ice Age. From the mountains flow 10 main rivers, some ultimately flowing into the Pacific Ocean, others far north into the Bering Sea.

The Haines Highway (from Haines, Alaska) meets the Alaska Highway at Haines Junction (Mile 1016), a town just outside the park. Mountain climbers and overnight hikers must register with park wardens at Haines Junction. (Mountaineering groups who want to tackle the St. Elias Mountains must apply in writing three months in advance.) Roads suitable for even four-wheel-drive vehicles are rare in Kluane so most visitors walk in. Planes and helicopters can be chartered, however; aside from days of wilderness hiking, they are the only way to see close-ups of Mount Logan and the other St. Elias peaks (although the range is visible—40 miles away—from roadside telescopes 110 miles northwest of Haines Junction).

The interior of Kluane is a place to confront, to meet on its own demanding terms. A 1972 resource study report warned: "The inner core is extremely rugged and beautiful but dangerous. Only the very experienced will brave the hazards of this area, and some of them have been killed by the mountains." Black and grizzly bears may attack when surprised. The temperature in the river valleys may reach 27°C. (80°F.) during summer days when the sunlight lasts 19 hours, but even in July sudden blizzards often sweep the mountainsides.

But hikers find stunning, stirring vistas and see a rich variety of wildlife when they walk in from the main roads. Using maps, you can reach the foot of the awesome Kaskawulsh Glacier in two or three days from the Slims River bridge at Mile 1055 of the Alaska Highway. An old packhorse trail follows the east bank of the river, past sand dunes, mud flats and cliffs to the windswept foot of the glacier, five miles wide, twisting like an icy blue-brown ribbon. Two rivers that begin at the glacier end hundreds of miles apart. The Kaskawulsh Glacier winds into the Alsek River and the Gulf of Alaska, 140 miles south; the Slims flows into Kluane Lake, then the Yukon River and eventually the Bering Sea, 1,400 miles west.

The park's only campground is off the Haines Highway, on the eastern shore of chilly, crystalline Kathleen Lake, laden with trout, Kokanee salmon and Arctic grayling. Set under 8,000-foot peaks, Kathleen is no lady: her waters can turn so fierce in sudden storms that canoeing is discouraged.

A two-hour climb from Kathleen Lake leads through spruce and up a sheer but safe gully to the King's Throne, a grassy expanse adorned with wild flowers. Below, like a huge azure carpet shimmering in the sun, is Kathleen Lake.

Pure white Dall sheep survey their range around Sheep Mountain, which can be reached by hiking down a sideroad from Mile 1060.5 of the Alaska Highway. Right: Near Duke River in Kluane Park.

Ground squirrels sass you on most Kluane walks and a hiker along willow-thick watercourses may sight some of the biggest moose on the continent. The giant mountain caribou is less plentiful but one band of about 125 is often seen on the 20-square-mile Burwash Uplands, excluded from the park but convenient to the Alaska Highway. Kluane shelters mountain goats, 500-pound grizzlies, black bears, and the odd Alaskan brown bear that meanders onto Canadian soil.

Birds abound, a unique mix of at least 170 varieties—such easterners as the spruce grouse, northerners like the rock ptarmigan and even that migrant from the grasslands, the magpie. Climbers once saw a hummingbird halfway up Mount Logan. John Theberge, a University of Waterloo, Ont., wildlife ecologist, becomes poetic when describing his observation of Kluane

Two arms of the Kaskawulsh Glacier meet and blend as they wend through the St. Elias Mountains. Earth and rocks create the dark strips (moraines) on the glacier.

birdlife one June: "Mew gulls diving at a bald eagle, golden-crowned sparrows singing their three-note song in the northern dusk, a spotted sandpiper guarding its nest of four splotched eggs, Arctic terns swooping down to ward off an intruder, a sharp-tailed grouse performing its broken-wing display, a red-necked grebe covering its eggs and slipping into the water of a pristine lake..."

In and around the park, the landscape constantly astonishes. The grasslands of the Slims River delta could have been borrowed from the prairies. White volcanic ash dates from an eruption about 1,400 years ago. Million Dollar Falls tumbles 200 feet into the Takhanne River, a half mile west of the Haines Highway.

The park's great mountains, its vast ice fields and awesome glaciers, its fine wildlife population and the variety of its vegetation and landscape . . . and the big fish that give Kluane its name . . . together they make this corner of the Yukon a showcase of nature's superlatives.

OTHER ATTRACTIONS

The Trail of '98— And Peaks Missed By the Ice Age

Chilkoot Pass Hiking Trail This 35-mile trail from Dyea, Alaska, to Bennett, B.C., follows the Chilkoot Pass route of the Klondike gold rush of 1898. Plaques and gold rush photographs are displayed along the way and some campsites are where sourdoughs had tent settlements. The three-mile ascent up the pass reaches a height of 3,740 feet. From the top the trail leads to Crater Lake, Long Lake and finally Lindeman and Bennett lakes, which form the headwaters of the mighty Yukon River. Hikers can return by foot or take a White Pass and Yukon Route excursion train to Whitehorse or Skagway, Alaska.

Dempster Highway Caribou Crossing Hundreds of caribou cross the highway at several places on their summer migration to calving grounds on the Alaska tundra to the west.

Haines Road The 115-mile Canadian section of the 160-mile highway between Haines, Alaska, and Haines Junction in the Yukon runs through tundralike terrain, rolling hills and sparse stands of spruce and aspen. Gizzly bear, wolverine and sheep inhabit the countryside.

Keno Mountain The spectacular view from the 6,200-foot mountain includes a valley 2,000 feet below, sparkling lakes and rolling hills covered with flowers.

Kluane Lake The 40-mile-long blue-green lake is hemmed in by the Kluane Range of the St. Elias Mountains. Dall sheep, grizzly bear, moose and wolf inhabit the mixed spruce-aspen forests around the lake; Canada geese, loons, ducks and trumpeter and whistling swans summer here.

Klutlan Glacier Forests of white spruce and poplar grow in a two-foot layer of ash that a volcano dumped on the glacier ice some 1,400 years ago. The ice is almost a mile thick in places. The five-mile-wide terminus (foot) is the widest of any glacier on the Canadian mainland.

Like some medieval fortress, this ridge in the Tombstone Range is granite, more resistant to erosion than the sedimentary rocks more common in the rest of the Ogilvie Mountains.

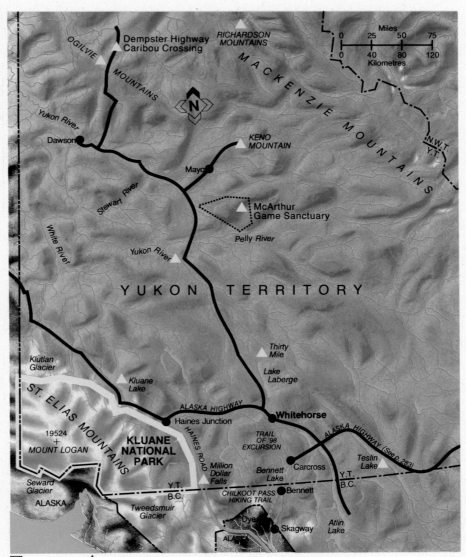

341

Richardson Mountains *These are composed mainly of dull-colored rocks but include the White Mountains, whose dolomite and limestone rocks are light colored.*

McArthur Game Sanctuary This 204-square-mile preserve was established to protect what once was considered a distinct species on the verge of extinction: the Fannin (saddle-backed) sheep. It now is known to be a product of interbreeding between Dall (white) sheep and Stone (black) sheep. Golden eagles, blue grouse, kingfishers and loons are also found in the sanctuary. The temperature of a small hot spring is 53°C. (128°F.). In the center of the sanctuary is 7,265-foot Grey Hunter Peak.

Million Dollar Falls The Takhanne River plunges 200 feet over a series of drops and rapids.

Ogilvie Mountains Stream beds here are bedrock, not glacial till or gravel, and there is no evidence of glaciers, because these mountains, like most of the northwest Yukon, survived the Ice Age relatively unscathed. There are a number of rare plant species. Picture preceding page.

Richardson Mountains Picture this page.

Teslin Lake Rolling, forested hills and the peaks of the Big Salmon Range form a backdrop to the clear, deep waters of the lake. Moose are abundant in the stands of spruce, poplar and pine.

Thirty Mile This section of the Yukon River flows from Lake Laberge to Hootalinqua through a winding 75-foot-wide channel rimmed by steep sand-and-gravel bluffs up to 300 feet high. Near Lower Laberge is an S-shaped curve below towering cliffs on both sides. Bald and golden eagles nest along the cliffs, and geese and ducks are found on lower lands along the Thirty Mile.

Trail of '98 Excursion The 100-mile train journey from Skagway, Alaska, to Whitehorse follows the path of the Klondike gold seekers. White Pass and Yukon Route passengers may leave the train at Bennett and be picked up by a train returning to Skagway, or may continue to Whitehorse past the spectacular scenery of mountain-fringed Lake Bennett. At Carcross passengers debark and take a steamer down the West Taku Arm of Tagish Lake.

Yukon River The 600-mile stretch between Lake Bennett and Dawson has rapids, gorges and magnificent scenery. In places the river boils through narrow canyons with sheer, 75-foot walls. At Five Finger Rapids, four 50-foot-high pillars of sandstone protrude from the river, dividing it into five streams. The swirling waters and rock walls of Miles Canyon are particularly impressive, as is 700-foot-high Eagle Bluff. Huge black basalt cliffs run for miles along the bank north of the Pelly River junction. Moose, bear, lynx and porcupine live in the forest and scrub brush; geese, hawks, falcons and eagles nest along the river.

The daily advance of a glacier is usually measured in inches—at most a few feet. But often many glaciers in the mountains of northwestern North America start to "gallop" at 10 to 100 times their normal rate. Some are in Kluane National Park.

More than half of the 8,500-square-mile park is covered by ice fields and alpine glaciers. Many Kluane glaciers and several in northwest British Columbia have speeded up in the last decade. Many are still galloping.

Unlike continental glaciers, which move slowly out from the center of an ice sheet no matter what the contours of the land, alpine glaciers tend to take the path of least resistance, usually through valleys.

A glacier up to two miles wide and as high as 1,000 feet surging down a valley at up to 75 feet a day is an awesome spectacle.

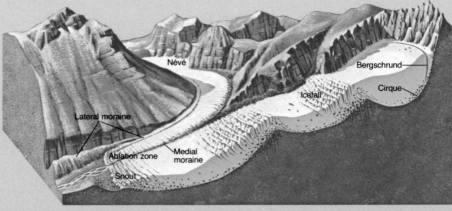

New snow that survives a year of melting is called firn. The snow accumulates in a **névé** or firn field, often a sheltered mountain slope which weathering and ice erode into giant depressions called **cirques**. A bergschrund is a large crevasse that separates the flowing ice from nearly stagnant ice above. **Icefalls** form when ice flows down a steep descent. Debris carried on the glacier creates a medial **moraine** (visible as a dark strip down the center of a glacier) and lateral moraines (dark strips at a glacier's edges). The lower part of the glacier is in the **ablation zone** (area of melting).

The Crawling Glaciers That Sometimes Break Into a Gallop

During its short-lived gallop in 1973, Tweedsmuir Glacier moved up to 20 feet a day. It dammed the Alsek River when its progress was halted by a mountain. Great slabs of ice (as much as 160 feet high) broke off at the edge, toppling into the water with roars that were heard for miles.

Snow crystal

Ice crystals

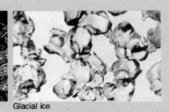
Glacial ice

A glacier is a mass of permanent land ice that sometimes moves. Unlike the frozen water of a lake or pond, glacial ice forms when snow (crystals of frozen water vapor) amasses to such an extent that more remains than melts in a season. After many years of accumulation, pressure changes the ice crystals (which were once snow crystals) into glacier ice. This mass begins to flow under the pressure of its own weight.

Resembling a breaking wave, the snout of Steele Glacier advances during a spectacular surge in 1965. Two miles wide and 1,000 feet thick in places, it accelerated from a near-stagnant rate to 75 feet a day, moving 4½ miles in less than three years.

Its surface fractured by its own movement, 45-mile-long Tweedsmuir Glacier heads across the Alsek River in northwest British Columbia during a surge in 1973. The glacier slammed into a mountain and effectively dammed the Alsek.

Cliffs of newly activated ice 150 feet high override the old terminus (foot) of Donjek Glacier on the northeast side of the St. Elias Mountains. In one surge, fast-moving ice formed deep crevasses and 200-foot-high pinnacles.

Staggering Beauty and Ominous Tales of a 'Shangri-la'

Tucked away in the Mackenzie Mountains, where the borders of British Columbia, the Yukon and the Northwest Territories come together, is a land long shrouded in mystery and legend, a Shangri-la (it was said) of tropical valleys, gold beyond dreams, and sudden death to all who would seek it—the Nahanni.

From the air it is a 14,300-square-mile jumble of rugged peaks and deep canyons—and the South Nahanni River crashing over a precipice almost twice as high as Niagara. The Nahanni's Niagara is Virginia Falls, a legend in itself, named for the daughter of the falls' discoverer, Fenley Hunter. All around the majestic waterfall are features whose names perpetuate the Nahanni legends: Deadmen Valley, Headless Range, Murder Valley, Broken Skull River, Funeral Range, Valley of No Return...

The headless bodies of two prospector brothers were found in their camp in 1908 (other men had disappeared without trace) and the Nahanni became known as a place to avoid. But one prospector in particular took little note of the tales that murderous mountain men ruled the Nahanni. Albert Faille went in scores of times between 1927 and 1973, when he died at age 85. "Didn't find any gold," he once said, "and for sure there's no tropical valley in there."

What *is* there is staggering natural beauty—and 1,840

Virginia Falls: the brink.

square miles of it was set aside in 1972 as Nahanni National Park. In it are such things as part of the saw-tooth Ragged Range, with a backbone of interconnected ice fields, and deep glacial lakes such as Hole in the Wall Lake, hauntingly lovely in a setting of snowcapped peaks.

There is Wild Mint Springs, a cluster of warm crystal-clear pools fringed with asters, delphiniums and mint.

There is the Devil's Kitchen, a litter of bizarre sandstone shapes on the slopes of the Liard Range. A banshee wind wails here and men are said to have plunged through a brittle crust of soil—and disappeared....

Adventurer Robert Patterson, who visited the Nahanni in the 1920s, wrote in *The Dangerous River* about "Wild Mountain Men" guarding gold. These were Indians who "never came in to any trading post," lords of the remote uplands of the Yukon-Mackenzie Divide, who "made short work of any man, white or Indian, who ventured into their country." Grandmothers in villages along the Liard tell of raiders who swooped from the hills to kill men and carry off women.

If such stories can be dismissed as legend, explaining the disappearances and the headless bodies is more difficult. Drownings, perhaps? Animals? No one knows.

Despite hair-raising legends and the difficulties of travel in the Nahanni, more and more tourists are visiting Shangri-la. They may drive the 960 miles from Edmonton along the Mackenzie Highway to Fort Simp-

A limestone pinnacle called Pulpit Rock stands 200 feet above the Nahanni River in Third Canyon. Many layers of rock in the steep walls of First Canyon (right) were sediment at the bottom of seas that flowed in and out of the Nahanni region over a 50-million-year period.

son, then go by charter aircraft to Nahanni Butte, 90 miles farther on at the confluence of the South Nahanni and Liard rivers. From Nahanni Butte it is 130 miles up the South Nahanni to Virginia Falls, in a steel-bottomed aluminum boat designed for Nahanni travel: 24 feet long, 6-inch draft, powerful engines. Each boat carries four or five tourists, a cook and a guide.

You set off through The Splits, where the river is wide and smooth and multichanneled but you fight a 12-to-15-knot current. (The river drops 960 feet—10 feet a mile—between Virginia Falls and Nahanni Butte.) Gradually the river narrows and you are in white water. Ahead is the Nahanni Range, gray and black, a maze of peaks marching to the horizon. Headless Range and Funeral Range lie out there, the river slicing through them between canyon walls hundreds of feet high.

You stop to see a hot spring at the foot of a bluff a few hundred feet in from the river. Luxuriant vegetation surrounds a pool and borders a stream that flows year round to the South Nahanni. There are ferns higher than a man, birch and spruce trees, a tangle of vines and acres of chokecherries.

Between the hot spring and Deadmen Valley lie the 17 spectacular, twisting miles of First Canyon. Here the river has laid bare layer after layer of pre-Ice Age rock—beds of yellow, gray, tawny brown and orange. Cliffs tower almost 3,000 feet above the river: 2,000 feet of solid dolomite is topped by limestone layers that soar another 700 to 800 feet and end in a craggy crest.

The canyon widens and the boat lurches through George's Riffle, a mad half mile of water at the upstream end of First Canyon. You are in Deadmen Valley. Headless bodies were found in 1908 just a few miles in from the river. But you camp here nonetheless.

Next day you push upriver through Second Canyon, its walls a sheer 4,000 feet. The valley opens up and ahead looms Third Canyon, guarded by The Gate, where the river makes a tight hairpin turn, narrowing through 800-foot vertical portals that glow brick red in an afternoon sun. Third Canyon is another 21 miles of fast water and beyond it is another campsite.

Next morning, the last 10 miles of white water, the surging waves of Hell's Gate and its double hairpin turn where many a boat has been smashed to kindling. Then, around a bend, Virginia Falls, one of the North's most magnificent spectacles, a great torrent crashing in twin waterfalls down a rock face 294 feet high and more than twice as wide, disappearing in an explosion of spray and mist.

The trip back is fast. You shoot through Hell's Gate, racing within a lick of canyon walls and jutting rocks, heaving, tossing in the torrent of cross-chop waves,

Rabbitkettle Hotsprings rises 90 feet out of the dark spruce forest, a giant layer cake of brittle, porous rock about 225 feet in diameter. Water that bubbles from the top spills gently down one foot-high terrace after another, depositing minerals that maintain the Rabbitkettle despite erosion. See also p. 351. Right: A cave in First Canyon.

swiftly down the river, through the canyons, through the valleys, across the floodplain to Nahanni Butte.

You look back to where you have been. The mountains are as dark and forbidding as before but you have experienced what lies behind that awesome façade. No longer can the Mackenzies conceal from the outsider their magnificence of rock and river, of thundering falls and roaring rapids, of dark canyons and deep pools, of caves and hot springs, the feast of wonder and beauty that is the Nahanni.

OTHER ATTRACTIONS

Rugged Canyons and Wild Rivers

Cli And Little Doctor Lakes These are fjord-like lakes, six miles apart, which glaciers carved in the Mackenzie Mountains some 10,000 years ago. Cli is 10 miles long, Little Doctor 6 miles long. Both are narrow and rimmed with near-vertical rock walls that soar 3,000 feet above the water.

Lafferty Canyon The canyon, 1,200 feet deep but only 1,400 feet wide at its downstream end, was carved from limestone by a tributary of the South Nahanni River.

Liard River Deep canyons and turbulent rapids, including the two-mile-long Portage Brûlé Rapids near Coal River, B.C., mark the wild Yukon and British Columbia sections of the 700-mile Liard. The most spectacular canyon is Hell Gate, in British Columbia, some 325 miles upstream from Fort Simpson, N.W.T. At Hell Gate the water rages through a 100-foot-wide channel between 150-foot-high rock walls. Below Hell Gate only a few sandbars and short portages block an easy canoe route to Fort Simpson, where the Liard joins the Mackenzie. Moose, beaver, marten, Canada geese, belted kingfishers, bald eagles and Canada jays are common in the coniferous forests along the river.

Nahanni Butte This limestone formation, 4,580 feet above sea level at its highest, is near the junction of the Liard and South Nahanni rivers. Dall sheep are sometimes seen atop the butte.

Norah Willis Michener Game Preserve In this rugged preserve, accessible only by float plane, are woodland caribou, wolverine, mountain grizzly, Dall sheep and moose. Songbirds nest in mixed forests on the lower mountain slopes. The Meilleur River rises in the Tlogotsho Range, descends through twisting gorges and meanders across the tundra to the South Nahanni River.

Ram River Canyon Dense boreal forest rolls back from the river and up to 2,500 feet above the river to near-vertical can-

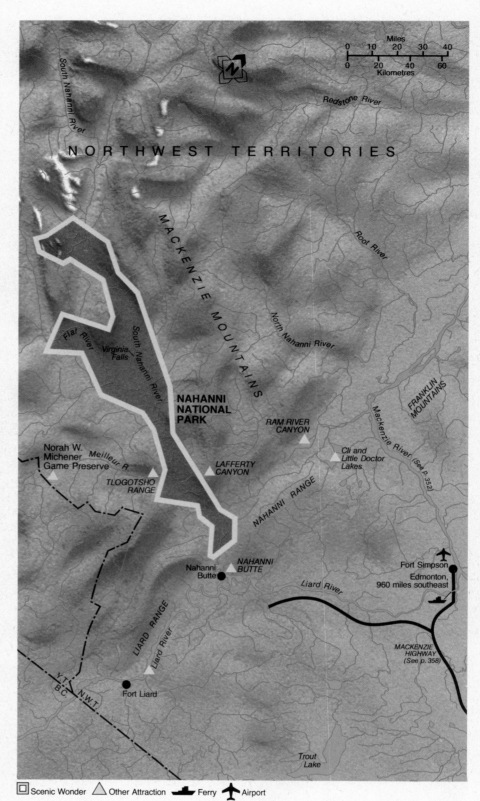

Scenic Wonder △ Other Attraction ⛴ Ferry ✈ Airport

yon walls 1,000 feet high. Sediment along the 10-mile-long canyon indicates it once was flooded with glacial meltwater. A one-mile section called Scimitar Canyon is narrow and impassable by boat. Its waters tumble over a waterfall and continuous rapids.

Tlogotsho Range Dall sheep are seen on a high, tundralike plateau fringed by steep slopes of red and silver-gray limestone. The graceful white animals summer on slopes as much as 6,000 feet above sea level and move down to drier, south-facing slopes in winter.

Newly-formed terraces at Rabbitkettle Hotsprings in Nahanni National Park resemble an elegant staircase. Pools behind the outer ridges will soon be filled with crystalline rock called tufa.

The Elegant Staircase at Rabbitkettle Hotsprings

Tropical valleys where snow never falls, where exotic plants grow in profusion year round...these are part of the Nahanni legend, a legend long accepted as truth. There are no such valleys. But there are hot springs and it is these that probably gave rise to tales of tropical Edens. In Nahanni National Park water heated far underground percolates to the surface at temperatures as high as 41°C. (106°F.)—and vegetation around these steaming pools is always green.

Some springs are simply pools of hot water that overflow into nearby streams and rivers. Others have deposited minerals and created fragile, terraced mounds. The most impres-

sive mounds are at Rabbitkettle Hotsprings on the sloping gravel bank of the Rabbitkettle River, a tributary of the Nahanni River. Two springs there have built a wide, low mound; a third has created a 90-foot-high mound that is one of the showpieces of the park. This formation, 225 feet wide at its base, is formed of tufa, a fine-grained crystalline rock made of calcium carbonate and other minerals. (Layered hot spring formations in other parts of the world, called travertine terraces, are of pure calcium carbonate.)

The building of the Rabbitkettle mounds probably started soon after the Ice Age

ended, some 10,000 years ago. Water from deep in the earth emerges in a 12-foot-wide pool at the top of the main mound. Laden with dissolved minerals, it flows as a thin sheet across a surface that is never completely level. Whenever it flows over a ridge, the sheet of water becomes thinner and it deposits minerals at a faster rate. These build up the ridge and the depositing of minerals quickens. The ridge becomes a dam and a pool forms behind it. Dissolved minerals settle to the bottom of the pool. When the pool is filled, the water starts to flow across an older, lower terrace and the entire process begins anew.

Tufa spills down one side of the large Rabbitkettle mound. At first iron red, tufa turns orange-red, then dull white as it dries. Rain and snow turn it gray.

Sulphur in the water bubbling from this spring near the mouth of First Canyon in Nahanni National Park cleans away tufa before it can form a mound.

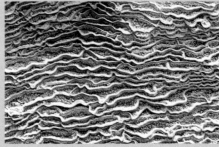

A series of small terraces creates a "French pastry" formation. The tufa deposits that build the Rabbitkettle mounds are fragile and easily damaged.

351

Sunset over the Mackenzie.

THE MACKENZIE

Canada's Mightiest River, a Highway to the Arctic

The wilderness is hushed, with just a whisper of wind, as the great Mackenzie, near the end of its long, relentless march to the Arctic Ocean, suddenly points itself straight into the sunset—and its ripples change to hammered gold.

It is a clear evening in August. The sun has waited until 10 p.m. for its long, lazy slide toward the rim of the world. And now: magnificence! High overhead, wispy tracers of cloud catch fire. Two snow geese rise, the rosy light tinging their dazzling white wings. Gold, orange, crimson—the colors shift and deepen. At last the sun dips into the river. The sky clings stubbornly to the last pink smudges until 11:30 p.m. Now a full moon offers its cool glow and the river turns to mauve.

This is sunset on a grand scale, like many works of nature here. Like the aurora borealis. It flashes on now,

353

not a feeble glimmer in the North but a sky-filling canopy of dancing green-white ghosts. Like the Mackenzie River system itself. The greatest in Canada, and second only to the Mississippi in all North America, it drains 696,700 square miles, an area 13 times the size of England. And it *seems* even more immense.

The mighty Mackenzie is born under other names, high in the British Columbia Rockies 2,635 miles from its outlet at the Beaufort Sea. One by one the Finlay, Parsnip, Peace, Athabasca and Slave rivers pour into the system—in British Columbia, Alberta and the Northwest Territories. Now they meld into Great Slave Lake. Finally, in Great Slave's northwest corner, the Mackenzie proper begins.

From there on, in its meandering 1,070-mile journey to the Arctic, it dominates the northwest. Fed by innumerable raveling threads of tributary rivers and streams, it twists and turns like a fat snake. It gives Great Bear and Great Slave—fourth and fifth largest lakes in North America—an outlet to the sea. It runs from spruce to tundra, through mountain cliff to soggy muskeg. It is life itself: its warming waters help nourish the tree line almost to the Arctic coast, and it is a main transportation artery for industry and settlement.

In all its long journey down north from Great Slave Lake, the Mackenzie drops only 500 feet, and so it moves with a deceptively measured pace. But its current is powerful. Its shallow waters are clogged with sandbars and can be churned into ugly whitecaps by sudden storms. Its environs seem uninspiring at first glance but they are teeming with life and subtle change.

As the Mackenzie leaves Great Slave, it flows west through flat land treed with spruce, poplar, tamarack and jack pine. Wild raspberries hang in red clusters, almost as thick as the clouds of mosquitoes and blackflies that plague animals and men throughout the mild summer. At Fort Simpson, some 200 miles along, the Liard plummets in from British Columbia, laden with silt and driftwood. For 70 miles its murky current hugs the left bank, next to clean water on the right, until they merge and the Mackenzie runs muddy to the Arctic.

Next the North Nahanni River adds its milky waters, and the Mackenzie rolls toward a splendid landmark: Camsell Bend, a 3,000-foot escarpment with the Mackenzie Mountains looming behind. Here the river turns sharply to the north, firmly committed to the sea, with the purple Mackenzies on its left and the Franklin Range taking up escort duty on the right.

The mountains will linger for several days' travel, but the river voyager will see little animal life. Through the short summer the Mackenzie is busy with supply barges for settlements and oil camps, and with adventurers in canoes and power boats or on rafts or aboard a cruise ship

A half-mile from the Mackenzie shore, these pillars form a part of The Ramparts, a seven-mile stretch of cliffs along the river.

that makes 18 trips each summer. So, by day at least, wild creatures stay shyly in the bush or along lesser streams: moose, wolves, lynx, martens, black bears and a few grizzlies. On the river one sees ducks, geese, wild swans—and geological curiosities.

Rising 1,200 feet out of the water near the village of Wrigley is a steep mass of Devonian limestone: *Roche-qui-trempe-à-l'eau* (rock soaking in the water), it is called. Hot springs issue from crevices in its base. Later, near Fort Norman, the air is sharp with sulphur and the east bank is oil-stained. Here the Great Bear River enters the Mackenzie from Great Bear Lake.

The Mackenzie winds on, spreading three miles wide as it passes the refinery towers of Norman Wells, then narrowing to churn through Sans Sault Rapids. Its entire length is tricky for inexperienced navigators, but this turbulent 10-mile stretch is the prime challenge, promptly followed by the Ramparts Rapids. Although seven miles shorter, these rapids must be carefully traversed down a central chute which has a jagged, 200-foot-long rock lurking underwater at the down-

Rain pouring over an overhanging rock near The Ramparts freezes to form a glistening curtain of icicles.

stream exit. Then river and travelers relax for the most spectacular sight en route: The Ramparts, a seven-mile corridor of limestone with vertical walls rising 200 feet.

On over the invisible Arctic Circle; past Arctic Red River where the sourdoughs turned off to Klondike in '98; on to Point Separation. Suddenly the river shatters into a multitude of lesser channels and 20,000 lakes. This is the Mackenzie Delta and here the true Arctic begins to show itself.

The trees are dwindling but a strange plant life clings to the surface: lichens, mosses, grasses, dozens of flower species from flaming fireweed to fuzzy white Arctic cotton, ferns, berry bushes, willows and junipers. A few inches beneath the surface lies permafrost, frozen ground that helps plants survive by harboring precious moisture. Like so many other aspects of Arctic ecology, permafrost is fragile. Even a building's warmth will thaw it, so northern houses perch on pilings driven into the frozen ground, and water, sewage and heating ducts are housed together in above-ground "utilidors."

The warming delta waters also foster plant and animal life in a continuous chain reaction. Thousands of muskrats thrive in the marshes; hares, voles, mice and other small rodents live off the land. Larger predators live off them. Caribou graze on the sedges and lichens.

Above all, the delta is bird country. Ducks, geese, swans, loons, sandpipers, gulls and terns nest here by the tens of thousands. Eagles, ptarmigans, owls, hawks, sparrows and warblers fly the region. And everywhere the raven, clown of the North, perches on rooftops or storage tanks, checking out garbage pails and croaking an amiable greeting to mankind.

Filtering through the delta sieve, the river finally pours into the Beaufort Sea. Beyond, in blue-gray emptiness, lies pack ice and the Arctic Ocean. At water's edge perches the old Eskimo whaling village of Tuktoyaktuk. Dome-shaped pingos pop up strangely on the flat landscape sometimes 100 feet high.

It is a chilly reminder of the river's alter ego. By October ice forms and the Mackenzie is locked to water traffic. The white dark months close in. The river is given over to snowmobilers, dogsleds, the occasional polar bear with his rolling sailor's gait, and temperatures to 60 below zero.

But spring comes with a rush. Warm water sneaks into the Mackenzie from the Liard, starting the thaw in midstream. Ice breaks like thunder in The Ramparts. Sunlight and long days work magic on Great Slave Lake. By June the watery heart of the northwest throbs again.

356

OTHER ATTRACTIONS

A Lonely Road, Two Great Lakes

Anderson River Bird Sanctuary Whistling swans and white-fronted geese arrive in May on the still snow-covered islands of this five-mile-wide delta, joining willow ptarmigans and snowy owls that stayed the winter. Soon other birds appear—phalaropes, jaegers, redpolls, Lapland longspurs. Wolves, lemmings and red foxes are common.

Camsell River Canoe Route Canoeists have two main choices. One is to fly from Yellowknife to Sarah Lake, where the Camsell rises. The other is to start at Rae, on Great Slave Lake, go up the Marian River and portage to Sarah Lake. This second route, from Great Slave to Great Bear Lake, covers 300 miles. The Camsell route can be treacherous (depending on seasonal flow) and difficult to follow; canoeists should employ a guide or carefully study topographical maps. Arctic grayling is abundant in the river.

Caribou Hills Rising abruptly from the Mackenzie Delta, the hills level off to a rolling plateau 500 to 850 feet above the river. Erosion gullies have scored the hills, giving them a ribbed appearance. The area is distinctive for its variety of plants, including those found in delta, scrub, boreal, tundra and fire-ravaged areas.

Great Bear Lake This 12,275-square-mile lake, eighth largest in the world, is extremely deep—1,356 feet (844 feet below sea level) at one place near Port Radium. It lies in a vast wilderness near the tree line. Many of the evergreens are stunted, gnarled spruce. The lake is the habitat of four relict marine species thought to have moved south from the Arctic Ocean, following glacial lakes ahead of the ice caps: the four-horned sculpin (a fish) and three tiny crustaceans are all found in abundance.

Great Slave Lake The fifth largest lake in North America (and eleventh in the world), this 11,269-square-mile lake is in a transition zone between the boreal forest of the Canadian Shield and the grasses of the Arctic tundra. The Lock-

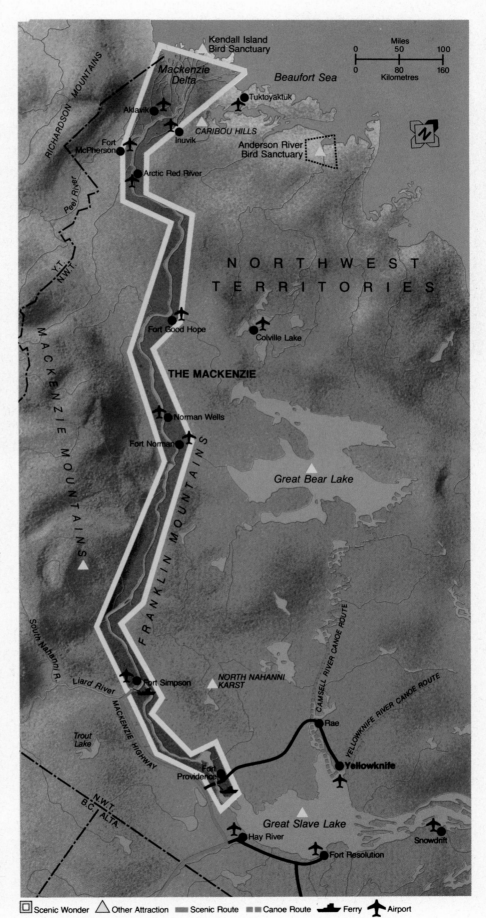

Its flat floor covered with bright green grass, the world's most northerly polje (a depression without outlets) appears to be a valley. But after eight days of rain in early July 1972, the polje (a part of the North Nahanni Karst) was transformed into a lake (below).

hart River drops a total of 700 feet, through rapids and over falls—including 130-foot Parry Falls—in the last 25 miles of its descent to the lake. Whitefish and inconnu (a food fish) are abundant.

Kendall Island Bird Sanctuary Snow and Canada geese summer on the coastal plains of this Beaufort Sea island and the adjacent mainland delta.

Mackenzie Highway Starting at Grimshaw, Alta., this road has been completed north to Fort Simpson, N.W.T. It is to eventually reach Tuktoyaktuk on the Arctic Ocean, 1,330 miles from Grimshaw. The route, the first 200 miles of which are paved, winds through dark forests, past lakes and sloughs and across miles of spongy tundra. Connecting highways lead to Hay River, Fort Resolution, Fort Smith and Yellowknife. The Hay River Highway passes scenic Alexandra Falls, a 300-foot-wide cataract that plummets 109 feet. Two miles away a trail leads to 46-foot Louise Falls and, below it, a 170-foot-deep gorge and three miles of rapids. To the northwest, 250-foot-wide Lady Evelyn Falls tumbles 48 feet. The Mackenzie Highway to Fort Simpson follows the Mackenzie Valley Escarpment. The area has wolves, foxes, black bears and moose. Campsites and food supplies are available along some stretches of the road, others lack even service stations.

Mackenzie Mountains In this 500-mile extension of the Rockies is 9,062-foot Mount Sir James MacBrien, the highest in the Northwest Territories.

North Nahanni Karst This eroded limestone formation, extraordinary in an area of limited rainfall and cold temperatures, extends for 31 miles and is up to seven miles wide. Some "corridors" in the limestone labyrinth are 600 feet deep, several hundred feet wide and as much as three miles long. Some limestone towers are as high as 330 feet. The formation includes several 100-foot-deep dolines, depressions that often have ponds or ice blockages at their bottoms. There are more than 200 caves, many blocked by ice or silt. Three that have been explored are more than 5,000 feet long. Pictures this page.

Yellowknife River Canoe Route Canoeists are flown to the river's source for a 150-mile journey to Yellowknife.

Permafrost, a layer of permanently frozen ground that underlies most of the Canadian North, determines the very shape of the land. Round hills called pingos, oddly patterned landscapes (polygons) and wedges of ice thrusting up from thin soil . . . all are evidence of poor drainage and the power of permafrost.

The Mackenzie Delta has both Arctic and sub-Arctic environments. The southern (upper) delta, blessed by an abundance of water (which absorbs the sun's heat) and shielded by stands of white spruce (which retain snow), is warmer than surrounding areas. Here permafrost may be 400 feet thick. In the northern (lower) delta, along the Beaufort Sea, the permanently frozen ground is up to 1,800 feet thick.

All plant life in the North depends on a surface layer of soil, a few inches to four feet thick, that thaws every spring. This surface soil is soggy, saturated by water that the permafrost prevents from seeping into the ground. Nor does the general flatness of the tundra make for much runoff. It is in this top layer of soil, which freezes and thaws with the seasons, that the unique landforms of northern Canada are created.

In summer, life abounds in the myriad ponds and looping streams of the Mackenzie Delta's 4,700 square miles.

Pingos and Polygons and the Power of Permafrost

A permafrost ice lense is exposed along the bank of a shallow pond on the Tuktoyaktuk Peninsula. Atop it is a mat of water-logged vegetation and silty material supported by a thin layer of thawed soil.

Pingos, dome-like mounds of ice (left), apparently are formed when shallow lakes dry up and become underlaid with permafrost. Water pressure forces pockets of ice (and covering soil) upward, just as the liquid in a can expands as it freezes. As cracks develop at the pingo's summit the ice core is exposed to the sun's warmth. The ice melts slowly; soil from the pingo slopes piles up at the outer edges, leaving a water-filled crater with a high rim (right).

Hummocky tundra stretches to the horizon on Ballie Island, northeast of the Mackenzie Delta. Arctic soils are generally poor, since they lack nutrients that warmth-loving bacteria normally supply.

Intense cold contracts the ground, causing fissures like the cracks in dried mud. During the spring thaws, trapped water enters the cracks. As it freezes, the water expands the openings, allowing more water to seep in. Eventually a network of ice-filled channels develops and soil is forced up on both sides of each channel, creating ridges. Polygonal islands (left) result, some filled with water (right).

A Desolate Wasteland in Winter, the Tundra Is Vivid and Vibrant While Summer Lasts

Vast and white and void, the tundra in winter stretches in infinite loneliness from horizon to horizon, a land as stark and still as a frozen sea. Barren Grounds seems *the* right name for this region of almost 500,000 square miles, extending from Hudson Bay northwest to the delta of the Mackenzie River, and from the tree line, the edge of the boreal forest, north to the Arctic Ocean.

Less than a century ago, when he crossed the Barren Grounds by canoe and snowshoe, James W. Tyrrell wrote, "of almost this entire territory less was known than of the remotest districts of 'Darkest Africa.'"

Only a handful of white men before Tyrrell and his brother, J. B. Tyrrell of the Geological Survey of Canada, had made the trek across the Barrens. The first was Samuel Hearne of the Hudson's Bay Company, who set out December 7, 1770, from Fort Prince of Wales on Hudson Bay, near the present town of Churchill, and *walked* to the mouth of the Coppermine River and back (more than 2,000 miles) in 18 months and 23 days.

It is now a land virtually without people. Some 800 Caribou Eskimos, who once inhabited the Barren Grounds, in camps scattered over an area about the size of Manitoba and Saskatchewan combined, deserted the land when the caribou herds declined in the late 1950s. They moved to coastal villages and to Baker Lake, the

*The Thelon River
in the central Barrens.*

361

only settlement in the Barren Grounds. But signs of long-ago men persist on the tundra: rings of stone that once held down the hems of Eskimo tents; low, semi-circular stone ambushes, where hunters crouched as caribou approached; and *inukshuks,* stone cairns built in the shape of men, to scare caribou toward the hunters.

In winter, the Barren Grounds seem utterly desolate. "A monotonous snow-covered waste," wrote the British explorer Warburton Pike, who traveled across the tundra in the winter of 1889-90. "A deathly stillness hangs over all and the oppressive loneliness weighs upon the spectator till he is glad to shout aloud to break the awful spell of solitude."

There is life on the Barrens in winter but most hunters and prey are in camouflage white. The Arctic fox, wrapped in a warm, white winter coat, trots silently across the land on furry paws, listening intently for the telltale squeak of mouselike lemmings in their nests and runways beneath the snow. The ermine, white except for the black tip of its tail, twists with sinuous grace around a pile of snow-covered rocks. It too is in search of lemmings. The ptarmigan, in white winter plumage, runs on densely feathered feet among stunted dwarf willows, snipping off buds and watching warily for an Arctic fox that may wait in ambush.

Not all tundra animals change to white in winter. The mighty musk-oxen, most numerous in the Thelon Game Sanctuary of the central Barren Grounds, where they feed on dwarf willow and sparse fallow grass, are cloaked in dark fur so thick that it makes them impervious to the cold. Ravens retain their glossy blue-black plumage all year. They mate earlier than other birds and in March circle and swoop in the ardor and exuberance of their courtship flight high above the frozen, solemn land.

In May and June, suddenly, the Barren Grounds are no longer barren, but vividly and vibrantly alive. Like a late-season blizzard, immense flocks of snow geese descend; nearly a quarter million nest in the delta of the McConnell River, near the Hudson Bay settlement of Eskimo Point. Ross's geese, among the smallest of North American geese, fly north to breeding grounds so isolated that they were not discovered until 1938.

Caribou have wintered in scattered bands in forests to the south. Now they start their migration to the tundra, small groups merging into larger groups that also unite. The great march becomes urgent and purposeful and in April the herds spread over the tundra like a living tide. Wrote James W. Tyrrell after seeing the caribou migration in 1893 (when there were an estimated two million): "The valleys and hillsides for miles appeared to be moving masses of caribou.... They could only be reckoned in acres or square miles." The caribou now have been reduced to some 400,000 on the Barren

Grounds but they are the last of the great wildlife herds in North America.

Elegant eider drakes, in black and white plumage with olive-green napes, croon their haunting love song along the coast. On the myriad tundra lakes, flashy male old-squaw ducks fill the air with chattering hoots and whistles as they court somberly dressed females. Sandhill cranes sound their bugling calls and horned larks pour out their liquid, lilting song. The voice of the Barren Grounds is a symphony of spring and new life.

Among the last to arrive are the northern phalaropes, little birds like sandpipers. The resplendent female has a snow-white throat and rufous-red bib; the male is more modestly in browns and grays. The female does the wooing, the male builds the nest. The female lays the eggs, the male broods them and "mothers" the chicks.

In mid-April, in black and white and dun, the tundra still looks stern and somber. But the days are long now and a strong sun quickly melts the snow. From mid-May

Musk-oxen head up a sandy rise in the Thelon Game Sanctuary deep in the Northwest Territories. Also in the sanctuary are caribou, Barren Grounds grizzly, Arctic fox, Arctic hare, moose and lemming.

to June a glistening lacework of runnels and rivulets carries the meltwater to rivers and lakes. Some moisture soaks into the slowly thawing soil and suddenly the first flowers are in bloom on hillsides and ridges—dainty rosettes of purple saxifrage. Grasses and sedges sprout and a green sheen spreads over the vast tundra meadows. Whole slopes are covered with the tiny bells of Arctic white-heather. Blooms of gold and white mountain avens glow on sandy ridges. The rounded cushions of moss campion are spangled with tiny pink petals. And, amid the deep green of wet sedge meadows near tundra ponds, silky bolls of cotton grass sway in the breeze.

The great tundra rivers break their icy bonds. Hardly more than two generations ago they were the highways of explorers who, like the Tyrrells in 1893, came to visit and map this "great mysterious region of terra incognita." Still used by Eskimos, they are also canoe routes for visitors. Some of today's venturesome travelers cross the Barren Grounds from west to east on the Thelon River. In the Thelon Game Sanctuary they often see musk-oxen feeding placidly near the river, or large herds of caribou. The fortunate may observe the rarely seen and cautious white Arctic wolf and the Barren Grounds grizzly, the grumpy, solitary, honey-hued monarch of the wilderness. Some canoeists go north on the great Kazan River, through Thirty Mile Lake and on to Baker Lake, portaging around Kazan Falls. A few of the most experienced and intrepid venture down the Back River, with its wild, swirling rapids, to the Arctic Ocean at Chantrey Inlet.

Summer days in the Barrens are long, nights are short and luminous. Summer itself is brief and everywhere there is urgency to multiply and mature within the season's short span. The Arctic poppy, with golden-yellow blooms on long slender stems, completes its cycle from germination to full growth and production of ripe seeds in less than a month. Snow buntings hunt insects for nearly 18 hours a day, to feed their fast-growing young in nests hidden among the tundra rocks. Orange and black bumblebees drone from bloom to bloom collecting nectar. Young ravens follow their parents on hunting trips across a land now rich in food. White gyrfalcons, largest of all falcons, swoop low over the tundra to pluck an unwary ptarmigan or lemming.

The Hood River drops 160 feet over Wilberforce Falls as it carves a canyon through the Canadian Shield in the far northern Barrens.

The lakes teem with whitefish and with trout that weigh up to 50 pounds. Arctic char descend to the sea in spring and return in fall, and the rivers are rich with fighting Arctic graylings, the delight of sports fishermen.

Near the Hudson Bay coast, milky-white belugas congregate in the shallows to have their young, occasionally in scattered pods of more than a thousand. These whales are easiest to see near the mouth of the Churchill River and north near the Seal River and Whale Cove. Farther north, narwhals swim into Repulse Bay. The male of this strangest of all whales carries a single, tapered and twisted ivory tusk as long as eight feet.

On the western tundra lakes, pairs of whistling swans swim with stately grace, followed by their downy cygnets. Little lemmings scurry along runways hidden by tundra grasses. Their populations increase and crash in roughly four-year cycles. The females bear three or four litters in a season; in peak years the tundra is aswarm with them and occasionally these lemming legions spill over the land in those apparently aimless migrations. But there is no evidence to suggest that these turn into the "suicide marches" attributed to European lemmings.

The fastest way to see the Barrens is from a small plane. This way you get a vivid impression of their immensity and diversity. Half the land seems covered by lakes, an infinite watery jigsaw puzzle—and all but the largest are still nameless. But the best way to see the Barrens is by canoe. Eskers meander across the tundra, sand and gravel ridges that look like railroad embankments but are the accumulated sediment of rivers that flowed under and through Ice Age glaciers. They are favorite denning areas of foxes, wolves and Barren Grounds grizzlies. Great green valleys alternate with brown, rolling hills. Sinuous rivers and brooks flow toward the lakes and out of them to other, larger rivers and, eventually, the sea.

Fall comes early. The animals lay up reserves for another long, hard winter or for their great, strenuous migration to the south. Flowers droop and their petals wither and drop, but plants (nearly all tundra plants are perennials) store starches and fats in their root systems for the next spring. The caribou, sleek after pasturing all summer in the great meadows, move toward the forests. Skeins of geese wing toward the south.

The berries are ripe: glossy black crowberries, watery and sour; sweet, blue bilberries; amber cloudberries. Foxes continue to gorge themselves. Grizzlies, already swathed in fat in preparation for their long winter sleep, munch methodically across whole acres of berries.

Now many parts of the tundra are aglow with the final flamboyance of fall, the brilliant scarlet of bearberry leaves, the bright yellow of the willows, the brick red of tiny, creeping dwarf birches.

The first frost touches the land. Delicately veined ice covers the tundra ponds. Ground squirrels retire to their burrows. The grizzly rolls up in his den. Flocks of snow buntings fly south. In October, the first snow snuffs out the vivid colors of fall, and the Barren Grounds are again mantled in white, infinite and still.

OTHER ATTRACTIONS

Huge Sanctuaries in a Huge Land

Banks Island Some 200,000 lesser snow geese nest on high ground some five miles inland from the Beaufort Sea, unusually far from water for this species of goose.

Bathurst Inlet Some of the inlet's mountainous islands have high, rocky cliffs where golden eagles and peregrine falcons nest. Treeless, rolling terrain is bedecked in summer with a variety of wild flowers, including Arctic poppies, lupines, blunt-leaf and early coralroot orchids and mouse-eared chickweed.

Canrobert Hills Minerals and soils give these ridges and valleys red and orange hues. Red sandstone, limestone and ironstone exist close to yellow, brown and orange siltstone and gray shale and weathered green sands. Bright red and purple silts and clays add color to some rivers through the 2,000-foot hills.

Central Barrens Calving Grounds As many as 225,000 caribou migrate here each May from the Manitoba-Saskatchewan-Northwest Territories border region. They calve on the tundra.

Chesterfield Inlet Raised Beaches Sand and gravel ridges along the west shore of Hudson Bay resemble gigantic stairs climbing up from the water's edge. Pronounced between Chesterfield Inlet and the Manitoba-Northwest Territories border, the steps rise as high as 700 feet. They began to form at the end of the Ice Age when the glaciers melted and the land, relieved of the weight of the ice, began to rise. The land still rises here about one foot every 50 years.

Cunningham Inlet Beluga whales enter the inlet each summer to calve.

Haughton Dome This 22-mile-wide crater was formed by the impact of a meteor more than two million years ago. Geologists call it a dome because rock at its center has been uplifted and is older than rock toward its rim. The outer edge rises more than 660 feet above the floor of the inner basin.

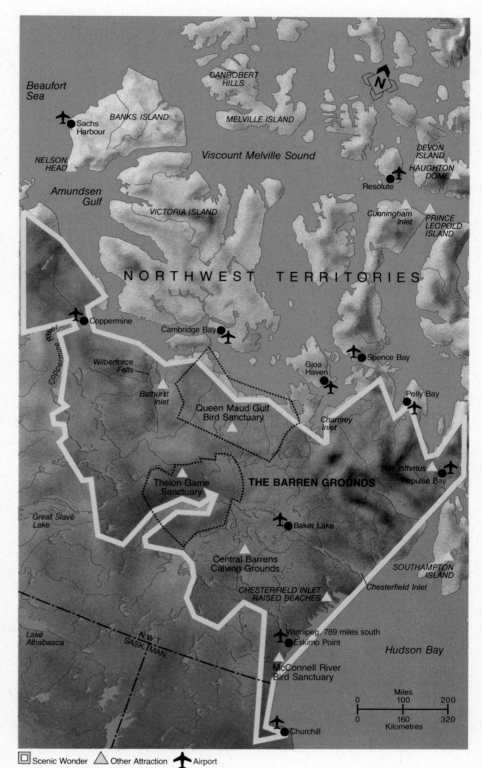

◻ Scenic Wonder △ Other Attraction ✈ Airport

McConnell River Bird Sanctuary Arctic terns that summer here between late May and early August migrate as far as the shores of Antarctica, making a round trip of 25,000 miles. Some 400,000 birds, mostly snow geese, nest on the hummocks and gravel ridges of the sanctuary. Other species include Canada geese and whistling swans.

Nelson Head Picture next page.

Prince Leopold Island Hundreds of thousands of seabirds nest on the narrow ledges of 1,000-foot-high cliffs. Northern fulmars, thick-billed murres, black guillemots, black-legged kittiwakes and glaucous gulls feed in the surrounding waters. Beluga whales, narwhals and

Rae Isthmus *This boulder-covered strip of land separates Melville Peninsula from the mainland. A strait once isolated the peninsula but land rising after the Ice Age created the isthmus.*

Nelson Head *These 1,400-foot-high cliffs are of Precambrian rock almost two billion years old—335 million years older than any other part of Banks Island.*

ringed seals inhabit the waters; polar bears den on the rocky shores.

Queen Maud Gulf Bird Sanctuary This 24,000-square-mile sanctuary was established to protect the Ross's goose (North America's smallest Arctic-nesting goose), whose breeding grounds were discovered here in 1938. Wet, marshy terrain is dotted with 30-foot-high drumlins (ridges of glacial debris) and thousands of shallow lakes, many no more than six feet deep. Birds that nest here from mid-May to August include Canada geese, peregrine falcons, gyrfalcons, whistling swans and sparrows.

Rae Isthmus Picture this page.

Southampton Island Two sanctuaries along the south coast—more than 1,000 square miles—support about 220,000 birds, mainly Canada, snow and white-fronted geese, whistling swans and terns.

Thelon Game Sanctuary This 21,512-square-mile preserve of tundra and boreal forest was established to protect the musk-ox, a relic of the Ice Age. Also in the sanctuary are caribou, Barren Grounds grizzly, Arctic fox, Arctic hare, moose and lemming.

Lichens: Rootless, Leafless Plants That Can Grow Without Soil

Plants that have no roots or leaves and can grow without soil? There are such plants, called lichens. They result when fungi and algae combine, each supplying something the other cannot.

Fungi are plants incapable of utilizing the sun's energy to produce food for themselves. Algae are rootless plants present in the air, in soil and in water. (Airborne algae without moisture simply drift in a suspended state.) When an alga and a fungus combine—scientists do not know exactly how the union takes place—a new plant is formed. It is different in appearance from that of the partners that created it, and has capabilities that neither partner alone possessed. Lichens assume a variety of shapes and colors, de-pending on what kinds of algae and fungi created them and the environment in which they exist.

To obtain minerals that other plants get from soil, lichens capture and retain minute dust particles from the air. Minerals are also secreted from the rocks to which many lichens cling. Over long periods, lichens even flake off fragments of rock and these combine with the accumulated dust particles and the remains of dead lichens to form a fine layer of soil—soil which can support higher forms of plant life.

Lichens anchor themselves to rocks, trees and soil with threadlike strands called rhizines. They need no roots to absorb water: moisture is absorbed over the entire surface of the plant, directly from rain and dew or, in some cases, from moisture in the air. Lacking leaves, lichens manufacture their food from carbon dioxide and sunlight (by photo-synthesis), by using chlorophyll in the algae.

Like mosses, some lichens manufacture spores, but it is not known whether the spores are functional in the reproduction process. All lichens can propagate through fragments breaking off and anchoring on other surfaces.

Because they can withstand great cold, lichens thrive in far northern climates, providing food for caribou and other grazing animals. But lichens are also found in forests and deserts and in the tropics. They are not found in large cities. For all their hardiness, lichens cannot endure air pollution.

THE HARDY OFFSPRING OF FUNGI AND ALGAE

Off the Auyuittuq coast.

AUYUITTUQ NATIONAL PARK

Where the Ice Age Lingers On and On: Our First Park North of the Arctic Circle

Auyuittuq, in the gloriously complex tongue of the Inuit, means "entirely without summer"— which is almost but not quite true of Auyuittuq National Park. Summer to the hardy Inuit is when the land comes bare of snow and the arctic flowers and the birds return. All this does happen in some areas of the 8,300-square-mile park (Canada's first national park north of the Arctic Circle) on Baffin Island's Cumber-land Peninsula but vast parts are sheathed year round in ice and snow. In summer the peculiar fascination of Auyuittuq (pronounced ow-you-EE-took) is that as you tread the soft tundra of its valleys you are always within sight of its gleaming white heights. Always in the background is the roar of glacier meltstreams and a tumbling of rocks down the mountainsides.

Here (or hereabouts) on Baffin Island was the birthplace of one of the two great ice sheets that eventually—18,000 years ago—covered most of Canada and have shaped so much of its landform and its destiny. If the suns of summer weaken and the snows of winter thicken, another age of ice could have its onset here.

Fourteen thousand years ago all Canada could have borne the name Auyuittuq. Then the ice sheet started to melt and plants and animals and men followed its northward retreat. But the ice lingered long on Baffin Island. Probably no human being camped on Cumberland Peninsula until about 1,500 years ago.

The stark landscape of Auyuittuq National Park is softened by fluffy Arctic cotton (near right) and colored by such wild flowers as purple saxifrage (far right). Below: Mount Odin towers over Pangnirtung Pass, one of the principal approaches to the park.

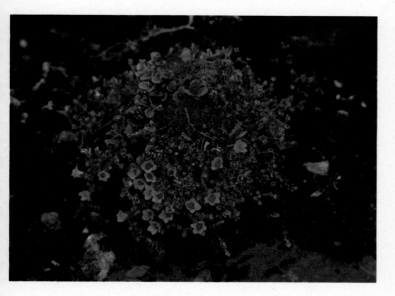

These Stone Age Dorset people hunted seals and warmed their dwellings with sealblubber-burning soapstone lamps. They apparently had no domesticated dogs, so their winter traveling must have been difficult. Yet they spread along the northern coasts where the Inuit now live, from their heartland around the Bering Sea to distant Greenland and Newfoundland. There must have been a camp or two of Dorset people who gazed in wonder at the square sail of a Norse vessel from Greenland about a thousand years ago. The Helluland of The Greenlanders' Saga was a land of rock and glaciers, likely Baffin Island at its nearest point to Greenland. However, the Norse did not tarry. In the 12th and 13th centuries a new wave of people spread over the island, the certain ancestors of the present Inuit. These were the Thule people, hunters of whales and caribou, dogdrivers, builders of houses of stone and whalebone.

The first white men since the Norse were Englishmen who came in the late 16th century. John Davis, in 1585, planted the first names on Baffin's map—Earl of Cumberland's Isles (the name has been transferred to the whole peninsula), Cape Dyer, Mount Raleigh, and Sunneshine and Mooneshine fjords—after his stout little vessels.

Whaling Capt. William Penny, after whom the Cumberland Peninsula ice cap is named, sailed into Cumberland Sound in 1840, the first visitor since John Davis. American whalers hired the Inuit to help them and gave them tools of iron, and guns, and songs and dances. They founded shore stations on both sides of Cumberland Sound. At Kivitoo on the Davis Strait coast of Auyuittuq Park sailors' graves and other relics of whaling days (such as vats used to boil blubber) can be seen. When the whaling industry declined, the Hudson's Bay Company moved in, trading furs and skins for the goods the native people now needed.

The hamlet of Pangnirtung is the southern gateway to the park, though there is a fine back door too at Broughton Island's little settlement.

The grandest feature of the park is Pangnirtung Pass, a 60-mile-long U-shaped trench across the peninsula. Filled with ice long ago, it now is a throughway partly blocked in places by the glaciers coming down from highlands to the east and west. They have built huge bouldery moraines that loop across the valley.

Between these moraine bulges are gravelly flats laced with the braided streams of the Weasel River, turbid with rock flour the glaciers have milled. At each moraine barrier the river foams through a narrow gorge—and in the depth of 40-below-zero winter is frozen into a series of fluted curtains. The first of these is at Crater Lake, where the glacier ends in a circular lake.

371

Just beyond Crater Lake the valley takes a gentle S bend. A triple waterfall leaps and tumbles 300 feet from a hillside to the west, and on the north rises the huge bulk of Mount Odin, at 7,050 feet probably the highest summit between the Carolinas and Ellesmere Island. From its ice-domed peak one can see all of the Cumberland Peninsula's jumble of peaks, an area nearly as big as Switzerland.

Southeast of the bend is Tirokwa (Corner) Peak and from its summit a view up the rest of the Weasel Valley. The huge wall of 5,500-foot Thor Peak leans out over the valley on the east. Beyond a huge moraine formed by Fork Beard Glacier, which drains a vast snowfield be-

Debris turns the pond at the foot of an Auyuittuq glacier milky. But the water in the lower pond is clear after being filtered through a natural dam of glacial sand and gravel.

hind Thor Peak, is another flat-floored portion of the valley.

Farther beyond the bend is another upward step, where a giant moraine curves down from the east. Summit Lake comes into sight, eight miles long, one wide, nestled in the mountains. In some years ice never leaves the lake, but always an open moat of water forms around its margin. Foot-long ice candles that look like upside-down icicles tinkle as the breeze breaks them.

Summit Lake was once two lakes, separated by the moraine of Turner Glacier, which withdrew between 1953 and 1961. Now all the meltstreams pour south to Pangnirtung. The northern part, formerly Glacier Lake, is a dried-up gorge beneath the curving moraine of Highway Glacier. From the shore of Glacier Lake is seen the fantastic 6,600-foot tower of Mount Asgard, a peak that has drawn climbers from many parts of the world. On the east the easily accessible rounded summit of 4,450-foot Mount Battle gives magnificent views—up and down the pass, across to Mounts Asgard and Loki, and up the huge Highway Glacier that leads the eye on to the thin white line of the Penny Ice Cap on the horizon.

Owl Valley opens up to the north; lush with vegetation, little obstructed by the moraines of the side glaciers. The land becomes less savage near the northern sea gateway. Here in certain years, at the peak of their four-year cycle, the valley crawls with lemmings frantically nibbling at grasses and other greenery, storing hay for their nests. When lemmings proliferate so do their predators, the agile ermine and the little Arctic fox. The great valley walls echo the deep hooting of *ukpik,* the snowy owl.

Many visitors see parts of Pangnirtung Pass; only the strongest see all of it. But Auyuittuq Park has other attractions. Maktak Fjord has a rich splash of high-arctic flowers on its northern shore. In Coronation Fjord and Okoa Bay tongues of ice cap end in spectacular ice cliffs in the sea. And there are the towers of Cape Searle, where hundreds of thousands of northern fulmars nest, whitening the rock and the air around. The little auk, the dovekie, which breeds in Greenland, is seen near here in winter in pools among the pack ice drifting slowly toward Newfoundland.

Beautifully sculptured icebergs march into Cumberland Sound, where in summer they enhance the blue of the sea, the gray of the cliffs, the eternal ice and snow on the heights.

Ice groaning on land, inching downhill; ice at sea, grinding piece against piece and against a ship's hull; the sweet music of ice crystals melting on myriad upland lakes.

Ice, always ice. Auyuittuq.

OTHER ATTRACTIONS

A Vast Ice Cap, Crater and Fjord

Admiralty Inlet Cliffs 1,000 to 1,500 feet high line stretches of the 230-mile inlet, thought to be the longest fjord in the world.

Baffin Bay The southwest part of the bay has a maximum depth of 9,000 feet and is one of the deepest spots in Canadian Arctic waters. Much of the bay is often so packed with ice as to offer no passage even to icebreakers. The North Water, an area at the north end of Baffin Bay, is kept ice-free year round by strong currents. It is a wintering ground for narwhals, walruses, beluga and bowhead whales and ringed, bearded and harp seals.

Bylot Island Some 800,000 thick-billed murres and 100,000 black-legged kittiwakes nest on ledges along sheer, 1,000-foot cliffs. Near a similar colony on the southeast coast are narwhals, polar bears and seals.

Cape Dorset Bird Sanctuary Northern eiders, black guillemots, Iceland gulls, snow buntings, water pipits, redpolls and king eiders inhabit a group of 20 islands off Cape Dorset.

Cape Searle Two near-vertical cliffs which tower 1,400 feet above the sea are laced with ledges and crevices where 200,000 northern fulmars nest, one of the world's largest colonies. The two-mile-long cliffs are also home to glaucous gulls, black guillemots and thick-billed murres.

Coburg Island Some 20,000 thick-billed murres nest on this mountainous, 22-mile-long island. Common eiders are found on the rocky shorelines and polar bears hunt walruses in open waters that currents keep ice-free all year.

Cornwallis Island Picture next page.

Devon Island About one third of this 21,000-square-mile island is covered by a 3,300-foot-deep ice cap and its numerous glaciers. Cliffs up to 1,000 feet high tower above fjords that cut into the

□ Scenic Wonder   △ Other Attraction   ✈ Airport

Ellesmere Island *On the rugged island's Fosheim Peninsula is a massive outcropping called The Falcon's Castle. The peninsula is on the west side of Ellesmere Island, the largest and most easterly of the Queen Elizabeth Islands. It is also the most glaciated.*

Cornwallis Island *Most of this 2,670-square-mile island is flat. But along the island's east coast steep cliffs are as high as 1,350 feet.*

island. Harp seals, polar bears, walruses and snow geese live on and around the island.

Dewey Soper Bird Sanctuary One million Canada geese, lesser snow geese and black brants nest in the world's largest goose colony.

Digges Sound Water emptying from tundra lakes plunges into the sea over near-vertical 800-foot cliffs that are the home of possibly the world's biggest colony of thick-billed murres, an estimated two to three million. Young murres spend the first month of their lives on narrow ledges, then plunge into the sea to follow the adults. Many jump before they should and do not survive the leap.

Ellesmere Island Picture this page.

Jones Sound This 250-mile-long body of water—60 miles wide—is a migratory channel for seals and walruses and is used year round by polar bears and ringed seals. Harp and bearded seals, belugas and narwhals summer in the sound.

New Quebec Crater The world's third biggest meteor crater, almost perfectly circular, is two miles across. At the bottom of its 300-foot walls is a lake 800 feet deep containing Arctic char and trout that are malformed and undersized due to an inadequate supply of plankton. Around the crater, formed 100,000 years ago, are acres of giant boulders, debris from the meteor's impact.

Reid Bay Some 400,000 thick-billed murres and 20,000 northern fulmars nest on the pinnacles and ledges of two 3,000-foot-high rock towers on shore.

Arctic hare   Snowshoe hare   Jackrabbit

In almost all mammals and birds the loss of body heat is controlled by insulation—hairs in mammals, feathers in birds. Hairs and feathers as such do not insulate but air trapped in them does, air being a poor conductor of heat. The Arctic fox is protected by long, oily guard hairs which waterproof and a wooly underlayer which traps air. The caribou has little or no underhair but each hair of its coat is larger at the top than the bottom and is filled with minute air spaces. The overlapping tips keep warmth in, moisture out.

The bigger a mammal's ears, limbs and tail, the more heat it loses. Thus arctic animals tend to have smaller appendages than counterparts to the south. The Arctic hare's ears are small compared to those of the snowshoe hare, or of the jackrabbit—whose huge ears help it to lose heat.

Arctic Animals Hoard Heat To Survive

Auyuittuq National Park on Baffin Island has few permanent residents—only those warm-blooded creatures able to maintain a body temperature of about 38°C. (100°F.) and the cold-blooded that assume the temperature of their environment and go into a dormant state in winter. In Auyuittuq, as in much of the vast Arctic that is more than a third of Canada, the temperature is below freezing for nine months every year and bitter winds often exceed 70 miles an hour, sometimes for days on end. But the eight land mammals and eight birds that exist year round in Auyuittuq have the ability to regulate body heat and to remain active when the outside temperature is too low for fish, amphibians and reptiles.

Heat is energy which cannot be created or destroyed but is transferred from one form to another. Animal energy comes from food that, directly or indirectly, contains the stored energy of the sun. As an animal's body cells break down food and energy, heat is produced. Some warms the body but some is lost into the air, ground or water through body surfaces—and the colder it is outside, the more heat is needed to maintain the temperature at which a creature functions. Arctic animals must produce heat (in a climate where energy-giving food is scarce) or evolve efficient ways of reducing heat loss.

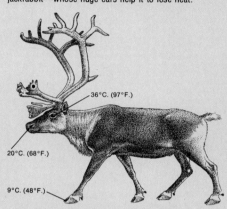

36°C. (97°F.)

20°C. (68°F.)

9°C. (48°F.)

The caribou's body temperature is about 38°C. (100°F.) but its extremities, in contact with ice and cold water, function at lower temperatures. Heat loss is minimized: blood from the heart warms incoming blood from the limbs—and is itself cooled as it travels toward the limbs.

The seasonal change of color in some arctic animals serves two purposes. The dark warm-weather coat and the white cold-season pelage both provide camouflage; cells filled with pigment in summer contain insulating air in winter. The rock ptarmigan, a year-round resident of Auyuittuq National Park, moults three times a year. The female turns speckled brown in spring but the male remains white well into summer, perhaps as a territorial display or as a decoy for predators that might attack young born in June or July.

The raven, like other arctic birds, has layers of insulating down and feathers but retains its conspicuous black coat year round. Many other birds depend on insects and aquatic plants for food and, because their diet is unavailable in winter, they must migrate. But the highly intelligent raven has adapted well. It survives winter by feeding off the remains of a predator's kill or by scavenging in garbage dumps on the outskirts of northern settlements.

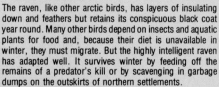

In many northern species, fetuses develop only when conditions favor survival. Polar bears mate in April or May when food is plentiful. Implantation of the fetus in the womb is apparently delayed for some months—until the female digs a den to protect herself from the elements. Cubs are born in December or January, are weaned at three months and emerge from the den about the time good weather returns.

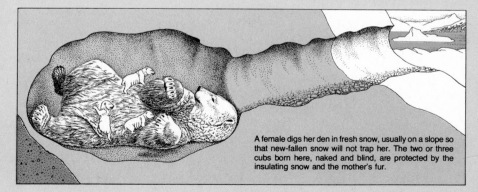

A female digs her den in fresh snow, usually on a slope so that new-fallen snow will not trap her. The two or three cubs born here, naked and blind, are protected by the insulating snow and the mother's fur.

Index

The page numbers in regular typeface are references to the text; in **boldface** to photos or illustrations; in *italics* to subjects described in greater detail. Page numbers followed by the letter *m* are references to the maps.

Abalone, pinto, 329
Abbot Pass (Alta.), 265
Abraham Lake (Alta.), 266m
Adams Lake (Alta.), **224-25**
Adams Lake (B.C.), 300m, 302
Adams River (B.C.), 302
Admiralty Inlet (N.W.T.), 373m
Aero, B.C., 330m
Agawa Bay (Ont.), 161m
Agawa Canyon (Ont.), 161m
Aguasabon River (Ont.), 161
Aiyansh, B.C., 322m
Aklavik, N.W.T., 357m
Alastair Lake (B.C.), 322
Albatross, 330
Alberni Inlet (B.C.), 312
Albertosaurus, **239**
Alder Peak (B.C.), 322
Alert Bay, B.C., 321
Alexander Bay, Nfld., 18, 19
Alexandra Falls (N.W.T.), 358
Alexandria, B.C., 291, 299
Allan Moses bird collection, 66
Alliford Bay (B.C.), 326, 330m
Allison Pass (B.C.), 302
Alma, N.B., **67**
Almonte, Ont., 109m
Alright Island (Que.). *See* Ile du Havre aux Maisons
Alsek River (Y.T.), 338, 343
Amadjuak Lake (N.W.T.), 373m
Amethyst Lakes (Alta.), 271
Amherst Island, Que. *See* Ile du Havre aux Aubert, Que.
Amphibians, **59**
Amundsen Gulf (N.W.T.), 365m
Andrew Bay (Ont.), 180
Angel Glacier (Alta.), 271
Annapolis Royal, N.S., 53, 57m
Annapolis Valley (N.S.), 57m
Anse au Griffon (Que.), 74, 75
Antelopes: pronghorn, 220, 222, 228, *229*, 230, **231**
Anthony Island (B.C.), 329
Appalachian Mountains, 74, 77
Aquariums: Kootenay, B.C., 258; Margaree Forks, N.S., 44; Presqu'ile Provincial Park (Ont.), 118; Quebec, Que., 93m, 94; Vancouver, B.C., 302
Arctic Red River (N.W.T.), 356, 357m
Arctomys Cave (B.C.), 276
Arêtes, 269
Argentia, Nfld., 21m
Arrowhead Lake (Ont.), 129
Arrow Lakes (B.C.), 257m
Aspy Bay (N.S.), 43m
Assiniboine River (Man.), 207m, 212, 214m
Astoria River (Alta.), 271
Asulkan Glacier (B.C.), 267
Athabasca Falls (Alta.), 272
Athabasca Glacier (Alta.), **269**, 275
Athabasca River (Alta.), 184, 191, 192, 195m, 265, 271, 272, 273, 275m, 354
Athabasca Sand Dunes (Sask.), 195m, **196**
Athabasca Tar Sands (Alta.), 195m
Atikokan, Ont., 172m
Atlin Lake (B.C.), 283m, 341m
Atnarko River (B.C.), 288, 290
Aubrey Island (Ont.), 119
Auklets: Cassin's, 322, 329; knob-billed rhinoceros, 329; rhinoceros, 314, 322
Auks: dovekie, 372; flightless great, *21-22*; razorbill, 21, 22, **23**, 36, 43, 77, 86

Aurora borealis, 186, **189**
Avalanches, 268, 274
Avalon Peninsula (Nfld.), 22
Azure Lake (B.C.), 276

Babine Lake (B.C.), 291m
Babine Range (B.C.), 291
Baccalieu Island (Nfld.), 21m
Back River (N.W.T.), 363
Baddeck, N.S., 43m
Badgers, 188, 212
Baffin Island (N.W.T.), 369-70, 371, 373m, 375
Baie de Gaspé (Que.), 73, 74, 76, 77m, 78
Baie de Penouille (Que.), 76
Baie de Plaisance (Que.), 36m
Baie des Chaleurs (Que.), 77m, 78
Baie Sainte-Marguerite (Que.), 87
Baie-Saint-Paul, Que., 81, 85m, 93m
Baker Creek (B.C.), 292
Baker Lake, N.W.T., 361, 363, 365m
Baldy Lake (Man.), **206**
Baldy Mountain (Man.), 207
Ballie Island (N.W.T.), 359
Balmoral Mills, N.S., 57
Bamfield, B.C., 313, 314m
Bancroft, Ont., 129m
Banff, Alta., 262, 263-64, 265, 266m
Banks Island (B.C.), 322m
Banks Island (N.W.T.), 365m, 366
Bare Summit (Ont.), 157
Barkley Sound (B.C.), 314m
Barnacles, **79**, 330; gooseneck, 310, **312**
Barnes Ice Cap (N.W.T.), 373m
Barren Grounds, The (N.W.T.), 183, 197, 335, **360-64**, 365m
Barrie, Ont., 153m
Barrier, The (B.C.), 301
Barrière du Diable (Que.), 98
Barron River Canyon (Ont.), 129m
Barry's Bay, Ont., 129m
Basalt Cliffs (B.C.), **291m**
Basin Head Sand Dunes (P.E.I.), 50m
Baskatong Reservoir (Que.), **109m**
Basque Islands (N.S.), 44
Basswood River (Ont.), 171
Bathurst, N.B., 65m
Bathurst Inlet (N.W.T.), 365m
Bats: brown, 220; Keen's, 42
Battle Mountain (B.C.), 276
Bay of Fundy, 53, 57m, 58, 61, 65m, 66, 67
Bay of Islands (Nfld.), 29m, **30**, 31
Bay of Quinte (Ont.), **117m**

Beachy Cove (Nfld.), 21m
Beamer Memorial Park (Ont.), 137m
Bear Glacier (B.C.), 284
Beargrass, **251**
Bears, 18, **45**, 65, 95, 107, 162, 172, 186, 205, 222, 250, 256, 268, 329, 330, 342; Alaskan brown, 340; Barren Grounds grizzly, 179, 362, 363, 364, 366; black, 42, 54, 76, 77, 78, 85, 86, *90*, **100**, 161, 170, 193, 214, 228, 248, **251**, 258, *265*, *273-74*, 288, 290, 321, 326, 338, 340, 354, 358; grizzly, 196, 227, 228, 238, 248, 258, 265, 266, *273-74*, 282, **288**, 290, 321, 338, 340, 341, 354; mountain grizzly, *350*; polar, 179, 302, **332-33**, 335, 356, 366, 373, 374, **375**
Beaufort Sea, 354, 356, 357m, 358, 359, 365m
Beausoleil Island (Ont.), 153
Beaver Lake (Alta.), 196
Beaver Lake (B.C.), 302
Beavers, 18, 42, **45**, 76, 85, 90, 100, 107, 108, 128, 129,130, 154, 161, 170, 172, 178, 186, 193, **209**, 222, 247, 265, 291, 321, 326, 350
Bella Coola, B.C., 288, 291m, 292, 321, 322m
Bella Coola River (B.C.), 292
Belleisle Bay (N.B.), 64
Belleville, Ont., 117m
Bell-Irving River (B.C.), 284
Bench (Sask.-Alta.), 227
Bengough, Sask., 218, 220, 221m
Bennett, B.C., 341m, 342
Bennett Lake (B.C.-Y.T.), 341m, 342
Berens River, Man., 179
Berg Lake (B.C.), 276
Bering Sea, 338, 371
Bideford River (P.E.I.), 50
Big Bar Creek (B.C.), 323
Big Beaver, Sask., 220, 221m
Big Brook (Nfld.), 17, 18
Big Falls (Nfld.), 30
Big Muddy Badlands (Sask.), 221m, **223**
Big Muddy Valley (Sask.), **216-20**
Big Rock (Alta.), 238m
Big Salmon Range (Y.T.), 342
Birch River (Alta.), 191, 192, 195m
Birchy Lake (Nfld.), 29
Bird Islands (N.S.), **43m**, 44
Bird nests, **259**
Bird Rock (Nfld.), 21
Bird Rocks, Que. *See* Rochers aux Oiseaux
Bird sanctuaries – *see box*

Birds Hill, Man., 180
Bison. *See* Buffalo
Bitterns, 154; American,118; least, **143**, 146
Black Beaver Falls (Ont.), 161
Blackbirds, red-winged, 142, 173
Black Brook Cove (N.S.), 40
Black Creek (B.C.), 315
Black Tusk Mountain (B.C.), 301
Blakiston Valley (Alta.), 246
Blomidon Mountains (Nfld.), 29
Blooming Point, P.E.I., **46-47**, 48
Bluebird, eastern, 144
Blue Hills lookout tower (Nfld.), 19
Blue Mountain Caves (Ont.), 153m
Bobcats, 54, 65, 180, 228
Boiestown, N.B., 66
Bonaventure Island (Que.), 76, 77m, 78
Bonavista Bay (Nfld.), 17, 19, 21m
Bonne Bay (Nfld.), **24-25**, 26-27, 29m, 31
Bonnechere Caves (Ont.), 129m
Bonnechere Park and River (Ont.), 129m
Borden, P.E.I., 50m
Boshkung Lake (Ont.), 130
Bosporus Strait (Alta.), **244-45**, 247
Boston Bar, B.C., 296, 299, 300m
Boundary Range (B.C.), 284
Bow Lake (Alta.), **260-61**
Bow Pass (Alta.), 266
Bow River (Alta.), 249m, 263, 265, 266m
Brackley, P.E.I., 47, 49
Brackley Beach, P.E.I., **48**
Brandon, Man., 207m
Brantford, Ont., 137m
Bras d'Or Lake (N.S.), 43m
Brent, Ont., 129m
Brent Crater (Ont.), 129m, 130
Bridal Creek, B.C., 300
Bridal Lake (B.C.), 258
Bridal Veil Falls (B.C.), 300m
Bridal Veil Falls (Ont.), 161
Bridge River (B.C.), 300m
Brier Island (N.S.), 57m, 58
British soldier. *See* Red jacket
Broad Cove (Nfld.), 18
Brockville, Ont., 113, 117m, 119
Broken Group Islands (B.C.), 309, 312, 313
Broken Skull River (N.W.T.), 345
Brome Lake (Que.), 101m

Brooks, Alta., 233, 234, 238m
Broughton Island (N.W.T.), 371
Brown's Bay (Ont.), 118
Bruce Peninsula (Ont.), 123, 148-52, 153m, 155
Bruce's Cave (Ont.), 152
Brule Rapids (Sask.), 195
Buckley Lake (B.C.), 282
Buffalo, 50, 138, 175, 188, 191, 196, 205, 220, 222, 227, 228, 230, 238, 245, 248
Buffalo Bay (Ont.), 179m
Buffalo Lake (Alta.), 238m
Buffalo Narrows, Sask., 186
Buffalo Park (P.E.I.), 50m
Buffalo Pound Lake (Sask.), 211, 213, 214m, 221
Bugaboo Alpine Recreation Area (B.C.), 266m
Bulkley River (B.C.), 291, 322m
Bulyea, Sask., 213
Bumblebees, **215**, 363
Buntings: indigo, 142, 161; lazuli, 302; snow, 144, 145, 363, 364, 373
Burgeo, Nfld., 29m
Burin Peninsula (Nfld.), 21m
Burke Channel (B.C.), 322m
Burlington, Ont., 137m
Burnaby, B.C., 300m
Burns Lake, B.C., 291m
Burntside Lake (Ont.), 171
Burwash Uplands (Y.T.), 340
Bushtits, 301
Butchart Gardens (B.C.), 314m
Butedale, B.C., 321
Butterfly: giant swallowtail, 144; olive hairstreak, 144; monarch, 144, 146, **147**; satyrid, *205*
Buttermilk Falls (Ont.), 129m, 130
Butternut Island (Ont.), 109
Buttes, **223**, 233, 350
Bylot Island (N.W.T.), 373m

Caamaño Sound (B.C.), 321
Cabot Head, Ont., 149, 152
Cabot's Landing, N.S., 43
Cabri, Sask., 229m
Cache Creek, B.C., 302
Cactus, 230, 231, **234**, 235, 243, 250, 301, 302; ball, 212; desert, 227; pincushion, 208; prickly pear, *144*, 212, 315
Calgary, Alta., 238m
Calvert Island (B.C.), 321
Cambridge Bay, N.W.T., 365m
Cameron Creek (Alta.), 246
Campbell Creek (P.E.I.), 50
Campbell River, B.C., 314m
Campbellton, N.B., 65m
Campobello Island (N.B.), 65
Camrose, Alta., 238m

Wildlife Sanctuaries and Wilderness Areas

Bird sanctuaries Alf Hole (Man.), 179m; Anderson River (N.W.T.), 357m; Bonaventure Island (Que.), 77m; Cap Tourmente (Que.), 93m-94; Cape Dorset (N.W.T.), 373m; Dewey Soper (N.W.T.), 373m, 374; Gault Estate, Mont-Saint-Hilaire (Que.), 102; George C. Reifel (B.C.), 300m, 301; Ile aux Basques (Que.), 85; Isle of Bays (Sask.), 221m; Jack Miner (Ont.), 145m; Kendall Island (N.W.T.), 357m, 358; Kortright (Ont.), 137m; Last Mountain Lake (Sask.), 214m; McConnell River (N.W.T.), 365m; Moore's (P.E.I.), 50m; Nechako River (B.C.), 291m, 292; Queen Maud Gulf, 365m, 366;

Round Hill (Alta.), 238m; Southampton Island (N.W.T.), 366; Vaseux Lake Provincial Park (B.C.), 302; Wascana (Sask.), 221m, 222; Witless Bay (Nfld.), 21m, 22
Conservation areas, wilderness areas, and wildlife preserves Buckhorn (Ont.), 117m; Cap Tourmente (Que.), 93m, **94**; Chapleau Crown (Ont.), 161m; Chignecto (N.S.), 57m; Condie (Sask.), 214m; Creston Valley (B.C.), 253, 254; Delkatla (B.C.), 329; Elora Gorge (Ont.), 137m; Fowley Mountain (Ont.), 118; Grand Forks (B.C.), 257m, 258; Inglis Falls (Ont.), 153m, 154; Lauder Sandhills (Man.), 207m;

Laurentian Lake (Ont.), 154; Liscomb (N.S.), 57m, 58; Luther Marsh (Ont.), 137m-38; McArthur (Y.T.), 341m, 342; Norah W. Michener (N.W.T.), 350m; Mitlenatch Island (B.C.), 315; Newfoundland, 21m, 22, 29m, 30; Oak Hammock (Man.), 179m, 180; Pipestone (Ont.), 179m, 180; Prince Edward Island, 58; Purcell Wilderness (B.C.), 257m, 258; Rattlesnake Point (Ont.), 137m, 138; Selwyn (Ont.), 117m, 118; Sifton (Ont.), 145m; Thelon (N.W.T.), 362, 363, 365m, 366; Tobeatic (N.S.), 57m, 58; Warsaw Caves (Ont.), 117m, 118; Wildcat Hill (Sask.), 187m, 188; Willmore (Alta.), 275m, 276

Camsell Bend (N.W.T.), 354
Camsell River (N.W.T.), 357
Canadian Shield, 83, 105, 110, 114, 119, 127, 159, 160, 167, 169, 176, 184, 185, 187, 193, 201, 357, 364
Canim Falls (B.C.), 276
Canoe routes: Boundary Waters (Ont.), 172m; Camsell River (N.W.T.), 357m; Cariboo-Quesnel (B.C.), 291m; Dease River (B.C.), 283m, 284; Granby River (B.C.), 257m, 258; Rearguard Falls (B.C.), 275m, 276; Steel Lake and River (Ont.), 161m, 162; Stikine River (B.C.), 283m, 284; Stuart-Nechako (B.C.), 291m, 292; Yellowknife River (N.W.T.), 357m
Canrobert Hills (N.W.T.), 365m
Cap-au-Corbeau, Que., 85
Cap-aux-Meules, Que., 34, 36m, 50
Cap Blanc (Que.), 78
Cap Bon Ami, Que., 76
Cap de Gaspé (Que.), 73, 76
Cap-des-Rosiers, Que., 76, 77m
Cap-des-Rosiers-Est, Que., 76
Cape Blomidon Lookoff (N.S.), 57m
Cape Bonavista, Nfld., 20
Cape Breton Island (N.S.), 41-42, 43m, 44
Cape Dorset (N.W.T.), 373m
Cape Dyer (N.W.T.), 371
Cape Knox (B.C.), 330m
Cape Norman (Nfld.), 20
Cape North (N.S.), 42, 43m
Cape Race (Nfld.), 21m, 22
Cape Ray, Nfld., 29
Cape St. Francis (Nfld.), 21m, 22
Cape St.George (Nfld.), 29m
Cape St. Mary's (Nfld.), 21m
Cape Searle (N.W.T.), 372
Cape Smoky (N.S.), 43m, 44
Cape Spear (Nfld.), 21m
Cap Eternité (Que.), 84
Cape Tryon (P.E.I.), 50m
Cap-Gaspé, Que., 76
Capilano Canyon (B.C.), 300m
Cap Trinité (Que.), 84
Carcross, Y.T., 341m, 342
Cardinals, 142
Cardston, Alta., 249m
Cariboo Mountains (B.C.), 275m, 292, 302
Cariboo Plateau, (B.C.), 243
Cariboo River (B.C.), 291
Caribou, 15, 22, 53, 58, 78, 94, 128, 282, 284, 335, 338, 341, 356, 361, 362, 364, 365, 366, 367, 371, 375; Barren Grounds, 27; Dawson, 326; giant mountain, 340; mountain, 273, 288; Newfoundland, 27, 28; woodland, 27, 77, 159, 162, 186, 188, 258, 350
Caribou Hills (N.W.T.), 357m
Carleton-sur-Mer (Que.), 77m
Carnelians (N.W.T.), 329
Carolinas, 372
Carp, 142
Carpenter Lake, B.C., 300m
Carp River (Ont.), 109
Carrying Place (Ont.), 117
Cascade Falls (Ont.), 160
Cascade Mountain (Alta.), 277
Cascade Mountains (B.C.), 300m, 302
Cassiar, B.C., 283m, 284
Cassiar Mountains (B.C.), 243, 283m, 284
Castle Butte (Sask.), 218
Castlegar, B.C., 257m
Castle Mountain. See Mount Eisenhower
Cathedral Grove (B.C.), 306-07, 315
Cave and Basin (Alta.), 264
Cavell Lake (Alta.), 271

Cavendish, P.E.I., 47, 48
Cavendish Beach, P.E.I., 48-49
"Cave of the Winds" (Ont.), 172
Caves and caverns, 43, 57, 74, 118, 129, 150-51, 152, 153, 155, 172, 220, 276, 315, 348-49
Cedar Island (Ont.), 119
Cedar Lake (Man.), 187m
Cedar Lake (Ont.), 129m
Centennial Range (Y.T.), 338
Central Barrens Calving Ground (N.W.T.), 365m
Chain Lakes Reservoir (Alta.), 249
Chamouchouane River (Que.), 83, 85m
Champlain Lookout (Que.), 105
Champlain Sea, 94, 119
Chandler Reach, Nfld., 20
Chantry Inlet (N.W.T.), 363, 365m
Chapel Island (N.S.), 43
Chapleau, Ont., 161m
Charlottetown, P.E.I., 33, 47
Charny, Que., 93m, 94
Chasm, The (B.C.), 300m, 302
Chasmosaurus, 239
Chatham, Ont., 145m, 146
Chats Rapids (Ont.), 109, 110
Chatterton Falls (Ont.), 171
Chaudière Falls (French River, Ont.), 130
Chaudière Falls (Chamouchouane River, Que.), 85
Chaudière Falls (Ottawa River, Que.), 110
Chaudière River (Que.), 93m, 94
Chebogue Point (N.S.), 57m
Chedabucto Bay (N.S.), 43m, 44
Chemung Lake (Ont.), 117m, 118
Chenal des Quatre Fourches (Alta.), 192
Chester, N.S., 58
Chesterfield Inlet Raised Beaches (N.W.T.), 365m
Chéticamp, N.S., 39, 40, 42, 43m
Chickadees, 114, 274, 313; boreal, 128, 161
Chicoutimi, Que., 83, 85m
Chignecto Bay, N.S., 58, 65
Chilcotin-Fraser River Expedition, 300m
Chilcotin Plateau (B.C.), 243, 292
Chilcotin River (B.C.), 291m, 292, 301
Chilko Lake (B.C.), 300m, 301
Chilliwack, (B.C.), 300
Chin Lakes (Alta.), 249m
Chipmunks, 42, 92, 173, 274
Chippawa Channel (Ont.), 139
Chiton, 79
Christina Falls (B.C.), 283m, 284
Christina Lake (B.C.), 257m
Christina Range (B.C.), 257, 258
Chukachida River (B.C.), 284
Churchbridge, Sask., 212
Churchill, Man., 361, 365m
Churchill Falls (Lab.), 114
Churchill Lake (Sask.), 187m
Churchill River (Sask.), 188, 189
Churchill River (N.W.T.), 364
Chute à Michel (Que.), 86
Chute aux Rats (Muskrat Falls) (Que.), 98
Chute du Diable (Que.), 98
Chutes Croches (Crooked Falls) (Que.), 98
Ciboux Island (N.S.), 43
Cirques, 247, 263, 268, 269, 271, 291, 343
Cisco, B.C., 299
Claresholm, Alta., 249m
Clark Mountains (B.C.), 247
Clear Lake (Man.), 205, 207m
Clearwater Lake (B.C.), 276

Clearwater River (Alta.-Sask.), 184, 195m, 266m
Clearwater River (B.C.), 275m, 276
Cleland Island (B.C.), 314m
Cli Lake (N.W.T.), 350m
Cloak Bay (B.C.), 326
Clode Sound (Nfld.), 19
Coal River, B.C., 350
Coast Mountains (B.C.), 243, 283m, 284, 286-87, 292, 295, 296, 300m, 301, 302, 316, 322m, 323
Coast Range (B.C.), 284
Cobequid Mountains (N.S.), 58
Coburg Island (N.W.T.), 373m
Cocoa Crater (B.C.), 281
Cody Cave (B.C.), 257m
Cody Creek (B.C.), 257
Coffee Crater (B.C.), 281
Coffin Island, Que. See Ile de la Grande Entrée
Cold Lake (Alta.-Sask.), 195m
Coleman, Alta., 249m, 250
Coleman Volcanic Deposits (Alta.-B.C.), 249m
Collingwood, Ont., 153m
Colpoys Bay (Ont.), 152, 153m
Columbia Glacier (Alta.), 269
Columbia Icefield (Alta.), 265, 266m, 269, 272, 275m
Columbia Mountains (B.C.), 243, 257m, 266m
Columbia River (B.C.), 257m, 265, 266m, 275m
Colville Lake (N.W.T.), 357m
Conception Bay (Nfld.), 21m, 22
Condie Reservoir (Sask.), 214
Condor Needle (Que.), 101m
Cone Head (B.C.), 329
Conk Lake (Ont.), 171
Connors, N.B., 62, 65m
Conservation areas. See box p. 376
Continental Divide (Alta.), 196, 247, 261, 263, 265, 272, 275, 284
Cooks Creek (Man.), 180
Coots, 142
Coppermine, N.W.T., 365m
Coppermine River (N.W.T.), 361, 365m
Corkscrew Island (Ont.), 175
Corkscrew Mountain (Alta.), 267
Cormorants, 28, 42, 76, 207, 325, 329; double-crested, 36, 85, 86, 214, 221; great, 36; pelagic, 313, 315, 322
Corn Creek Marsh (B.C.), 254
Corner Brook (Nfld.), 25, 29m, 30
Cornwallis Island (N.W.T.), 373m, 374
Coronation Fjord (N.W.T.), 372
Cougars, 95, 188, 247, 250, 251, 315, 316, 321
Coulees, 222, 230, 234-35, 250
Courtenay, B.C., 314m
Cowbird, brown-headed, 259
Cox Island (B.C.), 326
Coyotes, 142, 214, 220, 228, 231, 247, 256, 274
Crabs, 51, 79, 313, 315; dungeness, 329; hermit, 79
Cranbrook, B.C., 257m, 302
Cranes; sandhill, 212, 214, 222, 230, 329, 362; whooping, 196, 214
Crater Lake (N.W.T.), 341, 371, 372
Cree Lake (Sask.), 187m
Creignish Mountain (N.S.), 43m
Crescent Spire (B.C.), 266
Creston, B.C., 253, 254, 256, 257m, 258
Creston Valley (B.C.), 252-56, 257m, 259
Crooked Lake (Ont.), 171
Crooked Lake (Sask.), 211, 214m
Crows, 50; Northwestern, 313
Crowsnest Mountain (Alta.-B.C.), 249, 250

Crowsnest Pass (Alta.), 249m, 250, 302
Cuckoos, 212
Cul de Sac Lake (Ont.), 175
Cumberland House (Sask.), 186
Cumberland Peninsula (N.W.T.), 369, 370, 371, 372
Cumberland Sound (N.W.T.), 371, 372, 373m
Cunningham Inlet (N.W.T.), 365m
Cup and Saucer Lookout (Ont.), 154
Curlews, 49
Curtain Falls (Ont.), 171
Cyclops, 181
Cypress Hills (Alta.-Sask.), 224-28
Cypress Lake (Sask.), 228, 229m

Dale Marsh (B.C.), 254
Dall Island (Alaska), 329
Dalvay, P.E.I., 47
Daly Glacier (B.C.), 268, 269
Dardanelles Strait (Alta.), 247
Darky Lake (Ont.), 171
Dartmouth, N.S., 57m
Darwin Falls (Que.), 101m
Dauphin Lake (Man.), 207m
Dauphin Mountain (Man.), 206
Davis Strait (N.W.T.), 371, 373m
Dawson, Y.T., 282, 341m, 342
Dawson Bay (Man.), 207m
Dawson Creek, B.C., 283, 284
Deadman Falls (B.C.), 301
Deadman Valley (B.C.), 300m, 301
Deadmen Valley (N.W.T.), 345, 348
Dean Channel (B.C.), 291m
Dease Lake (B.C.), 283m, 284
Deep River, Ont., 129m
Deer, 45, 64, 75, 76, 77, 78, 85, 86, 90, 95, 107, 129, 131, 142, 196, 212, 214, 222, 227, 265, 315, 316, 321, 329; blacktailed, 326; Chinese water, 238; mule, 205, 207, 220, 230, 248, 250, 258, 273; Père David's, 179, 238; white-tailed, 42, 54, 65, 100, 128, 153, 207, 228, 247, 250, 256, 258
Deer Island (N.B.), 65
Deer Lake (Nfld.), 29m
Deer Park, B.C., 257
Della Falls (B.C.), 316
Delta Marsh (Man.), 207m
Dempster Highway Cariboo Crossing (Y.T.), 341m
Denali fault (B.C.), 331
Desmids, 181
Deschênes Rapids (Que.), 110
Deux Rivieres Portage (Ont.), 171
Devil Rapids (Sask.), 186
Devil's Bay (Ont.), 176
Devil's Hole (Que.), 93m, 94
Devil's Kitchen (N.W.T.), 346
Devil's Woodpile (B.C.), 300
Devon Island (N.W.T.), 365m, 373m
Diable River (Que.), 98, 101m
Diatoms, 181
Digby, N.S., 57m
Digges Sound (N.W.T.), 373m, 374
Dinosaurs, 233-35, 236, 239
Dipper Lake (Sask.), 185
Dixon Entrance (B.C.), 322m, 329, 330m
Dobbies, 230
Dog Lake (Ont.), 172m
Dolphins, 20, 85; Pacific striped, 302
Donjek Glacier (Y.T.), 343
Donnacona, Que., 94
Doré Bay (Ont.), 157
Douglas Channel (B.C.), 322m
Dove, mourning, 92, 250
Dove Lake (Sask.), 187m
Dowitchers, 18
Driftwood Creek (B.C.), 291
Drinking Falls (Sask.), 182-83
Drinking Lake (Sask.), 185

Drumheller, Alta., 234, 235, 236, 238m
Drummondville, Que., 93m, 101m
Dryden, Ont., 172m
Drysdale Falls (N.S.), 57m
Duck Lake (B.C.), 254-55
Duck Mountain (Man.), 207
Ducks, 42, 50, 58, 64, 86, 92, 110, 116, 137, 142, 145, 146, 154, 180, 192, 194, 195, 205, 248, 253, 256, 341, 342, 354, 356; black, 36, 49, 54, 85, 108; blue-winged teal, 36, 49, 188, 193, 197, 222; bufflehead, 207; canvasback, 207, 222; eider, 36, 85, 362; golden-eyed, 114, 207, 254, 325; green-winged teal, 36, 49, 208; harlequin, 325; king eider, 373; lesser scaup, 197; mallard, 138, 181, 186, 197, 207, 214, 222, 238, 250, 310-12; merganser, 14, 144, 160, 171, 325; northern eider, 373; old-squaw, 362; pintail, 36, 197, 207, 214, 222, 310-12; redhead, 197; ring-necked, 49; scaup, 325; scoter, 325; shoveler, 197, 207; teal, 254; wood, 254
Dufferin Islands (Ont.), 138
Duke Depression (Y.T.), 338
Duke River (Y.T.), 338
Dulse, 66
Duncan, B.C., 314m
Duncan Lake (B.C.), 266m
Dunes, 34, 47, 48, 50, 66, 74, 118, 123, 146, 155, 161, 207, 208; seif, 195, 196
Dunphy's Pond (Nfld.), 18-19
Dunvegan, Alta., 195m
Dutch Creek Hoodoos (B.C.), 257m, 258
Dyer Bay (Ont.), 152, 153m

Eagle Bluff (Y.T.), 342
Eagles, 144, 186, 222, 259, 273, 329, 356; bald, 27, 42, 44, 145, 163, 170, 172, 181, 188, 193, 205, 290, 310, 313, 321, 322, 325, 340, 342, 350; golden, 205, 220, 230, 248, 251, 268, 342, 365
Eardley Escarpment (Que.), 105-06
Earthquakes, 331
East Bay (N.S.), 43m, 57m
East Bay Hills (N.S.), 44
East Bluff Lookout (Ont.), 154
East Cranberry Pond (Ont.), 142
Eastend, Sask., 227, 229m
East Lake (Ont.), 118
East River (Ont.), 129
East Sister Island (Ont.), 145m
Ebenezer, P.E.I., 48
Eddontenajon, B.C., 282, 283m, 284
Edmonton, Alta., 194, 238m, 346
Edmontosaurus, 239
Edmundston, N.B., 61, 64, 65m
Edson, Alta., 275m
Eels, 78; moray, 302
Eels Creek (Ont.), 118
Egmont Bay (P.E.I.), 50m
Egrets, 142; American, 145
Elbow, Sask., 212, 214m
Elk, 45, 138, 162, 188, 204, 205, 207, 214, 222, 227, 228, 238, 248, 250, 251, 256, 258, 265, 266, 268, 273, 274, 316, 326
Elk Falls (B.C.), 316
Elk River (B.C.), 249m, 316
Elkwater Lake (Alta.), 228
Ellesmere Island (N.W.T.), 167, 372, 373m, 374
Emerald Lake (B.C.), 268
Englishman River (B.C.), 316
English River (Ont.), 179m
Englishtown, N.S., 44
Ennuyeuse Creek (Sask.), 195
Enon Lake (N.S.), 44
Entry Island, Que. See Ile d'Entrée
Erin Mountain (Nfld.), 29

Ermine. 205, 321, 326, 362, 372
Escarpment Lookout (Man.), **205**
Eskasoni, N.S., 43
Eskers, 53, 106, 162, 179, 188, 207, 266, 284, 364
Eskimo Point, N.W.T., 362, 365m
Eskimos, Caribou, 361
Esterhazy, Sask., 212
Estevan, Sask., 221m
Etang-du-Nord, Que., 36m
Euclataws Cave (B.C.), 315
Eva Lake (B.C.), 268
Eve Cone (B.C.), 280, 281, 282, 285
Eyebrow Lake (Sask.), 214m

Fairy Hole (N.S.), **43m**
Fairy Point (Ont.), 162
Falcons, 163, 342; peregrine, 145, 193, 248, **329**, 330, 365, 366; prairie, 220
Falcon's Castle (N.W.T.), **374**
Fatima, Que., 36m
Field, B.C., 265, 266m
Fife Lake (Sask.), 221m
Finches, 42, 212, 259; cross-bill, 144; red crossbill, 228, 313
Finlay River (B.C.), 283m, 284, 354
Fires, forest, **95**
Fireweed, 90, **95**, 212; flaming, 356; magenta, 265; red-purple, 288
First Canyon (N.W.T.), **346-47, 348-49,** 351
Fisher Range (Alta.), 267
Fishers, 321
Fish hatcheries, 77m, 78, 85m 86, 102, 257m, 258
Fishing Lakes, The (Sask.), 211, 213, 214m
Fitz Hugh Sound (B.C.), 322m
Five Finger Rapids (Y.T.), 342
Fjords, 26, **31,** 83, 84, 323, 350, 373
Flathead River (B.C.), 249m
Flat River (N.W.T.), 350m
Flickers, 49, 254
Flin Flon, Man., 187m, 188
Floating Heart Bay (Ont.), 157
Flowerpot Island (Ont.), 152, **153-54**
Flowerpots, 66
Flycatchers, 212; Acadian, 146; great crested, 54; olive-sided, 108
Fond du Lac River (Sask.), 192
Foothills Erratics Train (Alta.), 238
Forest: boreal, 45, 74, 98, 154, 161, 167, 188, 201, 282, 350, 357, 366; Carolinian, 144, 146; climax, 45, 95; decidu-ous, 161; evergreen, 44, 188; hardwood, 141; Krummholz, 27, 264; subalpine, 288; virgin, 58
Forest preserves: Belair Provincial Forest (Man.), 179m; Carleton Forest Area (Ont.), 118; Clearwater-Rocky (Alta.), 275m; Cypress Hills Provincial Forest (Alta.), 224-28; Kananaskis Research Forest (Alta.), 266m, 267; Limerick Forest (Ont.), 118; Missisagi Park Reserve, 154; Petawawa Forest Sta-tion, 129m, 130; Rocky Mountain Forest Reserve (Alta.), 250
Forester's Walk (B.C.), 314
Forestville, Que., 85m, **86**
Forillon Peninsula (Que.), 73, **74-75**
Fork Beard Glacier (N.W.T.), 372
Fort Chipewyan (Alta.), 194, 195m
Fort Erie, Ont., 137m, 138
Fort Frances, Ont., 172m
Fort Garry, Man. *See* Winnipeg, Man.

Fort Good Hope, N.W.T., 357m
Ford Liard, N.W.T., 350m
Fort Macleod, Alta.,249m
Fort McMurray, Alta., 194, 195m
Fort McPherson, N.W.T., 357m
Fort Norman, N.W.T., 355, 357m
Fort Prince of Wales, N.W.T., 361
Fort Providence, N.W.T., 357m
Fort Qu'Appelle, Sask., 213, 214m
Fort Resolution, N.W.T., 357m, 358
Fort St. Charles, Ont., 178
Fort St. James (B.C.), 291m
Fort Simpson, N.W.T., 346-48, 350m, 354, 357m, 358
Fort Smith, N.W.T., 194, 358
Fortune Bay (Nfld.), 21
Fortune Creek (Que.), 107
Fort Vermilion, Alta., **195m**
Fort Walsh, Sask., 227-28, 229m
Fosheim Peninsula (N.W.T.), 374
Fossils, 22, 30, 57, 58, 86, 94, 110, 118, 129, **138,** 153, 180, 207, 217, 220, 222, 227, 229, 233-34, 235, 238, **239,** 258, 291, 326
Fosthall Creek Falls (B.C.), 257
Foxe Basin (N.W.T.), 373m
Foxes, 17, 50, 95, 100, 107, 159, 193, 212, 321, 358, 364; Arctic, 268, 362, 366, 372, **375,** gray, 146; red, 42, 49, 76, 90, 118, 228, 357
Franey Peak (N.S.), 43m
Franklin Mountains (N.W.T.), 350m, 357m
Franklin Range (N.W.T.), 354
Frank Slide (Alta.), 249m, 250
Fraser Canyon (B.C.), 295-299, 300m
Fraser Plateau (B.C.), 287, 291m, 302
Fraser River (B.C.), 275m, 276, 291, 292, **294-99,** 301, 302, 303, **323**
Fredericton, N.B., 61, 62, 64, 65m, 66
Frenchman Butte (Sask.), 187m
French River (Ont.), 130, 153m
French River (Que.), 98
Friars Head, N.S., **41**
Frobisher Bay, N.W.T., 373m
Frog Portage (Sask.), 186
Frogs, 54, 114, 128, 146, 161; green, 108; leopard, **59,** 108; western gray tree, 205; wood, 105
Frontenac Axis, 114, 119
Front Ranges (B.C.), 266
Fry Creek Canyon Recreation Area (B.C.), 257m, 258
Fulmars, northern, 365, 372, 373, 374

Funeral Range (N.W.T.), 345, 348
Funk Island (Nfld.), 21-22

Gabarus Bay (N.S.), 43m, 44
Gabriola Island (B.C.), 314m
Gagetown, N.B., 64
Galiano Gallery (B.C.), 314
Gallinules, 114, **143;** common, 146
Gananoque, Ont., 113, 117m, 119
Gander, Nfld., 21m
Gannets, *21,* 22, **23,** 36, 42, *76,* 77
Gap, The (Alta.), 250
Gardiner Dam (Sask.), 229
Gargoyles, The (B.C.), 301
Garibaldi, Giuseppe, 301
Garibaldi Lake (B.C.), 301
Garson, Man., 180
Gaspé Peninsula (Que.), 26, 33, 71, 73, 74, 75, 89
Gatineau, Que., 109m
Gatineau Hills (Que.), **104-05**
Gatineau Park (Que.), 71, **105-08,** 109m, 111
Gatineau River (Que.), 109m, 110
Geese, 42, 58, 114, 144, 194, 205, 207, 248, 253, 256, 342, 354, 356, 364; black brant, 310-12, 325, 374; blue, 180, 207; brant, 85; Canada, 17, 36, 49, 50, 86, *93-94,* 105, 145, *179,* 180,193, **197,** 208, **212-13,** *214,* 222, 238, 250, 254, *292,* 302, 312, 329, 341, 350, 358, 365, 366, 374; em-peror, 137; giant Canada, 137, *179.;* lesser snow, *179, 365;* Ross's, **197,** *362, 366;* snow, *93-94,* 180, 207, 254, **256,** 353, 358, 362, 365, 366; white-fronted, 357, 366
Geological history. *See* box this page
George Bay (N.S.), 43m
George's Riffle (N.W.T.), 348
Georgian Bay (Ont.), 123, 127, 130, 149, 150, 152, 153m, 154, 155
Geraldton, Ont., 161m
Giant Cleft (B.C.), 300
Gillies Lake (Ont.), 152
Gilmour Lake (Ont.), 130
Gimli, Man., 179m
Gitnadoix River (B.C.), 322m
Gjoa Haven, N.W.T., 365m
Glacier Creek (B.C.), 291
Glacière Cave (Ont.), 118
Glacier Gulch (B.C.), 291m
Glacier Lake (N.W.T.), 372
Glaciers, **31,** 77, 89, 114, 247, 258, 261, 262-63, 267, 269, 272, 277, 287, 290, 292, 300, 340, **343,** 364, 371. *See also* specific glaciers
Glen Huron, Ont., 153
Goat Canyon (B.C.), 284
Goat Island (N.Y.), 135

Goats, 284; mountain, 248, 250, **251,** 266, 273, 282, 288, 340; Rocky Mountain, 248, 258; white mountain, 272
Godwits, 49
Golden, B.C., 266m, 268
Golden Ears Mountain (B.C.), 301
Golden Hinde (B.C.), **316**
Golden Mile Park (Ont.), 130
Goldenrod, 74, 90, 212, 284
Goldeye, 193
Gold River, B.C., 314m
Goldstream River (B.C.), 314
Good Spirit Lake (Sask.), 214m
Goodwin, Alta., 250
Gophers, pocket, 205; Richard-son's pocket, **231**
Gordon Island (Ont.), 119
Gore Bay, Ont., 153m, 154
Goshawk, **163**
Gouin Reservoir (Que.), 90
Gracefield, Que., 109m
Graham Island (B.C.), 325, 326, 329, 330m
Graham River (B.C.), 284
Granby, Que., 101m
Granby River (B.C.), 258
Grand Bay, N.S., 62
Grand Canyon of the Stikine, 282, 283m, 284
Grande Anse River (N.S.), 40, 41
Grande Cache, Alta., 275m
Grande Chute à l'Ours (Que.), 86
Grande Entrée (Que.), 36m
Grande Prairie, Alta., 195m
Grand-Etang Eel Pool (Que.), 77m, 78
Grand Falls, N.B., 61, **64,** 65m
Grand Falls, Nfld., 21
Grand Forks, B.C., 257m
Grand Harbour, N.B., 66
Grand Lake (N.B.), 62, 65m
Grand Lake (Nfld.), 29m
Grand Manan Island (N.B.), 65m
Grand-Mère, Que., 90, 93m, 94
Grand Pèlerin (Que.), 86
Grand Portage, Minn., 172
Grand Rapids, Man., 179
Grand Rapids (Sask.), 195
Grand-Remous (Que.), 109m
Grand River (Ont.), 137m, 138
Grass: blue-eyed, 152; blue grama, **251;** cotton, 27, 108, 363; dune, 34, 36; fallow, 203, 362; hay, 230; marram, *48,* 49, **51,** 58, 137; marsh, 44
Grasses of Parnassus, 288
Grass River (Sask.), 188
Great Bear Lake (N.W.T.), 354, 355, 357m
Great Bear River (N.W.T.), 355
Great Bras d'Or (N.S.), 43
Great Gorge (Ont.), 138
Great Island (Nfld.), 22
Great Sand Hills (Sask.), 229m, **230,** 231

Great Slave Lake (N.W.T.), 192, 354, 356, 357m, 365m
Grebes, 142, 144, 195, 205, 214; red-necked, 340; west-ern, 196, 222
Greenbrier, 54
Green Island (Nfld.), 22
Green Point (Nfld.), 27
Green Point (N.S.), 40
Grey Hunter Peak (Y.T.), 342
Grey Island (Nfld.), 153
Grice Bay (B.C.), 310
Griffith Island (Ont.), 152
Grimshaw, Alta., 195m, 358
Grindstone Island. See Ile du Cap aux Meules
Grosbeak, evening, 92
Gros-Cap, Que., 36m
Gros Morne Mountain (Nfld.), 26
Grosse Ile (Que.), 34, 36m
Groundhog, 76, 100
Grouse, 42, 86, 274; blue, 329, 342; ruffed, **45, 54-55,** 105, **173, 212;** sharp-tailed, *340;* spruce, 128, 340
Guelph, Ont., 137
Guernsey Island (Nfld.), **30**
Guillemots, 36, 43; black, 21, 22, **23,** 76, 85, 86, 365, 373; pigeon, 322, 325
Gulf Islands (B.C.), 302, **304-05,** 314m, 316
Gulf of St. Lawrence, 29m, 30, 33, 34, 36m, 37, 39, 43m, 50m, 71, 73, 75, 76, 77m, 79
Gull Island (Nfld.), 22
Gull Island (Que.), *See* Ile aux Goélands (Que.)
Gulls, 17, 21, 28, 42, 51, **65,** 114, **146,** 186, 214, 321, 322, 325, 329, 356; Bonaparte's, 162; California, 221; glau-cous, 365, 373; glaucous-winged, 366; great black-backed, **23,** 36, 50, 54; her-ring, 22, 36, 50, 76, 85; Ice-land, 373; mew, 340; ring-billed, 118, 162, 221
Gun Lake (B.C.), 300
Gyrfalcons, 27, 301, 335, 363, 366

Hadrosaurs, **239**
Haida, B.C., 326
Haines Junction, Y.T., 338, 341m
Halbrite Badlands (Sask.), 221m, 222
Haliburton, Ont., 129m, 130
Haliburton Highlands (Ont.), 129m, 130
Halifax, N.S., 57m
Hall's Lake (Ont.), 130
Hamilton, Ont., 137m
Hares, 76, 86, 107, 118, 356; Arctic, 27, 362, 366, **375;** snowshoe, 42, 49, 85, 92, **173,** 180, **375;** varying, 100
Harptree, Sask., 220, 221m
Harrison Lake (B.C.), 300m, 301

Geological History

Algonquin Provincial Park (Ont.), 127-28; Auyuittuq National Park (N.W.T.), 370-71; Banff National Park (Alta.), 261-63, 265, 269; Barron River Canyon (Ont.), 129; Big Muddy (Sask.), **216-18,** 223; Brent Crater (Ont.), 130; Bruce Peninsula (Ont.), 149, 150-52, 155; Canadian Shield, 167; Cape Breton Highlands (N.S.), 39, 40-41; Carp Lake Provincial Park (B.C.), 291; Chesterfield Inlet Raised Beaches (N.W.T.), 365; Coleman Volcanic Deposits (Alta.-B.C.), 249; Cypress Hills (Alta.-Sask.), 225-27; Driftwood Canyon Provincial Park (B.C.), 291; Foothills Erratics Train (Alta.), 238; Forillon National Park (Que.), 74; Fraser Canyon (B.C.), 296; Gatineau Park (Que.), 105-06, 108; Georgian Bay National Park (Ont.), 153; Grand Manan Island (N.B.), 65-66; Gros Morne National Park (Nfld.), 26-27, 31; Haughton Dome (N.W.T.), 365; Jasper National Park (Alta.), 272; Kejimkujik National Park (N.S.), 53, 56; Kluane National Park (Y.T.), 343; Lake of the Woods (Ont.), 176; La Mauricie National Park (Que.), 89; Magdalen Islands (Que.), 33; Mont-Saint-Hilaire (Que.), 101-02; Mont Tremblant Provincial Park (Que.), 98; Mount Edziza Provincial Park (B.C.), 279-81, 282, **285;** Nahanni National Park (N.W.T.), 346; Niagara Falls (Ont.), 135-36, **139;** Nipawin Provincial Park (Sask.), 47; Pacific Rim National Park (B.C.), 310, **314;** Peace-Athabasca Delta (Alta.), 193; Point Pelee National Park (Ont.), 141; Port au Port (Nfld.), 30; Qu'Appelle Valley (Sask.), 212; Queen Charlotte Islands (B.C.), 326, 331; Quetico Provincial Park (Ont.), 170; Red Deer Badlands (Alta.), **223,** 236, **239;** Riding Mountain National Park (Man.), 204-05; Rocky Mountains, 277; Saguenay River (Que.), 83, 84; Saint John River (N.B.), 62; Saskatchewan, 222; Scarborough Bluffs (Ont.), **137;** The Chasm (B.C.), 302; The Shoals Provincial Park (Ont.), 162; Thousand Islands (Ont.), 114, 119; Tseax River Lava Bed (B.C.), 322; Tyndall Stone Quarries (Man.), 180; Upper Churchill (Sask.), 185; Waterton Lakes (Alta.), 247; Whiteshell Provincial Park (Man.), 180; Wood Mountains Uplands (Sask.), 230

Hartland, N.B., 64, 65m, 66
Haughton Dome (N.W.T.), 365m
Havre-Aubert, Que., 36m
Havre aux Basques (Que.), 36m
Havre de la Grande Entrée (Que.), 36m
Hawk Cliff (Ont.), 145m
Hawkes Bay (Nfld.), 31
Hawks, 42, 137, 145, 207, 208, 248, 342, 356; broad-winged, 212; Cooper's, 212, 220; ferruginous, 220; marsh, 49, 160, 220; pigeon, 220; redtailed, **163**; sharp-shinned, 144, 160, 212; sparrow, 92, **163**, 212, 220, 254; Swainson's, 212, 220, 228
Hay Island (Ont.), 152
Hay River, Alta., 195m
Hay River (N.W.T.), 357m, 358
Hazelton, B.C., 292
Hazelton Mountains (B.C.), 291m
Headless Range (N.W.T.), 345, 348
Hearst, Ont., 161
Hébertville-Station, Que., 85m
Hebron, N.S., 57m, 58
Hecate Strait (B.C.), 322m, 326, 329, 330m, 331
Heckman Pass (B.C.), 288
Hell Gate (B.C.), 350
Hellroaring Creek (Alta.), 245
Hells Gate (B.C.), **298-99**
Hell's Gate (Y.T.), 348, 350
Helmcken Falls (B.C.), 276
Hepworth, Ont., 152
Hepworth Creek (Ont.), 152
Herons, 138, 247; black-crowned night, 85, 86, 145, 221; blue, **143**; great blue, 36, 48, 85, 86, 92, 108, 114, 118, 142, 153, 154, 160, 162, 188, 196, 207, 208, 212, 214, 301, 325; green, **143**; little blue, 146; yellow-crowned, 145
Hertford Island (N.S.), 43
High Falls (Ont.), 118
High Level, Alta., 195m
High River (Alta.), 238m
Highway Glacier (N.W.T.), 372
Highways, roads, scenic routes, trails, train excursions: Alaska Highway (B.C.), 283m-84, 338, 340, 341m; Algoma Central Railway (Ont.), 161m; Banff-Windermere Parkway, 267, 268; Beaupré Coast, 93m; Brockville-Morrisburg Scenic Drive (Ont.), 117m; Cabot Trail (N.S.), 38-39, **40-41**, 42, 43m, 44; Cariboo Road (B.C.), 299; Deadman-Vidette Road (B.C.), 301; Dewdney Trail (B.C.), 256, 302; Dinosaur Trail (Alta.), 236, 238m; Etienne Trail (Ont.), 130; Forestry Trunk Road (Alta.), 249m, 250, 266m, **267**, 275m; Fundy Trail (N.B.), 65m; Gaspé Trail (Que.), 77m, 78; Gatineau Parkway (Que.), 105; Haines Highway, 338, 340; Haines Road (Y.T.), 341m; Hanson Lake Road (Sask.), 186, 187m, 188; Hay River Highway (N.W.T.), 358; Icefields Parkway (Alta.), 265, 266, 272, 275; Island Highway (B.C.), 307, 341m, 316; Kootenay Skyway (B.C.), 257m, 258; Laurentian Autoroute (Que.), 101m; Lupine Trail (N.S.), 57m, 58; Lytton Road (B.C.), 299; Mackenzie Highway (Alta.), 195m; Mackenzie Highway, (N.W.T.), 346, 350m, 357m, 358; Malahat Drive (B.C.), 316; Marine Drive (Nfld.), 21m, 22; Nashwaak-Miramichi Trail (N.B.), 65m, 66;

Niagara Parkway (Ont.), 137m, 138; Otosquen Road (Sask.), 187m, 188; Ottawa-Wakefield Train (Que.), 109m, 110; Ottawa River Parkway (Ont.), 110; Riding Mountain Parkway (Man.), 203; River Route (N.B.), 65m, 66; Road Around the Bay (Nfld.), 22; St. Clair Parkway (Ont.), 145m, 146; Scenic Route (Nfld.), 30; Scenic Route (Que.), 93m, 94; Scenic Route (B.C.), 291m, 292, 300m, 302, 314m, 316; Stewart-Cassiar Road (B.C.), 279, 283m, 284; Thousand Islands Parkway (Ont.), 117m, 118; Trail of '98 Excursion (Y.T.), 341m; White Pass and Yukon Route, 341, 342; Yellowhead Highway (Alta.-B.C.-Man.-Sask.), 272, 275m, 276, 291m, 292, 322m
Highwood Pass (Alta.), 266-67
Hiking. See Trails, hiking
Hills Bar, B.C. 297
Hinton, Alta., 272, 275m
Hog's Back Park (Ont.), 110
Holden Lake (Ont.-Que.), 129m, 130
Hole-in-the-Rock (Ont.), 138
Hole in the Wall Lake (N.W.T.), 346
Honeybees, **215**
Honora, Ont., 153m, 154
Hoodoos, **218**, 220, **223**, 233, **236**, 250, **258**, 262, 268, 301
Hoodoo Valley (B.C.), 268
Hood River (N.W.T.), 364
Hootalinqua, Y.T., 342
Hope, B.C., 296, 297, 300m, 302
Hope Slide (B.C.), 302
Hopewell Cape (N.B.), 66
Horne Lake (B.C.), 155
Horne Lake Main Cave (B.C.), 315
Horses, wild, 58, 275
Horsethief Canyon (Alta.), 236
Horsethief Creek (B.C.), 258
Hot springs, 261, 264, 268, 284, 302, **342**, **348**, 351
Houston, B.C., 291m
Howe Sound (B.C.), 302
Howser Spire (B.C.), 266
Hoy Lake (B.C.), 284
Hudson Bay, 152, 159, 183, 184, 188, 196, 205, 227, 265, 275, 361, 362, 364, 365m
Hudson Bay, Sask., 187m, 188
Hudson Bay Mountain (B.C.), 291, 292
Hudsonian curlews. See Whimbrels
Hudson's Hope, B.C., 284
Hudson Strait (N.W.T.), 373m
Hughes Range (B.C.), 258
Hull, Que., 105, 109m, 110
Humber River (Nfld.), 29, 30
Humber Valley (Nfld.), 29m
Humboldt, Sask., 214m
Hummingbirds, 144, 154, 274, 340; rufous, **259**; ruby-throated, 212, **215**
Hunlen Falls (B.C.), **288-89**, 290
Hunter Island (B.C.), 321
Hunter River (P.E.I.), 50m
Huntsville, Ont., 153m
Hut Pool (N.S.), 44

Ibis: glossy, 142; scarlet, 142
Icebergs, 20, 22, 258, 372
Icefield Ranges (Y.T.), 338
Idaho Peak (B.C.), 258
Igloolik, N.W.T., 373m
Ile-à-la-Crosse, Sask., 184, 185, 186, 187m
Ile aux Basques (Que.), 85m
Ile aux Coudres (Que.), 85m
Ile aux Goélands (Que.), 36
Ile aux Grues (Que.), 94
Ile aux Loups Marins (Que.), 36

Ile aux Oies (Que.), 94
Ile Brion (Que.), 36
Ile de la Grande Entrée (Que.), 34, 36m
Ile de l'Est (Que.), 34, 36m
Ile d'Entrée (Que.), 34, 36m
Ile d'Orléans (Que.), 93m, 94
Ile du Cap aux Meules (Que.), 34, 36m
Ile du Havre Aubert (Que.), 34, 36m
Ile du Havre aux Maisons (Que.), **32-33**, 34, 36m
Ile du Jardin (Que.), 86
Iles aux Pèlerins (Que.), 85m
Iles de Kamouraska (Que.), 85m
Illecillewaet Glacier (B.C.), 267
Illecillewaet River (B.C.), 266m, 268
Imperial Eagle Channel (B.C.), 312
Inconnu, 358
Indian Harbour (N.S.), 57m
Indian Head Mountain (B.C.), 283
Indian Lake (Ont.), 172
Indian River (Ont.), 118
Infernal Point (Ont.), 175
Ingonish, N.S., 40
Ingonish Beach, N.S., 39, 43m
Ingonish Centre, N.S., 43
Ingonish Island (N.S.), 44
Inside Passage, The (B.C.), **318-21**, 322m
Interior Plateau (B.C.), 292
International Peace Garden (Man.-N.D.), 208
Inuvik, N.W.T., 357m
Iskut, B.C., 282
Isle Madame (N.S.), 43m, 44
Islet Rock (Ont.), 138
Ivy Lea, Ont., 112, 116, 117, 118

Jackass Mountain (B.C.), **296-97**, 299
Jackrabbits, 220, **375**; white-tailed, **231**
Jacques-Cartier River (Que.), 93m, **94**
Jaegers, 357
Jarvis Creek (Alta.), 276
Jasper (Alta.), 265, 272, 273, 275m
Jasper Lake (Alta.), **272**
Jays, 54; Canada, **274**, 350; Steller's, 313, 321, 326
Jean Creek (Ont.), 171
Jean-Larose Falls (Que.), 94
Jedway, B.C., 330m
Jellyfish, 28; Sun, 330
Jemseg, N.B., 62
Jervis Inlet (B.C.), 300m
Joe Lake (Ont.), 162
Joggins (N.S.), 57m, 58
Jones Sound (N.W.T.), 373m, 374
Juan de Fuca Strait (B.C.), 314m
Juan Perez Sound (B.C.), 330m
Jumping Brook, N.S., 41
Juncos, 144; dark-eyed, 54; slate-colored, 49
Juskatla, B.C., 326, 330m

Kahshahpiwi Lake (Ont.), 169-70
Kakiddi Lake (B.C.), 282
Kaministikwia River (Ont.), 172
Kamloops, B.C., 276, 300m, 302
Kananaskis Range (Alta.), 267
Kananaskis River (Alta.), 266m, 267
Kaskawulsh Glacier (Y.T.), 338, **340**
Kathleen Lake (Y.T.), 338
Kathlyn Glacier (B.C.), 291
Kawartha Lakes (Ont.), 117m, 153
Kazan Falls (N.W.T.), 363
Kazan River (N.W.T.), 363
Keg Lake (Sask.), 184-85

Kejimkujik Lake (N.S.), 53, 56
Kelowna, B.C., 300m
Kelsey Bay (B.C.), 307, 316, 319, **320-21**, 322m
Keno Mountain (Y.T.), 341m
Kenora, Ont., 172, 178, 179m
Kerouard Islands (B.C.), 326, 329
Kestrel, American, **163**
Keswick River (N.B.), 64
Kettle Point (Ont.), **145m**
Kicking Horse River (B.C.), 268
Killdeer Badlands (Sask.), 229m, **230**
Kimberley, B.C., 257m
Kingfishers, 114, 290, 342; belted, 207, 350
King Island (B.C.), 322m
King's Throne (Y.T.), 338
Kingston, Ont., 114, 117m, 118
Kingston Creek (N.B.), **62-63**
Kitchener, Ont., 137m
Kitimat, B.C., 322m
Kittiwakes, 21, 22, 36, 76, 77; black-legged, **23**, 365, 373
Kiusta, B.C., 326
Kivitoo, N.W.T., 371
Klastline River (B.C.), 282
Kleanza Creek (B.C.), 322
Klemtu, B.C., 321
Klondike (Y.T.), 319, 356
Kluane Lake (Y.T.), **334-35**, 338, 341m
Kluane Ranges (Y.T.), 338
Klutlan Glacier (Y.T.), 341m
Kokanee Glacier (B.C.), 258
Kokanee Lake (B.C.), 258
Kootenay Arch (B.C.), 257
Kootenay Lake (B.C.), 254, 257m, 258
Kootenay Ranges (B.C.), 258
Kootenay Summit (B.C.), 254
Kostal Lake (B.C.), 276
Kwadacha River (B.C.), 284
Kwatna Inlet (B.C.), 321

Labrador Current, 20, 29
Labyrinth Bay (Ont.), 175
Lac Antikagamac (Que.), 92
Lac au Renard (Que.), 74
Lac aux Brochets (Que.), 92
Lac Caché (Que.), **98-99**
Lac Cardinal (Alta.), 195
Lac des Femmes (Que.), 98
Lac des Mille Lacs (Ont.), 172
Lac des Sables (Que.), 102
Lachute, Que., 101m
Lac Ile-à-la-Crosse (Sask.), 185, 187m
Lac Kénogami (Que.), 85m
Lac La Biche (Alta.), 195m, 196
Lac la Croix (Ont.), 171
Lac Lapêche (Que.), 109m
Lac La Roche (Sask.), 183-84, 187m, 195m
Lac La Ronge (Sask.), 184, 185, 187m, 188
La Cloche Mountains (Ont.), 154
Lac Matawin (Que.), 98
Lac Mékinac (Que.), 92
Lac Monroe (Que.), 97, 98
La Corniche (Que.), 98
Lac Sainte-Marie (Que.), 109m
Lac Saint-Jean (Que.), 81, 83, 85m, 86
Lac Saint-Louis (Que.), 98, 101m
Lac Saint-Pierre (Que.), 101m
Lac Tremblant (Que.), 101m
Lac Vert (Que.), 85
Lac Wapizagonke (Que.), 92
Lady Evelyn Falls (N.W.T.), 358
Lafferty Canyon (N.W.T.), 350m
Lake Agassiz (Man.), 205
Lake Agnes (Alta.), 263
Lake Ainslie (N.S.), 43m
Lake Athabasca (Alta.-Sask.), 191, 192, 193, 194, 195m, 365m

Lake Audy (Man.), **203**, 205
Lake Chaplin (Sask.), 229m
Lake Claire (Alta.), 192, 195m
Lake Columbia (B.C.), 257
Lake Dauphin (Man.), 204
Lake Diefenbaker (Sask.), 212, 214m, 229m
Lake Erie, 123, 135, 137m, 138, 139, 141, 142, 144, 145m, 147, 155, 178
Lake Hertel (Que.), 102
Lake Huron, 123, 145m, 149, 150, 152, 153m, 154, 155
Lake Iroquois (Ont.), 119, 139
Lake Laberge (Y.T.), 341m, 342
Lake Lavieille (Ont.), 129
Lake Louise, Alta., 263, 265, 266m, **269**
Lake McArthur (Alta.), **276**
Lake Manitoba, 204, 207m
Lake Massawippi (Que.), 101m
Lake Mazinaw (Ont.), 129
Lake Memphremagog (Que.), 101m
Lake Newell (Alta.), 249m
Lake Nipigon (Ont.), 161m, 172m
Lake Nipissing (Ont.), 129m, 130, 153m, 155
Lake of Shining Waters (P.E.I.), 49
Lake of the Dead (Sask.), 186
Lake of the Hanging Glacier (B.C.), 258
Lake of the Rivers (Sask.), 221m
Lake of the Woods (Ont.), 172, **174-78**, 221
Lake O'Hara (B.C.), 265
Lake Ontario, 114, 117m, 119, 123, 135, 137, 139, 149
Lake Rossignol (N.S.), 57m
Lake St. Clair (Ont.), 145m
Lake Simcoe (Ont.), 153m
Lake Superior, 123, 157, 159, 160, 161m, 172m, 176-78
Lake Uist (N.S.), 44
Lake Winnipeg (Man.), 171, 176, 178, **179m**, 180, 184, 187m, 188, 207m, 265
Lake Winnipegosis (Man.), 187m, 207m
La Malbaie, Que., 85m
Lambeosaurus, **239**
Lancaster Sound (N.W.T.), 373m
Langara Island (B.C.), 325, 326, 329, 330m
Langenburg, Sask., 212
Laredo Channel (B.C.), 321
Lark, horned, 49, 92, 362
La Roche Noire (Que.), 98
Last Mountain Lake (Sask.), 213, 214
La Tuque, Que., 90, 94
Laurentian Mountains, **68-69**, 71, 85, 93, 94, **98-99**
Laurentide Ice Sheet, 119
Lava, 26, 101, 276, 279, 280, 281, 282, 285, 288, 301, 310, 329; pillow, 176
Lava Lake (B.C.), 322m
Lavallée Lake (Sask.), 188
Lawnhill, B.C., 330m
Leach Lake (B.C.), 254, 256
Leader, Sask., 229m
Leamington, Ont., 145m
Leaves, **103**
Le Bassin (Que.), 36m
Lebret, Sask., 211, 214m
Lemming, 335, 357, 362, 363, 364, 366, 372; northern bog, 205; southern bog, 146
Lena Island (B.C.), 326
Lennox Passage (N.S.), 44
Lenoir River (Que.), 98
Le Petit Mort Rocks (Ont.), 157
Les Caps (Que.), 85m
Les Escoumins (Que.), 87
Leslie M. Frost Natural Resources Center, 129m, 130
Les Pèlerins (Que.), 86
Les Sept Chutes (Que.), 94
Lesser Slave Lake (Alta.), 195m

Les Six Chutes (Que.), 101
Les Taureaux (Que.), **94**
Lethbridge, Alta., 249m
Lewis Mountains, 247
Liard Plain (B.C.), 284
Liard Range (N.W.T.), 346, 350m
Liard River (B.C.-N.W.T.), 284, 346, 348, 350m, 354, 356, 357m,
Lichens, 30, 50, 58, 74, 106, 167, 170, 172, 186, **235**, 248, **251**, 259, 264, 281, 282, 288, 329, 356, **367**
Lièvre River (Que.), 109m
Life Zones, Waterton, **251**
Lilies, 180, 217; avalanche, 247; bluebead, 160; pond, **126-27**; prairie, 212; wood, 159; yellow-blossomed glacier, 288
Lillooet, B.C., 295, 296, 299, 300m, 301
Lillooet River (B.C.), 300m
Lily Pond (Man.), **180**
Limestone, 29, 30, 43, 73, 74, 110, 118, 119, 129, 136, **138**, 139, 145, 149, 150, 152, 153, 155, 162, 180, 187, 188, 238, 250, 257, 258, 264, 267, 272, 310, 342, 346, 348, 350, 356, 358, 365; Devonian, 141, 355
Lindeman Lake (B.C.), 341
Lineham Creek (Alta.), 245
Lions, The (B.C.), 300m, 302
Lions, 222; mountain, 228
Lions Den (Nfld.), 20
Lion's Head (Nfld.), 21
Lions Head, Ont., 150
Little Bow River (Alta.), 249m
Little Codroy River (Nfld.), 29
Little Divide, The (Alta.), 195m, 196
Little Doctor Lake (N.W.T.), 350m
Little Kashabowie Lake (Ont.), **168-69**, 171
Little Manitou Lake (Sask.), 214m
Little Missinaibi River (Ont.), 162
Little Quill Lake (Sask.), 214
Little Vermilion Lake (Ont.), 172
Little Wawa Lake (Ont.), 162
Liverpool, N.S., 53, 57m
Livingstone Creek (Alta.), 250
Livingstone Falls (Alta.), 250
Livingstone Mountain Range (Alta.), 250
Lizards, 59; short-horned, **231**
Llewellyn Glacier (B.C.), **284**
Lloyd George Icefield (B.C.), 284
Lloydminster, Sask., 187m
Loch Lomond, (N.S.), 43m, 44
Lockhart River (N.W.T.), 357-58
London, Ont., 145m
Lonesome Lake (B.C.), 290
Long Beach (B.C.), 307, **308-09, 310-11**, 313, 317
Long Island, N.Y., 119
Long Lake (B.C.), 341
Long Pond (P.E.I.), 49
Long Pool (N.S.), 44
Long Range Mountains (Nfld.), 25-27, 29m, 30, 31
Long Reach (N.B.), **60-61**, 62-64, 65m
Longspurs, Lapland, 144, 357
Loons, 17, 53, 54, 78, 92, 144, 145, 160, 167, 173, 196, 205, 247, 325, 341, 342, 356; common, **259**; red-throated, 313
Lost Horse Creek (Alta.), 245
Lost Lagoon (B.C.), 302
Loudoun Channel (B.C.), 312
Louise Falls (N.W.T.), 358
Low, Que., 109m
Lower Elk Lake (B.C.), 266
Lower Falls (Ont.), 109
Lower Jade Lake (B.C.), 268
Lower Prairie Lake (Ont.), 162
Lundbreck Falls (Alta.), 249m, 250
Lunenburg Harbour (N.S.), 57

Lupines, 57, 58, 365; blue, **251**, 268; blue-purple, 288
Lynx, 42, 76, 95, 100, 159, 161, 180, 228, 288, 342, 354; Canada, 18, 90, 205
Lytton, B.C., 296, 299, 300m

Macaza River (Que.), 98
McConnell River (N.W.T.), 362
McCreary, Man., 203
McGregor Lake (Alta.), 249m
McIntyre Bay (B.C.), 329, 330m
Mackenzie Delta (N.W.T.), 356, 357m, 359, 361
Mackenzie Mountains (N.W.T.-Y.T.), 341m, 345, 348, 350m, 354, 357m, 358
Mackenzie River (N.W.T.), 114, 184, 192, 265, 271, 284, 335, 350m, **352-56**, 357m
McLeod River (Alta.), 275m
McLeod River (B.C.), 291
Mactaquac Dam (N.B.), 64, 66
Mactaquac Lake (N.B.), 64
Mad River (Ont.), 154
Magdalen Islands (Que.), **14-15**, **32-36**, 50
Magnetic Hill (N.B.), 65m, 66
Magnuson Island (Ont.), 178
Magog, Que., 101
Magpies, 340
Mahone Bay (N.S.), 57m, 58
Main River (Nfld.), 30
Maktak Fjord (N.W.T.), 372
Malaspina Strait (B.C.), 314m
Maligne Lake (Alta.), 272, 273, 275m
Maligne River (Ont.), 171
Mallorytown Landing, Ont., 116, 117m
Malpeque Bay (P.E.I.), 50m
Mandarte Island (B.C.), 314m, 315
Manitoba Escarpment, 204
Manitoulin Island (Ont.), 123, 149, 152, 153m, 154
Maniwaki, Que., 109m
Manning, Alta., 195m
Manuels River (Nfld.), 21m, 22
Manyberries, Alta., 239
Maple Creek (Sask.), 228, 230
Marathon, Ont., 157, 161m
Marble Canyon (B.C.), 267
Margaree Forks, N.S., 43m, 44
Marian River (N.W.T.), 357
Marine Lake (Sask.), 214
Marmots, 85, 248, 265, 288; hoary, **251**, 274
Marten, 128, 163, 178, 248, 321, 326, 350, 354; pine, 42
Martin Head (N.B.), 65m, 66
Maskinongé River (Que.), 102
Massacre Island (Ont.), 178
Masset, B.C., 326, 329, 330m
Masset Inlet (B.C.), 326, 330m
Matane, Que., 77m
Matapédia Lake (Que.), 77m, 78
Matapédia River (Que.), 77m, 78
Matawin River (Que.), 90, 92, 93m, 98
Mattawa, Ont., 129m
Mattawa River (Ont.), 130
Mayflower Lake (Ont.), 129
Mayo, Y.T., 341m
Meach Lake (Que.), 108
Medicine Hat, Alta., 229m
Medicine Lake (Alta.), 273
Meductic, N.B., 61, 64, 65m
Meelpaeg Lake (Nfld.), 29m
Meilleur River (N.W.T.), 350m
Melanistic Peak (B.C.), 284
Melville Island (N.W.T.), 365m
Melville Peninsula (N.W.T.), 366, 373m
Mer Bleue Peatland (Ont.), 109m, 110
Mersey River (N.S.), 56
Mesas, **223**

Mess Creek (B.C.), 282, 285
Métabetchouane River (Que.), 82, 85m
Mice, 95, 163, 288, 356; deer, 326; field, 49; meadow jumping, 92, **173**; northern grasshopper, 205; white-footed, 92, 107; woodland jumping, 50, 92
Michichi Creek (Alta.), 235
Michipicoten Harbour and Island, Ont., 157, 161m
Middle Head (N.S.), 43m, 44
Middle Island (Ont.), 146
Middle River (N.S.), 43m, **44**
Midge, phantom, **181**
Midland, Ont., 154
Midway Range (B.C.), 258
Miles Canyon (Y.T.), 342
Milford Dollar Falls (Y.T.), 340, 341m, 342
Milk River (Alta.), 249m, 250
Milligan Creek (Sask.), 214
Million Dollar Falls (Y.T.), 340, 341m, 342
Milfoil, **181**
Minaker River (B.C.), 283
Minas Basin (N.S.), 57m, 58
Minesing Swamp (Ont.), 153m, 154
Minks, 18, 42, 49, 100, 107, 118, 128, 142, 161, *171*, 178, 186, 193, 222, 247, 290, 313
Minnedosa Valley (Man.), 207m, **208**
Minton, Sask., 220, 221m
Mira Bay (N.S.), 43m
Mira Hills (N.S.), 44
Miramichi River (N.B.), 66
Mira River (N.S.), 43m, 44
Missinaibi Lake (Ont.), 162
Mississauga, Ont., 137m
Mississippi River (Ont.), 109m
Mistaken Point (Nfld.), 22
Mistassibi River (Que.), 85m
Mistassini River (Que.), 83, 85m
Mockingbird, 92
Moles, star-nosed, 118, 154
Monarch Mountain (B.C.), 287
Monashee Mountains (B.C.), 257m, 302
Moncton, N.B., 65m
Montague, P.E.I., 50m
Mont Albert (Que.), 78
Mont Condor (Que.), 101
Mont Jacques-Cartier (Que.), 77
Mont-Laurier, Que., 101m, 109m
Montmagny, Que., 93m, 94
Montmorency Falls (Que.), 94m
Montmorency River (Que.), 94
Mont Orford (Que.), 101
Montreal, Que., 97, 98, 101m, 102, 107, 114
Montreal Lake (Sask.), 187m
Montreal River (Ont.), 161
Mont Sainte-Agathe (Que.), 102
Mont Sainte-Anne (Que.), 78, 94

Mont Saint-Hilaire (Que.), 101m-02
Mont Saint-Joseph (Que.), 77
Mooneshine Fjord (N.W.T.), 371
Moon jellies, 28
Moonstones, 129
Moose, 18, 27, 42, 45, 58, 65, 75, 76, 77, 78, 85, 86, 90, 95, **100**, 101, 109, 128, 129, 131, 154, 159, 161, 162, 170, 172, **173**, 186, 193, 205, 214, 222, 228, 248, 250, **251**, 256, 265, 273, 282, 284, 288, 340, 341, 342, 350, 354, 358, 362, 366
Moose Jaw, Sask., 213, 214m, 221m, 222
Moose Mountain Creek (Sask.), 221m
Moraine Lake (Alta.), 263
Moraines, 26, 263, 266, 269, 284, 340, 343, 371, 372
Moran Canyon (B.C.), 301
Morden, Man., 207m
Moresby Island (B.C.), 325, 326, 329, 330m, **331**
Moricetown Falls (B.C.), 291m
Moths: barred sallow, 228; ribbed underwing, 228; mountain beauty, 228
Mountain Lake (Ont.), 152
Mountain Lake (Sask.), 186
Mount Albert Dease (B.C.), 284
Mount Arrowsmith (B.C.), 315, 316
Mount Asgard (N.W.T.), 372
Mount Assiniboine (Alta.-B.C.), 263, 268, 269
Mount Athabasca (Alta.), 272
Mount Battle (N.W.T.), 372
Mount Blakiston (B.C.), 247
Mount Buxton (B.C.), 321
Mount Carleton (N.B.), 66
Mount Crandell (Alta.), 247
Mount Edith Cavell (Alta.), 271, 274
Mount Edziza (B.C.), 279, **280-81**
Mount Eisenhower (Alta.), 265
Mount Fryatt (Alta.), **274**
Mount Garibaldi (B.C.), **301**, 302
Mount Hoy (B.C.), 284
Mount Kitchener (Alta.), 272
Mount Lloyd George (B.C.), 284
Mount Logan (Y.T.), 335, **336-37**, 338, 340, 341m
Mount Loki (N.W.T.), 372
Mount McNamara (B.C.), 284
Mount Newton (B.C.), 316
Mount Norquay (Alta.), 263, 265
Mount Odin (N.W.T.), **370-71**, 372
Mount Palmerston (B.C.), 321
Mount Raleigh (N.W.T.), 371
Mount Robson (B.C.), 275m, 276
Mount Rundle (Alta.), 264
Mount Seemore (Nfld.), 29

Mount Seymour (B.C.), 302
Mount Sir James MacBrien (N.W.T.), 358
Mount Sykes (Nfld.), 29
Mount Temple (Alta.), **262-63**
Mount Vedder (B.C.), 300
Mowdale Lake (B.C.), 282
Mowry Sea, 236
Mud hens, 250
Mummichog, 29
Muncho Lake (B.C.), **283**
Munson, Alta., 236
Murder Valley (N.W.T.), 345
Murrelets, ancient, *329-30*
Murres, 21, 22, 36, 77; common, **23**, 322; thick-billed, **23**, 365, 373, *374*
Murtle River (B.C.), 276
Museums: Algonquin Provincial Park (Ont.), 128; Banff Natural History (Alta.), 263; Cowichan Valley Forest (B.C.), 314m; Dinosaur Park (Alta.), 238; Drumheller (Alta.), Dinosaur, 235; Eastend (Sask.), High School, 229; Grand Manan, 66; Medicine Hat (Alta.), 229; Miracle Beach Provincial Park (B.C.), 315; Morden (Man.), 207; National Museum of Natural Sciences (Ottawa, Ont.), 109m, 110, 235; National Museum of Science and Technology (Ottawa, Ont.), 110; of the Highwood (High River, Alta.), 238m; Parrsboro (N.S.), 58; Quebec Fauna (Hébertville-Station, Que.), 85; Presqu'ile Provincial Park (Ont.), 118; Rondeau Provincial Park (Ont.), 146; Round Hill Bird Refuge (Alta.), 238; Saskatchewan Natural History (Regina), 221m, 222; Sir Andrew Macphail Provincial Park (P.E.I.), 50; Swift Currrent (Sask.) Natural History, 230
Muskeg, 42, 188, 238, 331, 354
Muskeg Bay (Ont.), 179m
Muskoka Lakes (Ont.), 153m, **154**
Musk-oxen, 335, **362-63**, 366
Muskrats, 42, *49*, 54, 64, 92, 108, 118, 128, 142, 154, **181**, 193, 222, 247, 254, 259, 326, 356
Mussels, 21, 79; blue California, 310

Nahanni Butte, N.W.T., 348, 350m
Nahanni Range (N.W.T.), 348, 350m
Nahanni River (N.W.T.), 346, 351
Nakusp, B.C. 257m, 266
Nanaimo, B.C., 314m
Narwhals, 335, *364*, 365, 373, 374

National Parks

Alberta Banff, 226, **260-65**, 266m, 268, 272, 275m, 276, 277; Elk Island, 238m; Jasper, 265, 266m, 268, **270-74**, 275m, 276, 277; Waterton Lakes, 245, 246, **244-48**, 249m, 251; Wood Buffalo, 191, 195m, 196, 337
British Columbia Glacier, 266m, 267, 268; Kootenay, 257m, 266m, 267-68, 276; Mount Revelstoke, 266m, 268; Pacific Rim, 307, **308-13**, 314m, 318; Yoho, **242-43**, 265, 266m, 268, 269, 276
Manitoba Riding Mountain, **202-06**, 207m
New Brunswick Fundy, 65m, 66; Kouchibouguac, 65m, 66
Newfoundland Gros Morne, 15, **24-28**, 29m, 31; Terra Nova, 15, **16-20**, 21m
Nova Scotia Cape Breton Highlands, 15, 33, **38-42**, 43m, 89; Kejimkujik, 15, **52-56**, 57m
Ontario Georgian Bay Islands, 152, 153m-54; Point Pelee, 123, **140-44**, 145m, 147; Pukaskwa, 123, **156-60**, 161m, 163; St. Lawrence Islands, 116
Prince Edward Island Prince Edward Island, 47, 48, 50m
Quebec Forillon, 71, **72-76**, 77m, 79; La Mauricie, 71, **88-92**, 93m
Saskatchewan Prince Albert, 187m, **188**
Northwest Territories and Yukon Territory Auyuittuq, 335, **368-72**, 373m, 375; Kluane, 335, **336-40**, 341m; Nahanni, 335, **344-49**, 350m, 351; Wood Buffalo, 191, 195m, 196, 337

Nashwaak River (N.B.), 66
Nass Ranges (B.C.), 322
Nass River (B.C.), 322m
National parks. See box p. 380
Nature trails. See Trails
Nechako River (B.C.), 291m, 292
Nelson, B.C., 257m
Nelson Head (N.W.T.), 365m, **366**
Nelson River (Man.), **187m,** 188
Nestor Falls, Ont., 178, 179m
Nettibing Lake (N.W.T.), 373m
Névé, 343
Newman Sound (Nfld.), **16-17, 18-19,** 19-20, 21m
New Quebec Crater (N.W.T.), 373m, 374
New Westminster, B.C., 282
Niagara Escarpment, **136, 137,** 138, 139, 149, 153, 154, 155
Niagara Falls (Ont.), 123, **132-36,** 137m, 138
Niagara Glen Park (Ont.), 138
Niagara-on-the-Lake, Ont., 137m, 138
Niagara River (Ont.), 123, 133, 134, 135, 136, 137m, 138, 139
Nickel, 154
Nighthawks, 145
Ninstints, B.C., 329
Nipekamew River Sand Pillars (Sask.), 187m, 188
Nipew Lake (Sask.), 186
Nipigon, Ont., 161m
Nipigon Palisades (Ont.), 161
Nistowiak Falls (Sask.), 188
Noire River (Que.), 94
Nordegg, Alta., 267, 275m
Norman Wells, N.W.T., 355, 357m
North Aspy River (N.S.), 41, 44
North Battleford, Sask., 229m
North Bay, Ont., 129m, 130, 153m
North Bend, B.C., 299, 300m
North Channel (Ont.), 153m, 154
Northern lights. See Aurora borealis
North Mountain (N.S.), 57
North Nahanni Karst (N.W.T.), 357m, 358
North Nahanni River (N.W.T.), 350m, 354
North Saskatchewan River (Sask.), 187, 214m, 229m, 265, 275
North Sydney, N.S., 43m
North Thompson River (B.C.), 275m, 302
Northumberland Strait (N.B.-P.E.I.), 50m, 65m, 66
Northwest Angle Inlet (Ont.), 178
Notikewin River (Alta.), 195
Notre-Dame-de-la-Salette (Que.), 109-10
Nottawasaga River (Ont.), 153-154
Nuthatches, 274; red-breasted, 228
Nuttlude Lake (B.C.), 282

Oak Point (N.B.), 60
Ocean Falls, B.C., 322m
Octopuses, 302
Ogilvie Mountains (Y.T.), 341m, 342
Ojibway Prairie (Ont.), 145m
Okanagan Lake (B.C.), 300m
Okoa Bay (N.W.T.), 372
Okotoks, Alta., 238m
Old Harry Head (Que.), 36m
Oldman River (Alta.), 249m, 250
Old Perlican (Nfld.), 22
Old Wives Lake (Sask.), 218, 221m
Olympic Mountains (Wash.), 316
Omineca Mountains (B.C.), 243, 283m, 291m

Oolichans (candlefish), *322*
Ootsa Lake (B.C.), 291m
Opeongo Lake (Ont.), 129m
Opossums, 146, 302
Orchids, 64, 152, 154, 227, 228; Arethusa, **111;** blunt-leaf, 365; bog, 18; broad-lipped twayblade, 18; early coral-root, 365; fairy slippers, **111,** 162; grass pink, 90, 108, **111;** green adder's mouth, **111;** hooded ladies tresses, 18; ladies tresses, **111;** lady's slipper, 54; Loesel's twayblade, **111;** pink lady's-slipper, **111,** 162; purple-fringed, **111;** ragged fringed, **111;** round-leaved, **111;** showy lady's-slipper, 27, 108, **111;** spotted coralroot, 18, 54, **111;** yellow lady's-slipper, 27, 162, 215
Orchis, round-leaved, 162, 205
Orient Bay, Ont., 161m, 162
Orioles, 114; Baltimore, 142, 154, 250; orchard, 142
Oshawa, Ont., 137m
Osoyoos, B.C., 300m
Osprey Peak (B.C.), 266
Ospreys, 27, 54, 85, 92, **163,** 172, 186, 188, 205, 254, 259, 290, 310
Ottawa, Ont., 105, 109m, 117m, 118, 119
Ottawa River (Ont.-Que.), 71, 98, 101m, 105, 107, 109m, 110, 118, 127, 129m, 130, 155
Otter Island (Ont.), 157
Otter Lake (Sask.), 184, 185, 186
Otter Rapids (Sask.), 184, 186
Otters, 18, 42, 54, 76, 85, 100, 107, 128, 159, 161, 171, 178, 186, 193, 290, 310, 321; river, 326; sea, 85, 302, 326
Ouareau River (Que.), 101
Ouiatchouane River (Que.), 86
Ouimet Canyon (Ont.), **162**
Ovens, The (N.S.), **57m,** 58

Owen Sound, Ont., 149, 153m
Owl Hoot Hill (Alta.), 195m, 196
Owls, 92, 208, 326, 356; barred, 42; burrowing, 230; great horned, **163,** 207, 250; hawk, **163;** saw-whet, **163,** 326; snowy, 230, 357, 372
Owl Valley (N.W.T.), 372
Oxytrope, alpine, 280
Oysters, 43, 50, 79
Oyster catchers, black, 313, 314, 315, 322, 330

Pachyrhinosaurus, **239**
Paintbrush: Indian, 152, **251,** 265, 268, 288; scarlet, 212
Painted Rock Island (Ont.), 176
Paint Pots (Alta.), 268
Pangnirtung, N.W.T., 371, 372, 373m
Pangnirtung Pass (N.W.T.), **370-71,** 372
Parc Montmorency (Que.), 94
Park Lake (Alta.), 250
Parksville, B.C., 314m, 316
Parrsboro, N.S., 57m, 58
Parry Falls (N.W.T.), 358
Parry Sound, Ont., 153m
Parsnip River (B.C.), 354
Parsons Pond (Nfld.), 31
Partridge, 86; Hungarian, 250
Pasquia Hills (Sask.), 188
Peace-Athabasca Delta, **190-94,** 195m, 196, 197
Peace River (Alta.), **166-67,** 184, 191, 192, **195m,** 196, 239, 354
Peace River, Alta., 184, 195m
Peaked Butte (Sask.), 218, 220
Pearl Island (Nfld.), 30
Peel River (N.W.T.), 357m
Peggy's Cove (N.S.), 57m, 58
Pelee Island (Ont.), 145m, 146
Pelican Narrows (Sask.), 186
Pelican Rapids (Sask.), 195

Pelicans, 180, **185;** white, **181,** 186, 188, 196, 207, 212, 221, 254
Pelly River (Y.T.), 341m, 342
Pelly Bay, N.W.T., 365m
Pembroke, Ont., 129m
Penguin, king, 302
Penny Ice Cap (N.W.T.), 372, 373m
Penouille, Que., 74
Penstemon, **215**
Penticton, B.C., 300m
Percé, Que., 77, 78
Percé Rock (Que.), 77m, **78**
Péribonka River (Que.), 81
Periwinkle, rough, **79**
Permafrost, 187, 356, 359
Peterborough, Ont., 117m, 118
Petitcodiac River (N.B.), 65, 66, **67**
Petit-de-Grat Island (N.S.), 43m, 44
Petite Pond Lake (Sask.), 187m
Petit Sault River (Que.), 94
Petrels. See Storm-petrels
Peyto Glacier (Alta.), 265, 269
Peyto Lake (Alta.), **264-65, 269**
Phalaropes, 49, 357; northern, 362
Pheasants, 142; ring-necked, 138, 250
Philomène's Cave (Que.), 86
Photosynthesis, 103, 181
Phytoplankton, **181**
Pic de l'Aurore (Que.), 77m, 78
Pic River (Ont.), 157, 161m
Pictou County (N.S.), 58
Pigeon, passenger, 230
Pigeon Falls (Ont.), 172m
Pigeon River (Ont.), 172
Pijitawabik Bay (Ont.), 161
Pijitawabik Palisades (Ont.), 161m, 162
Pikas, 248, 288
Pillar Rock (B.C.), 330
Pilot Mound (Man.) 207m
Pincher Creek, Alta., 249m

Pine Lake (Alta.), 196
Pingos, 356, 359
Pink Mountain (B.C.), 283
Pitcher plant, 18, 27, 90, 108, 146
Pitman River (B.C.), 284
Pitt Island (B.C.), 322m
Pitt Lake (B.C.), 302
Pitts Pond (Nfld.), 19
Pitt River (B.C.), 300m, 302
Placentia Bay (Nfld.), 21m
Plain of the Six Glaciers (Alta.), 265
Plains, salt, **196**
Plains, The (Ont.), 118
Plateau Mountain (Alta.), 250
Pleasant Bay (N.S.), 40, 41, 43m
Pleasant Grove, P.E.I., 48
Plovers, 49, 76, 310; black-bellied, 28, 301; semipalmated, 28
Poboktan River (Alta.), 272
Pointe-au-Loup (Que.), 36m
Pointe La Canadienne (Ont.), 157, 159, 160
Point Isacor (Ont.), 157
Point Michaud (N.S.), 43m, 44
Point Pelee (Ont.), **140-41, 142, 144,** 146
Point Separation, N.W.T., 356
Poljes, 358
Polygons, 359
Pond Inlet, N.W.T., 373m
Porcupine Hills (Alta.), 249
Porcupines, **45,** 54, 76, 100, 212, 265, 321, 342
Porpoises, 315, 330; harbor, 325
Portage Brûlé Rapids (B.C.), 350
Portage La Loche (Methy Portage) (Sask.), 184
Portage la Prairie, Man., 207m, 276
Port Alberni, B.C., 155, 307, 314m, 316
Port Alice, B.C., 322m
Port au Port, Nfld., 29m, 30

Provincial Parks

Alberta Beauvais Lake, 249m; Bow Valley, 266m; Chain Lakes, 249m; Cypress Hills, 229m; Dinosaur, 234, 238; Long Lake, 195m; Lesser Slave Lake, 195m; Park Lake, 249m, 250; Police Outpost, 249m, 250; Saskatoon Island, 195m, 196; Taber, 249m, 250; William A. Switzer, 275m, 276; Willow Creek, 249m, 250; Writing-On-Stone, **249m,** 250

British Columbia Atlin, 283m, 284; Bowron Lake, 275m; Bugaboo Glacier, 266; Cape Scott, 322m; Carp Lake, 291m; Cathedral, 300m; Driftwood Canyon, 291m; Elk Lakes, 266m; Englishman River, 316; Garibaldi, 300m, 301; Golden Ears, 300m, 301; Goldstream, 314m; Hamber, 275m; Horne Lake Caves, 314m, 315; Kleanza Creek, 322m; Kokanee Glacier, 257m, 258; Kwadacha, 283m, 284; Liard River Hotsprings, 283m, 284; Little Qualicum Falls, **315,** 316; MacMillan, 314m, 315; Manning, 300m, 302; Miracle Beach, 314m, 315; Mitlenatch Island Nature, 314m; Monashee, 257m, 258; Mount Assiniboine, 266m, 268; Mount Edziza, **278-82,** 283m; Mount Robson, 272, 275m-76; Mount Maxwell, 314; Mount Seymour, 300m, 302; Muncho Lake, 283m, 284; Naikoon, 329; Pinnacles, 291m, 292; Qualicum Falls, **315;** St. Mary's Alpine, 257m, 258; Spahats Creek, 275m, 276; Stagleap, 257m, 258; Stone Mountain, 283m, 284; Strathcona, 314m, 316; Tatlatui, 283m, 284; Top of the World, 257m, 258; Tweedsmuir, **286-90,** 291m, 292, 322m; Vaseux Lake, 300m, 302;

Wasa Lake, 257m, 258; Wells Gray, 275m, 276

Manitoba Asessippi, 207m; Birds Hill, 179m; Clearwater, 187m; Duck Mountain, 207m; Grand Beach, 179m; Grass River, 187m, 188; Hecla, 179m, 180; Spruce Woods, 207m, **208;** Turtle Mountain, 207m, 208; Whiteshell, 179m, 180

New Brunswick Bore View, 65m; Mactaquac, 64, 65m, 66; The Rocks, 65m, 66

Newfoundland Backside Pond, 21m; Barachois Pond, 29m; Bellevue Beach, 21m; Blow Me Down, 29m; Blue Ponds, 29m; Cataracts, 21m; Crabbes River, 29m; Frenchman's Cove, 21m; John T. Cheeseman, 29m; Mummichog, 29m; Otter Bay, 29m, 30; Piccadilly Head, 29m, 30; Sandbanks, 29m, 30; Sop's Arm River, 29m, 30; Windmill Bight, 21m

Nova Scotia Five Islands, 57m, 58

Ontario Algonquin, **124-28,** 129m, 131, 154; Antoine, 129m; Arrowhead, 129m; Black Sand, 161m; Blue Lake, 172m; Bon Echo, **129m;** Bonnechere, 129m; Craigleith, 153m; Cyprus Lake, 150, 152, 155; Darlington, 137m; Driftwood, 129m, 130; Earl Rowe, 153; Fitzroy, 109m; Frontenac, 118; Ipperwash, 123; Iroquois Beach, 137m; John E. Pearce, 145m; Kakabeka Falls, 172m; Killarney, 153m, 154; Killbear Point, 153m, 154; Lake of the Woods, 179m, 180; Lake on the Mountain, 117m; Lake St. Peter, 129m, 130; Lake Superior, 161m; Long Point, 137m; MacLeod, 161m, 162; Mattawa Wild River, 129m, 130; Middle Falls, 172; Missinaibi Lake,

161m, 162; Mississagi, 153m, 154; Neys, **122-23,** 161m, 162; North Beach, 117m; Obatanga, 161m, 162; Ojibway, 172m; Ouimet Canyon, 161m, 162; Outlet Beach, 117m, 118; Petroglyphs, 117m, 118; Pinery, 145m, 146; Presqu'ile, 117m, 118, 123; Queen Victoria Falls, 136; Quetico, **168-71,** 172m, 173; Rainbow Falls, 161m, 162; Rideau River, 118; Rock Point, 137m, **138;** Rondeau, 123, 145m, 146; Sandbanks, 117m, 118; Sandbar Lake, 172m; Serpent Mounds, 117m, 118; Sibley, 161m, 162; Silent Lake, 129m, 130; The Shoals, 161m, 162; Turkey Point, 137m, 138; Wasaga Beach, 153m, 154; Wheatley, 145m

Prince Edward Island Devil's Punch Bowl, 50; Green Park, 50m; Andrew Macphail, 50m; Strathgartney, 50m

Quebec Bic, 85m; Chibougamau, 85m; De la Gaspésie, 77m; Laurentides, 71, 81, 85m, 93m, 94; La Vérendrye, 71, 109m, 110; Mastigouche, 90, 93m, 101m; Matane, 77m, 78; Métis, 78; Mont Orford, 101m; Mont Sainte-Anne, 93m, 94; Mont-Tremblant, 71, **96-100,** 101m; Papineau-Labelle, 101m, 109m, 110; Paul Sauvé, 101m, 102; Port-Daniel, 77m, 78; Portneuf, 93m, 94; Rimouski, 85m, 86; Saint-Maurice, 90, 93m, 94

Saskatchewan Buffalo Pound, 213; Cypress Hills, 228, 229m; Danielson, 229m; Douglas, 229m; Duck Mountain, 214m; Echo Valley, 213; Grass Greenwater Lake, 214m; Katepwa, 213; Lac La Ronge, 184, 187m, 188; Moose Mountain, 221m; Nipawin, 187m, 188; Rowan's Ravine, 214m; Saskatchewan Landing, 229m

Port au Port Bay (Nfld.), 29m
Port Clements, B.C., 326, 330m
Port-Daniel River (Que.), 78
Port Hardy, B.C., 321
Port Hope, Ont., 153
Portland Creek Pond (Nfld.), 31
Portland Inlet (B.C.), 322m
Port Radium, N.W.T., 357
Port Renfrew, B.C., 313, 314m
Powell River, B.C., 314m
Prairie Dog Town (Sask.), 229-30m
Prehistoric Parks (Alta.), 236
Prescott, Ont., 117m
Price Island (B.C.), 321
Primrose: evening, 160; western yellow evening, **215**
Primrose Lake (Sask.), 187m, 195m
Prince Albert, Sask., 187m
Prince Charles Island (N.W.T.), 373m
Prince Edward County (Ont.), 117
Prince George, B.C., 276, 291m, 292
Prince Leopold Island (N.W.T.), 365m
Prince of Wales Falls (Ont.), 110
Prince of Wales Island (Alas.), 329
Prince Rupert, B.C., 276, 307, 319, 322m
Princess Royal Island (B.C.), 322m
Princeton, B.C., 302, 300m
Project Nisk'u (Sask.), 214
Provincial Park. See box p. 381
Ptarmigans, 248, 288, 356, 362, 363; rock, 340, **375**; willow, 357
Puffins, 21, 22, 36, 43, 77; bright-billed tufted, 329; common, **23**; tufted, 314, 322
Puget Sound (Wash.), 319
Pukaskwa River (Ont.), 159
Pulpit Rock (N.W.T.), **346**
Pumas, 179
Pumice, 285
Purcell Mountains (B.C.), 253, 257m, 258, 266m, 267

Quadra Island (B.C.), 316
Quandary Bay (Ont.), 175
Qu'Appelle, Sask., 211
Qu'Appelle River (Sask.), 211, 212, 213, 214m, 221
Qu'Appelle Valley (Sask.), **210-13**, 214m, 215
Quebec, Que., 81, 93m
Queen Charlotte Islands (B.C.), 197, 303, 307, 319, **324-29**, 330m
Queen Charlotte Ranges (B.C.), 326, 330m
Queen Charlotte Strait (B.C.), 322m
Queen Elizabeth Islands (N.W.T.), 374
Queen of Prince Rupert, 319, **321**
Queenscup, **251**
Queenston, Ont., 139, 153
Quesnel, B.C., 291m, 292
Quesnel Highland (B.C.), 302
Quesnel Lake (B.C.), 275m
Quesnel River (B.C.), 291
Quetico Lake (Ont.), 171
Quiddy River (N.B.), 66
Quill Lakes (Sask.), **214m**
Quinsam River (B.C.), 316
Quinte's Isle (Ont.), 123

Rabbitkettle Hotsprings (N.W.T.), **348-49, 351**
Rabbits, 95, 163; cottontail, 118; Nuttall's cottontail, 220; white-tailed, 220. See also Jackrabbits
Raccoons, 49, 54, 92, 100, 107, 142, 222, 313, 321, 326
Radium Hot Springs (B.C.), 268

Rae, N.W.T., 357m
Rae Isthmus (N.W.T.), 365m, **366**
Ragged Range (N.W.T.), 346
Rail: sora, 142, **143, 146;** Virginia, 142, 146
Rainbow Falls (Ont.), 162
Rainbow Range (B.C.), **288**
Rainy River (Ont.), 172m, 176, 179m
Rainy River, Ont., 179m
Ramparts, The (B.C.), 300, **354-55**, 356
Ramparts Rapids (N.W.T.), 355
Ram River Canyon (N.W.T.), 350m
Random Island (Nfld.), 21m
Rapides du Joli Fou (Alta.), 195
Rapid River (Sask.), **188**
Raspberry Pass (B.C.), 281, 282
Raptors, **163**
Rats, kangaroo, 225, **231**
Rattlesnakes, 302; massasauga, 153
Ravens, 163, 205, 313, 325, 329, 356, *362*, 363, **375**
Ravenscrag (Sask.), 217
Rearguard Falls (Alta.), 276
Red Deer, Alta., 223, 238m
Red Deer Badlands (Alta.), **223**, 232-37, 238m
Red Deer River (Alta.), **200,** 223, 233, 236, 238m, 266m
Red Deer Valley (Alta.), 223, 239
Red Indian Lake (Nfld.), 29m
Red jacket, **18**
Red Point (N.B.), 65-66
Red Point, N.B., 65-66
Redpolls, 145, 357
Red River (Man.), 179m
Red Rock Canyon (Alta.), **248**
Red Rock Cuesta (Ont.), 161m, 162
Red Rocks (Nfld.), 29m, 30
Redstone River (N.W.T.), 350m
Regina, Sask., 214m, 221m
Reid Bay (N.W.T.), 373m, 374
Reindeer Lake (Man.-Sask.), 186, 187m
Reindeer River (Sask.), 186
Renfrew, Ont., 129m
Rennell Sound (B.C.), 330m
Reptiles, **59**
Repulse Bay (N.W.T.), 364, 365m
Resolute, N.W.T., 365m
Restigouche River (N.B.), 65
Revelstoke, B.C., 266m, 268
Reversing Falls Rapids (N.B.), 62, **67**
Rhododendron Flats, B.C., 302
Rice Lake (Ont.), 117m
Richardson Mountains (Y.T.), 341m, 342, 357m
Richelieu River (Que.), 101m, **102**
Rideau Falls (Ont.), 118
Rideau Lakes (Ont.), 117m
Rideau River (Ont.), 109m, 110, **118**
Riding Mountain (Man.), 203, 204
Rimouski, Que., 85m
Ripple Passage (B.C.), 321
Rivers Inlet (B.C.), 321
Rivière aux Saumons (Que.), 86
Rivière des Rochers (Alta.), 192
Rivière-du-Loup (Que.), 101
Rivière-du-Loup, Que., 85m
Robb, Alta., 275m
Roberval, Que., 85m, 86
Robins, 54, 114, 142, 144, 274
Roche Percée, Sask., 217
Rochers aux Oiseaux (Que.), 36
Rock Pile (Sask.), **228**
Rockport, Ont., 117, 118
Rock Wall (B.C.), 267
Rocky Mountains, 89, 113, 183, 192, 201, 225, 236, 238, 239,

243, 249, 257, 265, 266m, 267, 269, 272, 275m, 277, 283m, 284, 323, 354, 358
Rogers Pass (B.C.), 266m, 268
Rondeau Bay (Ont.), 146
Root River (N.W.T.), 350m
Roseau River (Man.), 179m
Rose Blanche, Nfld., 29m, 30
Rose Harbour, B.C., 330m
Rose Point (B.C.), 329, 330m
Rouge Lakes (Ont.), 171
Rouge River (Que.), 98, 101m
Roughbark Creek (Sask.), 222
Round Lake (Ont.), 129m, 214m
Round Lake (Sask.), 211
Royal Botanical Gardens (Ont.), 137m, 138
Roy Island (B.C.), 321
Ruby Ridge (Alta.), 245
Ruisseau Froid River (Que.), 98
Rustico Island (P.E.I.), 47, 48

Saanich Peninsula (B.C.), 314m, 316
Sable Island (N.S.), 34, 57m, 58
Sachs Harbour, N.W.T., 365m
Saguenay River (Que.), 71, **80-94**, 85m, 87
St. Ann's Bay (N.S.), 43m, 44
St. Ann's Harbour, N.S., 43m, 44
St. Catharines, Ont., 137m
St. Catherines, P.E.I., 50m
St. Clair River (Ont.), 145m, 146
Saint-Donat, Que., 97, 98, 101m
Sainte-Agathe-des-Monts, Que., 101m, 102
Sainte-Anne du Nord River (Que.), 94
Sainte-Anne Falls (Que.), 94
Sainte-Croix, Que., 93m, 94
St. Elias Mountains (Y.T.), 337, 338, 340, 341m, 343
Sainte-Marguerite Mountain (Que.), 84
Ste. Rose du Lac, Man., 203
Sainte-Ursule Falls (Que.), 101m, 102
Saint-Fabien-sur-Mer, Que., 85
Saint-Faustin, Que., 97, 101m
Sainte-Féréol-les-Neiges, Que., 93m, 94
St. George's Bay (Nfld.), 29m
St. George's Island (Alta.), 238m
Saint-Jérôme, Que., 101m
Saint-Joachim-de-Tourelle, Que., 78
Saint John, N.B., 65m, 66
Saint John River (N.B.), 15, **60-64**, 65m, 66, 67
St. John's, Nfld., 17, 20, 21m, 22
Saint-Jovite, Que., 101m
St. Lawrence River, 71, 77m, 78, 81, 83, 85m, 86, 87, 90, 93m, 94, 101m, 113, 114, 117m, 119
St. Lazare, Man., 212, 214m
St. Leon Falls (B.C.), 257
St. Mary River (Alta.), 249m
St. Marys, Ont., 145m
St. Mary's Bay (Nfld.), 21m
St. Mary's Bay (N.S.), 57m
Saint-Maurice River (Que.), 71, 89, 90, 93m, 94, 98
Saint-Méthode, Que., 85m, 86
Saint-Nicolas, Que., 93m, 94
St. Pauls Inlet (Nfld.), 29m, 31
Saint-Pierre-de-Broughton, Que., 93m, 94
Saint-Siméon, Que., 81, 85m
St. Stephen, N.B., 65m
St. Thomas, Ont., 145m
St. Victor, Sask., 221m
Salamanders, 54, 114, 128, 161; four-toed, **59**; red-backed, 107
Salmo, B.C., 258
Saltspring Island (B.C.), 314, 316

Samuel de Champlain Park (Ont.), 129m, 130
Sand, **51**. See also Dunes
Sandbar Lake (Ont.), 172
Sanderling, 49
Sandpipers, 49, 92, 160, 310, 356; spotted, 28, 340
Sandspit, B.C., 325, 326, 330m
Sandstone, 34, 47, **48-49**, 57, 58, 65, 78, 110, 118, 119, 218, 221, **223**, 235, **236**, 250, **292**, 314, 330, 342, 346, 365
Sandy Bay (Sask.), 186
Sandy Hook (Que.), 36
Sandy Lake (Nfld.), 29m
Sandy Pond (Nfld.), 18
Sans Sault Rapids (N.W.T.), 355
Sarah Lake (N.W.T.), 357
Sarnia, Ont., 145m, 146
Saskatchewan Glacier (Alta.), 269
Saskatchewan River (Sask.), 178, 186, 187m
Saskatoon, Sask., 214m, 229m
Sault Ste. Marie, Ont., 161m
Saxifrage: encrusted, 129; purple, 363, **370-71**
Sceptre, Sask., 229m
Schist Falls (Ont.), 159
Scimitar Canyon (N.W.T.), 350
Sculpin, **79**, 315; four-horned, 357
Sea anemones, 28, **79**; green, 310, **312**
Sea Lion Rock (Ont.), 162
Sea lions, 310, 315, 321, 325; northern, 313, **328-29**
Seal River (N.W.T.), 364
Seals, 76, 85, 302, 310, 322, 326, 330, 335; bay, 20; bearded, 373, 374; freshwater, 238; gray, 44, 58; hair, 315; harbor, 58, 315; harp, 20, **37**, 373, 374, northern elephant, 330; ringed 366, 373, 374
Sea stacks, 28, 50, **317**
Sea urchins, 28, **79**, 315, 329
Sechelt Peninsula (B.C.), 300m, 302, 307
Seebe, Alta., 267
Selim Lake (Ont.), 162
Selkirk, Man., 179m
Selkirk Mountains (B.C.), 253, 254, 257m, 258, 266m, 267, 268
Sewell, B.C., 330m
Seymour Inlet (B.C.), 321
Seymour Narrows (B.C.), 316
Seymour Narrows Lookout (B.C.), 314m, 316
Sharks, lemon, 302
Shawinigan, Que., 90, 93m, 94
Shawinigan River (Que.), 90, 93m
Shearwaters, sooty, 330
Sheep: bighorn, 248, **251**, 266, 272, 273, 278; Dall, **338**, 341, 342, 350; Fannin, 342; mountain, 250; Rocky Mountain, 258, *265*; Stone, 282, 284, 342
Sheep Mountain (Y.T.), 338
Sheet Harbour, N.S., 58
Sheffield Lake (Nfld.), 29, 30
Shepody Bay (N.B.), 65
Shickshock Mountains (Que.), 74, **77m**, 78
Shigawake, Que., 77m, 78
Shoal Lake (Ont.), 179m
Shrews, 50, 205, 326; masked, 92, 146; smoky, 146
Shrikes, 212; northern, 144
Shubenacadie, N.S., 57m, 58
Shuswap Highland (B.C.), 302
Shuswap Lake (B.C.), 300m, 302
Side Lake (Ont.), 171
Sifton Botanical Bog (Ont.), 145m, 146
Silver City, Y.T., 338
Simcoe, Ont., 137m
Similkameen River (B.C.), 243, 300m

Similkameen Valley, 302
Sinclair Canyon (B.C.), 267, **268**
Sinkholes, 29, 196
Sioux Lookout, Ont., 172m
Sioux Narrows, Ont., 176, 178, 179m
Sir Richard Squires Memorial Park (Nfld.), 29m, 30
Siskins, pine, 228
Six Mile Slough (B.C.), **254**
Skagway, Alas., 341m, 342
Skeena Mountains (B.C.), 243, 283m, 284
Skeena River (B.C.), 322m
Skidegate Channel (B.C.), 325.
Skidegate Inlet (B.C.), 325, 326, 330m
Skidegate Mission (B.C.), 326
Skidegate Plateau (B.C.), 331
Skink, northern prairie, 208
Skunks, 49, 100, 142, 212, 256; striped, 220
Skylark, 316
Skyline Park (Ont.), 130
Slatechuck Mountains (B.C.), 326
Slate Island (Ont.), 161m, 162
Slave River (Sask.), 192, 195m, 354
Sleeping Giant (Ont.), 162
Slims River (Y.T.), 338, 340
Slocan Lake (B.C.), 257m, 258
Smeaton, Sask., 187m, 188
Smithers, B.C., 291m, 322m
Smiths Falls, Ont., 117m
Smoky River (Alta.), 275m
Snafflehound Spire (B.C.), 266
Snakes, 123, 128; black rat, 114; bull, 220; fox, 142; garter, 315; green, 220; hognose, 225; northern ringnecks, **59**; plains garter, 220; red-bellied, 205; ribbon, 54; water, 142; western hognose, **231**. See also Rattlesnakes
Snow Dome (Alta.), 265
Snowdrift, N.W.T., 357m
Soda Creek, B.C., 296, 299
Solomon, Que., 36
Solomon's seal, 144, 212
Somerset Island (N.W.T.), 373m
Souris, Man., 208
Souris, P.E.I., 33, 50m
Souris Agate Pit (Man.), **207m**, 208
Souris River (Man.), 207m, 208
Souris River (Sask.), 221m
Southampton, Ont., 149, 152, 153m
Southampton Island (N.W.T.), 365m, 366
South Bay Ingonish, N.S., 43
South Bentinck Arm (B.C.), 291m
Southern Indian Lake (Man.), 187m
South Granville, P.E.I., 50m
South Nahanni River (N.W.T.), 345, 348, 350m, 357m
South Saskatchewan River (Sask.), 214m, **229m**, 230
South Thompson River (B.C.), 302
Southwest Brook (Nfld.), 19
Southwest Miramichi River (N.B.), 65m
Spahats Creek (B.C.), 276
Sparrows, 145, 356, 366; chipping, 49; fox, 312; golden-crowned, 340; Ipswich, 58; Savannah, 49; song, 49, 114, 144, 312; swamp, 108, 142; vesper, 92; white-throated, 49, 92
Spectrum Range (B.C.), **278-79**, 281, 282, 285
Spence Bay, N.W.T., 365m
Sphinx, twin-spotted, **215**
Spirit Island (Alta.), 272
Splake, 128
Splitfrock Falls (Ont.), 171
Splits, The (N.W.T.), 348
Spotted Lake (B.C.), 300, 302

Spring beauty, **251**
Spring Creek (Ont.), 152
Spring peepers, 105, **181**
Spuzzum, B.C., 299, 300m
Squid, 87; giant, 20
Squirrels, 95, 321, 326, 330;
brown, 100; Columbian
ground, **251**, *274*; flying, 42;
Franklin's ground, 212;
ground, 188, 205, 248, 340,
364; northern flying, 54; red,
54, 90, 100, 107, **173**;
Richardson's ground, 220;
southern flying, 54; thirteen-
lined, 212; tree, 248
Stanhope, P.E.I., 47
Stanley Mission (Sask.), 184,
186
Stanley Park (B.C.), 300m, 302
Starfish, 28, **79**, **312**, 329; com-
mon purple, 310
Stave Lake (B.C.), 300m
Steamboat Mountain (B.C.),
283
Steele Glacier (Y.T.), 337-38,
343
Steeples, The (B.C.), 257m,
258
Stettler, Alta., 238m
Stewart, B.C., 283m, 284
Stewart River (Y.T.), 341m
Stikine Plateau (B.C.), 283m,
284
Stikine River (B.C.), 279, 282,
283m, 284
Stockholm, Sask., 212
Stone City (B.C.), 300
Stony Rapids (Sask.), 195
Storm petrels, 21, 322;
Leach's, *22*, **23**, 77, 314
Strait of Canso (N.S.), 43m
Strait of Georgia (B.C.),
300m, 302, 307, 314m, 315,
316
Stratford, Ont., 137
Stuart Lake (B.C.), 291m, 292
Stuart River (B.C.), 291m, 292
Sturgeon, 175, 188
Sturgeon Lake (Ont.), **170-71**
Stutfield Glacier (Alta.), 272
Sudbury Basin (Ont.), 153m,
154
Sugar Loaf (N.S.), 43
Sulphur Mountain (Alta.), 261,
263, 264
Sullivan Lake (Alta.), 238m
Sumas Mountain (B.C.), 300
Summit Creek (B.C.), 254, 256
Summit Lake (B.C.), 284
Summit Lake (N.W.T.), 372
Summit Viewpoint (Alta.), 272
Sunneshine Fjord (N.W.T.),
371
Sunrise Valley (N.S.), 43m, 44
Sunset Park (Ont.), 130
Sunwapta Falls (Alta.), 272,
275
Sunwapta Pass (Alta.), 265,
272
Sunwapta Peak (Alta.), 268
Sunwapta River (Alta.), 272
275m
Sutherland Falls (B.C.), 266m,
268
Swale Tickle (Nfld.), 20
Swallows, 142, 145; bank, **259**;
cliff, 146, **259**; sea, 76
Swan Hills (Alta.), 195m, 196,
238
Swan Lake (Man.), 207m
Swans, 194, 208, 214, 247, 250,
253, 354; mute, 222; trum-
peter, 254, *290*, 302, 325, 329,
341, whistling, 137, 144, **192-
93**, **197**, 222, 254, 341, 357,
364, 365, 366; white whis-
tling, **256**
Swartz Bay, B.C., 314m
Swift Current, Sask., 229m
Swifts, chimney, 92
Swindle Island (B.C.), 321
Sydenham River (Ont.), 145m,
154
Sydney, N.S., 39, 43m
Synclines, 277

Taber, Alta., 249m

Tableau (Que.), 84
Tadoussac, Que., 81, 83, 84, 87
Tagish Lake (Y.T.), 342
Tahltan Highland (B.C.), 280
Takakkaw Falls (B.C.), 268,
269
Takhanne River (Y.T.), 340,
342
Takla Lake (B.C.), 291m
Tanagers, scarlet, 54, 142, 161
Tatlatui Range (B.C.), 284
Teetering Rock (B.C.) 283-84
Telegraph Creek, B.C., 282,
283m, 284
Terns, 42, 114, *142*, 186, 356,
366; Arctic, 340, 365; black,
143; common, 118
Terrace, B.C., 322m
Terrace Bay, Ont., 161m, 162
Terra Nova River (Nfld.), 19,
21m
Teslin Creek (B.C.), 283m
Teslin Lake (B.C.-Y.T.), 283m,
341m, 342
Tête Jaune Cache, B.C., 276
Thames River (Ont.), 145m
Thelon River (N.W.T.), **360-61**,
363
The Pas, Man., 187m, 188
Third Canyon (N.W.T.), 346,
348
Thirty Mile (Y.T.), 341m, 342
Thirty Mile Lake (N.W.T.), 363
Thirty Thousand Islands
(Ont.), 123, 153m, 154
Thompson, Man., 187m
Thompson Plateau (B.C.), 302
Thompson River (B.C.), 299,
300m, 302
Thornbush Pool (N.S.), 44
Thor Peak (N.W.T.), 372
Thousand Islands (Ont.), 71,
112-16, 117m
Thrashers, 212
Thrushes, 42, 259; hermit, **64**,
144; Swainson's, 49; wood,
54, 92
Thunder Bay, Ont., 161m, 162,
169, 172m
Thunder Bay Amethyst Mine
(Ont.), 161m, 162
Thunder Mountain (B.C.), 288
Ticouapé River (Que.), 86
Tidal bores, 58, 65, 67
Tides, 67, **79**, 83
Tiger fish, **181**
Tip Top Mountain (Ont.), 159
Tirokwa Peak (N.W.T.), 372
Titmouse, tufted, 142
Tlell, B.C., 326, 329, 330m
Tlogotsho Range (N.W.T.),
350m
Toadflax, **215**
Toads, 54, 60, 114, 128, 161;
horned, 225; spadefoot, **231**
Tobermory, Ont., 149, 152,
153m
Tobique Reservoir (N.B.), 66
Tobique River (N.B.), 65m, 66
Tofino, B.C., 310, 314m
Tokumm Creek (B.C.), 268
Tombstone Range (Y.T.), **341**
Tona Kela Lake (Ont.), **128**
Tonawanda Channel (Ont.),
139
Tonquin Valley (Alta.), 271
Topsail, Nfld., 22
Topsails, The (Nfld.), 29m, 30
Toronto, Ont., 137m
Tower of Babel (Alta.), 263
Towhees, rufous-sided, 144
Tow Hill (B.C.), 329
Townshend Woodlot (P.E.I.),
50m
Tracadie Bay (P.E.I.), 48
Trade Lake (Sask.), 186, 187m
Trail, B.C., 257m
Trails, hiking and nature:
American Pacific Crest
(B.C.), 302; Blue Heron,
(Sask.), 221; Bonshaw Hills
(P.E.I.), 50m; British Colum-
bia Centennial 300m; Bruce
(Ont.), 138, **148-49**, 152, 153m;
Chilkoot Pass (Alas.-B.C.),
341m; Etienne (Ont.), 130;
Ganaraska (Ont.), 153m;

La Vase Portage (Ont.), 129m,
130; Monument 78 (B.C.),
302; Mountain Meadows
(B.C.), 268; Muhkwa (Ont.),
179m, 180; Old Princetown
Road (P.E.I.), 50; Ottawa
River (Ont.), 110; Rideau
(Ont.), 117m, 118; Telegraph
(B.C.), 282; Trail of the
Voyageurs (Ont.-Que.),
109m, 110; West Coast
(B.C.), 309, 313
Trent-Severn Waterway
(Ont.), 118
Triangle Island (B.C.), 322m
Trinity Bay (Nfld.), 21m, 22
Trois-Rivières, Que., 90, 93m,
94
Trout Lake (Ont.), 129m, 130
Trout Lake (N.W.T.), 357m
Trout Lake (Sask.), 186, 187m
Trout River (P.E.I.), 50
Trumpeter Mountain (B.C.),
290
Trutch Mountain (B.C.), 283
Tsawwassen, B.C., 314m
Tseax River Lava Bed (B.C.),
322m
Tsitsutl Peak (B.C.), 288
Tuaton Lake (B.C.), 284
Tufa, **351**
Tuktoyaktuk, N.W.T., 195, 356,
357m, 358
Tuktoyaktuk Peninsula
(N.W.T.), 359
Tundra, 25, 167, 251, 354, 357,
358, 359, 362, 363, 364, 365,
366, 369, 374
Tunnel Mountain (Alta.), 264
Turner Glacier (N.W.T.), 372
Turner Lake (B.C.), 288, 290,
291m
Turtle Mountain (Alta.), 250
Turtles, 114, 128, 146, 171;
Blanding's, 54, **59**; painted
142, 172; sea, 302; snapping,
154; spotted, 142, 154;
western painted, 205, 302
Tweed Island (Nfld.), 30
Tweedsmuir Glacier (B.C.),
341m, **343**
Twelve Mile Lake (Sask.),
221m
Twin Falls (B.C.), 291
Tyndall, Man., 238
Tyndall Stone Quarries
(Man.), 179m, 180

Ucluelet, B.C., 310, 314m
University River (Ont.), 157
Upper Churchill River (Sask.),
182-86
Upper Elk Lake (B.C.), 266
Upper Falls (Ont.), 109
Upper Hot Springs (Alta.),
264
Upper Jade Lake (B.C.), 268

Valin Mountain (Que.), 84
Val-Jalbert Falls (Que.), 86
Val-Jalbert Park (Que.), 85m,
86
Valley of a Thousand Falls
(Alta.), 276
Valley of No Return (N.W.T.),
342
Valley of the Dinosaurs
(Alta.), 234, 236
Valley of the Ten Peaks (Alta.),
263
Valleyview, Alta., 195
Val Marie, Sask., 229m, 230
Vancouver, B.C., 296, 300m,
302, 307, 314m
Vancouver Island (B.C.), 300m,
302, 303, 307, 310, 312, 314m,
315, 316, 321, 322m
Vancouver Island Ranges
(B.C.), 314m
Vanderhoof, B.C., 291m
Veeries, 54
Verdigris Coulee (Alta.),
249m, 250
Vermilion Valley (B.C.), 267
Vernon, B.C., 300m
Victoria, B.C., 307, 314m, 316
Victoria, P.E.I., 50m

Victoria Glacier (Alta.), 263,
269
Victoria Island (N.W.T.), 365m
Victoriaville, Que., 93m
Vimy Peak (Alta.), 247
Vincent Massey Park (Ont.),
109m, 110
Violets: blue, 18; Canada, **215**;
hooded, 90
Virago Sound (B.C.), 330m
Vireos, 259; red-eyed, 49;
white-eyed, 142, 146
Virginia Falls (N.W.T.),
344-45, 348, 350m
Viscount Melville Sound
(N.W.T.), 365m
Volcanoes, **285**
Voles, 356; meadow, 50, **251**;
red-backed, 92
Volvex, **181**
Vultures, 144; turkey, 145, 146,
205, 207, 214

W.A.C. Bennett Dam (B.C.),
194, 284
Wakefield, Que., 109m
Walruses, 335, 373, 374
Wapella, Sask., 212
Wapiti. See Elk
Warblers, 42, 49, 54, 212, 356;
Audubon's, 228; Kentucky,
142; MacGillivray's, 228;
myrtle, 92, 144; Nashville,
92; parula, 142; prothonotary,
142, 146; yellow, 114, **259**;
yellowthroat, 142, 228
War Lake (B.C.), 291
Wasaga Beach (Ont.), **120-21**
Wasagaming, Man., 203, 205
Wascana Lake (Sask.), 222
Waskesiu Lake (Sask.), 188
Waterloo, Ont., 137m
Waterloo Mountain (B.C.),
314m, 316
Waterton-Glacier International
Peace Park (Alta.-Mont.),
245, **246-47**
Waterton Lakes (Alta.), 245-
46, 248
Waxwing, cedar, 92
Weasel River (N.W.T.), 371
Weasels, 100, 118, 180, 222,
248; least, 205; short-tailed,
42, 49
Weasel Valley (N.W.T.), 372
Welland Canal (Ont.), 136
Wellesley Island (Ont.), **116**
West Bay (N.S.), 43m
Western Brook Gorge (Nfld.),
26, 29m, **31**
West Escarpment (B.C.), 282
West Hawk Lake (Man.),
179m, 180
Wetaskiwin, Alta., 238m
Weyburn, Sask., 221m
Whale Cove (N.W.T.), 364
Whales, 321, 371; beluga, **87**,
302, 335, *364*, 365, 373, 374;
blue, **87**; finback, **87**; gray,
310, 330; humpback, 87, 330;
killer, 20, 87, 302, 314, **315**,
329, *330*; minke, 76, **87**, pilot,
20, 76, **87**; sei, **87**; sperm,
330; bowhead, 373
Whale-watching, 86
Whelk, common northern, **79**
Whimbrels, 28, 301
Whirlpool Peak (Alta.), **274**
Whistlers, The (Alta.), 272, 273
Whitbourne Crossing (Nfld.),
22
White Bay (Nfld.), 29m
White Cloud Island (Ont.), 152
Whitefish Bay (Ont.), **176-77**,
179m
Whitefish Falls (Ont.), 162
Whitehorse, Y.T., 284, 341m,
342
White Mountains (Y.T.), **342**
Whitemouth Lake (Man.), 179m
Whitemud Formation (Sask.),
217
White Otter Lake (Ont.), 172m
White River (Ont.), 159, 161m,
341m

White River (Y.T.), 341m
Whitney, Ont., 129m
Wiarton, Ont., 155
Wilberforce Falls (N.W.T.),
364, 365m
Wilderness areas. *See* box p.
376
Wild Horse Creek (B.C.), 302
Wildlife preserves. *See* box p.
376
Wild Mint Springs, (N.W.T.),
346
William River (Sask.), 195
Williams Lake, B.C., 288,
291m, 292
Willison Glacier (B.C.), 284
Williston Lake (B.C.), 283m,
284, 291m
Williwaws, 330
Willow Bunch, Sask., 218,
221m
Willow Bunch Lake (Sask.),
221m
Willow Creek (Alta.), 236
Willow Creek (Ont.), 154
Windsor, Nfld., 21m
Windsor, Ont., 145m
Winnipeg, Man., 179m, 180,
207m, 211
Winnipeg River (Man.-Ont.),
176, 179m, 180
Wisconsin Glacier, 106
Wollaston Lake (Sask.), 187m,
192
Wolverines, **251**, 288, 316, 321,
341, 350
Wolves, 85, 95, 100, **131**, 159,
160, 162, 205, 274, 288, 316,
321, 338, 341, 354, 357, 358,
364; Arctic, 268, 302; gray,
188, 268; timber, *128*, 161,
172, 180, 193, 214, 222, 282;
white Arctic, 363
Wood, petrified, 207, **235**
Wood Islands (P.E.I.), 50m
Wood Mountain Formation
(Sask.), 217
Wood Mountain Uplands,
(Sask.), 229m, 230
Woodpeckers, 42, 212; Arctic
three-toed, 161; black-backed
three-toed, 205; hairy, 326;
northern three-toed, 205;
pileated, 54; white-headed,
302; yellow-bellied sap-
sucker, **259**
Woodstock, N.B., 64, 65m
Woodstock, Ont., 137m, 145m
Woodwards Cove (N.B.), **65m**,
66
Wrens: Carolina, 142; long-
billed marsh, **259**; marsh,
142; winter, 312
Wrigley, N.W.T., 355

Yaku, B.C., 326, 300m
Yale, B.C., 296, 297, 298, 299
Yarmouth, N.S., 57m, 58
Yarmouth County (N.S.), 58
Yellowhead Pass (Alta.-B.C.),
276
Yellowknife, N.W.T., 357m,
358
Yoho Glacier (B.C.), 268
Yoho River (B.C.), 268
York Factory (N.W.T.), 184
Yorkton, Sask., 214
Young Creek (B.C.), 288
Yukon-Mackenzie Divide
(N.W.T.), 346
Yukon River (Y.T.), 338,
341m, 342

Zig Zag Island (Ont.), 175
Zooplankton, **181**
Zoos and wild animal parks:
Alberta, 238m; Assiniboine
(Winnipeg, Man.), 179m;
Calgary, 238; Nova Scotia,
57m, 58; Saint-Félicien, Que.,
85m, 86; Salmonier, Nfld.,
21m, 22; Saskatchewan,
221m, 222; Stanley Park
(Vancouver), 302;
Toronto, Ont., 137m, 138;
Wildlife Unlimited (Alta.),
268

Picture Credits

Engravings: Herzig Somerville Limited
Typesetting: The Graphic Group of Canada Ltd. / Compoplus Typesetters Inc.
Printing: Pierre Des Marais Inc.
Binding: Harpell's Press Co-operative
Binding material: Columbia Finishing Mills Limited
Paper: Rolland Paper Company Limited